D1489990

For Mother, Milton and Berta

Frank Gehry

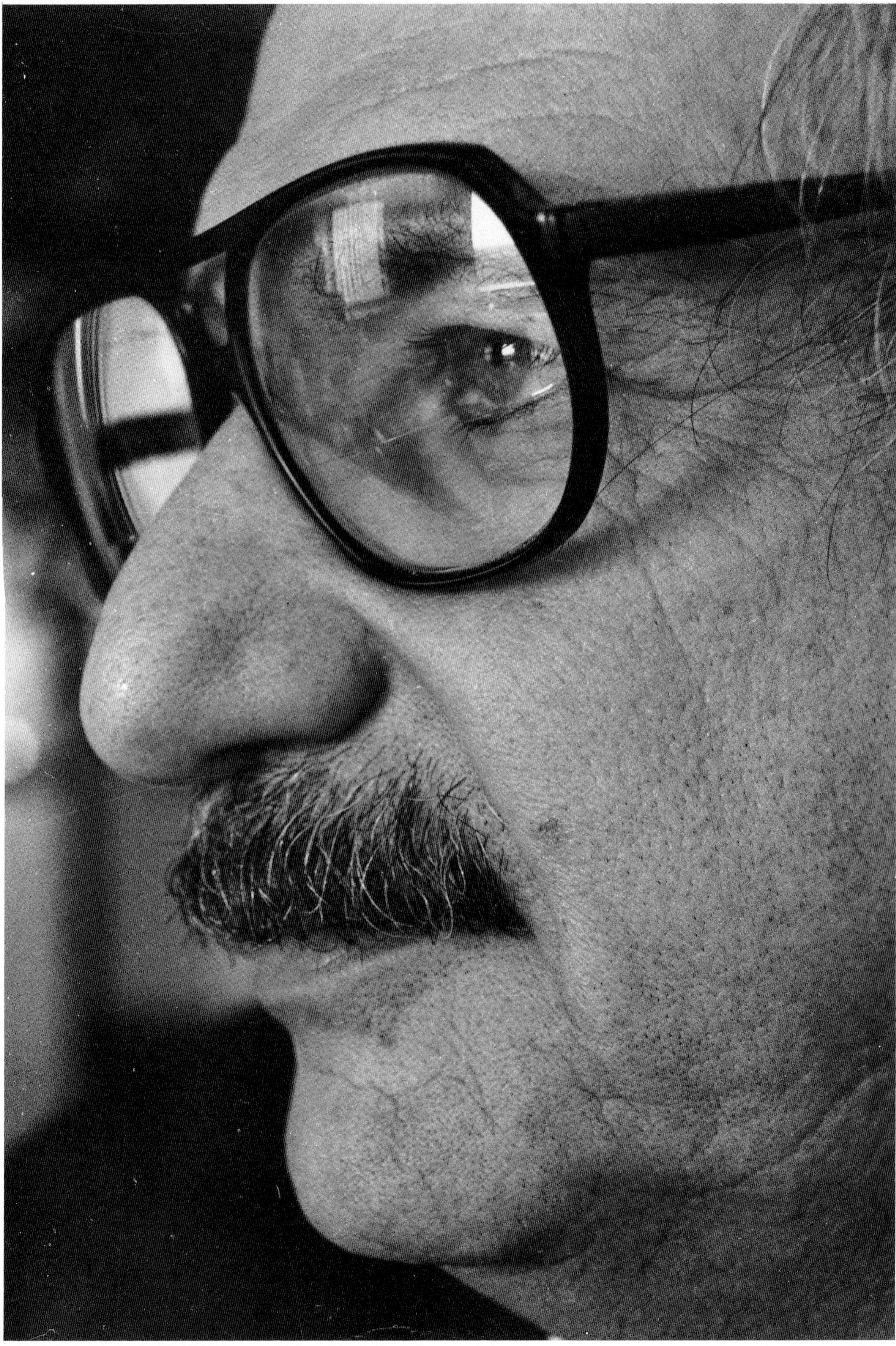

Frank Gehry
Buildings and Projects

Compiled and Edited by Peter Arnell and Ted Bickford

Essay by Germano Celant
Text by Mason Andrews

Recent Work Photographed by Tim Street-Porter

Rizzoli
New York

For Mallory too.

First published in the United States of America in 1985 by
RIZZOLI INTERNATIONAL PUBLICATIONS INC.
597 Fifth Avenue, New York NY 10017

Library of Congress Cataloging in Publication Data

Gehry, Frank O., 1929-
Frank Gehry, buildings and projects.

Bibliography: p.
1. Gehry, Frank O., 1929- . 2. Architecture, Modern—20th century—United States. I. Arnell, Peter. II. Bickford, Ted. III. Title. IV. Title: Buildings and projects.
NA737.G44A4 1985 720'.92'4 84-42646
ISBN 0-8478-0542-5
ISBN 0-8478-0543-4 (pbk.)

Set in Simoncini Garamond by Circle Graphics, Washington, D.C.

Printed and bound in Japan by Dai Nippon Printing Company

Reprinted 1987

We would like to extend a special thanks to Berta Gehry, Stanley Tigerman, Greg Walsh, Fred Hoffman, Eamonn O'Mahony, Tim Street-Porter, Bob Hale, Mason Andrews, Raffaella Pozzi, Germano Celant.

P.A. T.B.

Executive Editors:
Peter Arnell
Ted Bickford

Associate Editor:
Catherine Bergart

Design:
Peter Arnell
Raffaella Pozzi
Arnell/Bickford Associates

Design Coordination:
Holly Jaffe

Contents

Index of Buildings and Projects

The following is a complete chronological listing of all projects undertaken by Gehry's office. Listings of those projects illustrated in this volume are followed by the page number on which they are illustrated.

Rouse Investment Corporation Offices 1967
Los Angeles, California

Simi Valley Ranch 1967
Ventura County, California

Central Business District 1967
Hermosa Beach, California
Page 46

Greber Studio 1967
Los Angeles, California

Amusement Park 1967
Los Angeles, California

Billy Al Bengston 1968
Los Angeles County Museum of Art
Page 36

O'Neill Hay Barn 1968
San Juan Capistrano, California
Page 40

Clark County Housing 1968
Henderson, Nevada

Rose Gardens 1968
Las Vegas, Nevada

Joseph Magnin Store 1968
Costa Mesa, California
Page 42

Joseph Magnin Store 1968
San Jose, California

American School of Dance 1968
Los Angeles, California
Page 38

Bixby Green 1969
Garden Grove, California
Page 46

Easy Edges 1969–73
Page 64

University Park 1970
Irvine, California
Page 50

Vernon-Central Redevelopment 1970
Los Angeles, California
Page 50

Hollywood Bowl 1970–1982
Hollywood, California
Page 52

Ron Davis House 1972
Malibu, California
Page 58

Town Center 1972–1978
Woodlands, Texas
Page 70

Handler House 1972
Los Angeles, California

Town Center 1973
Cochiti Lake, New Mexico
Page 71

Larkspur-Greenbrae Mall 1973
Larkspur, California
Page 74

Illinois Center 1973
Chicago, Illinois
Page 74

Hollydot Houses 1973
Hollydot Park, Colorado
Page 76

Westinghouse Distribution Services 1974
El Monte, California

Janss House 1974
Los Angeles, California
Page 76

The Rouse Company Headquarters 1974
Columbia, Maryland
Page 78

Horton Plaza 1974
San Diego, California
Page 74

Performing Arts Pavilion 1975/1977
Concord, California
Page 84

Gemini G.E.L. 1976/1979
Los Angeles, California
Page 86

Norton Simon Guest House & Gallery 1976
Malibu, California
Page 90

Harper House 1976
Baltimore, Maryland
Page 94

Placement and Career Planning Center 1976
University of California at Los Angeles
Page 96

Shoreline Aquatic Park Pavilions 1976
Long Beach, California
Page 98

Thornwood Mall 1976
Park Forest South, Illinois
Page 102

Pier Rehabilitation 1976
Santa Monica, California

Golden Cove Shopping Center 1976
Palos Verdes Estates, California

Manhattan Tower 1976
Los Angeles, California

Hotchkiss House 1976
Santa Monica, California

Jung Institute 1976
Los Angeles, California
Page 100

San Francisco Pier Project 1976
San Francisco, California

The Atrium 1977
Lincoln, Nebraska
Page 102

Berger, Berger, Kahn, Shafton & Moss Law Offices 1977
Los Angeles, California
Page 104

The Vineyard 1977
Escondido, California

Weisman House 1977
Beverly Hills, California

Frederick Weisman Beach House 1977
Trancas, California

Beach House 1977
Trancas, California

Ed Ruscha House 1977
Los Angeles, California

Cheviot Hills House 1978
Los Angeles, California
Page 110

Nelson House 1978
Los Angeles, California
Page 116

Treasures of Tutankhamen 1978
Los Angeles County Museum of Art

Heeramaneck Collection 1978
Los Angeles County Museum of Art

Mid-Atlantic Toyota Distributors 1978
Glen Burnie, Maryland
Page 112

Weisman Offices 1978
Los Angeles, California

Wagner House 1978
Malibu, California
Page 122

Gunther House 1978
Encinal Bluffs, California
Page 118

The Main Street 1978–1984
Venice, California

Familian House 1978
Santa Monica, California
Page 128

St. Ives House 1978
West Hollywood, California
Page 116

Gehry House 1978
Santa Monica, California
Page 134

Carriage House 1978
New York, New York
Page 146

Warner Ranch Valley Cultural Center 1978
San Fernando Valley, California

Arts Park 1978
San Fernando Valley, California
Page 152

"No, I'm an Architect"

Frank Gehry and Peter Arnell: A Conversation

In thinking about Frank's work and of its evolution as shown in this book, it seems an expression of what we would like to call the work of the "New Perspective"—most easily understood by referring to the explorations of Cubism. In questioning the presumption of a fixed position from which one sees, it brought into question the very nature of perception, proposing the indisputable fact that the eye moves constantly, that perception is based on a composite of "takes" on an object garnered as one moves around it. The pioneering work Frank has executed seems to us to extend these ideas to architecture—a field in which their truth seems most emphatic. For as the eye moves constantly, so, in architecture, does the observer. In architecture the constantly shifting perspectives of spaces are further affected by the passage of time as one moves through them. So while most contemporary architecture is static—presuming essentially a series of fixed, atemporal readings of flattened multi-colored compositions—Frank has steered a course—clearly visible in the work presented in this book—of exploration in which the roles of the observer and observed are taken as a basic criterion and resource. Indeed, Frank sees design as a process of ongoing collaboration in which each viewer brings their own sensibilities and experiences to his work, in which clients react to and act upon his spaces so that the collaborative design process is ongoing. In a sense, an undertaking as vast as this monograph has proven to be a similar sort of collaborative venture. Taking the raw data of the enormous body of work produced by the several firms that have been formed around Frank and his special sensibilities, a number of individuals have each brought their own perspectives and "takes" on the material to it and thus shaped the final project. It seemed that in keeping with the nature and the subject of the work that, rather than including presumptively "definitive" explanations of the work by Frank and ourselves as introductions, it would be more useful to present the following conversation between us. Essentially "unretouched," it offers insights into both the priorities of the architect—his "take" on his work, his career, and his profession—and the sort of communication—sometimes clear, sometimes synaptic, sometimes revelatory to us all—between Frank and ourselves which has had as its result the book you now have before you.

Peter Arnell
Ted Bickford
January 1985

PA: Interview with Frank Gehry...

FG: February 24, 1984. Four days before his 55th birthday.

PA: You like New York City?

FG: Ya.

PA: Do you like being inverviewed?

FG: Ya.

PA: Seriously.

FG: It depends who's doing it. Certain people I like being interviewed by and certain people I don't like being interviewed by. And I can't tell until I'm into the interview. I'll let you know in a little while.

PA: How long have you been in practice?

FG: Practicing what?

PA: Architecture.

FG: I used to practice the guitar. When I was a kid I took guitar lessons and I practiced a lot then. Architecture? I practice every day.

PA: How long have you been in practice?

FG: At least 12 hours a day—like a fine pianist.

PA: For how long?

FG: 12 hours.

PA: How many years have you been in practice?

FG: With my own office, since 1962; but I started working for other people in 1952.

PA: What was the first office you worked in?

FG: William Morris. Not the famous William Morris. This was the schlock William Morris in Los Angeles. The office was next door to William Saroyan's office when he was writing "Come on to my house, my house, come on."

PA: What I'm going to do now is I'm going to ask some dumb questions and the questions shouldn't at all...

FG: Be answered.

PA: No. What I'm looking for is for you to expand on them. So I'm going to say things that have come out of our recent talks and things that Mason has been writing and so forth, and you're just going to go from it. Okay? "Expressive potential of raw structures."

FG: I don't know what you're talking about... Okay: Buildings under construction look nicer than buildings finished.

PA: When did you first recognize that?

FG: I've always... But everybody says that... When you start looking at buildings, when you start being interested in architecture, you walk down the street and you say, "Oh look at that great structure. Isn't that great? Too bad they can't leave it like that." How many times have you heard that in your life? Buildings that are just done by ordinary people—they look like hell when they're finished—but when they're under construction they look great. So that's part of it. Another is that I look at painting a lot... There's an immediacy in paintings, you feel like the brush strokes were just made. I think about paintings all the time, so one part of architecture that I felt an interest in exploring was how to bring these ideas to buildings. The tradition of Mondrian's paintings affecting architecture is an old story. I wanted to see what else we can learn from paintings. In particular, how could a building be made to look like it's in process? And how can the expressive and compositional attitudes of painting be explored in a building? That's what led me to explore opening up the structure and using the raw wood techniques and developing buildings that look like they just happened. They look like in the normal building process somebody just stopped.

PA: And that interests you a lot?

FG: Ya. More than is legal to contemplate.

PA: Do you think that to see something in that state is more expressive of our culture than to see something finished?

FG: A lot of people don't see it that way. But to me it seems we're in a culture made up of fast food and advertising and throw-aways and running for airplanes and catching cabs—frenetic. So I think there's a possibility that those ideas about buildings are more expressive of our culture than something finished is. On the other hand, because of all the freneticism, people may really need something more relaxed—less taxing, more in repose. I'm not against that but sometimes it leads to complacency—and you know where that leads. We need a balance.

PA: You said something about the way we see things. I think there's a kind of natural contradicatory process that goes on within the mind of someone trying to expand their architectural ideas. It's a concern about using too much of, or relying too much on, one's own traditions and history—on what's already there—even though these things are exactly what shape one's judgments—in order to propose an original or transforming judgment of what is about to happen and of what is happening at the moment. It seems we're trying to generate ideas to proselytize about a new vision. But I find the complete opposite in your architecture. It's an acceptance, in a way, of the culture—an attempt to work within it.

FG: I think all of us are, finally, just commenting in our own way about what's going on in our cone of vision. I tend to have this particular way of looking at it . . . I don't look for the soft stuff, the pretty stuff. It puts me off because it seems unreal. I have this socialistic or liberal attitude about people and politics: I think of the starving kids and that do-gooder stuff I was raised on. So a pretty little salon with the beautiful colors seems like a chocolate sundae to me. It's too pretty. It's not dealing with reality. I see reality as harsher; people bite each other. My take on things comes from that point of view.

PA: When we started this project—the book—about three years ago, it seemed like the work wasn't as accepted or known or publized as it is today. It's amazing what's happened over the last couple of years: you've really become a major architectural figure in America. Worldwide, recognized now as one of the leaders in architecture. Why has this happened recently? Is it because you've had more built by now? Because people finally recognize things you're doing? As a second, and more important, part to the question: has anything really changed because of it? Isn't it true that the work is still the same as it was five years ago, and that it's the work that is still most important to you?

FG: I came out of school and out of apprenticeship feeling that architecture was a service business, that as an architect you serve clients: you listen to programs, solve problems, and make buildings. And there's an even bigger picture in urban design and city planning—you know I studied city planning, not architcture, in graduate school. I had this sense of being involved with the political and social structure, and not—well, in the beginning the whole idea of doing houses for rich people was just abhorent to me. I was more interested in this bigger thing which I saw as lying with urban design and large-scale projects. What I found out was that it just meant going to those meetings which only led to a lot of planning reports and a lot of grandiose dreams that never got realized. There didn't seem to be a cause and effect relationship between the work and reality. You'd lay out these ideas; people would say "ya," but there was no way of getting it to happen. It was too complicated. So you start back-pedaling to something that's more realistic, and end up doing smaller buildings, which you *can* do one at a time in our culture. There are very few people who get to do those big complexes; they have to be really high-powered business types; and ironically they have to look like, and act like, they fit in with the business corporate structures they serve. It actually seems an unsound business decision to go after architecture produced by something aspiring to corporate structure. Any final result has to be compromised because so many people are involved. I've always wanted to mesh with the innovative, creative side of business—the part that really counts. I found more gratification and more excitement accessible in the smaller projects, even though I did get a few big ones, like Santa Monica Place, built. If you look at the firm's work from the beginning of my practice through the period Santa Monica Place was built you'll see I was doing matter-of-fact developer work at the same time I was doing projects like the Danzinger building and the O'Neill Hay Barn . . . I had these little projects which for me were very beautiful, where I could really be expressive. My house was a turning point; it was my money and I felt I could use the project for R & D—research and development. I was completely in control—budget, time, the look. But it freaked out my developer clients. The Rouse Company guys just fled the pasture after they saw it. They said, "If you like that, you don't want to deal with our stuff." In a way they were right. I had to start over again—literally start over again. So in the last five years I've had to rebuild the practice from scratch. It has been scarey financially and gratifying personally.

PA: But you are an artist, right?

FG: I'm an architect. I get that a lot because I've hung around with a lot of artists and I'm very close to a lot of them. I'm very involved with their work; I think a lot of my ideas have grown out of it, and that there's been some give and take. So sometimes I get called an artist. Somebody'll say, "Oh, well, Frank's an artist." I feel in a way that's used like a dismissal. I want to say I'm an architect. My intention is to make architecture.

PA: Your intention is to make architecture, but I think you love and always loved being involved with the art world: your closest friends are part of it. I think you understand it. You understand artists much better than most architects. I think you live a life which is similar to theirs—like the way you work in your studio, the way you work with pieces and models and parts and paintings. You create things. Not just in the way we think of an American architect following a program. You do it in a way that is a creative drive, much stronger than a business dirve.

FG: Well, I don't know if that's . . . the business drive isn't there very much—that's true. The drive to solve the client's problem *is* there. The drive to make buildings come in on time and on budget, to be in context—all those traditional things that architects deal with, I deal with. I consider all those given things; I don't even talk about them, because they're givens. If you're going to do a building for a client you gotta be responsible to the client. You gotta do something that they're gonna (a) like, (b) get their money's worth from, and (c) get something that'll last and serve their purposes. On the other hand, I question them. I'm probably more contentious with a client than most. I find myself questioning their programs, questioning their intentions . . . I get into a real intense relationship, which finally ends up synergistically giving more positive results, I think, because the client's spent more time thinking about the program and what they want—they get more involved.

PA: Do you like being on the beach?

FG: No, I don't like the office being in Venice. I'm jammed in with too much anatomy. Actually, I think if somebody really spent some time with me they'd find out that I'm very conventional. I even go to Brooks Brothers. I'm intense about my work and I spend every waking hour on it. I love my kids, my wife, but I'm so intensely involved with my work that I forget birthdays, anniversaries—I never remember anything personal. On the other hand, my projects come in on time, on budget—really on budget—I really take those kinds of things seriously. I *will* try to take a client's program and re-evaluate it in terms of what kind of expression is appropriate: I try not so much to fight the program as to re-order the priorities. And then I take great pleasure in being able to get the things to function in conventional terms and to have a certain visual character—all within a budget; what I like to do is develop a project's potentials. I think any good architect does that; but I think that's the thing that a lot of conservative clients don't understand. Any of the guys doing architecture we know that we have any respect for can do that. They can be really effective, and they can get more bang for your buck. You see, conservative clients feel more secure talking to those guys who seem to build more conventionally; they think they're going to get what they want. They don't. They don't. It's just that they're afraid to get involved in this kind of . . .

PA: But about the work—something that always strikes me is a parallel between Robert Venturi and Aldo Rossi and you. Take Venturi—his office understands very well how to make a building, both how to build it well and how to make a building that accepts its environment and has that play between scales that goes on in his architecture. Rossi, too, is very much part of his society. When I watch you sketch or when I watch Rossi sketch, I see something very similar: when you see the sketch and then the final building—there ain't much difference. If—and it also happens with Venturi—if he makes a sketch, it turns out to be a building. That's a very important side in creation, that there's a way . . .

FG: It hasn't always been that way, though. In the early days, my drawing techniques were very glib; I spent time learning renderings and perspectives. I can do those real well, and I did them as a professional renderer for people like Portman. The drawings were so glib that they tricked me. I would get excited about the rendered drawing but it never translated into the building. So in the early 60's, I began to try something different: Have you ever seen a structural engineer's architectural drawings? They're just awful. They have no character—they're just ugly and mean. There's nothing—there's just lines. So I began to have our structural engineer make the plans and elevation drawings of the buildings. I would look at those drawings, couldn't get snowed by the technique and the glibness of my own, and instead would have to concentrate on the final building. That's still what I concentrate on—the final building, not the drawings. I do a different kind of drawing now. They are a searching in the paper. It's almost like I'm grinding into the paper, trying to find the building. It's like a sculptor cutting into the stone or the marble, looking for the image. At least it feels like it to me. I never think of the drawings as a finished product—they're a process to get to an idea. If you watch me draw—actually draw—you'll see it's a frantic kind of searching. I let that lead, and then make models of the idea scratched out of the paper, and then go back to the drawing, and so on. The gallery had a hard time selling my drawings—probably because they're not finished drawings—they're part of a process. The models are the same way. Just lately we've forced ourselves to make more finished models and do some more refined presentation drawings because we find our clients really need them. I've begun to realize that publishing the work of our normal process has led to misunderstandings. For instance, the model of my house that we used in design was published. It's rough and ragged because we worked it over so much. But I think it's caused trouble because when I showed the publications with it to clients, they's say, "Well, Jesus, what's that all about?" They don't relate to it.

PA: Okay, but I think that a lot of times the buildings have a lot of wit and fun in them. I think they have two things going on: on one hand, they're very very serious responses to program made with the intent of building a good building; on the other hand they make commentaries on what those programs are about. The Aerospace project is amazing to me because it seems to express the essence of flight, and Loyola has the grandeur and the simplicity and the classicism of a law school or of a courthouse. And you find the same thing as you go on and you review all the projects: the Cabrillo Museum has the understanding of the marina and the lightness and transparency you see and feel by the water. The houses that are by the beach have an understanding of the horizon and the beach and the street *and* urban scale. Each project has these amazing connections.

FG: The irony is that that interest of mine has been so misunderstood. Some people don't see what you were talking about in my work; they get instead a reading of discord, of disjunction from the environment. Now maybe it's just my house, and maybe that's...

PA: The problem with the house is typical of the first project that any architect pays for: you have a lot of ideas that you've never had an opportunity to explore, so it becomes intense. It's especially true of your house. But I think a lot of its notoriety and a lot of what gets published about it has to do with its providing what I would consider good visuals for the media, not because the media understands its good ideas. So because the house is a special case, let's set it aside and consider the major work—like Santa Monica Place with its relationship of that facade to the bridge, or the museum, or the houses, or Bubar's jewelry store with the relationship of a little street within a store. It seems to me that the notion of shopping, the boutique, has been captured with that store. With most of your work it seems like the idea or topic or the category or the qualification of that project—whether it be jewelry store, fire house, house, museum, whatever—always ends up being characterized as what it's supposed to be. It's very unusual because in some very simple moves, without getting too decorative, without trying to apply itself too much to anything, it ends up having the characteristics of that topic which you started out with.

FG: Yeah, I'm very careful about that. I look for that.

PA: But I want you to try and comment on it because that for me is what a lot of the work's about.

FG: You already said it better than I can, Peter. When I began work at Loyola I was working with a bunch of law students who seemed to be looking for a home. The students and the faculty and the administration were in a pitiful environment. What they were in made you cry: there was just nothing there that had anything to do with what they were studying or what they were doing. It reads on their faces—the way they dressed, the way they acted. It was kind of like a second-class law school, and they acted like it. The problem didn't seem to be the curriculum and the program. There was just this feeling of desperation that we discussed in the very first meetings. I said, "What I think the key issue here is trying to create a place that gives you a better background for what you're doing, that gives you a feeling of dignity and is uplifting, that complements the curriculum, that provides, as you walk from class to class, the feeling that you're in an environment of the law." With the Aerospace project, the client said that they only had enough money to build a tiny part of what was needed to make an Aerospace museum, but that they really wanted the building to have the characteristics, to be expressive of, flight. It had to be expressive of what they were going to show because they didn't think they were going to have enough money to even put exhibits in. It seemed possible that for two or three years the building itself would be the exhibit. So in that case, what I try to do in a design anyway, was exactly the task given to me. I usually present a project and in my head I duck; I think, "Boy these guys aren't gonna..." But with this one, they applauded when I finished. I think that I have gotten better with this stuff, Peter, and I think the last projects are getting better—the library for Hollywood I think is really expressive of Hollywood, of library, and of the client that paid for it.

PA: Anyway, why a fish Frank?

FG: The fish uh...

PA: Is it Man Ray?

FG: Oh no no no.

PA: Who is it—Magritte?

FG: The fish is more complicated than that. I can tell you how the fish came about, I can trace the steps, and you can read into it whatever you want. Tigerman asked me to do the Chicago Tribune Competition Revisited. I thought of the power of the press and the Chicago Tribune—and the eagle came to mind. I drew a sketch of a building that grew into an eagle. An eagle represented the power of the press in America and all that. I didn't get the drawing finished; I just sent a sketch. Soon after I did the Smith House in which I decided there should be a colonnade, at the driveway in front of the little buildings—a first line of objects, smaller in scale. Since I was never able to finish the Tribune drawing, I started making the colonnade with the eagle. And then I decided—well I should have more columns. And that's when I drew the fish standing up....

PA: As a better representation of a column.

FG: I started thinking about the fish and realized how beautiful it was. And then came the bridge project with Richard Serra. We needed a building to anchor the thing and I couldn't get the fish out of my mind. I just made the sketch as a fish and Richard was really supportive of it. The fish evolved further: I kept drawing it and sketching it and it started to become for me like a symbol for a certain kind of perfection that I couldn't achieve with my buildings. Eventually whenever I'd draw something and I couldn't finish the design, I'd draw the fish as a notation.

PA: As a security blanket.

FG: Not as a security blanket. As a notation that I want this to be better than just a dumb building. I want it to be more beautiful.

PA: But you know Magritte's fishes, right?

FG: Yes I know Magritte's fishes.

PA: But that's not the way it happened.

FG: Well I'm not conscious of it.... Also, when I was a kid I used to go to the market with my grandmother on Thursdays. We'd go to the Jewish market, we'd buy a live carp, we'd take it home to her house in Toronto, we'd put it in the bathtub and I would play with this goddamn fish for a day until the next day she'd kill it and make gefilte fish. I think maybe that has something to do with it.

PA: Did you love her?

FG: Yes.

PA: How long did you play with the carp?

FG: Every Thursday.

PA: Were you fascinated with it?

FG: Yeah.

PA: The shape of it?

FG: Yes.

PA: And the movement?

FG: Un huh.

PA: The fact that it was floating?

FG: I suppose. Also there are other factors. If you believe in astrology, since I was born February 28th that makes me a Pisces. If there's anything in that then that's—the fish is—I don't really believe in that, but... I'm a good swimmer too. My favorite sport is swimming. I'm a sailor, I'm a water person.

PA: So it's a symbol.

FG: So, I think that it's all reinforced for me. The first time I saw the real potential of it was when I made the model of the scales out of glass for the bridge project. I loved the look of that layering of the glass. I don't know that I really want to build a fish building. I was invited to build a pavilion in Australia, a gazebo, that looked like a fish, and somehow I never did it. And I don't know whether that's because I don't really want to do it. When Formica asked me to design something with ColorCore I went through all the traditional stuff of cabinets. I had to do something different. I have an intense need somehow to change things and to transform them. And so in frustration I broke the ColorCore and then I loved it. It was just so beautiful when it shattered—it looked like flints. I started layering it and we made a fish. And fish lamps and snake lamps.

PA: Why a snake? The same scaling thing?

FG: The scaling thing but no... it was part of the afterlife of the collaboration with Richard Serra: we fantasized doing another project in LA. It was going to be a nursery school, and we were going to make two objects. He was going to make one and I was going to make the other. I wanted to explore further the fish form as a building and he got all excited about a coiled snake form next to the fish. Nothing ever happened with it, so when the Follies Show came up through the Castelli Gallery, I then put the fish and the snake together. And once you're in it, you're in it. I now still want to make the eagle, so I'm going to make an eagle out of Formica. I'm working on that now. I think that the primitive beginnings of architecture come from zoomorphic yearnings and skeletal images, and you know, the fish preceded man on this earth. So there's historic content to it, too. There are a lot of reasons which keep reinforcing the image. For me it's a symbol of perfection.

PA: Collaborations for a second, okay? More than any other architect in America, you've had many, many working relationships with artists, both intellectual as well as collaboration on projects: the Artist/Architect collaboration, the Venice Biennale, with Claes Oldenburg, with Serra. Is it because you think along the same lines they do? Because there's a respect for each other's work? Do you feel you're addicted to it?

FG: I don't know that I've ever sought out the collaborations—you know, gone out and said, "I should collaborate with somebody." It always just happened. Whether it's that something I do attracts that kind of relationship, I don't know. I'd guess that's part of it. I find a great common language with artists and I'm excited by the intensity and the directness and the economy of moves in someone like Richard Serra; the intensity is very inspiring to me. I think when I get excited about an artist's work, I'm interested in how they think and what they do and the process they go through: my interest is in learning from them as role models; I've always looked beyond just the product of the collaboration. I've learned a lot that way. I've never gone out and sought out a particular artist to work with. Like with Serra—we started talking to each other and then the Architectural League, which was sponsoring the Collaboration, heard about Richard and me working together and at the last minute included us as an afterthought. As for the new collaboration with Claes Oldenberg and Coosje van Bruggen: Claes and I were friends in the sixties and had tried to work together then but circumstances never allowed it to happen; we ran into each other two or three years ago and started talking again. He came to see the house and then we just sort of fell into a working relationship that Germano witnessed; Germano's sort of been promoting the collaboration. I think Claes and I probably wouldn't have done it on our own, even though we tried in the sixties and we were talking about it. I've also worked with Ed Moses and Bengston and other artists in LA and I try to include them in projects. Until recently, I was never very successful: when I did the Rouse Headquarters Building I commissioned Larry Bell to do a piece as a gift for the Rouse Company. They rejected it. Instead they put two little pewter pigs in the courtyard—just awful; and they could've had a nice Larry Bell sculpture, a prismatic piece of glass that refracted the sun. Only now am I starting to get a little power in that direction. People are starting to say, "Well what kind of art do you want?" Maybe in the next few projects....

PA: It's kind of wonderful that you're so closely associated with and so supportive of all your artist friends. You speak of it all the time. You're excited by the work, you're stimulated by it, new ideas come into your head by it...

FG: In fact if we could finish this *!@&# interview I could go and see Jasper's show.

PA: When you do installations in museums—which you have done a lot of—why are they always so good? Is it because you understand the work that you're about to play with?

FG: Yea, I understand the work and what it's about and what it needs as a background. I've seen it in its best environments. I've looked at so much of that stuff that I think I do understand about showing art and how it should be displayed and how it should be lit. I want to do a museum so badly and nobody will give me one. They give it to all the other guys. Please give a museum to do, world.

PA: All right, Gehry, ready for the next question? Big question. 1984. There's going to be a major book on your work, all right? Major major major monograph. 350 pages of Frank Gehry, 30 years. I don't want to consider it a retrospective because you're not dead. You're just beginning. In fact for me only six to eight years of the book represents the most powerful work, the recent work. The rest is necessary because it explains how one arrived at that work. You're one of the most consistent */@#s I've ever seen and I think that from the first sketch in the book to the sketch that you showed me at this moment in 1984 it's the same Frank Gehry, the same hand, the same eye. You've changed your ideas about form, not about architecture; and so the representations of those ideas have changed their forms, but the space, the feeling, the hand, it's all the same for me. Looking back and looking at all this 30 years of work—amazing accomplishment of 30 years, of 105 products that are about to go into this monograph, and every possible conceivable type, from office buildings to residential work, to high-rise, to libraries, museum...

FG: Peter, is this an advertisement for the monograph?

PA: No—with 4,000 illustrations, designed, edited and compiled and—listen. You ready? What I want to know is, do you feel that you've made a significant contribution to our urban landscape, and if so, how do you feel—hear me out—think about it for a second—how do you feel it's going to affect us in the future?

FG: God, Peter, that's a hard one. I don't know about a contribution—I think I've worked my ass off and made as good buildings as I know how to do. I consider it a personal effort. I don't think about it in megalomaniac terms of taking over the world. I think maybe what's been successful about it is that I have been able to keep on a sort of personal course. I've had little forays into somebody else's thing but I pull back and have been intensely involved with keeping it a personal expression. I've been consciously pushing this personal signature, or whatever you want to call it. I don't know what its impact is going to be; it's been so personally satisfying, that that's plenty for me. And I have a lot of good clients who seem to like the work and are very supportive. I haven't got yet a landslide following, I just have, you know...

PA: Is it the greatest thing you can be doing now? Is it the most important?

FG: Yeah, I can't imagine doing anything else. That's why when somebody calls and says, "You're an artist" I say, "No, I'm an architect." I don't see it any other way. I see what I'm doing as the only thing I could do. I'm intensely involved with it, I don't understand anything else.

"Reflections on Frank Gehry"
An Essay by Germano Celant

The Architectural City

The architectural creations of Frank Gehry seem idealized cities—essences of urbanity which, refracted and re-presented through Gehry's aerial vision, throws open new ways of understanding the spatial and temporal dimensions of architecture. In them one can hear the voice of the city speaking of its streets and its intersections, of its traffic and its flashing lights, of its commerce, and its familiar forms and stereotypes. They are "house-cities"—places of osmosis between macrocosm and microcosm, in which analogous typologies and formal congruence have been deduced and induced from their natural and man-made surroundings. They are like paraphrases of the city, with each building an individual village—a summation of independent contrasting entities.

His architecture reveals itself as an image of a city, but a city in which boundaries between both buildings and neighborhoods are broken: instead of a dominating central nucleus, there exists fusion and a positive sort of confusion between them. Within individual buildings, Gehry introduces the text of the city, with its ambivalences, ambiguities, masquerades, and sport. He re-creates them at a personal scale, producing a kind of residential layout that is open, unpredictable, and full of surprises. Looking at the course of his work—from the Gehry House in Santa Monica, through private houses like Benson, and Wosk, and even in the Loyola Law School—one finds a translation of urban character, composition, and organization into residential complexes that restore to individual spaces symbolic, technical, and material integrity and organize them according to a criterion that rejects homogenization in order to exalt diversity and multiple readings.

They are present-day acropolises, in which private agoras discordant and tumultuous forms and colors are composed into harmony under the vigilant hand of the architect, who controls chaos, restrains fractions, and smoothes over differences to create a "hortus conclusus" of earthly delights. The resulting ensembles are composed of discontinuities that are married through synthesis and through the reconciliation of opposing forces. Gehry takes architecture back to a kind of neutrality or a zero-degree state, in order to allow the unfolding of the building process as a pluralistic event free of continuities generated exclusively by logic.

If one considers the "voyage" that Gehry makes from the Steeves House of 1959 to his 1981 proposal for an addition to it, called the Smith House, one sees him pass from a uniform to a multi-form architecture. The Steeves House is a compact bundle of spaces embedded in a single mold, with its exterior defined by homogeneous walls and facades. It acquires an identity by suppressing the individual characteristics of living room, bedroom, kitchen, bathroom, study, foyer, and garage, utilizing and arranging them instead according only to their interior values. Although inspired by Wrightian theories, the house remains passive with respect to its context; potential residential chaos is supressed in favor of a unitary, morphological order. The Smith House, by contrast, is a chain of architectural units—units that accept the plastic and visual disorder of their surroundings. It exploits the hazardous nature of the site's slope, and splits into organisms adaptable to the contours. Each organism lets itself be "seduced" by topographical relativism, neither aligning with a compositional whole nor becoming subsumed by it; each, therefore, seems to exult in its individuality. These architectural entities detach themselves and disperse, assuming the form of huts, temples sanctuaries, portals, towers, and bridges. Thus, their roles and characteristics are expressed on the exterior by innumerable variations in color and material. The row of structures gives the multiple impressions and "takes" on diverse forms passed along a highway, becoming an architectural representation of flux rather than of stasis.

Gehry's architectural creations seem to split open and break apart, to burst out of closed containers and shoot off in all linguistic directions, as if seduced by the urban eroticism of Los Angeles. They become bodies that reflect the city, actors participating in the life of the street and assuming its divisions and tensions, its gaps and disorder. Gehry says, "If you walk out on the street, there are a lot of cars, lots of dumb walls. But if you look at that street atmosphere and if you are an artist . . . your eye starts to make pictures and you edit and you find beauty out there. We're commentators on that beauty, on what's around us. That's all we're able to do. And this other thing called 'design' is a sort of forced attitude—the values are all wrong. It demands things to be made of fancy, not reality"(1). If the works are to reflect the total reality of the city, they must tell of its entrance and exit ramps, its intersections and close scrapes, its traffic jams and gas stations, and they must exemplify a style of planning based on gaps and incisions rather than density and solidity. Of his own house, the apogee of this sort of planned osmosis, Gehry wrote, "I wanted to blur the edges . . . between the old and the new . . . you're not sure what you're looking at. I guess that's the game I'm about in this house: to try and blur those edges—real and surreal"(2).

These reflections on daily urban life distinguish Gehry from architects like Charles Moore and Michael Graves, who are interested not in shattering and interweaving architectural elements but, rather, in extracting them from their historical contexts. In contrast, for Gehry a quotation taken out of context or distorted by personal interpretation has a suprahistorical and transcendent connotation: a sign disconnected from the present. He avoids such quotation; when references to forms such as columns and trabeations, porticoes and cloisters seem to appear, one cannot read them as historical or narrative in context; they can be taken only as what they are—primary, elementary forms and volumes.

Gehry designs with a sharp, double-edged scalpel that penetrates and splits open, slices and separates, probes and carves its way to the heart of spatial phenomena. It is an instrument of change and understanding. Like sharp-pointed beaks, his buildings pierce through the thick, blind atmosphere of architecture and its empty simplemindedness, upsetting perception with creations that set the imaginary and the real on the same level. This cohabitation makes possible a synthesis of the visible and invisible, the reproduced and reflected, the natural and artificial, the old and the new, the opaque and transparent, the solid and void.

The collection of structures that constitute a Gehry "house-city" preserve an interdependence by transparency: one observes the other and glimpses details through apertures or lattices, panels or filters, through chain link or glass. With these transparent perimeters Gehry achieves an adimensionality that sometimes creates optical illusions in which one can question one's manner of perceiving the simplest phenomena. Thus, the effects created in the Gehry House in Santa Monica are real "surprises" (as Mason Andrews justly defines them), that put the manner of perception to the test. Through them, Gehry seems to encourage concentration on his construction as a site of self-contained experiences (and one can understand the sense of this attitude by considering his dialectical relationship with the client, who is always urged to "collaborate"). This invitation to the inhabitant or the visitor to participate in an individual and energetic dimension can be attributed to Gehry's contact, during the sixties, with such Californian environmental artists as Bell, Orr, and Irwin, who worked on projects which seem aspatial and aphysical cocoons where one feels a sort of sensory deprivation—as if every optical and acoustical reference had been eliminated. In these spaces, as in Gehry's incisions—those gaps that allow outside phenomena to enter—take on meaningful signification.

Gehry's surgical incisions and the gaps they make upset the traditionally linear manner of perceiving space and objects. They demarcate the territory and the autonomous spheres of individual zones, intensifying their differences. One could say that by incision Gehry suggests an anatomical view of architecture, as a body that can be divided at will; he thus takes into consideration not organic architecture, but the architectural organism. Armed with a scalpel, Gehry poses real questions to its skin, its intestine; he exposes the muscle layers, the nerves, and the bones. He does not perform grafts, but instead folds back the membranes and commits the outrageous act of turning whole architectural organisms inside out, letting each appear in all its crudity, raising questions about its concrete identity and physical form. Conventional conceptions of a building as an abstraction of place or cube, or as a sign or container, are rejected; instead each is disemboweled and laid open like a body made of walls, plumbing, tiles, attics, stairs, windows, entraces, and insulation. Its material configurations appear as absolutes, setting off shock waves by their leaps and turns.

As an instrument of architectural augury, Gehry moves his blade between the fleshy layers of forms and materials. He cuts through them and dissects them to render them expressive, bringing to light their organic vitality. While he differs from Frank Lloyd Wright by cutting into a body, he nonetheless has adopted Wright's suggestions for achieving a vital and subjective architecture—an architecture preserved from dissolution in abstraction and the pursuit of objectivity, one that achieves the status of protagonist, displaying a range of conscious and unconscious gestures, like all individuals, with their contradictions and spontaniety.

In Gehry's surgery, he wrenches joints until the body shatters, giving primacy to the individual elements. He then cuts through even these elements, breaks them, messes them up; he upsets the squareness of the walls, distorts perspective, breaking ties and making everything vulnerable. The clarity of such a method appears in the O'Neill Hay Barn and the Ron Davis House, in which space is attacked, cut, decomposed, and disarticulated. The ghosts of environmental apathy vanish and the architectural object abandons visual and structural orthodoxy. He pierces the sky and the landscape with wedges and beams; he scrapes their surfaces and torments their contours. The result is the undeniably pleasing qualities of both buildings' sharp edges, as well as their mirror-like roofs and walls of corrugated metal, which distance and reflect the natural scene. Designs like these concern the factual analysis of space; they are carried out by detailing and by the specification of the concrete entities. Initially this cognitive operation is nonfigurative, and involves establishing the phonemes of the architectural idiom. It is an inquiry into the existence and behavior of lines, pilasters, planes, walls, and roofs, which are transformed from standard elements into material to be molded and carved.

It must be said, however, that even if Gehry intends his architecture to be original and autonomous, it seems clear that from a technical point of view his association with Native American culture has been influential. For example, the O'Neill Hay Barn and the Ron Davis House pay tribute to the architectural tradition of the Indians of the Northwest. The O'Neill Hay Barn continues the Nootka attitude toward building, which is "based on the construction of sturdy residences in cedar where a balanced relation is achieved between permanent elements (the support poles) and moveable ones (the wall boards)(3)." The architectural language of the Ron Davis House is linked to the craftsmanship tradition of tribes living from California to Alaska, who consider the shaping of their environment to be one of the highest artistic expressions.

If art is seen as a "space" in which images are printed and volumes are formed, then in it images and volumes can be organized according either to an optical perspective that does not permit modifications, or according to a psychological perspective that alters and blends the representations of surfaces and forms, colors and lines. As Gehry wished to "project" Ron Davis's own artistic statement into the design of his house, he constructed it according to an "imaginary model" that follows the visual principles of a Davis-like painting with multiple viewpoints. He set out to create a multidirectional space, offering infinite variety and complexity by the simultaneous use of multiple points of perspective. He has said of the house: "the trapezoid grows out of his painting. The tilted roof grows out of my preoccupation with the tilted roof. The idea of forced perspective grew out of Palladio"(4). From this burst forth an architecture that symbolizes the continuous flux and transformation of things in time. Since the components of an individual residence here arise from the reciprocal and cyclical action of opposing forces, their typologies are continuously transformed. Here, then, are the different views and angles of the roof and walls, the spatial and luministic agitation of the windows and skylights, the multiple angulations of the interior divisions: all work together to let each residential element retain a fluid and continuously changing character. The traditional mechanics of movement, containment, seeing, and lighting are ignored. With incisions and joints, Gehry has created real stage sets along with stage machinery and trap doors. Here stairways are transformed into catwalks and platforms over the void, while balconies become medieval walkways above the moat of the floor, while the angles of the walls turn the paths into a maze. It all resembles a huge stage in the process of being set up; the dramatization is entrusted to Davis, the actor/inhabitor/artist, whose action and finishing touches are continually being added to the scene.

This reliance on interaction and on unfinished statements in the design is a further example of Gehry's ability to use the incoherencies arising from architectural communication which, like art, does not have great means at its disposal and cannot presuppose conclusive declarations. In fact, Gehry confirms that "I guess I was interested in the unfinished—or the quality that you find in paintings by Jackson Pollock, for instance, of de Kooning, or Cezanne, that look like the paint was just applied. The very finished, polished, every-detail-perfect kind of architecture seemed to me not to have that quality. I wanted to try that out in a building. The obvious way to go about it was the unfinished wood studs. We all like the buildings in construction better than we do finished—I think most of us agree on that. The structure is always so much more poetic than the finished thing"(5). While the linguistic relationship between Gehry's work and minimal art has been underlined elsewhere, these discussions emphasize formal issues. Attention should also be brought to a reading of his buildings that takes into consideration their "intersections" and their joints, which tend to push his architecture outside the anonymous, reductive communication of spatial phenomena. The contours of the O'Neill Hay Barn and Ron Davis House are diagrams gone mad, enclosures of twisted volumes, which liken Gehry to an architect-sculptor who wishes to renounce the functional organization of his working methods in order to concentrate on subverting volumetric and material rules and paradigms. He creates neither cubbyholes nor boxes, but rather, openings, paths, pauses and interruptions, which give the architecture room to breathe and make it a dialectical experience. Each building is an agglomeration of diversified functions and properties, a circuitous conversation that can be arranged in sequence or interrupted, creating rhythmic relations between the phases. Many practitioners of contemporary Western architecture, who tend to concentrate on constructive discourse, have not reflected sufficiently on the varied meanings of the pause and of emptiness, which can so amplify the power of pronouncement. Gehry has certainly understood its potential, in part by observing the traditions of the artisan and the Oriental mentality, both of which collect and combine fragments into a single corporality, be it an artifact or icon. Gehry believes intermittence can lead toward discovery: "I guess I appraoch architecture somewhat scientifically—there are going to be *breakthroughs* and they're going to create new information. It's adding information to the pot—not necessarily regurgitating other, older ideas"(6). To obtain these openings Gehry has introduced interrelational space between wall and wall, house and house, house and wall, wall and street, house and street, in order to divide one from the other and explore the reciprocal intervals.

In projects like the Norton and Benson House, intervals between one nucleus and another are activated by corridors, paths, and tunnel-like constructions, as well as by the presence of drawbridges and aerial passages activated by hinges, pulleys, and wheels—all of which serve to awaken significant connections among the "actors" of Gehry's architectural choreography. Reading the instructions concerning screens and volumes suspended by cords, which were prepared with the design of the House for a Filmmaker (all of which, as it happens, were ignored by the client), one notes the architect's continual attention to the collection and dispersal of images. It seems almost as if the choice of images derived from many thousands of passages, as in a film montage, that return to the same point—as in cinema, so in architecture.

Gehry's references continually draw on Los Angeles. He follows it so as not to forget it and shapes his houses with its ebb and flow, giving to each residential component the form of a barge being drawn along. In this way, each project comes to resemble a city of houseboats, in which the living room might become a golden temple, the study an industrial shed in corrugated metal, and bathroom a medieval alchemist's tower, the corridors arches and drawbridges, the windows the portholes of ships—all realized in unusual materials, like cardboard, fiberglass, polyester, teak, raw plywood, or cement.

This phantasmagoria of materials is a further indication of the "happy science" of architecture. Creating unusual effects with them, he breaks the heaviness of massive, dark stucco facades, obtaining rhythmic sounds and silences that give way to involved and unexpected visual orchestrations. Such a symphony of effects is reminiscent of the sixteenth-century villas of Pratolino and Boboli, the designs of which seem to attempt, with their incessant metamorphoses, to account for the complex laws that regulate the world. Gehry tries to document the contemporary equivalent, the indeterminism and discontinuity that hold together a particular city: Los Angeles. If New York can be called the last European city and Los Angeles the first American city, then Frank Gehry—who has sought to compose a statement that unifies the consolidated creations of architecture and the ungraspable qualities of the latter city, defining their relationship in irridescent figurations—can be called the "first" American architect.

The Architectural Labyrinth

Another important aspect of Gehry's architecture not explored in the preceeding analysis revolves around images based on memory and on mythological archetypes. The idea of a variety of sensations jumbled into a single container, which can stand for the spatial-temporal framework, recalls the vase in *Time Regained,* the last volume of *Remembrances of Times Past,* which reminds Proust of the mosaic of sensation and memory, a mosaic the writer should recall in linking together each word in every sentence. The architect must perform a similar task—more than merely collecting and storing images in a vase, he must also blend and mix them to create something new and fresh. For architecture, moving beyond simple containment makes it possible to attract and absorb all possible contacts and hypothetical textures, thus enabling one to pass from one space or surface to another. The process becomes in effect a spiraling daydream that recalls the archetypal labyrinth.

The labyrinth was invented by Daedalus, whose name means "cunning craftsman." Its web of corridors and doors is a tangled knot of streets and crossroads, forks and dead ends, at each of which one is free to choose which path to take. As a result, losing one's way or reaching the center is determined by one's own choices. The idea of a labyrinth can be taken as a metaphor for architecture itself, for to work in architecture means following a difficult path; to set out on this path is to embark on a trouble-filled adventure filled with impediments and nightmares.

On a symbolic level, the path of a labyrinth expresses, through its configuration, the relationship between interior and exterior; it is the site of hopes and fears, desire and guilt, pleasure and pain, reason and madness. To travel here is to take part in an initiatory process through which, after penetrating its complexity, one may finally achieve self-awareness. Aside from its dead ends and sidetracks, the labyrinth evokes the image of a world concentrated on the self, built up of visible and invisible layers that participate in a progressive appropriation of space: the body, bed, table, chair, room, corridor, house, office, street, neighborhood, city. It is the individual, social, and public space that revolves in the constellation of architectural spaces assigned to different individuals, in the multiple paths of which one is as likely to encounter sensuality as monstrosity.

Gehry's architecture presents the traveler with a labyrinthine, almost indecipherable structure: in a voyage through one of his creations one must make choices to chart the proper path, which the memory of the labyrinth infuses with the suggestions of peril or freedom. The imagery of the labyrinth appears in the background of Gehry's work as the common denominator in the evolution from the private world of the Gehry House to the public realm of the Los Angeles Children's Museum.

The Gehry House in Santa Monica is certainly the point of departure in this evolution. But as with all of Gehry's works, it has a double *raison d'etre:* it is a pleasure dome as well as a metaphor of bewitched architecture. Entering, one penetrates into a sensual retreat (where only friends and initiates are admitted), filled with exotic animals and plants, carved and molded substances, tools and materials summoning images of preconscious life. The house seems to bring to mind both the origins of human life and the development of consciousness: it is the safe womb from which we were separated and toward which we are drawn back by a semiconscious desire for self-forgetfulness.

Gehry populates the house with surprises and marvels that produce new types of earth and new plants, expressions of a Garden of Adonis which, during the summer, blooms and creates a festive architecture where the systematic violation of constructional rules is more conspicuous than ever. Walls are uprooted and transplanted like flowers and plants, stairs and terraces dangle as if suspended from the sky, facades sprout and crawl up the sides of other houses, entryways spread out their roots in different terrains. The kitchen has been sewn with asphalt, the cupboards are trees with chicken-wire foliage, and the rooms are trunks and branches from which the bark and cork have been hacked away with a hatchet.

The gesture that carves its surface or plows its soil is an act of intense passion between two "beings" that collaborate in life much as in architecture, bound together, like the two houses, by a passionate relationship. When asked, "Can you tell us what your intentions were there?" the architect replied: "It had to do with my wife. She found this nice house—and I love my wife—this cute little house with antiques in it. Very sweet little things"(7).

I mention this foray into sentimentality because I want to call attention to another feature in Gehry's architecture: its capacity to place on trial the architect's attitude toward himself and toward the object (both client and building). The subject is the identity, the identification, the unitary and totalizing instance that molds all differences into a general statement. By contrast, the object is the dissimilarity, the opposite pole of identification, the particular and resulting instance, the extraneous element that has not yet been assimilated. The object is, therefore, that which activates the reevaluation of differences. Gehry's intuitive and sentimental interpretation derives, on one hand, from the totality of meaning and, on the other, from its deconstruction. That is what makes his work a risky adventure—it dismantles structure to reach an architecture that discards and demolishes, positions and shuffles, diffuses and diverges. Thus is revealed a type of design that functions both as a personal and cultural emblem without, however, settling into a rigid framework: "life of building, aging, decreption, demolition, these above are all parts of architecture, dialogue between the two"(8).

What then is the text of this building in Santa Monica? What does it designate? Besides helping to personalize architecture, does it try to depersonalize it as well? Or else does it methodically attempt to open a space and a scene in the world of signs, where objectivity and subjectivity are no longer antithetical contenders in a fight to the finish?

Gehry's endeavors at Santa Monica involve a double violence: the violence of a statement controlled by desire and the violence of desire in the order of a statement. The first has been commented upon; the second remains to be discussed. Architectural trends since the seventies—the rejection of ideologies based on geometrical simplification, the right angle, and programmatic accumulation of functional standards—have been regarded as a more than justified defense of historical consciousness, as well as a "new style," seen as a summation of all others. In the end, however (except for the work of Venturi and Rossi), postmodernism has degenerated into forms of decorative narcissism. Monuments to period styles have arisen, along with real pocket encyclopedias of academic architecture, and feats of virtuosity with ceremonial and hermetic meanings. These have all given rise to a neomannerism that seems to leave the architect on the sidelines rather than presenting real challenges. How did this occur? Certainly by legislating and formalizing in monumental buildings the schizoid attitude of a culture that no longer believes in the unity of meaning, but instead in "three-dimensional puzzles, with their pieces stuck violently inside one another, always local and never specific, with pieces that do not match up, and are forces, manipulated, jammed into each other, always with pieces left over"(9). If it is true that the schizoid period coincides with a period in which the sketching of architectural designs in pencil and pastel predominates, it is also true that the thrust toward the unspeakable and the singular, which creates architectural nets of multiple meanings interwoven among themselves, has been trapped in the congealed forms of the contemporary monoliths in many styles and has been subsumed in a single, unidirectional code.

If the suggestion of the infinite proliferation of reason gone mad has been a way of avoiding any definition or imprisonment of architectural meaning, unfortunately the series of identical and repetitive neoclassic and hermetic projects, which are incapable of expressing "irrationality", has aborted the triumphant strategy that would have turned planning not toward a new equilibrium, but toward the ecstatic excitement of destroying fundamental principles. I believe that Gehry has been one of the few, if not the only one, to allow himself to lose both himself and architecture in the giddiness brought about by the antagonisms of the divided nature—the schizophrenia—of architecture. That is, he has rejected formulas and taken account of the dynamics of things themselves, as well as of the investments of desire. More than merely proposing, he tried to specify the indices, the residual traces, the transverse flights, of a demolition or decomposition of architecture seen as a mutating, regenerating organism. From this specification he derives his exaltation of surgical cutting as a subtle means of radicalization: he anatomizes the architectural body in order to double and multiply it to impress upon it an immortality based on fast traffic and reflected reproduction.

The representation of this movement seems to agree with the declaration of Baudrillard in which he affirms that in order to radicalize the world, "we do not oppose the beautiful and the ugly, we seek the ugliest of the ugly: the monstrous. We do not oppose the visible and the hidden, we seek the most hidden of the hidden: the secret. We do not seek chance and we do not oppose the fixed and the mobile, we seek the most mobile of the mobile; the metamorphosis. We do not distinguish the true from the false, we seek the most false of the false: illusion and appearance."(10).

Returning to the Gehry House, the multidimensionality that characterizes both its content and its formal dispersions could be interpreted as polyhedric architecture: in it space advances and recedes, is transfigured, and even causes bizarre mechanisms and apparitions to appear that are typical of a haunted house (similar to the illusionistic, eighteenth-century galleries of Paul Decker).

One box inside the other, the house in Santa Monica, with its optical and volumetric games of solid and void, sets itself up as the land of illusion. It opens itself, pliable and chameleon-like, to every interpretation, yet always remains ungraspable. Through the play of appearances and depths between one house and the other, the potential of fusion between the two is promoted, making the artifice of the new plausible with respect to the old. The autonomy of each is deliberately confused in order to make them both instruments to strain and challenge the "rules" consider architecture as the *mise en scene* of either spaces or the concrete realities of volumes and functions. "I got fascinated with the idea that the old house should appear to remain totally intact from the outside, and that you could look through the new house and see the old house as though it was now packaged in this new skin. The new skin and the windows in the new house would be of a totally different aesthetic than the windows in the old house. So they would constantly be in tension with each other"(11).

The phantasmagoria of the encounter between old and new, interior and exterior, reaches its peak in the kitchen/dining area. One finds oneself here on an asphalt passageway surrounding the exterior of the old house, but closed within the walls of the new one, with its windows reflecting the lights and shadows of the street. The perceptual complexities are multiplied little by little as one rises to the level of the gallery that surrounds the bedrooms. Here, standing on chain link, spaces open that are in turn multiplied and expand as one looks down into the abyss of the prismatic glass corner of the dining area. It is thus nearly impossible to arrive at the truth of this architecture, which is entangled and always interrupted, but finished and in a period of possible mutation. According to Gehry, "The house is complete although I continue to fantasize about it, like removing the interior and replacing it with a Miesian box, then tearing down the outside; or finishing it in conventional terms by painting it pink and convering it with gypsum board. There's some bite in that for me"(12). Moreover, while setting one building inside another could suggest a hierarchy between the two, Gehry excludes this possibility by making one an obstacle to the other. In order to maintain its autonomy, each one opens and closes the road to the other, producing a deceptive situation that finally results in a new architectural consanguinity.

With this house, architecture opens up to a series of dialectical conjectures. It ventures courageously onto deceptive and enigmatic paths and offers itself as a place in which the "sense" of building is subject to torsion and distortion. The vision of architecture that emerges here is entirely conditioned: the building is an unbound, mobile energy; it functions by involving all types of entities (beings, places, and concepts) in its movement—from the double entrance staircases in cement and wood rotating around different forms to the solid but transparent roofs in glass and chain link. The principle of circulation and fluidity governs the ensemble. In it, Gehry conducts undifferentiated floods of images, materials, and objects. He derives from it an effect of instability and of fragmentation of substances (for example, the edges of the chain link wedge themselves into the solid-void of walls and spaces) and of visual identities (the view of the diagonal windows/ceiling of the bedroom terrace seen from the ephemeral wall panels of the garden, for instance, differ with the view of these garden elements from the terrace).

The visual and spatial dismemberment that is born of the encounter between the old and new nuclei suggest a continuous conflict. And, in fact, if architecture is not to become moribund, it must promote the continual semination and dissemination of pieces and parts that are born, grow, change, and interact endlessly. The pursuit of this architectural organism, whose paroxysm of life threatens the equilibrium of the parts, must not stop. Here again one flirts with the desire for an uncontrollable transformation. One does not follow the direction of history, but rejects it and its ideology in order to work on displacement and disorientation. The consequence is not a return to the past or a "remake" of the academy or of classicism, but a personalization and discontinuity that spread out from the present.

It became evident at the 1980 Venice Biennale that Gehry does not use history as a tracing element. His project for the Strada Novissima succeeded in redeeming the spatial and temporal inertia of the Arsenale with a "screen" in rough wood. While other architects illustrated a romanticized reading of architecture, with their pictorial and cinematic annotations based on ancient icons and stories (the facades were all produced at Cinecittà), Gehry refused to translate archiecture into either a realistic or abstract "representation." His construction, transparent and unfinished—in the Michelangelesque sense—tried instead to frame the tangible aperture of the sixteenth-century window in the wall of the Arsenale beyond. It was not created as polemic against the architectural intellectuality of the exhibition, but, rather, to satisfy the demands of his instinct, for vitality and the architectural organism—which sees experience as the purpose of planning and building.

While both radical and essential, his Biennale project was, in a sense, nonetheless a "historical" response: the "facade" disappeared as structure and became instead a visual experience and an existential mechanism for testing space (in the tradition of the tenets of Californian environmental art). This artistic process of perceiving architecture recalls Rothko's new construction material and color, as well as Wright's plastic masses, in its attempt to achieve a desired light and natural synthesis of the two that shifts an architectural problem from history and structure to the visual plane.

From this direction came the "unexpected" (to use Philip Johnson's adjective) figurations of Gehry's plan for the Beverly Hills Civic Center. Like the whole competition, these figurations revolve around a rhetorical motif: the lofty style of public architecture that can accept only the good manners, forms, and ethics of polite language (indeed, of the language of the competition's winner, Charles Moore, who was ready to work with "the given collective parts" without changing them). As counterpoint, Gehry proposed his eighteenth-century staircase, which is both a scapegoat for and a reflection of Enlightenment and neoconservative journalistic criticisms of architecture. By inserting the staircase, Gehry tried to protect himself from this neoconservative malaise. The "sordid" quotation reflects his awareness of a position that is always intolerable, even to defenders of contemporary postmodern eighteenth-centuryism—that of inflexible moribund decorum. The stair itself is both literally and analogically a sidetrack, leading nowhere, with disorientation as its only purpose. Indeed, competition critics spoke of the project's "awkward" transitions and "engaging or irritating" spatial tensions (13), having failed to understand that this blind, exitless nucleus was intended to question, or even threaten, a form of historical quotation that is meaningless today. While the presence of the staircase may imply that Gehry's attitude mixes repulsion and attraction, it must be remembered that he still hopes to reconstruct a new harmonious order through the experience of an architectural rupture. He is searching for a dialectical and contradictory architecture that gushes from the decomposed and disjoined body, but which is still based on pulsation and on uncontrolled moments of pleasure.

This is not to suggest, however, that Gehry abandons the historical and structural method; only that for him this method is inadequate because it prohibits the study of facts and objects that go against the grain of history. Gehry operates in this direction because he is attracted by objects extraneous to history. New directions generated throughout architectural history from Borromini to Wright, have been based on this "extraneity," precisely because they do not rehash existing geneologies, but move in the opposite direction from the main roads of architecture. Similarly, Gehry's planning is not based on the manifest and artificial "residues" that are typical of postmodern quotationism, but plunges into the intuitive, profound archaeological zones (as Foucault defines archaelogical) of the unknown. It raises questions about the excavated materials of building in order to seek another logic. All his architecture turns, then, on something like Foucault's "uncomfortable reason... in order to traverse [which] one must renounce the comfort of terminal truths"(14). There is no break between reason and non-reason, just as no "caesurea" exists in Gehry's work (his house in Santa Monica providing the strongest example) between architecture and non-architecture.

That Gehry's work involves excavating in the realm of the subjective, from the irrational to the surreal, can be verified by his manner of drawing and sketching. His pencil or pen scrapes across the page as if torturing it to make it speak—as if the image of the building were hidden or sunk in the pulp of the paper and could be brought to light through a series of graphic furrows. His sketches are a universe filled with whirlpools and twisted lines, from which he clips out architectural outlines and larvae little by little as the graphite or ink breaks up and unravels the forms. He has said: "The process of doing architecture is to work through a set of ideas, a set of finished drawings, and give them to the field for the construction. Everything's got to be on that drawing, or else you get killed with extras. So the process forces a kind of precision. I can see why architecture tends to be so precise and finished, because the idea of building in the unfinished is very much against the system of building, unless you get there and work hands on with the materials. It is something I have been urging students to do, rather than go to work with a big office and become cynical in two years.... When the artists and sculptors I know work, there's sort of a free play idea. You try things; you experiment. It's kind of naive and childish, it's like kids in a playpen. Scientists work that way too—for example, genetic scientists that I have been involved with (through a genetic foundation that I work with) seem to work similarly. It's kind of like throwing things out and then following the ideas, rather than predicting where you're going to go"(15).

The graphic and chromatic substances of the page, which begin as formless, ephemeral figures, emerge from their prelinguistic definition through Gehry's continual manipulation, eventually blooming in the form of towers and domes, stairs and windows, banks and houses, animals and beings in motion. On the surface the drawing is forced to change—it is examined obsessively, isolated and scrutinized, in order to extract an image that can give meaning to the plan. Hence the action is never rectilinear, but is defined organically until the transition to a more objective and generalized system of communication is achieved: the passage from a nuclear image to fixity. It is removed from the flow of the imagination and then defined; it is disarmed and rendered non-obsessive.

As in the paintings of Archille Gorky, the Armenian-born American artist, the eventual pictorial arrangement comes from the iconography of the depths, whose meaning is connected to the variabilty and transience of signs. One could even affirm that Gehry's drawings continue, within the medium of architecture, the path suggested by Gorky. In his renunciation of the question of origins and of history, Gehry has assumed the task of verifying architecture as "continuous existence." His is an architecture in which the signs, cells, and molecules of planning continually change, are made and unmade, grow and shrink, are born and die. Yet it is not merely a case of the "organic" principle that recurs throughout American culture; for Gehry, becoming is a dissociating process. As a result, the surfaces never lie on a single plane, the lines are not definitive, the spaces are cracked and interrupted, the joints misfire or vacillate; in sum, figures and images are uncertain in their connotations. It is from this discordant and choppy rhythm that the monsters of architecture rise to the surface: Gehry's eagles, snakes and fishes.

In his designs for the Jung Institute, the Lafayette Street lofts, the *Chicago Tribune,* and tract houses, Gehry's graphic practice seems to use an automatic writing that permits him to render his lyricism objective. He designs or opens a space to give the stage to signs, and marks where architectural subjectivity and objectivity can no longer be considered actors in a battle typical of modernism, but protagonists in a revelation and integration of the interior, general design. His operation is therefore "without reservation," with total attention to the signals of the unknown and the game: "I go where my explorations take me—I never go back. I never turn off the searching until, like a mathematician, I've solved the problem. When faced with a new problem to explore I feel like a curious cat that has been given the freedom to play. I feel like a voyeur"(16).

To be a voyeur of one's own pleasurable efforts enables one to speak of the object—the image—not as a product, but as an event that arises from a fortuitous collision of effects and of secret and intimate correspondences: Voyeurism for Gehry is a means to multiply the opportunities for contact with one's own imaginative topology. He uses it to bring about the vision of marvelous architectural prototypes, like animals. In this vision, the abstract and functionalist burden of the rationalism is eschewed to give life to a foreign body capable of bringing about—as a privileged sign—a semantic redistribution of architectural iconography: within the imaginary landscape of this architecture, the unusual figure—the foreign body—is capable of provoking irritation in the field of ordinary buildings. In response, the architecture may discharge its own secretions against it, and in this way turn into pearl.

Just as the voyeur is presumably acquainted with group coupling, then architectural voyeurism as a method of research may be seen as reproposing the component of uniting many architectural individualities, which is peculiar to Gehry's "city-houses." It is accepting the situation of buildings that are thrown on one another, establishing varied relations and practices through which the amorous process of architecture lives. In Gehry's work the whirlpools of metaphors and allusions of iconic stratifications and enigmatic games, take shape, beginning in 1979, with the zoomorphic metamorphism of the *Chicago Tribune*'s eagle and, later, the fish and the snake.

The global display of architectural zoomorphism is a constant theme in Gehry's collaboration with Richard Serra. This confrontation with postminimal sculpture seemed to compel Gehry to make a definitive break with rationalist, modern iconography. Each of the bridgeheads supporting the spans that were proposed to pass through both the Chrysler Building and the World Trade Center presume and accept the same creative process, yet they represent poetic antitheses. One is the objectivization of volumes made aesthetic by nudity and essentiality, by abstraction and impersonality—a constructive utopia. The other is a Duchampian ready-made, cumbersome and unjustifiable—a dreamy, erotic object, personalized through surrealism. To plan a skyscraper in the form of a fish involves, then, empirical testing of the relative appropriateness of the "found" object's image for a certain use or purpose. A progression from the whole to the part, from the shape to the function that finally becomes congruent with the collaboration, was similarly considered and attempted in 1968 in a design for the Pasadena Museum in the form of a cigarette package; this process was finally realized in 1984 in Milan, with Claes Oldenberg – the artist who attributes an architectural sense to commonplace, everyday objects.

Gehry, like Oldenberg, renders the banal and the marvelous interchangeable; in this the ascending journey from banality toward banality, from stasis toward flight, from the aquatic toward the terrestrial. With such interchange the diagonal is not to be considered a sign of detachment or separation as much as—like the chain link—an index of transition and of the function of the glance and of desire. The position that Gehry and Oldenberg seem to share must be examined by studying the relation to the contextual determinations that the ojbect—icon has as it interacts with its context in reality. What matter are the reflexes and stimulations of the extraordinary sign that has landed in a certain place. This is how the meaning of Oldenberg's Bat Column and Flashlight may be understood in their dialogues with, respectively, Chicago and Las Vegas; the meaning of Gehry's fish may be deduced from its functioning with respect to the aquatic element that surrounds Manhattan. Its image recalls the subterranean world and the confusion of New York's urban elements; it is the index of a discipline— architecture—that for Gehry comes from the depths and from secrecy.

The criterion, is therefore, to test empirically the degree to which the architectural icon conforms to a certain use and a certain goal—like the Chinese restaurant on Melrose that Gehry has planned in the form of a snake. This image evokes the iconography of the Oriental world and recalls, like food itself, the dynamic between life and death. Even if this contribution is situated in Los Angeles, the city of supericonic architecture, the image succeeds in implying the continual metamorphosis—the skin-shedding—of design work. In addition, the snake, like the fish, is a symbol of love and libido. It is no surprise then that their sacred qualities have been transmuted in Gehry's work into a design of light, impalpable ghosts of a body that glows from within. Finally, in pagan and Christian bestiaries, the snake and the fish are always incarnations of the great creator or the great initiate—symbolic elements congenial to Gehry.

The Architectual Earthquake

The fact that Los Angeles is an area of seismic activity has its own influence on Gehry's work. The eminence of the earthquake in California culture is apparent in its building codes and in its spaces and materials; it shapes the physical and methodological terms of urban construction. Potential geological alteration is presupposed, and thus becomes the premise underlying formal and volumetric design.

For Gehry, architecture is itself an earthquake, travelling and spreading by waves, striking in all latitudes, cutting deep crevasses into buildings and environments, causing irreparable breaks and irreversible effects. It is a radical upheaval. When such upheaval occurs, as it has periodically in avant-garde movements throughout history, it subverts systems, alters the orderly character of the aesthetic territory, deconstructs and dislocates walls and spaces, forms and directions. Sometimes, at its highest level, from Brunelleschi to Borromini, from Behrens to Gropius, it brings about events of exceptional significance that shake society down to its foundations.

Since 1963, Gehry has adopted the earthquake as a model; he has used its concentrated, instantaneous efficacy against closed, banal constructions and has created cataclysms of dramatic violence in response to order and to functionalist mutations. Starting with knowledge of a preconceivable image, he has succeeded with projects like the Loyola Law School in crumbling an image, in tearing it to pieces, so that every cohesion corresponds not to a logic of "good forms," but instead to the enchanted plurality of processes and problems.

In designing a "hortus conclusus" for the school, Gehry has suggested—and provided an experience of—the stratified language of law as an exalted process in which legal decisions are made by reconstructing fragments of evidence (as opposed to a view of law as a series of hard and fast rules). He uses a process of simultaneous action on time and space that, like a seismic disturbance, places all elements on the same level, decomposes and deconstructs them according to their personifiable character: they are civil and religious buildings, classrooms and court buildings, offices and student center. Each is separate and isolated as well as traversed by clefts and fissures. The crevasses between one element and another create optical and perceptual distortions, dislocate entrances and split volumetric unities, while materials sway and slip like sheets of colors to form skins and transparencies. This chain reaction sets up correspondences between the subterranean and the superficial, interior and exterior, microcosm and macrocosm. The architecture unfolds and illuminates what is hidden, creating zones of brilliance. It becomes a vital diagram that opens to vision and to planning the secret processes of both legislation and construction, with columns and walls quotations of architecture in an abstract, objective sense rather than of architectural history. In this way, the tendencies of volumes are revealed and attention is drawn to their hidden solidity. Endowing splinters and fragments of buildings with corporality is an obvious consequence of architecture as a telluric occurrence that comprehends the seismic approach apparent in a work like Oldenberg's balanced staircase. Like that staircase, which appears on the verge of overturning a jar of paint, the architecture recalls the precarious fluctuations and difficult balance of law-making.

The campus also presents itself as a tribe of buildings with different identities reflecting the congregation of students and teachers from all over the world to practice the same creed—the law. This type of aggregation recalls the vital cultural progress of the Hebrew people—a historical collection that can be seen as shaping his design work in general. The implications of this theory point to another symbolic dimension in his way of working. The facade of Loyola's Burns Building can be seen, in its solidity, as a rock from which waters gush forth: the green stairs that burst naturalistically through the split wall of the faculty building become a fluid emanation. The stair is also the primary connection between the faculty and student "bodies": the former is represented by the construction in glass—on high—which can be identified as a clear, transparent mind (a true solar, cosmic dome that illuminates the entire universe of the school); the latter is identified with the classrooms, sites of the accumulation of knowledge as well as of architectural vocabulary (columns, facades, volumes, materials, colors, towers, paintings, and icons). Gehry has said, "With the center stair we wanted to make a statement about entrance, processions, identify the center of the building, and that centerpiece relates more to the future buildings—when they are in place, it becomes the center object"(17).

The glass architecture that dominates the Burns Building is not a quotation from the Bauhaus, but, rather, a recollection of the magic circle and the crystal cathedral that, from the Middle Ages to the twentieth century, have both been viewed as jealously guarding and protecting the secrets of human beings. It is an Enlightenment motif that floats above the structural web and is seen in much of Gehry's work, from the Smith House to the Frances Goldwyn Regional Branch Library. At Loyola, the classrooms are designed in a succession of levels and cubes, recalling the cosmological symbolism of sanctuaries and temples in which initiatory rites take place. Similarly, the reading boxes at the Goldwyn Library are surrounded by water; they also signal a reciprocity between nature and the knowledge that comes from reading (at Loyola it comes from teaching). Interpreted in this way, the glassed-in building—in the Wosk Residence it appears as the artist's studio—becomes a skylight-cupola as well, a center from which light radiates.

But compared with Rossi's scenographic orgy of cone-towers—in projects like the Carlo Felice Theater at Genoa and the Modena Cemetery, where the light component operates from the peak of a sacred mountain consecrated to the theater or to death—Frank Gehry shows a decided preference, typical of Californian environmental culture, for the real light that exists not only in the remote antiquity of temples, but in the daily life of houses and schools. This explains his preference for natural light as well as those colors (like the yellow, white, blue, and green of Loyola) that tend to lighten the architecture in order to attune it to the natural and urban landscapes. He has explained that at Loyola "the colors also have to do with trying not to upstage the neighborhood or the Martin Building. The intention was to try and make it as quiet a building as possible, relatively, because it is a large object, and make it fit in and not push the neighborhood. As for the interior colors, when you get bright blasts of sunlight into an interior that has light greens and blues, it's very pretty . . . the light has been a consistent tool in our work"(18).

Loyola is therefore a "city of the sun," where the parties confront each other in the central space, as a Taut's Stadkrone, across a bridge between tradition and the future of a renewed society. More than a city, it is the ideogram of a city founded on an open pattern, in which the ornamental inlays are integral and autonomous, capable of imitating the forms of the past as well as living in the future. It is here that the root of Gehry's refusal to characterize the columns and the sacred path of the chapel formally and historically lies; it is as if he wished to design only the beginning of an energetic process whose directions and prospects are unknown. He understates masses and emphasizes movement, in order to exalt the relationships through which the volumes and systems attract and repel one another: the classrooms and flowerbeds, for example, seem to draw as near as possible to one another, while intervals are left—as in the open space between the Burns Building, the classrooms, and the chapel—to allow free movement that seems to revolve around the tree of life. At Loyola the unity and interlacing of the components participate in a higher design—the hope for just legislation, as much as just planning and building—that cannot be crystallized, but must be left to act, as Taut put it, so that "the building contains nothing but a splendid space" (19).

The seismic splaying of buildings with unsettling, asymmetrical compositions opens furrows and craters in architecture that can be compared to the unexpected unhingings of Dadaism. For Gehry, architecture is a ready-made—it is formed of objects that can be extracted from time and space to be inserted into a different, uncodified, and unexpected territory. His orchestrated changes in context, in fact, allow the ready-mades to be reconsidered and perceived from a different material and physical angle, as well as a functional and artistic one (e.g. the Gehry House and the Easy Edges products). As a result, and as projects like the Cabrillo Marine Museum illustrate, the architectural ready-made can be turned over or rotated, multiplied or embedded, preserved or sliced, carrying out multiple operations that offer a possibility of decodifying it.

The intentional casualness and transiency with which Gehry relegates architectural elements find an almost metaphysical justification in the spider web in which the buildings of the Cabrillo Marine Museum are lodged. Here the visual labyrinth of tubular structures and chain link, with aquatic transparency seen from an industrial perspective, defines the infinity of a world submerged in a cultivated play of allegories. The underlying notion in the scenario of the museum is the fluctuation and reflection of bodies in space. The open links of its chain-link "netting" and the reflective glazing scan volumes of infinite dimensions. They are reflections of an "irridescent" architecture, in which the splendor of light circulates and the transparency of material elements are underscored—Material elements which also serve, on the building's interior, to enclose and make visible the marine flora and fauna displayed. The sparkle that unifies the exhibition and service areas almost recalls the Impressionist brilliance of Monet's Waterlilies; here, too, the objects seem to float on a surface; they break down formally into prismatic parts and live in the explosion of reflections and infinite modulations of light. This naturalistic combination finds further confirmation in the typology of the museum complex which recalls, with its triangular waves and its lobster-pot-shaped amphitheater, Buontalenti's "water theaters," where surprises and sudden apparitions of figures and automata constitute the performance. The museum becomes in this way a site of sensual and optical solicitation as much as a stage for scientific and didactic investigation of marine life.

The prismatic complexity of science in the theater becomes interpretative faceting, which Gehry translates into an apparatus in the World Expo Amphitheater in New Orleans, and into perspective complexity, induced by frontal and lateral vision, in the stage for Lucinda Childs' "Available Light."

This aptitude for fluidity reinforces Gehry's preference for working principally with the disorienting transfer of a manufactured space, volume, or surface, or one salvaged from the demolition or destruction of a building; he has, in fact, insisted that "these are all valid parts of architecture"(20). He removes them from their typical habitats and subjects them to a process of recodification, inserting them into surprising and upsetting systems of relations. This altering of the connections serves to demonstrate the differences in weight, color, and density that exist between different materials; as a result, spaces seem to open, explode, and become nuclei of energy—autonomous and heedless of the logic of conventional construction. The intent is to rebaptize architecture in accordance with a disinterested and antidogmatic attitude. Nonetheless, the explosion of the monolithic building into many fragments scattered over a site is dictated not only by a personal or artistic desire, but by a social one as well.

Many of the architectural projects planned by Gehry are offices, shopping centers, and museums that must withstand the impact and the movement of thousands of persons. The mass dimension in an exhibition or a super-market requires, in fact, the subdivision of the visual spaces as well as the selling spaces, in order to legitimize the fragmentation and disorder of the structures; Gehry personalizes them, in order to reassert the human scale in a sea of anonymity. In projects like Santa Monica Place and Mid-Atlantic Toyota, Gehry has therefore concentrated on shattering in order to exalt the variety of products and departments. He has split surfaces by inserting oblique, vertical, and polydimensional elements that force open the cubic resistance of spaces. He has, that is, accepted the disintegration of work as well as of the market, and instead of debasing them with anonymous and indifferent volumes and paths, he has exalted them. With the simultaneous use of incisions, materials, trespassings and redoublings, he has infused into the orthogonal severity of the Toyota Building an orchestration of isolating and transparent devices that permit him to definitively overcome the old, dated system of cellular cubicals and workstations. The recourse to psychoplastic screens and partitions capable of creating a kaleidoscope of environmental effects has produced a macroscopic jungle interrupted by panels, windows, and chain link that, with their interlacing, make the work "stage" explode. On two levels, across the infrastructure of steel pillars, industrial dynamism has been developed. In comparison with other office interiors, the Mid-Atlantic Toyota, like the Berger, Berger, Kahn, Shafton & Moss Law Offices, does not stop at suggestion, but represents the action of individual work activities, so far as to identify them with the user's special interests or even personality. In fact, in the Law Offices ribs and spaces cut out for the individual character of the lawyer project from its organizing spine: the log cabin and the temple of justice, the cactus garden and the black box—all determined by paths of pastel color, in which the benches are designed anthropomorphically so as to create a design that is not only organic, but also in movement.

It is evident that the effort to confer order on disorder and vice versa, for which chaos defines the structural identity of every service and use, is part of a stereo-vision that Gehry uses to open architecture to all views and perspectives. It is a hyper-condition of a vision determined by electronics and aeronautics, a future which is influencing the representation and construction of reality. If Gehry's architecture can be seen as characterized by this n-dimensional space, at its base must be recognized a vision in which space and the human being are projections of a machine: the death, therefore, of the univocal space of the Renaissance in favor of a spherical and extraterrestrial evolution of perception. Here lies true postmodernism. For this reason Santa Monica Place as well as the California Aerospace Space Museum cannot be conceived as "determined" but must be understood as discontinuous, but potentially infinite wholes.

In particular, the recent complex of the Aerospace Museum in Los Angeles represents a border-line case of aggregation, precisely because it is tied to a conception of space and volume that negates the cognitive value of perspective and traditional perception. The typological context of this architecture is in fact determined by the projectual itinerary through which space travel has passed, from aeronautics to astronautics, from gravitational to antigravitational movement. The building is not only an anthology of images, but appears horizontally like a rocket or a three-stage spaceship, in which each stage retains its identity as a spatial unit. The building is thus a vehicle hooked up to the old space station of the previous museum, which one approaches through the typical entrances of airplanes and spaceships—small hatches and steep airport stairs. Furthermore, looking at the individual stages of the museum, it is not difficult to identify other precedents. The form of a large irregular volume suggests parachute cords, a geometrical section of a dirigible, etc. The central stage appears as a summation, floating in the void delimited by glass partitions, of elementary volumetric affirmations, the primary inventions of flight seem to have descended—the metallic sphere, a reminiscence of the dirigible, as well as the turbine and the shield of a supersonic airplane—from this area. All three stages are assembled so that they seem to be "resting" on one another; they are therefore ready to break apart, like rockets, in order to enter the next orbit with the necessary propulsion. Thus the Aerospace Museum is definitively transformed into a "flight" of architecture. The underlying desire in this construction is therefore to exalt not just a portion of the building, but its operative globality, as if the eye wished to carry out an acrobatic tour around its walls, roof, and foundations. Gehry's idea is, therefore, to rotate architecture without recourse to any supporting base, so as to configure it as a perfectly spherical architecture that revolves, opens, and closes before us in astral spaces.

Germano Celant

February-June 1984

Footnotes

1. F. Gehry, interviewed by C. Souker King, "Getting Tough with Economics," *Designers West,* 6/82, pp. 150–51.
2. Frank Gehry, "Suburban Changes: Architect's House in Santa Monica 1978" in *International Architect,* vol. 1 no. 2, 1979, p. 40.
3. E. Guidoni, *Architectura Primitiva,* (Milan Electa, 1975), p. 326, M. Murray, trans.
4. F. Gehry, interviewed by Barbaralee Diamonstein in *American Architecture Now,* Rizzoli (New York): 1980, p. 41.
5. Ibid, p. 36.
6. Ibid, p. 37. author's emphasis.
7. Ibid, p. 43.
8. F. Gehry, unpublished notes.
9. Deleuze-Quarttari, Antiedipo, M. Murray, trans.
10. J. Baudrillard, *Les Strategies Fatales,* Paris: 1983, G. Celant, M. Murray, trans.
11. F. Gehry, interviewed by Diamonstein, op. cit, p. 43.
12. F. Gehry, interviewed in *Transaction,* February 1983, p. 23.
13. J. Giovannini, "Beverly Hills to Remodel Its Image?" *Los Angeles Herald Tribune,* Oct. 4, 1982.
14. M. Foucault, *Histoire de la folie a l'age classique* (Paris: Plon, 1964), p. 8
15. F. Gehry, interviewed by Diamonstein, op cit, pp 41–42.
16. F. Gehry, interviewed by Susan Grant Lewin, *"California Condition,"* La Jolla Museum of Contemporary Art: Nov. 13, 1982, p. 35.
17. F. Gehry interviewed by John V. Mutlow, *L.A. Architect* (January 1982).
18. Ibid
19. Bruno Taut, *Die Auflosung der Stadte,* (Hagen, i.w., 1920).
20. F. Gehry, unpublished notes.

Old paint on canvas, as it ages, sometimes becomes transparent. When that happens it is possible, in some pictures, to see the original lines: a tree will show through a woman's dress, a child makes way for a dog, a large boat is no longer on an open sea. That is called pentimento because the painter "repented," changed his mind. Perhaps it would be as well to say that the old conception, replaced by a later choice, is a way of seeing and then seeing again.

That is all I mean about the people in this book. The paint has aged now and I wanted to see what was there for me once, what is there for me now.

Lillian Hellman
Pentimento

Steeves House

Brentwood, California 1959

The reasonable thing to do is to learn from those who can teach.
—Sophocles

In the design of their first major project "from scratch," Gehry and associate Greg Walsh cite a heavy influence from Frank Lloyd Wright, Harwell Harris, and Japanese architecture. These influences can be seen particularly in the wood detailing and in an emphasis on the horizontal. The site is a promontory along the face of a bluff, commanding views of the Santa Monica Mountains to the southwest. The house, following level site area, is cruciform in plan. Entry is from the northeast, through an open entry court excised from the longer bar of the house, which contains the living area. Beyond the living room, the horizontal bands of the roofs extend to frame a reflecting pool. Bedrooms, dining room, and kitchen are in the building mass intersected by that of the living room; its lower height is marked within the living room as the bottom edge of a band of clerestory windows. Twenty years after the house was completed, Gehry was asked to design an addition to it for new owners. The addition, illustrated as the Smith House in this volume, illuminates an evolution from what Gehry describes as the "preoccupation with hierarchical spaces and formal planning organization" of the Steeves House.

1.View from south 2.Entrance court with service yard beyond 3.Plan 4.North elevation 5.Perspective

1

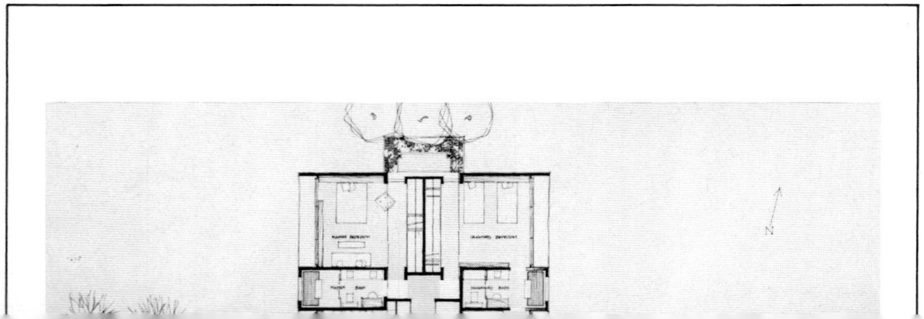

2

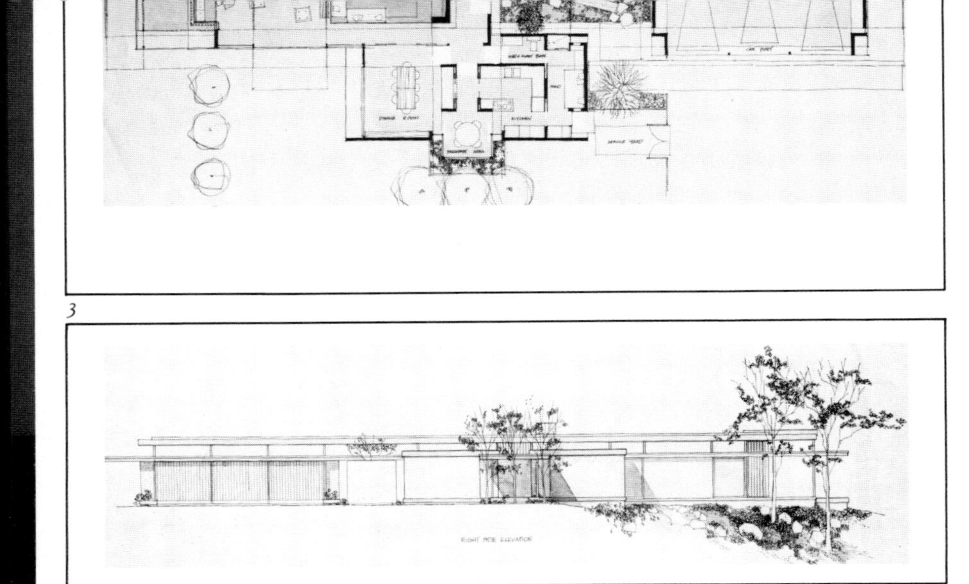

3

4

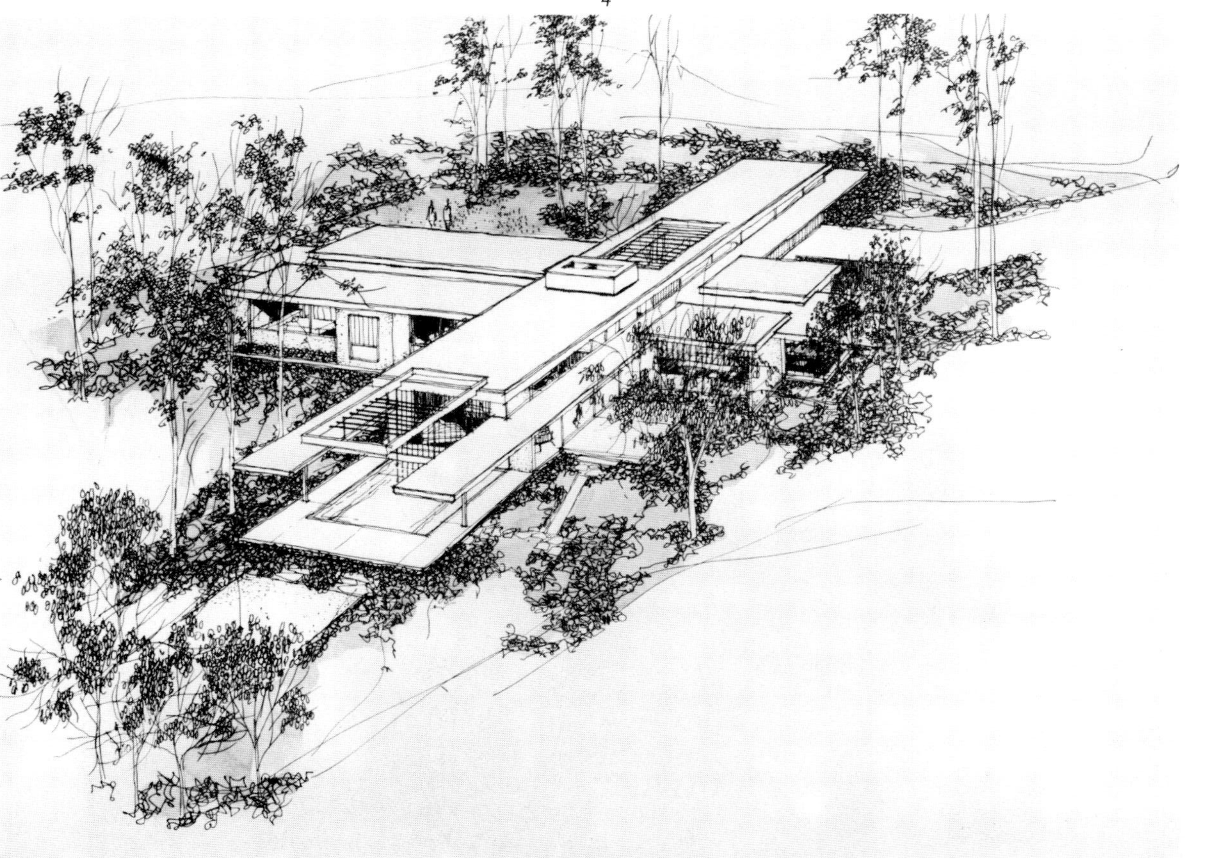

5

Resort
Clifton Springs, Australia 1960

Before establishing his own firm, Gehry worked as a staff architect at the office of Victor Gruen Associates. One of the last projects on which he worked there was a resort and clubhouse in Australia. The construction was intended to spur marketing and development of a large ocean-side tract of land. Work on the design was a collaborative effort with delineator Carlos Diniz. One of their principal interests was an exploration of Spanish-style roofs as used in Australia. Although the built project "does not," according to Gehry, "look anything like the drawings," the design represents an incident in Gehry's ongoing interest in extrapolating contemporary forms from vernacular architectural traditions. The Hillcrest Apartments, the Kay Jewelers Offices and Warehouse, and the Faith Plating Company and Danziger buildings, shown on subsequent pages, illustrate the progress of this interest.

1.Site plan 2.Guest cottages

Hillcrest Apartments
Santa Monica, California 1962

To generate work for his newly opened office, Gehry created a development project with some friends—architect-planner Fereydoon Ghaffari, engineers Joseph Kurily and Moshe Rubenstein, and developer Wesley Bilson. The site was in a neighborhood of houses built in the vernacular style called California Bungalow, many of which were being converted into or replaced with apartments. The priority in designing a six-unit apartment building for the site was to respect the existing architectural character of the neighborhood and to blend the new building into its context. So successfully were those goals realized that, according to Gehry, "when it was finished people thought we had remodeled an old house." The mayor of Santa Monica was moved to write his thanks and congratulations to the architect, adding his hope that "we can look forward to a continued improvement of an historically favorable location." The improvement, however, came in the form of a nearly complete replacement of all old buildings with new structures of heterogeneous aesthetics. The Hillcrest Apartments are now the only "bungalow" on the street, standing testament to a vanished neighborhood. The fate of the project, says Gehry, made him realize "how hopeless we were to try to contain the forces of change."

3-4.Views from Hillcrest Avenue 5.Interior 6.Ink sketch

1

2

3

4

5

6

Kay Jewelers Offices and Warehouse
Los Angeles, California 1963

For a jeweler's regional executive offices and warehouse, no design guidelines were specified other than the usual concern for economy. The building is a single, relatively inexpensive (total project cost: $42,000) concrete structure. The company president's admiration for Japanese culture suggested a means to create an appropriate scale and character for the executive offices, distinct from the warehouse area and sheltered from the adjacent highway's traffic: Some of the forms, details, and planning principles of Japanese architecture were used. The building is sited back from the street, a walled "Japanese" garden providing a buffer to the street. The garden designed by Gehry's office was originally to be surrounded by high walls, with entrance to the building from the street through the garden under a tiled pergola—ideas vetoed by the building department. The interiors are open office spaces given scale, character and flexibility by details derived from Japanese architecture. A wood band at cornice height is both set onto white walls and also continues as part of free spanning woodwork which organizes open office spaces. Used in conjunction with sliding panels, the banding provides defined open office areas adaptable to office reconfigurations. Japanese architecture is evoked, not imitated: the columns, formed in cardboard "sonotubes," are undisguised, untreated concrete, with their "capitals" boxed in redwood. As in the design strategy now called postmodernism, another architectural style is recalled through proportion and detail in contemporary materials.

1.Entrance

Kay Jewelers Stores
Redondo Beach, California 1963
Buena Park, California 1964

The layout and overall sizes of display cases being predetermined by management, the latitude in the design of the stores was largely in the details. Working in teak and oak, says Gehry, "we detailed the place like a beautiful cabinet. I actually had it built by a Finnish cabinet man who did high-priced furniture." The clients approved their furniture, but sought to lower its price for a second store in the Buena Park Shopping Center the following year. With interiors primarily drywall, an appropriately precious environment was created with the use of glass mosaic tile on the exterior and entrance gallery.

2-3.Redondo Beach store 4.Buena Park store

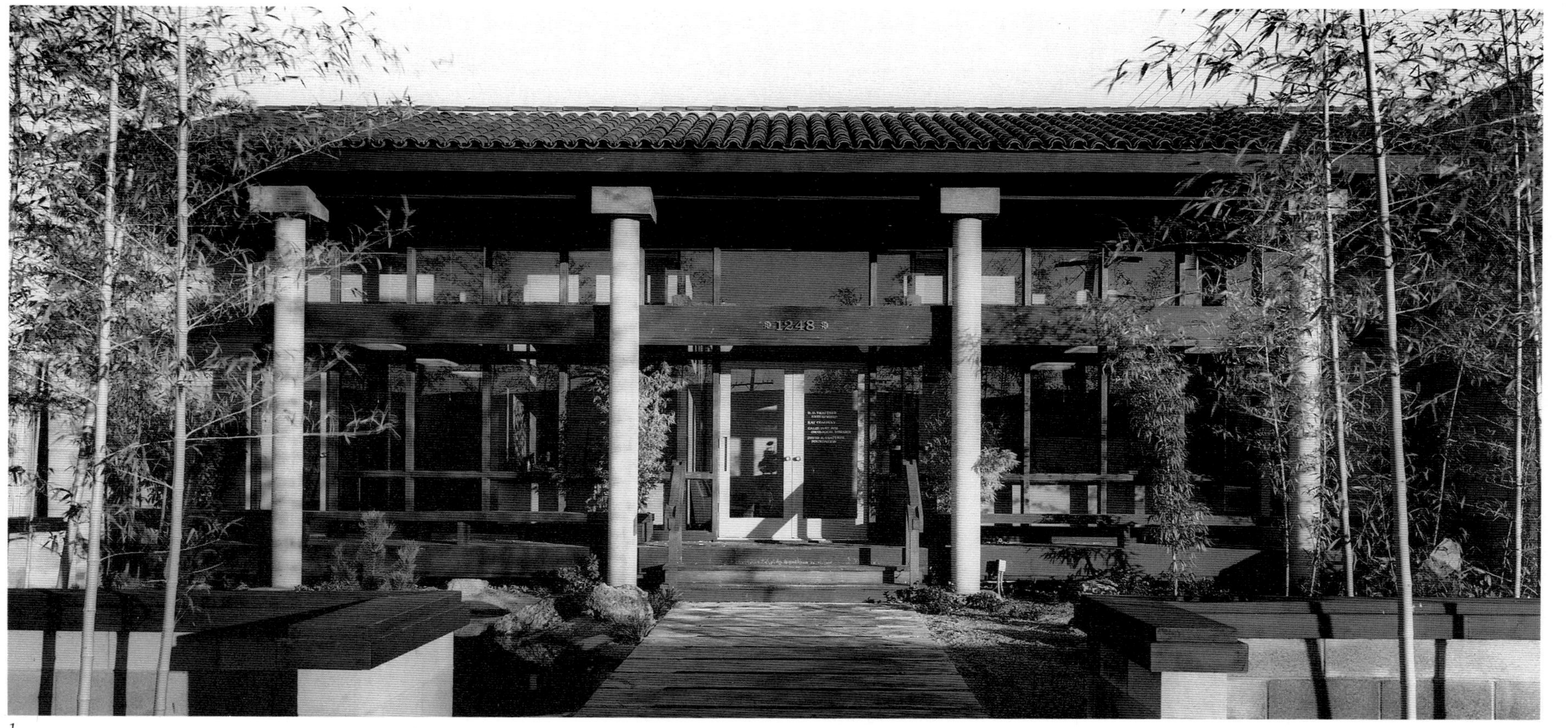

1

2

3

4

KAY Jewelers

Steeves Office Building
Santa Monica, California 1963

Having designed the Steeves House with "a preoccupation with horizontal banding," Gehry designed an office building for the same client which "was an opportunity to explore a more vertical building." The major materials of the five-story office building were to be glass with stainless steel mullions and concrete. Two treatments of the concrete were specified to provide contrasting textures—sandblasting for a relatively uniform surface, and bush-hammering for a heavier texture. Unfortunately, the size and construction type ran the projected costs and profits too close to risk, and the project was abandoned.

Gehry reports that teaching architecture has convinced him that young designers must work their way through existing architectural aesthetics by first designing in known vocabularies. Only by exploring accepted idioms can a young architect come to understand what does and does not seem personally appropriate or interesting, in order to reach personal styles and design priorities. Gehry now describes his early projects as such mimetic exercises.

1-4.Model

1

Faith Plating Company
Hollywood, California 1964

Gehry has noticed that for "many of our projects which seem to reach notoriety, there are several back-up projects that point towards a direction, and we use them for proving grounds for new ideas." The design for the Faith Plating Company was such a precursor to Gehry's first widely acclaimed project, the Danziger Studio and Residence. Explored in the designs is the archetypical Los Angeles building—what Gehry calls the "dumb box," and Reyner Banham "the plain plastered cube." Banham explains its genesis and its status as "a firm vernacular basis from which a more conscious architecture can develop" as follows:

"Schindler and Neutra had done so much to domesticate international modern architecture in Los Angeles that they might, almost unconsciously themselves, have put these forms into circulation and imitation.... If it is possible to put up a simple stuccoed box in Los Angeles and regard the result as architecture, it is as much due to what the pioneer modernists have done as it is to plain avarice stripping the Hispanic tradition of its ornamental detail.

"Very large areas of Los Angeles are made out of just these kind of elementary cubes—they nestle among the foothills and line the straight avenues of the plains. They are economically, structurally, and—given the sunshine—architecturally, the local norm and vernacular.

"Anyone who begins to understand Los Angeles visually has to accept, even celebrate, their normative standing—as David Hockney has done in his paintings of the city."

In his work for the Faith Plating Company, Gehry began to explore the architectural and sculptural potential of that vernacular—the evocative power of mute and stolid forms.

The project was a remodeling and rewrapping of an existing plant which remained in operation during construction. Offices for the company constituted the work on the interior, including a conference room and reception area. Furniture was also designed for the project, a first foray into a field to which much attention was later turned. Most importantly, however, was the experience gained in seamless stucco detailing and the initial encounter with an articulate dumb box.

5.Exterior

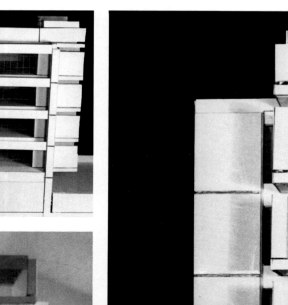

2

3

4

5

Atkinson Park Recreation Building

Santa Maria, California 1964

Unattached side walls become something independent, no longer enclosing walls. They're separate supporting screens, any one of which may be shortened, or extended or perforated, or occasionally eliminated. These free-standing screens support the roof. What of this roof? Overhead it becomes emphasized as a splendid sense of shelter, but shelter that hides nothing when you are inside looking out from the building. It is a shape of shelter that really gives a sense of the outside coming in or the inside going out.
—Frank Lloyd Wright

As part of its city parks and recreation program, Santa Maria sought to strengthen use of Atkinson Park as a community resource (with the motto, "Recreation for everyone!"). The structure in the park was built to house a wide variety of activities, scheduled at all hours, often concurrently. The building, then, was to provide shelter over open, easily divisible space, and attendant service areas. The building is comprised of four basic elements: the roof covering the main space, concrete block walls supporting it, concrete block "buildings" containing ancillary service rooms, and glazed panels between the latter. The roof appears an independent entity, with most of the ancillary blocks independent of its perimeter and elevation. It is as though an arbitrary part of a continuous park had been claimed attracting a collection of sheds camped at its edges. The project was done in collaboration with Eckbo, Dean, Austin & Williams, Landscape Architects, principals of which had been professors of Gehry, and had recommended him for the project.

1.Entrance 2.West elevation 3.North elevation 4.Plan

Kline House

Bel Air, California 1964

To replace a house destroyed by fire, Gehry echoed the original design by Calvin Straub, his mentor at USC, with some interior finishes and the sloping planes of the roof. Designing the house also provided an opportunity to further study refined detailing in oak and teak and to explore the exposed wood ceilings native to California tradition. In addition, an exploration of vertical spaces was begun: the stairhall, with the change in altitude accentuated by vertical wood members and a sharp contrast made between white wall planes and the rhythm and color of wood framing, invites comparison with later work—the stair at Gemini G.E.L., for example.

5.Side elevation 6.Entrance 7.Stair hall

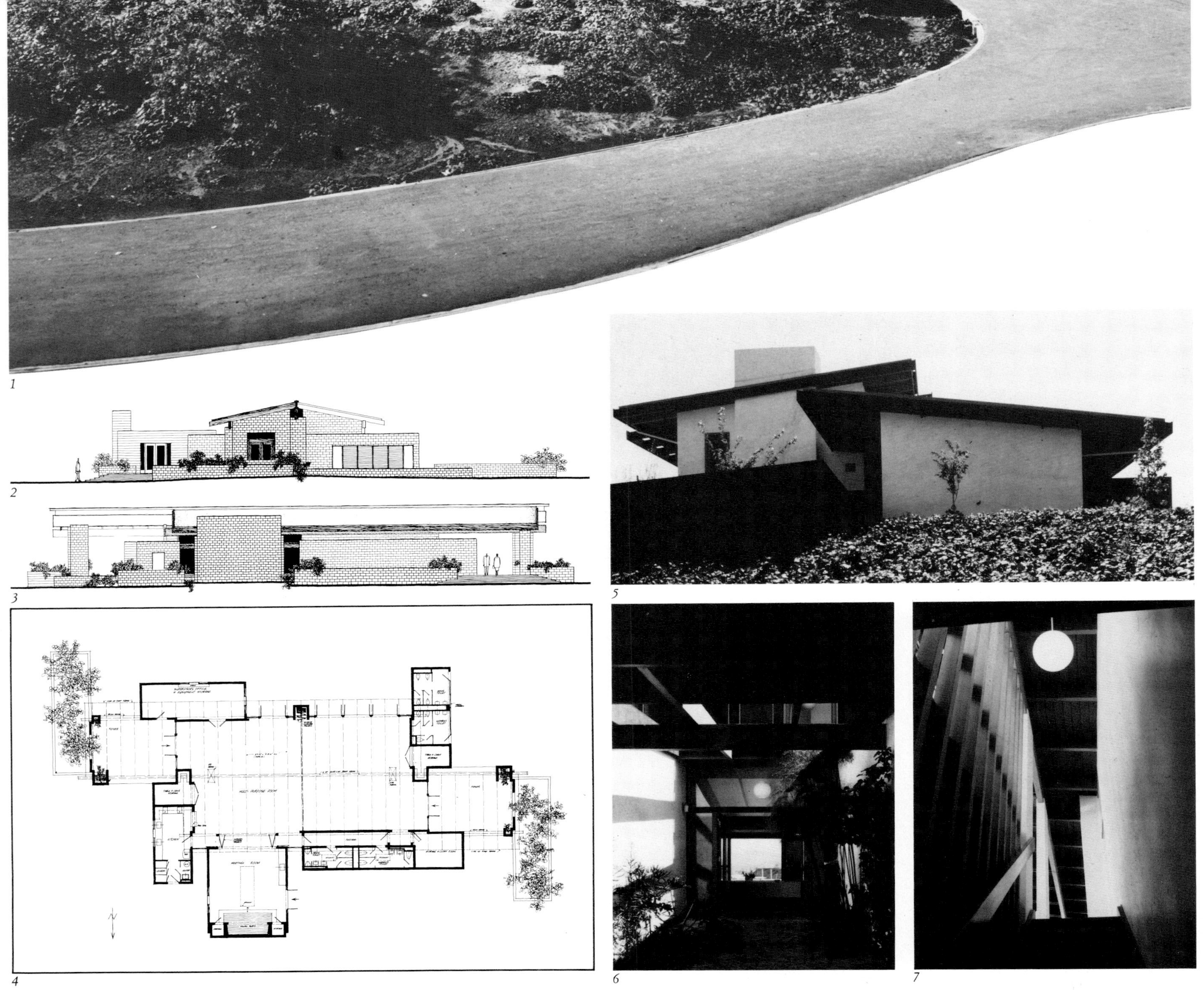
1
2
3
4
5
6
7

The Challenge of Our Cities and Towns

New York World's Fair 1964

The challenge for Gehry—and collaborators planner Richard Berry and exhibit designer Frederick A. Usher—in preparing an exhibit for the United States Pavilion called "Challenge for Progress," was to state the major problems confronting cities, using minimum words. The material was to be readily translatable into visual representation for exhibition. Two weeks were allotted for the preparation of the statement, which is excerpted below.

Introduction

The apparent problems of today's cities and towns are manifestations of the vast growth America has undergone in the past, which, predictably, will continue in the future. The intricate details of our social and economic structure creates growing complexity in the cities housing the overwhelming majority of our population. To approach an understanding of the urban phenomenon would require far greater knowledge of the city than is available today, yet the urbanization process continues at a relentless pace, multiplying problems to a critical magnitude.

The aim of this analysis is to explain the needs and conflicts in our cities in terms of the fundamentals of our system of free enterprise and our democratic political structure. It would be misleading to only deal with isolated symptoms when they actually stem from a more basic set of issues. The intention here is to provide a framework within which problems (slums, overcrowding, traffic, housing, etc.) can be more clearly understood.

The American System of Private Property Ownership Democratically Regulated by the Majority

The city is made of many individuals who have rights to separate pieces of property. The American political system has encouraged the development of great cities and towns, but it is also the source of many conflicts—prototypically, the conflict of the individual property owner serving his family's needs, which may differ from his neighbors' needs.

- A property owner builds a fence for privacy and obstructs his neighbor's light and view.
- A property owner opens a music studio next to a convalescent home.

Good neighbors compromise some of their individual rights and agree to the necessity of democratic control by the majority, enforceable by police power.

- A property owner is required to leave space for light and air between his building and other buildings (setbacks).
- The height of a building is limited so the view from another is not blocked (height controls).
- The building of a slaughterhouse is not permitted on a property which is surrounded by family homes (land use zoning).
- A barricade is required around a property during construction of a building to protect children from injury (building and safety codes).

The individual property owners must give up the rights to some or all of their land so that the needs and wants of the majority can be met; sometimes it is necessary to allow their property to be purchased for public use (eminent domain).

- A property owner gives up a portion of his land to provide enough space for widening the street for automobile use.
- Many property owners sell their homes to provide space for a needed freeway.

Each individual property owner relies on the majority to provide him with necessary services which he himself cannot provide; and each person agrees to pay a portion of the costs of city services (taxation).

- The property owner without children helps to pay for the education of his neighbor's children.
- All building owners pay for fire protection through taxes, regardless of whether their buildings are wooden or concrete.
- Water is carried many miles from a distant reservoir to supply both the industrial building and the private family home.
- Each owner agrees to rely on the skill and judgement of the specialist to balance the needs and different requirements of all the property owners and helps to pay his salaries (the judge, city planner, policeman, street engineer, librarian—city councilmen, school board staff, etc., usually serve their neighbors without salary).

Directing the Cumulative Knowledge of Modern Civilization Toward a Plan for Orderly Growth

The city, as the center of a vast social and economic system, reflects American ideals and technological progress. As the size and complexity of the city grows, so does the demand for a variety of specialists who are competent in planning for the many needs of the city-dwellers and in analyzing the problems constantly confronting our elected officials.

City Hall houses the working quarters of elected officials who have available to them extensive technical staffs for counsel and assistance.

- The financial staff administrates city income and expenditure for schools, libraries, roads, water mains, and all service requirements.
- The legal staff prepares and interprets the city laws which regulate the construction of buildings, zoning and the other elements which influence a city's growth patterns.
- The planning staff coordinates all the general requirements of the city into an outline for guiding long-range physical development.

The free university is a center for the distribution of knowledge and insight into the problems of our complex urbanized civilization. A new field of urban science is emerging which embraces all the specialized fields of study necessary for an understanding of the city.

- The social scientist.
- The life scientist.
- The physical scientist.
- The legal scholar.
- The engineer.
- The artist.

As elected officials increasingly depend upon the recommendations of the scientist and expert, greater emphasis is placed upon the education of the electorate (who ultimately make the decisions guiding the city).

- The public school system can provide the first insights into social understanding and democratic responsibility.
- It can provide the foundation upon which scientific knowledge is later built.
- It can provide the first awareness of living in a complex environment.
- It can foster an appreciation for an orderly and attractive city.

Reconciling our Cities' Present and Future Needs with Conflicts Inherent in Rapid Growth and Change

Social, economic, and technological progress is continual, forcing old forms to be adapted to new conditions. Immediate needs conflict with goals and desires for the future, creating extensive problems.

The city's taxation of private real estate is relative to improvements made. Deterioration of buildings ultimately means lower tax payments for the landlord, as well as a loss of revenue for the city.

- This traditional form of taxation penalizes new development and encourages property vacancies.
- This form of taxation encourages the "slum-landlord" by making physical deterioration profitable.

Small units of local government give the urban citizen a strong voice in his city or town. However, through urban sprawl, these small units run together creating the "megalopolis" with its myriad of uncoordinated, independent governmental units operating without any clear method for guiding growth or providing broad services on a regional basis.

- Traffic moves smoothly in one township but is snarled as it moves into the next.
- Fire trucks stop at a political boundary while across the street, in another jurisdiction, a house burns.
- Public transportation serves the community, but not the region—the bus line stops at the town line.
- Freeway construction, designed to benefit all, is hampered by rivalry between political entities.

Most American families want to own their own house. They seek increased prosperity to achieve this goal, which is made possible by this country's continued prosperity. However, enormous quantities of land are needed to satisfy a booming housing market, seriously straining the financial ability of the city to provide services over increasingly large areas.

- Housing tracts infringe on choice agricultural and scenic land.
- Surburbia continually expands, as does the demand for new roads and transit facilities.
- Sprawl perpetuates itself by encouraging further decentralization of the workplace and the marketplace.
- The ability for cities to provide public transit decreases with the expansion of the area that needs to be served.

The convenience and efficiency in housing and business attracts competition for choice locations and adequate space in prime areas of the city. The central core, traditionally the most desirable, has the highest land values, which in turn foster a high density of building and activity. New market demands and shifting distribution requirements strain the archaic patterns of streets and structures within the city's concentrated core.

- Inadequate to handle automobile traffic and service demands, narrow streets create traffic congestion and confusion.
- High concentrations of daytime workers need extensive car parking.
- The congestion of the center city drives out many businesses, which are replaced by marginal commercial enterprises.

Finding a Simple and Attractive City Form Which Will Provide for all our Daily Needs and Activities

Streets, buildings and both natural and man-made landscapes combine to create the physical form of the city.

The street system provides the structure and connecting link for the many physical parts and complex functions of the city. The street itself is a reference for understanding all the interrelating elements of the changing city.

- The street is the public link between private properties. Onto it open the front doors of homes and places of work, commerce, entertainment and leisure.
- The street is a carrier of a network of essential utilities providing water, electric power, telephone lines and waste disposal.
- The street is a total distribution system, a path for pedestrians, automobiles, trucks, buses and streetcars.
- The street is a wholesale and retail market place (the central produce market, the garment district, used car lots, flower vendors, newsstands, the Good Humor Man).
- The street is the nucleus of the neighborhood, a meeting place for children playing, mothers strolling with baby carriages, neighbors talking politics.

Our cities are burdened with a street system inherited from a less complicated past, conflicting with our present requirements for moving vast numbers of people and meeting the constantly changing and unpredictable needs of a dynamic technology. The pattern and system of streets reflects both the hierarchy of functions served and the pressures placed upon the system by constant change and growth.

- The freeway is a specialized street for high-speed automobile traffic.
- Some streets provide service access to shops and homes by delivery trucks: the narrow alley.
- The transit right-of-way provides for moving many people in a smaller space.
- The pedestrian mall separates shoppers from the fast moving automobile.
- The residential street discourages heavy traffic, providing a safe path for children.
- The ordinary street is multi-purpose, simultaneously serving the pedestrian, the private car, the delivery truck, while providing for loading and unloading, parking, advertising.

The street is the primary public space from which the city is perceived. It can provide an image of order or disorder, of quietness or activity, of attraction or repulsion.

- The street may be a path of bright lights and throngs of people at night. The street may be a deserted and dark canyon in the early morning hours.
- The street may offer an invitation to walk slowly—the tree-lined street of small shops.
- The street may offer an invitation to move quickly—the street of abandoned buildings.
- The street may be an enclosed corridor, tall and long, or wide and low.
- The street may be an endless repetition of identical units (tract houses).
- The street may be a sequence of surprise and change (a curved street).
- The street may contain reservoirs for people and activities (the public square or park).

Danziger Studio and Residence
Hollywood, California 1964

I always fall for the strong silent type.
—Hollywood Lady

The area of Los Angeles where the graphics trade has developed is a busy section of Hollywood. The site of designer Danziger's studio and residence is the heavily trafficked, noisy intersection of Melrose and Sycamore. The complex was designed to be "introverted and fortress-like." The walls are a double thickness of stucco on wood frame with an air space between for acoustic protection from the street. Street-side windows are above eye level, save that of the kitchen which is recessed within a recess.

The complex consists of a studio of one thousand square feet and a townhouse of sixteen hundred square feet. The two are connected only by one soundproof door. The studio, which is entered either from the street or from a small parking lot to the rear, was conceived as a totally open and flexible space; a darkroom is its only partitioned room. Clerestories admit light; the north-facing clerestory-and-skylight takes the form of a monitor popped up from the volume of the studio. The entrance to the townhouse is through a small garden, sheltered from the street by high walls. Facing the garden through a glazed wall is the two-story living area. At the rear of the residence is a garage, over which is a bedroom, lit by a second "pop up" monitor facing east.

With this project Gehry continued his exploration—begun with his design for the Faith Plating Company—of the simple stucco cubes which constitute the vernacular of Los Angeles's commercial strips. By accentuating the attributes of the building type—simple geometric volumes with unadorned surfaces—he succeeds in amplifying, as it were, the silence of what he calls "the dumb box." Fidelity to the model and context extends to the finishes: According to Gehry, "Heavy textured stucco was machine-applied to exterior walls and left exposed. The resulting surface is reasonably compatible with the dirt and grime of the location." Thus camouflaged, a sort of undercover architecture, the building on Melrose Avenue can almost be passed without notice. "I had a funny notion," explains Gehry, "that you could make architecture that you would bump into before you realized it was architecture." Post-bump, compositional subtleties of volumes toward and past which walls slide and the changing relationships of shadows cast by and against them are the reward.

1.At Melrose 2.Studio entry 3.Garden wall

1

2

3

1. Ground floor 2. Second floor 3. Neighbors on Melrose 4. "Picture of Melrose Avenue in an Ornate Gold Frame" by David Hockney, 1965 5. Garden wall 6. Residence, from Sycamore 7. Door between studio and residence 8. Garden gate, entry to residence 9. View from rear 10. View of residence from court 11. View from living room 12. Working studio

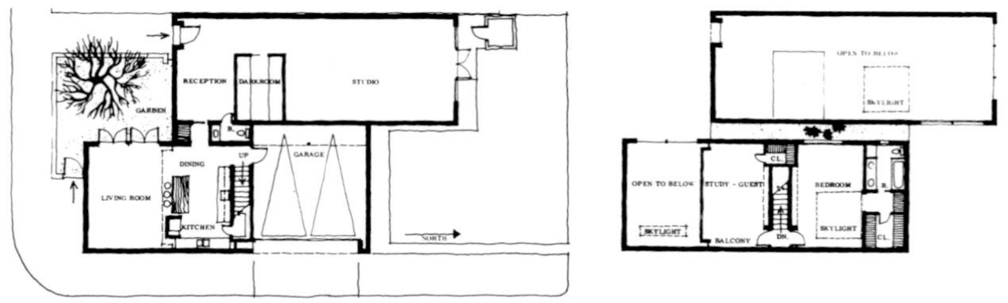

1-2.

3

4

5

6

7

8

9

10

11

12

420 Rodeo Drive
Bel Air, California 1965

Advertised as "the first condominium office in the West," the perimeter of the building proposed for development was dictated by parking requirements on a small, interior lot. Gehry describes the project as growing out of his design of the Danziger Studio and leading to that of the Cochiti, New Mexico, Town Center. Like the former, its party walls are held back from neighboring buildings to underscore its compositional independence, and, like both, it is composed of unadorned, large scale, geometrically pure forms on which light and shadow play a primary collaborative role. Unfortunately, like the Steeves Office Building, the floor area possible on the site proved too small to assure a profit, and the project was abandoned.

1.Promotional rendering

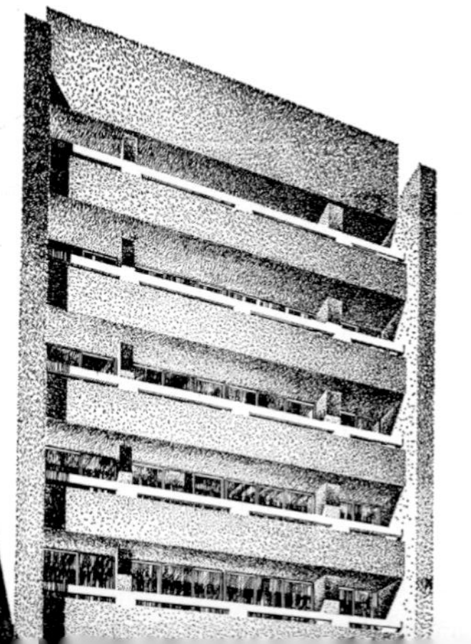

Merriweather Post Pavilion of Music
Columbia, Maryland 1967

If you have time to only solve the problem you don't get hung up with frills or become symbol-oriented. You try to get to the essence of how we're living today, of what's happening. It becomes a reductive process, an aesthetic manipulation of space. The materials don't matter too much. The forms and sculpting of space—with any material—are what count in art and architecture.... If we had more time we might have done better; but more probably not as well.
—Frank Gehry, 1968

Once the Rouse Company had donated land and a long-term construction loan to the National Symphony for a summer music festival home, eight months were allowed the architects, Gehry, Walsh and O'Malley, for design and construction. "Our approach," explains Gehry, "was to problem solve: to create a strong sculptured space that meets the... requirements of visual and aural comfort. And, to bring it in on schedule at a very economical figure." The pavilion was designed for a sloping site in a park near Columbia's town center, and is oriented on a northeast axis to shield audiences from western sun and prevailing winds. It seats three thousand under its roof and five thousand more on the grassy, sloping parkland around it. The roof area, trapezoidal in shape, is three-quarters of an acre of gravel over wood decking; its longspan trusses and joists are supported by six steel and concrete columns—two at the stage and four behind the seats. The slope of the fanning roof and its height in relation to the natural "dish" of the terrain were designed in collaboration with acoustical engineer Christopher Jaffe. Also designed in collaboration was the canopy of individual baffles, eight feet by six feet, which hangs over the stage and extends thirty feet out over the audience. The baffles, made of fiberglass reinforced polyester, are adjustable to "tune" the pavilion to the requirements of different performances. The pavilion's acoustics are considered among the best of outdoor music halls. From the full house of (muddy) dignitaries on opening night, *New York Times'* music critic Harold Schonberg reported: "An anti-art, anti-music rain started an hour or so before the concert. Soon it was a downpour, then a deluge, then a typhoon.... [But] The Merriweather Post Pavilion turned out to be an unqualified architectural and acoustical success. Even in the downpour, which can make an orchestra's sound duller than normal, the acoustics were clear and well-defined, with plenty of "throw" from the stage, good bass and an unusual degree of presence. In addition, the shed is exceptionally handsome, with pleasing proportions, clean lines and an unobtrusive kind of finish that fits perfectly into the landscape."

2–3,5,7.Views from Park 4.Opening night 6.Acoustic Canopy

1

2

3

4

5

6

7

Art Treasures of Japan

Los Angeles County Museum of Art 1965.

An installation for a major exhibition of Japanese art objects was the first of what proved to be a series of projects for the museum. Large crowds were expected; a comprehensive route for an orderly flow of visitors was required, as well as security for the artifacts from the touch of the curious. Complicating the design was the scale of the art objects, many of which were quite small and intricately detailed. The exhibit was designed as a clear route leading by a series of discrete areas of varying scales. Intermittently, partitions formed framed views of one of the most striking of the artifacts—the eighth-century "Healing Buddha," which was displayed beneath a scarlet silk canopy—providing a point of orientation for the visitor touring the rooms of the exhibit. To create a more intimate scale, lowered partitions were capped with redwood. Silk, suspended as canopies, reduced glare and varied the quality of light. Low redwood rails, used to restrict the public, were made less apparent as barricades by a coherent display method: smooth pebbles covered the carpet surrounding the sculpture rendering the rail an apparent part of a box holding pebbles. Tatami mats, raked white sand, and silk were used on display platforms.

1.General view 2–3.Sculpture groups

Billy Al Bengston

Los Angeles County Museum of Art 1968

There was something about the anonymous galleries of the museum that seemed inappropriate to Gehry for Bengston's exuberant, automobile-metallic paintings. "I was interested," explains Gehry, "in breaking down the institutional look of the Los Angeles County Museum so that it would be a nice environment for Billy's work, which grows out of motorcycle racing. His whole aesthetic comes out of his involvement with the motorcycle track. And the Los Angeles County Museum's institutional quality just fought it." Gehry's strategy was twofold. He used materials more compatible with the artist's favored environment: the installation marked Gehry's first use of the raw plywood, corrugated metal, and exposed wood studs prominent in his later work. Second, Gehry tried to create the illusion of being in the artist's studio. Furniture and objects owned or chosen by Bengston were installed in a series of "rooms" made of plywood panels on which the work was displayed. The rooms, some with lowered ceilings to mask the unattractive acoustic tile and lighting grid of the museum, provided more intimate and varied spaces for display of the work. The museum staff objected to the unorthodox materials, particularly the raw plywood. According to Gehry, "They wanted to paint it. They threw me a curve and brought up plywood that had already been used in other shows. It was partially painted. They thought that would throw me." They were wrong: Gehry found the material compatible with the rough, unfinished "hands on" aesthetic he intended, and installed the profferred panels half-painted.

4.Entrance 5.Exhibit room 6.Wax figure of Bengston at entrance 7.Exhibit niche

1

2

3

4

5

6

7

Reception Center
Columbia, Maryland 1967

While a portion of Howard County, Maryland was being transformed from farmland to a new town, its planners' intentions were on view and promoted in a lake-side building designed by Gehry, Walsh and O'Malley at the spot which became the town center. Plans of the new city were displayed in a large exhibition space, which, with offices for the developer, the Rouse Company, and a lounge, comprised the original building program. The interior, however, was designed with sufficient flexibility to accommodate later uses or tenants once the new city became established. Two building areas under shed roofs lie on either side of a tall glass-roofed spine. The spine runs between an entrance portico and a glass wall with views of the lake and the woods beyond. The structural elements of the skylight over the spine wash its white walls with geometric shadows, evoking the promise of dynamic structures to come from the domestic-scaled building by the water's edge.

1-2.Views from lake 3.Interior spine 4.Plan

Public Safety Building
Columbia, Maryland 1967

For their third building in the new town of Columbia, Gehry, Walsh and O'Malley designed four thousand square feet of space to house Columbia's volunteer fire department. In the original design, the modest public building was given civic character by transfiguring the forms of the surrounding neighborhood of domestic buildings. Their forms were extrapolated and simplified to primary, irreducible elements. Boldly scaled gable roofs of black asphalt shingles were to rest atop simple building masses of natural finish concrete block. A third equipment bay was planned for the facility's expansion. The final design—comprised of two fire fighting equipment bays, a hose drying tower, and firemen's living quarters—was a response to a firm request by the client for a more conventionally "contemporary" structure.

5.Model, preliminary design 6.Exterior

American School of Dance
Hollywood, California 1968

An established dance school in Los Angeles spawned a new ballet company and expanded its staff and curriculum. To accommodate these changes a new facility was planned for a site in Hollywood. Gehry's plan separates building masses to create an internal cruciform arrangement. Externally, the building appears as a pair of "dumb boxes," providing both privacy for the dancers and contextually compatible Los Angeles architecture. A glass spine provides light, the focal spatial and social area of the school, and an effective sculptural contrast to the solid building volumes. Its comparative delicacy, and its appearance of sliding out of the higher building mass and along the top of the lower, evoke the lightness and motion of ballet, a point reinforced by a super-scale photographic frieze of dancers hung within the glazed hall.

7.Model

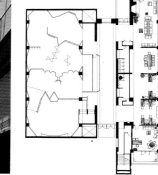

1

2

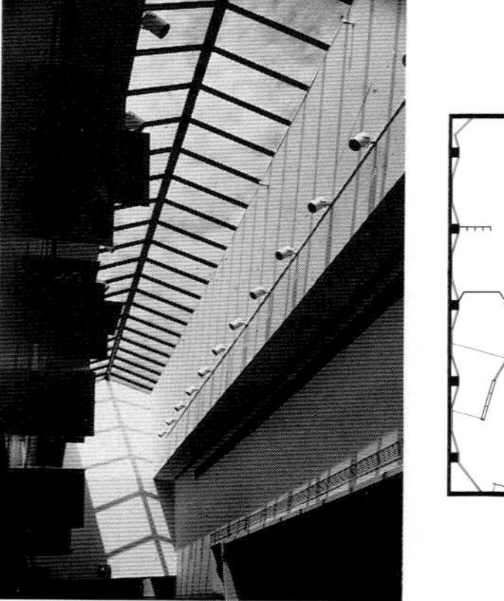

3

4

5

6

7

O'Neill Hay Barn

San Juan Capistrano, California 1968

As part of a master plan for a ranch which was to include ranch house, guest house, stables, and ancillary buildings, Gehry designed "a structure to cover up some bales of hay." Since the budget was as minimal as the program, modest materials were used—telephone poles sheathed in the kind of corrugated metal used for the Bengston exhibit. Given the simplicity of the program, "the form," explains Gehry, "could have gone anywhere." Where it went—a simple, rectangular enclosure with a roof that is tilted between diagonal corners—Gehry says, "I think... grew out of my fascination with Frank Lloyd Wright, actually—the way he played with roof structures was a very important part of his architecture." Whatever its genesis, the tilt of the roof in conjunction with the corrugated metal provided intriguing results. Not only does the shape and color reflect that of the surrounding hills, but also, according to Gehry, "the reflections of the sky on the metal make the building disappear sometimes."

Many, including Gehry, have remarked on the project's apparent affinity with the work of contemporary minimalist sculptors. Offering neither polish nor pedestal, minimalist sculpture exploits the power of the simple and bare. Unadorned, geometrically pure, constituent parts, and everyday materials leave the interested viewer little distracting detail. The result can be a heightened perception of critical proportion, pure form, craft, relation between parts, light, shadow, the immediate environment, and the viewer's active role in discovering relationships while moving about the object. In what seems similar fashion, attention turned to the hay barn's simple form is drawn to reflections and refractions, to the patterning of cast shadows, and to the perspective illusions of the tilted roof. But, despite the similarities, two distinctions must be made. Gehry's building is architecture, not sculpture. First and foremost, it is a functioning structure built within a client's budget. Gehry is now troubled by the confusion: "I hate to use the word sculpture. I've used it before, but I don't think it's really the right word. I'm not comfortable using it. [I'd prefer to call it] just an architectural element of some kind. It's a building." Secondly, the apparent similarity to the work of sculptors Carl André and Donald Judd, which he admires, is more a coincidence of means—in a different medium—toward an end Gehry has consistently pursued in his architecture: beyond the responsible satisfaction of program and budget, his best work, in all its diversity, seeks to stimulate and invite those who encounter it to share in the pleasure of visual phenomena.

1-4.Exterior views 5.Detail

1

2

3

4

5

Joseph Magnin Stores

Costa Mesa, California 1968
San Jose, California 1968

The designs for the Magnin stores grew out of an analysis of the ailments of traditional department store interiors. The custom of making each department appear a distinct "store" resulted, by Gehry's analysis, in visual chaos which served mainly to distract shoppers from merchandise. The high cost of renovation imposed any department design as a more or less permanent store component, unresponsive to changes in display requirements and opportunities. Most notably, stores thus designed were deemed woefully inadequate to make timely and effective use of changes in market trends. To facilitate marketing, Gehry sought to create envelopes sufficiently open and neutral to allow the merchandise itself to star and to make the space flexible for display. His goals were high visibility throughout the store and the creation of lighting and display systems which would allow inexpensive and relatively uncomplicated display alterations.

With the collaboration of Gere Kavanaugh on color for the Costa Mesa store and of Deborah Sussman at San Jose on color and graphics, these ideas were developed as follows: The store at Costa Mesa is designed around a central, skylit court. Views into every department are provided from the central circulation paths in and around it. Most lighting is indirect, reflected off the white ceilings from a number of concealed sources. Most notably, structural columns were boxed out to create light "fixtures;" uplighting troughs span between them. Concealing light sources not only allowed initial savings on fixtures, but also provides for simple alterations to lighting such as the insertion of gels to highlight merchandise or change the store's "color" for special occasions. At the store in San Jose's Almaden Plaza, an entire display system with integral lighting was designed. The fixtures are moveable and have interchangeable display and graphic parts. The system allows for the increase, decrease, interchange, or termination of departments by adding, subtracting, or shuffling display "trees." According to Gehry, "The new display system . . . enables the client to control his own environment. He can experiment, change, and refine the display systems, the departmental relationships, and the decor. He doesn't just have to make the best of a given, inflexible environment which doesn't permit him to change his mind."

Costa Mesa store: 1–4. Atrium 5. Light fixtures 6. Ground floor plan 7. 2nd floor plan

1

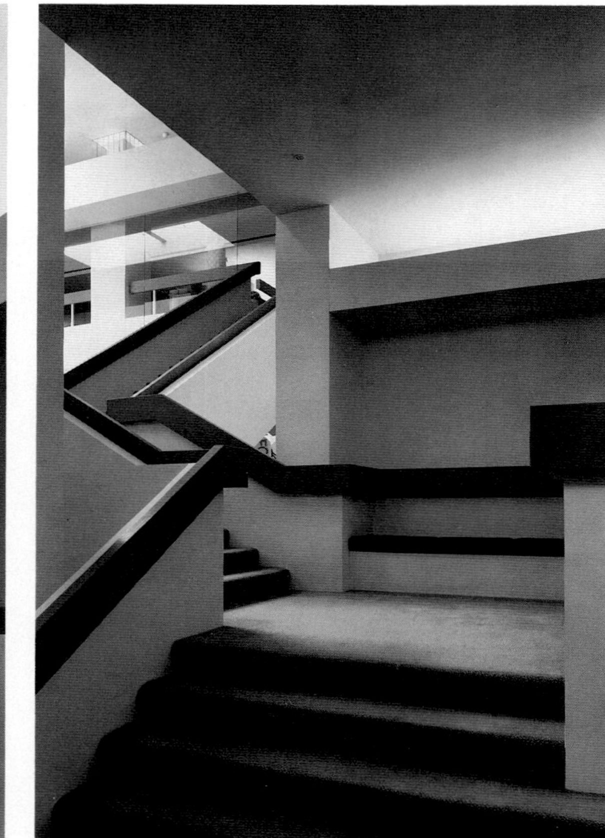

2

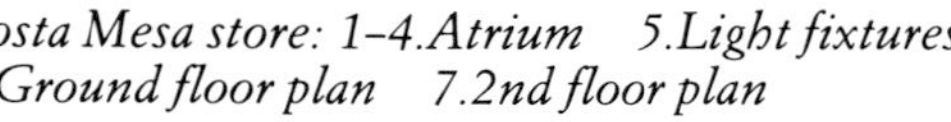

3

4

5

6

7

San Jose store *1.Interior with display "trees"*
2.Plan

1

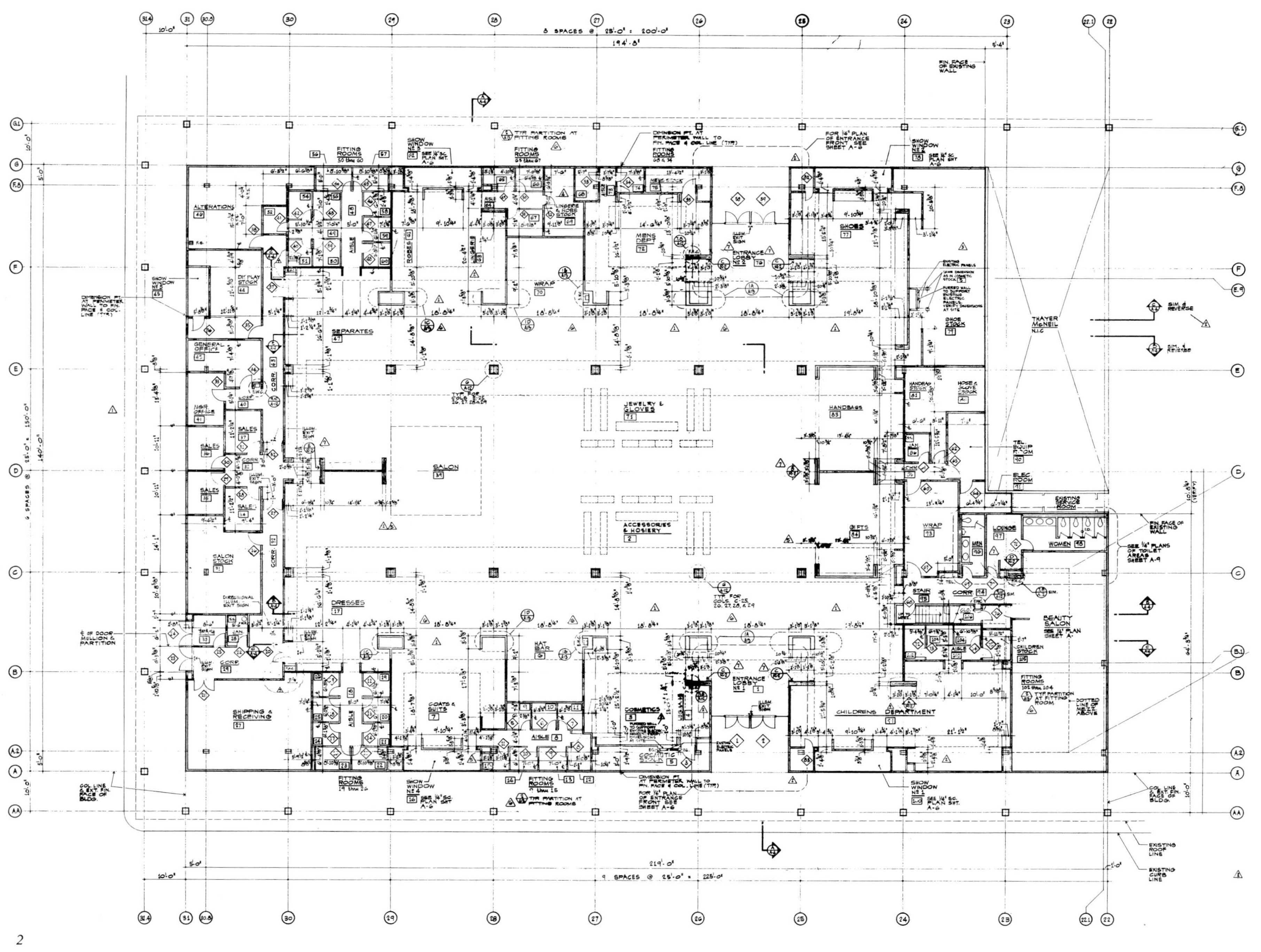

Central Business District
Hermosa Beach, California 1967

The business district of Hermosa Beach suffered from a problem not uncommon among small beachfront towns: the seasonal nature of retail opportunity creates an unstable business mix and an area susceptible to vacancies and a consequent decline in the quality of both the town and the tourist trade.

The four-block area which was the subject of the study is on the ocean front by the town's pier. It was hoped that careful planning and redevelopment could establish it as the nucleus of a rejuvenated business district and a more profitable tourist attraction.

The urban-design proposal developed by Gehry and planner Radoslav Sutnar calls for a recognition of the difference between seasonal, beachfront service and retail facilities, and those that serve the town year-round. By taking advantage of the site's slope, the latter is designed to extend, by colonnaded ambulatories, from the inland edge of the site to the waterfront, while the former could be fit at beachfront ground level beneath. At ground level behind the beachfront stores are parking, service stores, and storage. The plan conforms to the organization of the four city blocks which constituted the site at the time of the study. The city street bisecting the site on axis with the pier is, in the plan, closed to traffic but reasserted as the primary pedestrian thoroughfare. The bisecting street parallel to the beach continues uninterrupted through the site at grade, providing access to service stores fronting the street at ground level and to parking. In the interior of each block are three-level parking structures. Also included in the plan are housing, a two-hundred-room hotel, office space, and the redevelopment of the pier: shopping stalls, on the model of the Ponte Vecchio, line the pier, which is connected with the colonnade and shopping bridges. The Italian precedent notwithstanding, the architecture proposed for the buildings of the scheme was, according to Gehry, "more of my Spanish period."

1.Site model 2.Conceptual diagram

Bixby Green
Garden Grove, California 1969

In the competitive multihousing market, one developer had an intriguing idea. Instead of luring buyers with styling, the Bixby Ranch Company, with Gehry, sought to invest in more durable solutions to problems of multifamily housing. Specifically, they concentrated on creating a relatively traffic-free, park-like setting, on providing maximum living space in each unit, and on acoustical and visual privacy. The eighty-four units face landscaped park areas, some over the two subterranean parking structures. Adjacent units were staggered, and wing walls extended to block paths of sound transmission. Each townhouse is structurally an independent unit: "party" walls between units are in fact two walls with an air space. Acoustical sealant was used at wall seams. So effective was the attention to acoustic privacy that salesmen were able to demonstrate that a mariachi band playing in one unit could not be heard next door. Given the built-in costs of this acoustic protection and of below-grade parking, substantial cost juggling was done to create a community of aesthetic harmony.

3.Site plan 4.Site model

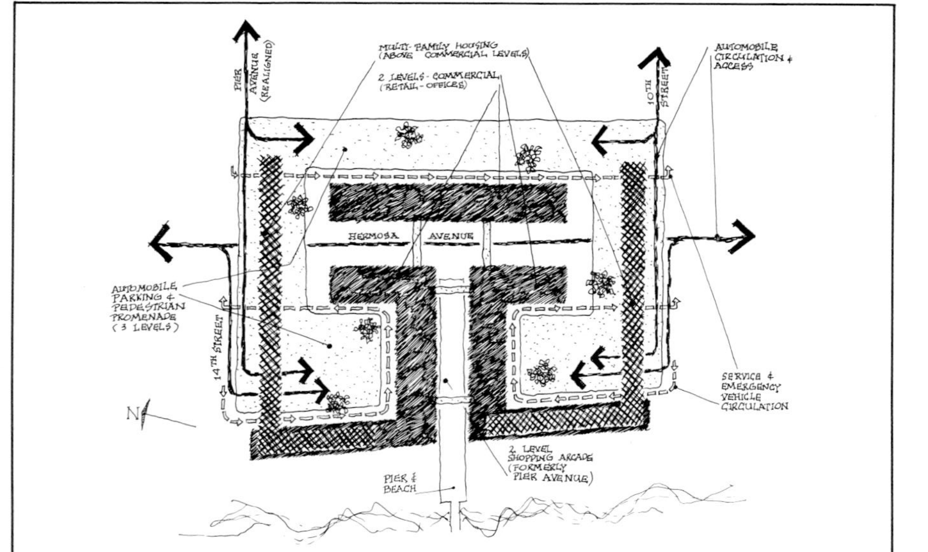

2

1

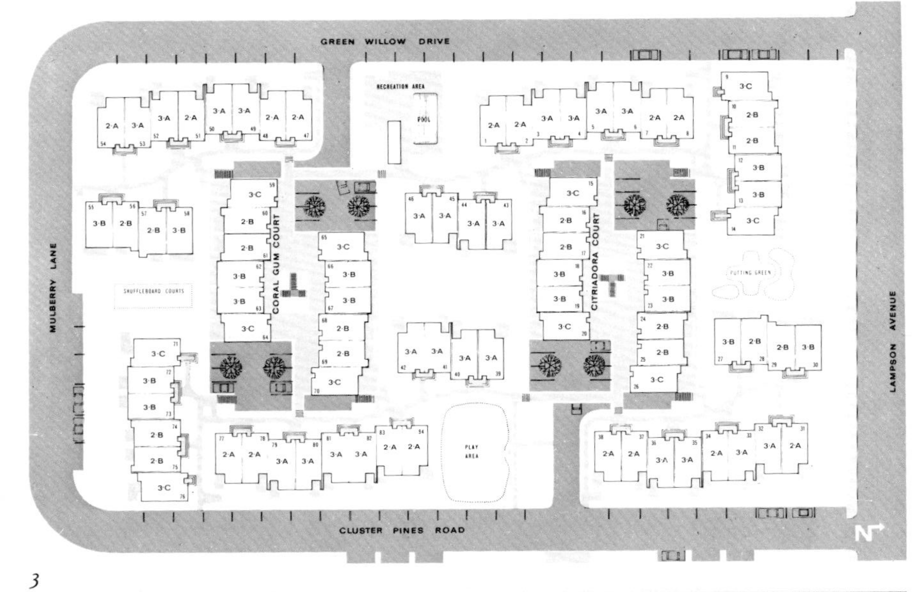
GREEN WILLOW DRIVE
RECREATION AREA
POOL
CORAL GUM COURT
CITRIADORA COURT
SHUFFLEBOARD COURTS
PUTTING GREEN
PLAY AREA
MULBERRY LANE
LAMPSON AVENUE
CLUSTER PINES ROAD
N

3

4

1.Party walls between units 2.Parking structure
3-4.Exterior elevations

1

2

3

4

University Park
Irvine, California 1970

The first multi-family residential areas of the new town, Irvine, were designed by Gehry. As the site was immediately adjacent to the San Diego freeway, a major challenge was to screen residential areas from highway noise. Rather than pulling building areas away from the freeway to the insignificantly small extent possible or resorting to fencing, Gehry designed a special "wall building" which screened the site from the highway and contained apartments with a blind wall to the freeway, opening instead onto green areas of the site. Similarly, instead of attempting to evoke an impression of suburban density with winding roads, scattered parking, and isolated buildings, compact building clusters were designed. From a single central boulevard, drives lead to parking at the center of each cluster. Open parking areas are heavily planted and ringed with linear carports: from the surrounding apartments, trees and pitched roofs, rather than cars, are the primary vista. The compactness and efficiency of site planning and a prefabricated building component system both reduced the costs significantly and netted one-third of an acre for additional green space. Gehry also designed the project's four-acre recreation area and its twelve thousand-square-foot recreation center, housing health club, dance floors, library, and assorted meeting rooms.

1.Projected site plan   2–3.Exterior views

Vernon-Central Redevelopment
Los Angeles, California 1970

The Redevelopment Agency of Los Angeles was charged with planning for the area around a station of the proposed city rapid-transit system. The project director experimented with a strategy to stimulate agency project members' ideas about possible development strategies. Three firms, including Gehry's, were hired to give schematic proposals. The firms were given thirty days, two meetings with the agency, and low fees to prepare plans. Gehry proposed a megastructure of stores, offices, and high-density housing over structured parking around the station, with a mixture of housing densities toward the periphery of the site. The charrette was felt to be a successful strategy for enriching the agency's planning process.

4.Diagrammatic plan   5.Study model

2

3

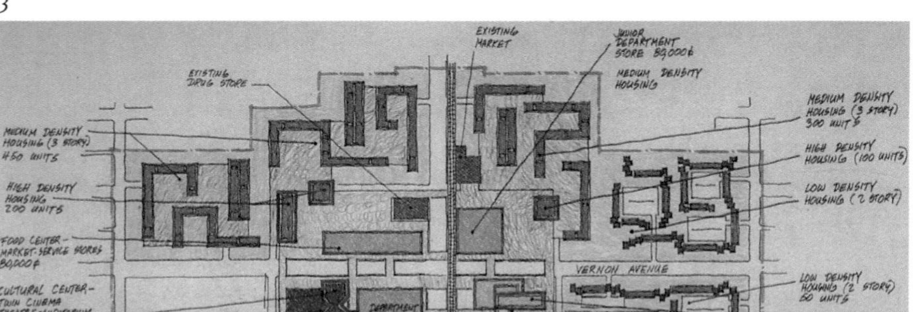

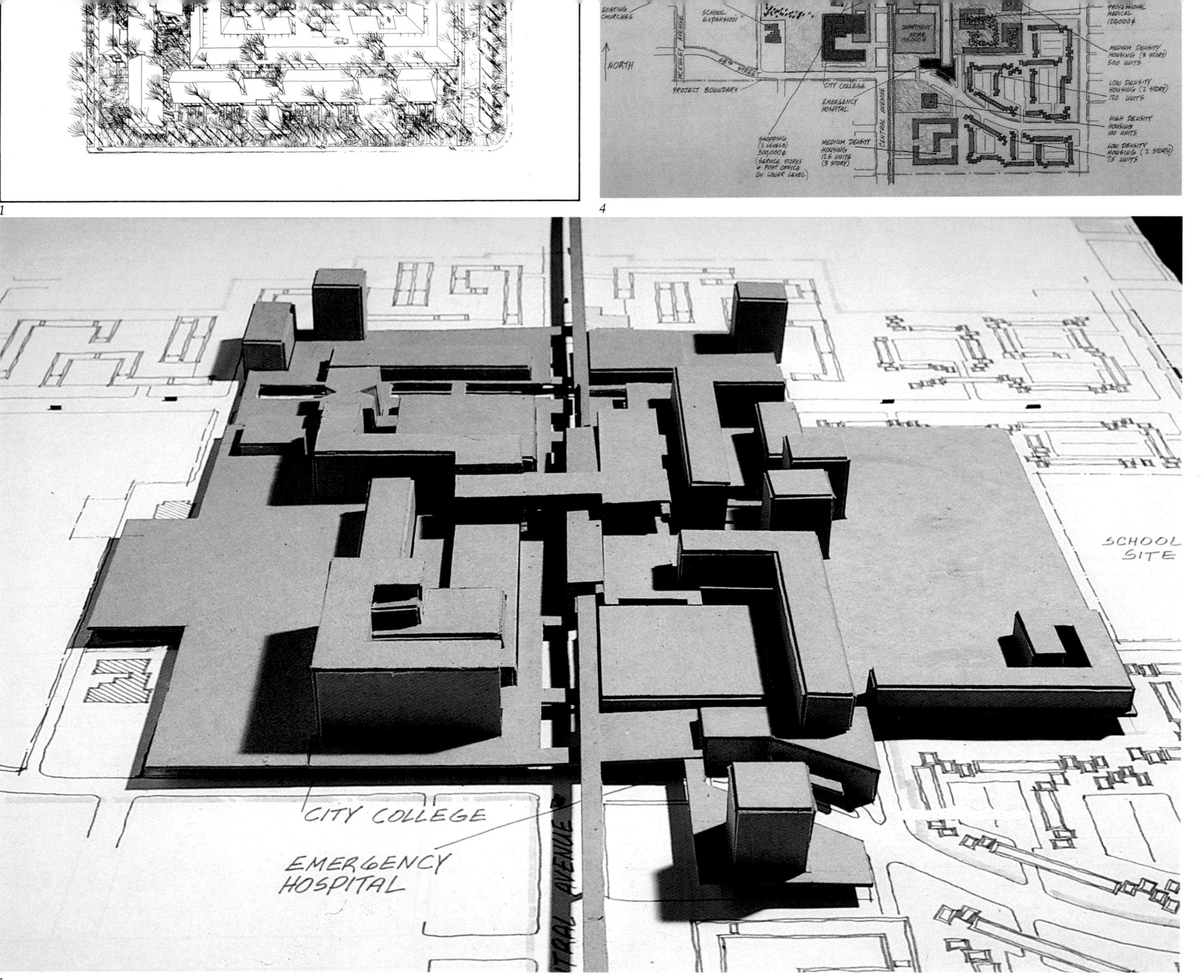
EXISTING CHURCHES
SCHOOL EXPANSION
NORTH
MCKINLEY AVENUE
PROJECT BOUNDARY
CITY COLLEGE
EMERGENCY HOSPITAL
CENTRAL AVENUE
PROFESSIONAL MEDICAL
MEDIUM DENSITY HOUSING (3 STORY) 500 UNITS
LOW DENSITY HOUSING (2 STORY) 120 UNITS
HIGH DENSITY HOUSING 100 UNITS
LOW DENSITY HOUSING (2 STORY) 75 UNITS
MEDIUM DENSITY HOUSING 125 UNITS (3 STORY)
SHOPPING (2 LEVELS)
(SERVICE STORES & POST OFFICE ON LOWER LEVEL)
SCHOOL SITE
CITY COLLEGE
EMERGENCY HOSPITAL
AVENUE

1

4

5

Hollywood Bowl

Hollywood, California 1970–82

[The] heiress to the Pittsburgh Paint fortune . . . arrived in Hollywood in 1918 with the idea of bringing culture to the community by presenting religious plays. In 1919, she established the Theater Arts Alliance with several other leading citizens and set out to find a Hollywood location suitable for the presentation of outdoor theatrical performances. The site chosen was the property that now contains the Hollywood Bowl; it then bore the euphonious name of Daisy Dell. . . . The alliance tested the dell's acoustics by setting up a rough platform in the sage brush, dragging a grand piano up the hill, and inviting a prominent local contralto to sing to the field mice. The natural acoustics were perfect.

—Bruce T. Torrence, *Hollywood, The First Hundred Years*

Although the acoustics of the site's natural amphitheater may be perfect, those of the series of shells built to shelter performers have not been. The present shell, in continuous use since 1929, is in the form of a series of nested quarter-spheres. Developed with water gardens between stage and audience, the shell lent itself to a fine impersonation of a sunset during the traditional flame-and-fountain shows served at intermission.

Unfortunately, as the shape of the natural bowl was changed to extend seating, as highway and air traffic noise increased, and as amplified sound was introduced, musicians began to have difficulty hearing themselves and other performers on stage, and performances became unevenly audible to audiences. Gehry was called in for a quick and inexpensive temporary solution for the 1970 season, pending development of, and financing for, further improvements. Gehry, who was experimenting with cardboard as a material for furniture, worked with acoustical engineer Christopher Jaffe on exploiting its acoustical properties. Cardboard sono-tubes, manufactured as formwork for concrete columns, were arranged fanning out from the shell at its sides and as a canopy above. The tubes, sufficiently durable for the summer season, not only solved the most pressing on-stage acoustical problems, but also, with the assistance of an electronic "sound reinforcement" system, markedly improved the quality of sound reaching the audience. As one critic reviewed the work: "The enclosure serves as a highly effective stage set, looking particularly well at night. . . . As it stands, the quality of sound is remarkable for an outdoor area as vast as the Hollywood Bowl. The orchestral personnel find their work easier, and Joseph Krips, veteran conductor of the opening concerts, ranks the installation as the best outdoor enclosure in his experience."

So successful—and inexpensive—was the installation that the tubes were replaced yearly until 1980 when a more permanent solution was installed. In the interim, Gehry designed a new shell, which was not constructed, and a master plan for the complex, much of which has been built. The first phase of renovation upgraded backstage areas and administrative offices and added sound and lighting control booths, additional seating, and restrooms. The second phase planned was building a replacement for the old shell. Gehry proposed a trussed frame from which stage equipment and a variety of demountable orchestra shells and proscenia could be hung. Considerations of budget and nostalgia led to the demise of the scheme.

Gehry's latest, and apparently final, design for the shell is now in place. A collection of fiberglass spheres of varying sizes are hung within the shell to reflect and distribute sound to the orchestra. Acoustically, the design has been held a success equalling the temporary installation. Visually, the spheres seem contextually appropriate effervescence in the architectural champagne cocktail that is the Hollywood Bowl.

1.Early temporary shell 2-3.Present shell 4.Sketch 5-7.Sonotube installation

1

2

3

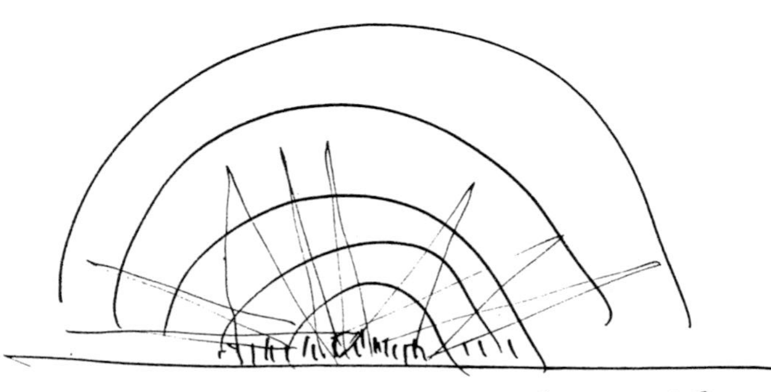
HOLLYWOOD BOWL –
1930 – 1970
ORIGINAL SHELL. – BASED ON A DESIGN BY LLOYD WRIGHT
PROBLEM: FOCUSED SOUND – NO ORCHESTRAL BALANCE.

TEMPORARY SOLUTION: INTENDED FOR 1 YEAR
1971 – 1979
CARDBOARD SONOTUBES
AS SOUND DIFFUSERS
BY JAFFE & GEHRY

4

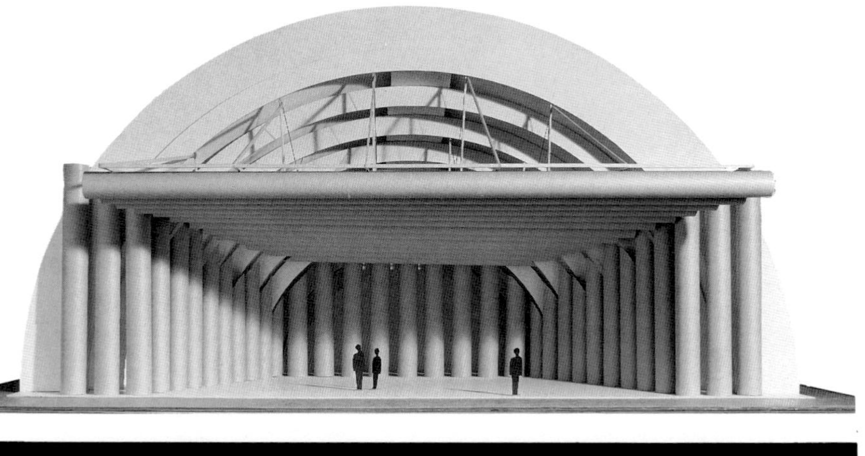

5

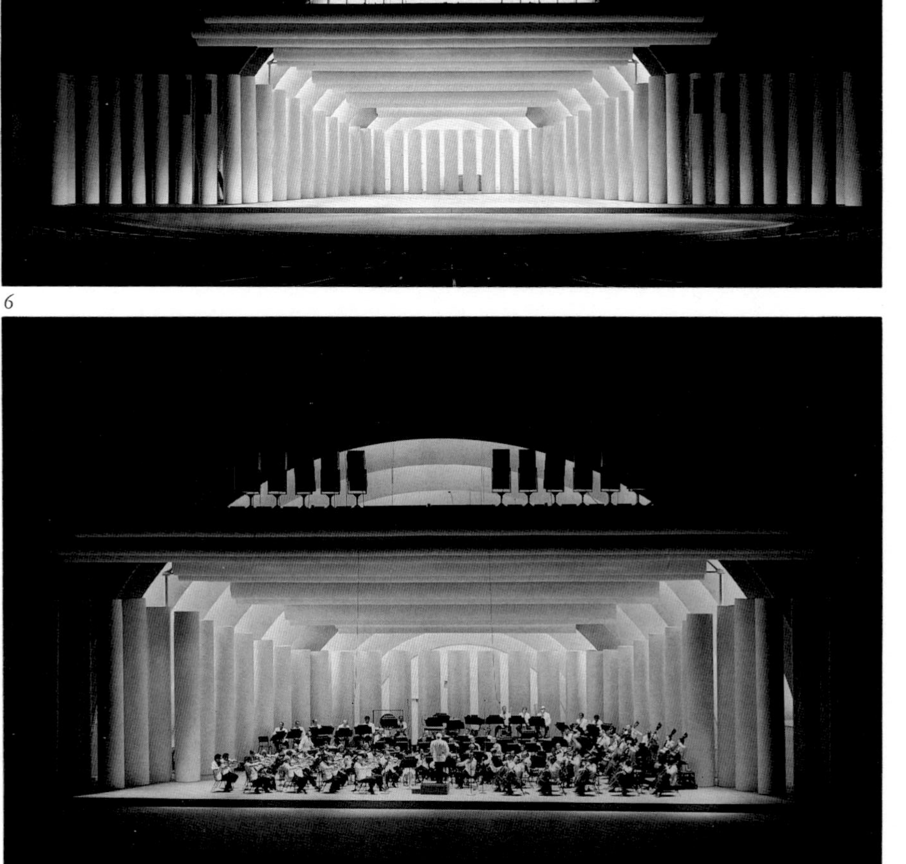

6

7

1.Temporary installation 2.Study for replacement shell 3.Permanent amendments.

1

2

3

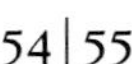

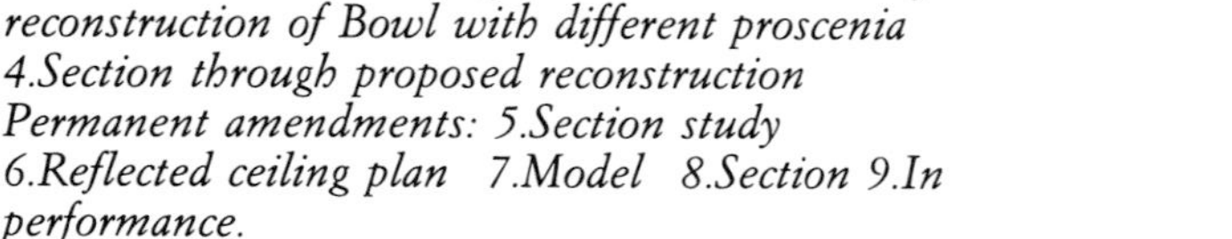

1.Zubin Metta conducting at the Bowl 2-3.Proposed reconstruction of Bowl with different proscenia 4.Section through proposed reconstruction Permanent amendments: 5.Section study 6.Reflected ceiling plan 7.Model 8.Section 9.In performance.

1

2

3

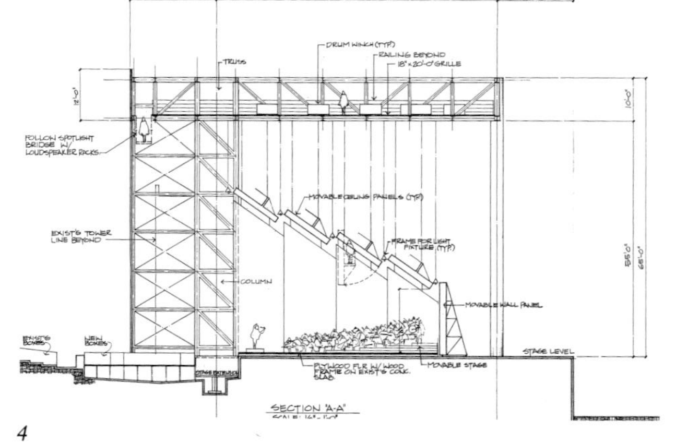

4

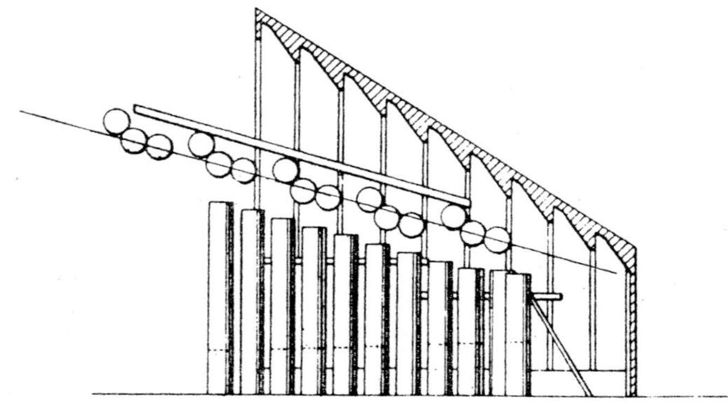

5

6

7

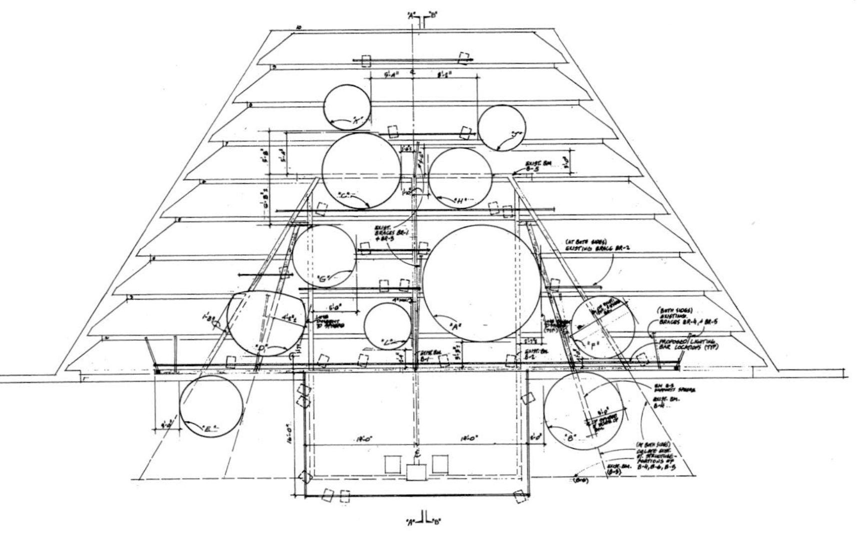

8

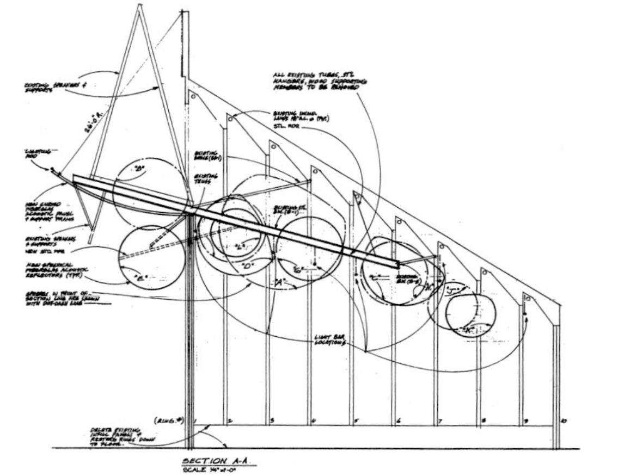

9

Ron Davis House

Malibu, California 1972

After seeing the O'Neill Hay Barn, painter Ron Davis commissioned Gehry to work with him on a design for a house. Gehry and Davis share an interest in manipulating perceptions of perspective, a major focus of Davis's paintings. Working together on Davis's site in Malibu, they staked out vanishing points for perspective illusions, which established the rhomboidal perimeter of the house. In addition, the shaping was a response to the site—" a large hockey stick shape" beside a lake—on which two buildings, a house and studio, were conceived and positioned as related objects.

As the design and project scope evolved, the original interest in perspective and perception continued and the distorted trapezoidal plan developed. In the final design, the roof is tilted from a height of thirty feet in one corner to ten feet at the corner diagonally opposite. Window openings, located to frame views of the mountains and ocean, contribute to the perspective illusions created by the walls and roof.

The project was conceived as an open loft space delivered vacant by the architect. To accommodate any necessary or spontaneous reorganization, the idea of designing a neutral container, developed for the Magnin stores, was pursued. Equally important was Gehry's idea that the collaboration with Davis should be ongoing, that Davis's use of the space—as artist, resident, and designer—would constitute a reaction to Gehry's design which would in turn effect the way the architecture was perceived. Gehry explains, "I built the most beautiful shell I could do, and then let him bring his stuff to it, and convert it to his use. In its optimum, it's a kind of confrontation between the client's aesthetic and values and my own. I'm idealistic in thinking that there's a value in that interaction." Originally constructed were the shell; an on-grade deck outside; and inside, a bedroom and a kitchen and bath core which separated living and bedroom spaces. The volume enclosed was designed as sufficiently capacious to allow both fabrication of large-scale artworks and also subsequent building within the shell. A crawl space under the floor allows alteration or addition to mechanical and electrical systems. Originally, interior partitions were to be on wheels so that Davis's reactions to and designs for the interiors could be a continuous process, with no arrangement ever permanently fixed. Gehry had intended that subsequent building would be done by Davis himself, "that the stuff that went in it would be aesthetically different from the shell, so there would be a kind of confrontation between two ideas." As it turned out, Gehry was called back when more room was needed within the building—twice after initial construction.

Of the interior, Paul Goldberger wrote, "While Gehry has designed a space that offers a significant amount of freedom—and has thus made a strong statement in favor of a passive, rather than active, role for the architect—he has subtly kept himself in control at the same time. The unusual space is never neutral; it forces one to think of the nature of space, the nature of walls, the nature of enclosures. Doing this is a primary mission of serious architecture, and for all its play at being casual this is serious architecture indeed."

Another visitor challenged to consider aspects of architectural elements was the architect himself: "I was nervous about that project; I thought the degree of the angles might be bizarre, and make you feel uneasy. In fact, it was very restful. The building unlocked a whole lot of other possibilities for me. I spent a lot of time there, sitting and looking for a lot of days and evenings, watching the reflections. That helped me in my house. Because nothing was parallel, you couldn't predict where the shadows and sunlight and reflections would fall. If you've got a straight rectangular box, with rectangular windows, you sense where these things come from. But if things aren't all straight then you get a different take. That's become an interesting part of my work. In my new work I am working with those reflections."

1.Early study model 2-5.Construction 6.Interior 7.Plan 8.Splash block

1

2

3

4

6

5

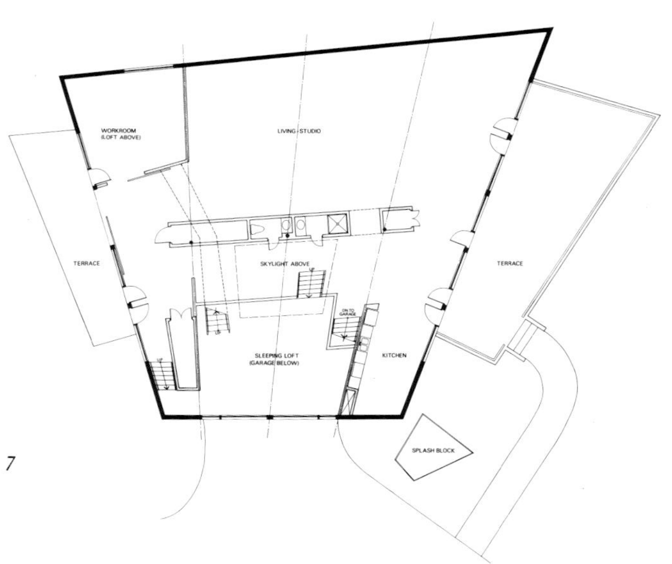
WORKROOM
(LOFT ABOVE)
LIVING | STUDIO
TERRACE
SKYLIGHT ABOVE
TERRACE
SLEEPING LOFT
(GARAGE BELOW)
KITCHEN
SPLASH BLOCK
7

8

1. Terrace 2. Window 3. Skylight 4–6. Interiors
7. Axonometrics, phased construction

2

3

4

5

6

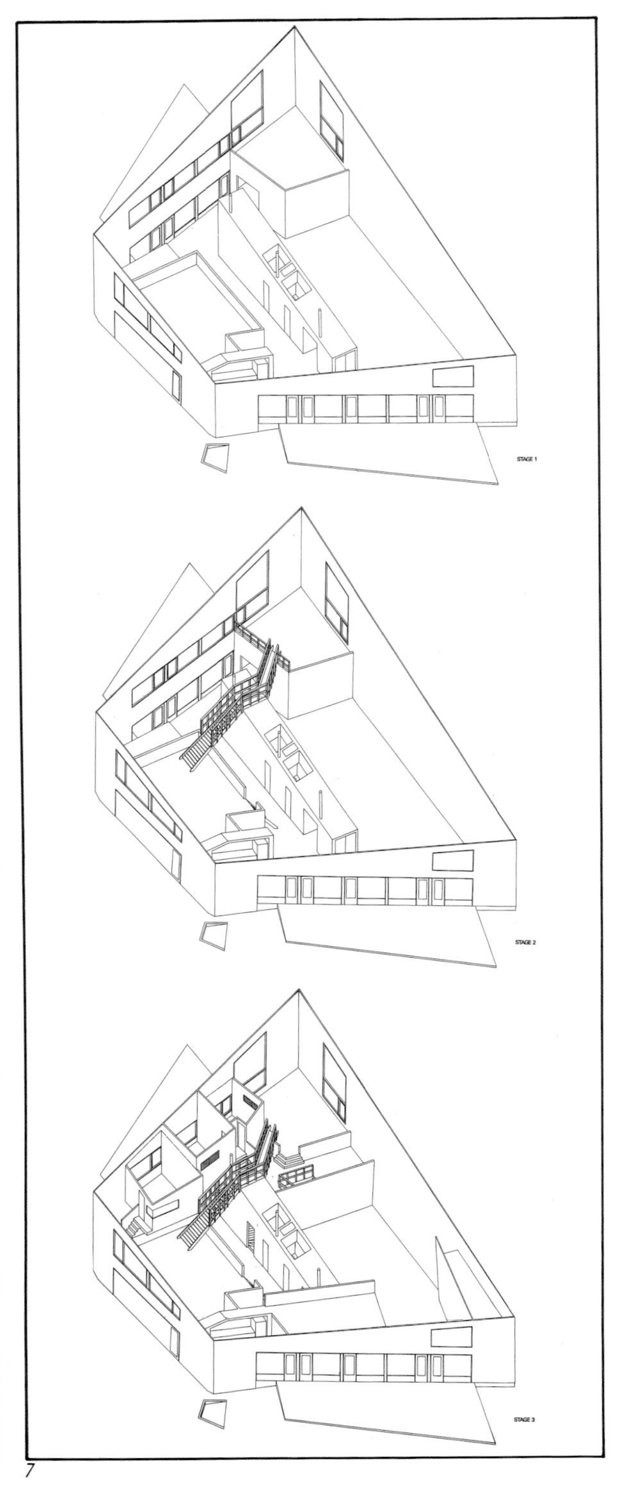

7

1–2,4.Interior 3.Painting by Ron Davis

1

2

3

4

Easy Edges
1969–73

For a symposium between artists and NASA scientists on art, technology, and habitability in space, part of Gehry's contribution was the transformation of the site of the discussion—artist Robert Irwin's studio—with cardboard floors, an operable cardboard garage door, and stacks of cardboard for furniture.

Later, in the course of model building, Gehry became intrigued with the appearance of the raw edges of corrugated cardboard. On the speculation that more might be better, he glued a number of sheets together and made a couple of larger artifacts: a desk and a file cabinet. Not only was the appearance of the raw edges still interesting, but the paper furniture proved to be remarkably strong. More furniture followed. Enthusiasm for the project infected friends Irwin, Josh Young, Larry Bell, and Alexis Smith. Gehry remembers, "We all had a lot of fun playing with it. We started with tables and chairs, then got into partitions and flooring. It was endless, like a disease."

Since discovering that an inordinate portion of building budgets is usurped by fixtures and furniture, Gehry had been interested in developing some inexpensive alternatives. With the cardboard furniture, a solution was found. The material is cheap, fabrication simple, and products durable, strong, and lightweight. The process of fabrication is straightforward: sheets of corrugated cardboard are glued together into a stack which can then be cut to any form with a jigsaw. Although the smooth, regular surface is relatively fragile (hardboard facing proved necessary), the surfaces of exposed corrugation are tough, with demonstrated resistance to everyday mishaps, from food spills to assault with a blow torch. If stained or marred, they can be spot-sanded; crumbs in the exposed webbing of a table surface are susceptible to vacuuming. These surfaces appear and feel like something related to suede and, when cut thin, are virtually transparent. Permutations of shape and function appear boundless.

Says Gehry of his time in the furniture business: "I love working with materials directly. The cardboard furniture allowed that to happen. I could design a shape and build it in the same day. Test it. Refine it. And the next day build another one. The two or three years I spent doing that were some of the most rewarding times of my life. My intention was to design the ultimate inexpensive furniture, something that could be sold cheaply and that would be acceptable to a mass market. . . . It was market-tested . . . and lots of different kinds of people bought it. It reinforced all my feelings about trying to build cheaply in architecture. I knew somewhere there was a key to building inexpensive architecture; uncompromising forms that would be acceptable to the mass market."

But if the idea seemed irresistibly straightforward, marketing, in fact, proved to be anything but. Much time was devoted to finding a company capable of production and distribution. Eventually the furniture was made available at two department stores where it excited much curiosity but moderate sales. Research and development continue on the product. Recently a line was shown which explored shaggier, less machined designs, playing more explicitly with the material and expectations about the appearance of a paper chaise.

SACK CHAIR

OUTGOING
INCOMING

Town Center
Woodlands, Texas 1972–78

For an area near Houston being developed as a new town, Gehry has been involved in two stages of planning the town's center. Given the vagaries of development at so large a scale, preliminary studies involved designing an easily accessible service network of utilities and conceptual images for a transportation system sufficiently flexible to accommodate changes and modifications during the course of development. Later work involved town center buildings, designed to accommodate incremental additions. Among buildings planned for sites along a man-made lake were a hotel, office building, amusement park, company headquarters building, and a regional shopping mall. About one million square feet of building is scheduled for phased construction.

1.Model, town center and lake

Town Center
Cochiti Lake, New Mexico 1973

In the high desert of New Mexico the climate is harsh, the scenery awesome. For a new town being built on the Cochiti Indian Reservation near Albuquerque, the town center was designed to provide shelter from the heat and wind and to harmonize with the surrounding landscape. Screen walls block wind and shelter entrances; trellises and building masses cast shade; light is admitted through terraced north- and east-facing clerestories. These elements, as well as the breezeways and patios around which they are planned and the rough wood and stucco of which they are made, are functionally and aesthetically the progeny of native- and nouveau-American building in the region. Further, the extended unadorned walls and the restrained terraced massing reflect the sweep of desert and sky and the mountains rising in the distance.

At the town center, clusters of buildings were designed to create a sheltered plaza. The buildings—to contain a market, offices, housing, shops, and restaurant—open onto an ambulatory shaded by trellises, screen walls, and the buildings themselves. The side of the plaza not bounded by the building opens to a view of the mountains to the east.

The first building to be built in the center, and nearly the first in the town, was the recreation center. A multipurpose room is the main element in the project—a large clerestory-lit area designed to be hospitable and divisible. The terraced roof form gives the room a variety of ceiling heights and, through the clerestories, even daylighting. Also within the compound are a kitchen, lockers, and a swimming pool. Solid screen and building walls block the heat of the sun from south and west; to the north the building opens onto patios and game courts. The stucco is painted an ice blue, which perceptually cools the building, and, on the irregularly terraced massing, melds the form with the distant mountains. In addition, the walls limit peripheral views, drawing attention to the sweep of the desert sky.

2-3.Recreation center

1

2

3

1.Model, town center 2.View from west 3.View from southeast 4.Plan 5.View toward entrance from pool patio

1

2

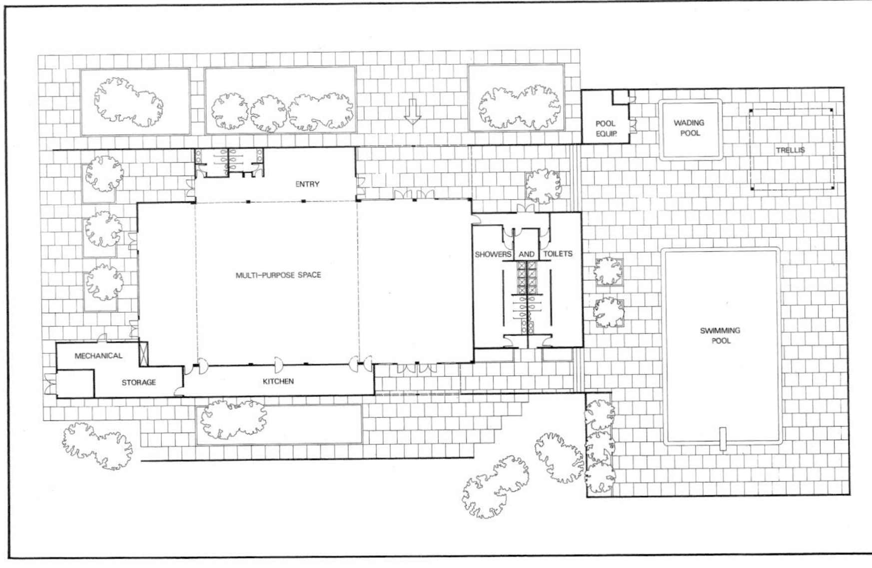
POOL EQUIP
WADING POOL
TRELLIS
ENTRY
SHOWERS AND TOILETS
MULTI-PURPOSE SPACE
SWIMMING POOL
MECHANICAL
STORAGE
KITCHEN

Larkspur-Greenbrae Mall
Larkspur, California 1973

In the preliminary design for an 800,000-square-foot enclosed Rouse Company shopping mall, priority was given to enhancing the natural environment and achieving maximum integration of the interior spaces with the out-of-doors. The sixty-five-acre site is bounded on one side by commercial and residential developments and on the other by a lagoon and creek. It was intended that the project create a village center for shopping and recreation, and that the open-air ambience of the Bay Area be promoted. Extensive landscaping within the parking and commercial areas—including the rooftop—and paths along the water were planned. The two-story enclosed mall, designed to house three major department stores and about one hundred shops, was oriented toward the lagoon. The mall was to be skylit and open to fresh air in many places. Around the perimeter of the mall building, restaurants, boutiques, terraces, and plazas were planned. A system of paths by the water's edge; docks along the lagoon; and planting, paths, and tennis courts on roof tops, further extended the unusual idea of orienting an enclosed mall to its natural environment.

1.Site model

Illinois Center
Chicago, Illinois 1973

To take advantage of available air rights over a portion of Illinois Central Railroad land, a large-scale development project was studied for feasibility. Working with the Mies van der Rohe architectrual offices and developers Metro Structures and the Rouse Company, Gehry and Associates participated in preliminary planning for a regional shopping center. The shopping center was to include two department stores totalling 200,000 square feet in area, 300,000 square feet of mall and tenant stores, and the expansion of a third, existing department store. Critical in the study was the interrelation with parking structures below, a commuter train station, and several office and residential high-rise towers above.

2–3.Site model

Horton Plaza
San Diego, California 1974

A twenty-two acre site in downtown San Diego was studied as a site for redevelopment intended to revitalize the city's core. The fifteen-block area is adjacent on one side to San Diego's "Gas Lamp Quarter" of small-scale buildings suitable for prime retail specialty shops, and on another to hotels and government buildings at one end of the city's downtown commercial corridor. The site's three stops on a rapid transit system would connect the area with the planned bay-side marina at Navy Field, three blocks to the south, and to other points in the city. A full range of urban amenities was planned, with facilities for living, working, and recreation. Another venture with the Rouse Company, the project, taken through schematic design, planned for 1,000,000 square feet of construction as a first phase, with an additional 750,000 square feet to be built subsequently. A similar study for Santa Monica's downtown, which preceded that of Horton Plaza, led to the development of Santa Monica Place.

4.Site model

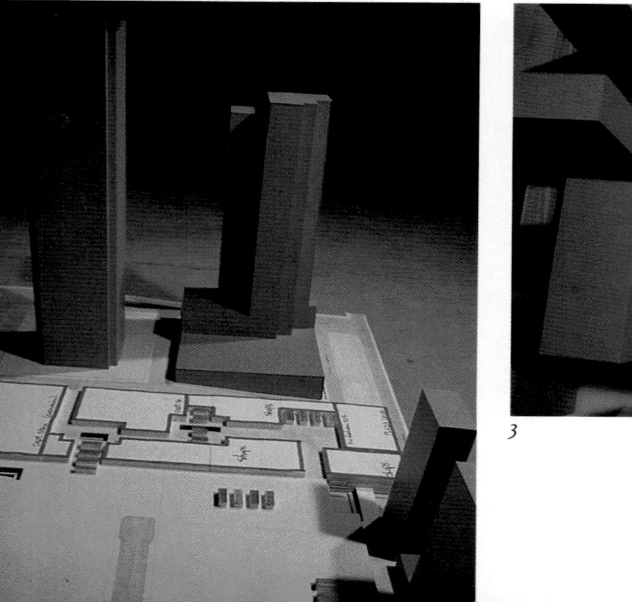

3

2

4

1

Hollydot Houses

Hollydot Park, Colorado 1973

Hollydot Park is a development of luxury townhouses near Colorado Springs. Its particular amenities are facilities for horseback riding, and a rolling, wooded site. Two hundred units were planned. The initial fifty units were sited to overlook a stream which runs through the site, and to preserve existing trees. Buildings are arranged in clusters around entry courts and open toward the stream at the rear. Roofs are steeply pitched to shed snow; skylights cut into them offer views of the treetops. Siding and shingles are of wood, to blend with the landscape.

1.Sketch 2.Model

Janss House

Los Angeles, California 1974

The site for an art collector's house is in a very typical West Los Angeles suburb. Gehry and client Ed Janss, who participated in the design process, developed a rather austere building envelope, to be covered in natural gray "cemesto" cement asbestos board. Offering a marked contrast, the building was to be surmounted by a trellis of rough logs on the roof.

The house was built, although not as designed. The major room of the house, a living room and gallery, however, "looks the way it was intended." A spacious, open room with high ceilings, even, diffused natural daylighting for the art is provided by a strategy which years later became the basis of the gallery scheme developed for the Médiathèque-Centre d'Art Comtemporain in Nîmes, the final project illustrated in this volume. A tall light well is projected substantially above the ceiling of the gallery space. Within the volume of the light well, direct sunlight is reflected off and between its surfaces, so that the light is even and diffused when it reaches the gallery.

3.Side view 4.Entrance view 5.Living room/ gallery

1

2

3

4

5

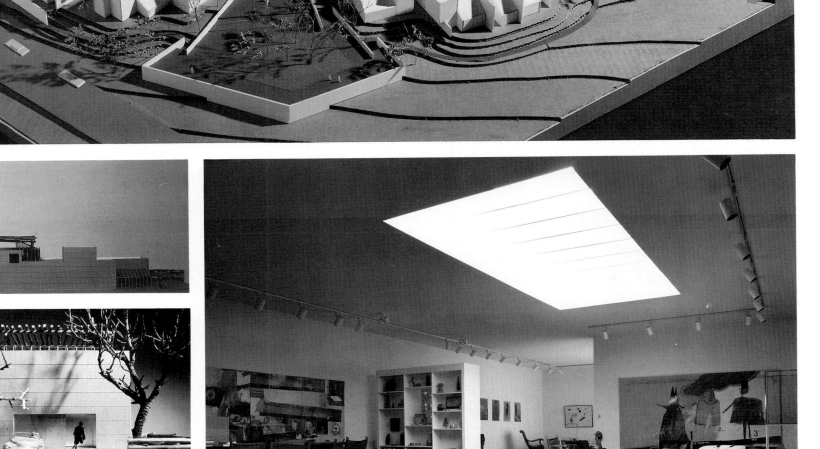

Rouse Company Headquarters

Columbia, Maryland 1974

The Rouse Company has made its mark and its success by building new towns and shopping facilities which promote human contact. The words "people" and "festival" loom large in the stated intentions of its enterprises. Its projects, at all scales, are based on networks for pedestrians along which built, spontaneous, and programed "events" occur. For the design of the company's headquarters at a lakeside site in its new town, Columbia, these ideas were incorporated.

To insure that the diversity of the individuals working within the building could be to some extent accommodated and made visible, and to allow necessary departmental shuffles, the building envelope was conceived, like the Magnin stores and the Davis House, as a neutral shell. A skylit central atrium provides the zone of vertical circulation, the "community" center, and, with the zone allocated on each floor as a "street" connecting open offices areas within the atrium, a coherent organization. Mechanical systems were designed to support this idea of a neutral, flexible interior and to keep the ceilings free of visual clutter. Structural columns were boxed out to include HVAC ducts and registers, leaving the ceiling free of ductwork. A raised flooring system was designed for electrical and telephone lines, to accommodate changes in layout. Several lighting systems were considered; the one adopted is a combination of fluorescent wall-wash fixtures with quartz iodide fixtures—the sort used in museums because of their pure light. The quartz iodide fixtures are integrated with the partitioning panels developed for the project. Light reflects off the unbroken white plane of the ceiling onto the desks below, providing ambient light around the work station as well. The system has proven energy efficient in that, as each work station is its own light source, light intensity is related directly to work areas. Fabric covered partitions were designed to be easily reassembled for use in conjunction with drywall partitions. Panels and partitions, erected directly on the raised floor, provide a varied palette of interior spaces—from low, open stations to completely enclosed offices and conference rooms——possibilities amply explored in scores of rearrangements carried out by the company. To keep the space light and visually open, many enclosed offices are made of panels with butt jointed glazing. Visiting the project after two years of occupancy and many reorganizations, critic Sharon Lee Ryder reported that "the overall impression is one of a carefully established balance between an almost endless variety and a consistent set of design components. The clustered, village-like character of the various departments has a warmth and ease rarely encountered in work environments."

It was intended that the building be expanded, although the date and extent of expansion could not be predicted. The thirty-by-thirty-foot modules of the building were massed in a manner sufficiently picturesque to escape present or future formal "completeness." When the company chooses to expand, the building may be enlarged at either end of the internal "street," to any extent required. The exterior wood trellises are demountable for use in other locations when expansion occurs. They, and the shadows they cast, constitute a changing abstract decoration on the planes of the building.

1. Waterfront 2.Entrance 3.Planned expansion site

1

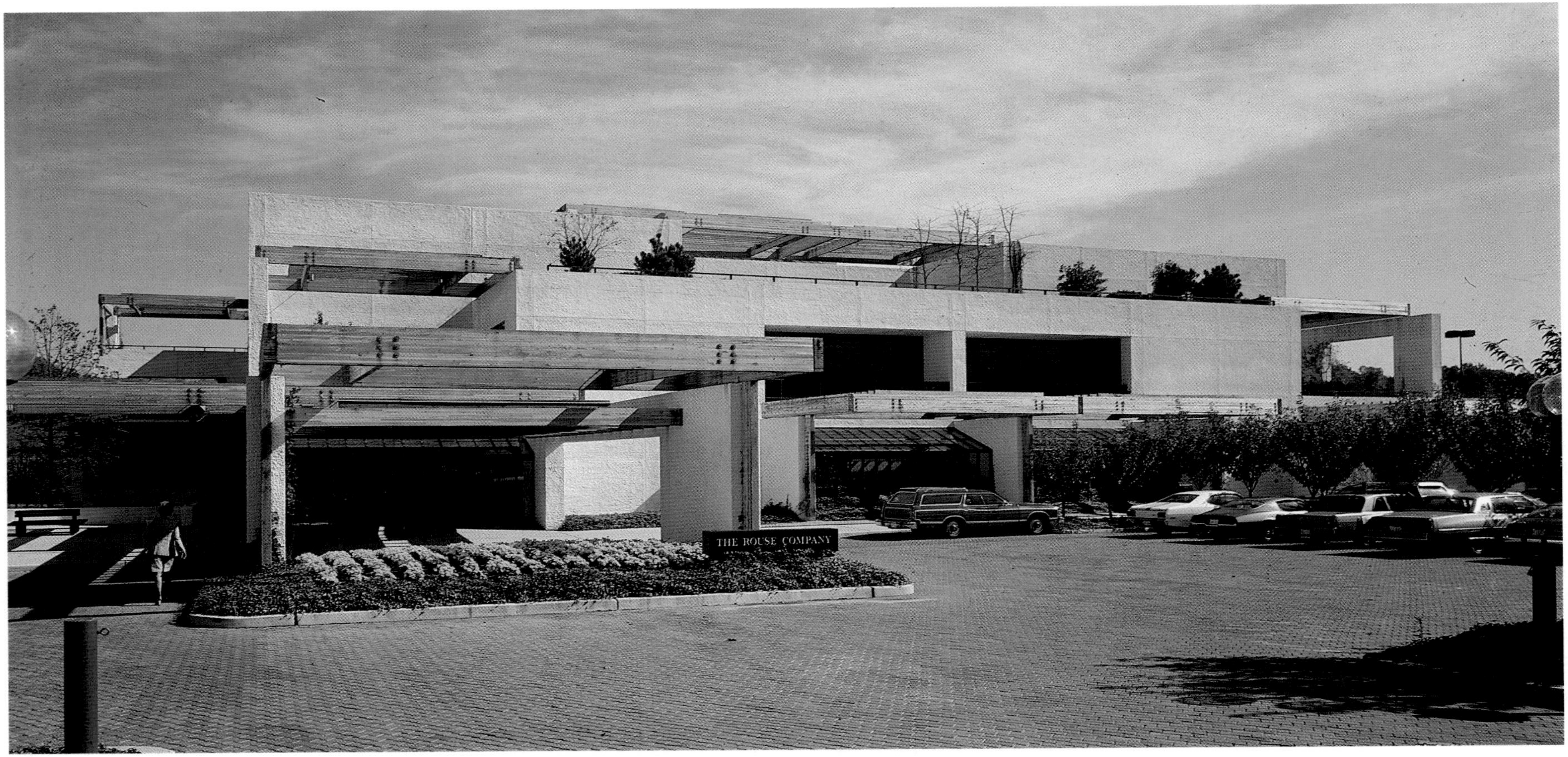

2

3

1-3.Study models 4-5.Interior models study lighting and layout options 6.Full-size mockup in Gehry's office studying interior lighting 7.Typical floor plan 8.Typical department layout 9.Section through workspace

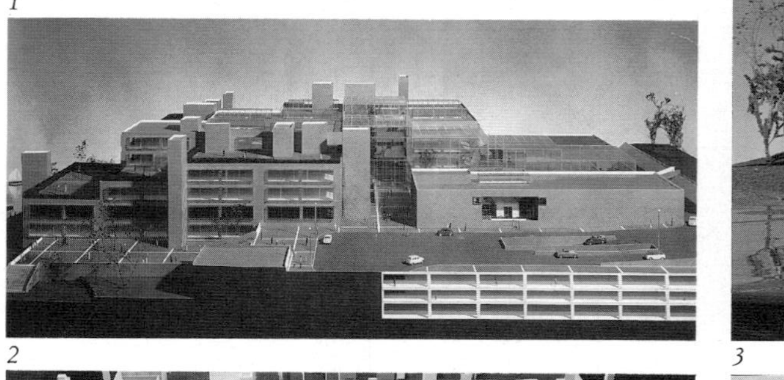

1

2

3

4

5

6

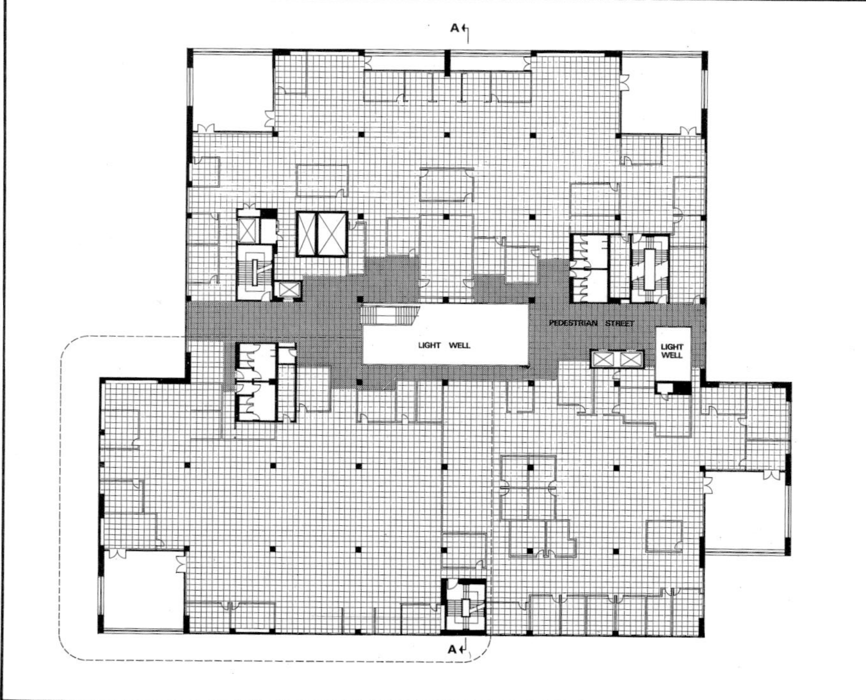
A
LIGHT WELL
PEDESTRIAN STREET
LIGHT WELL
A

7

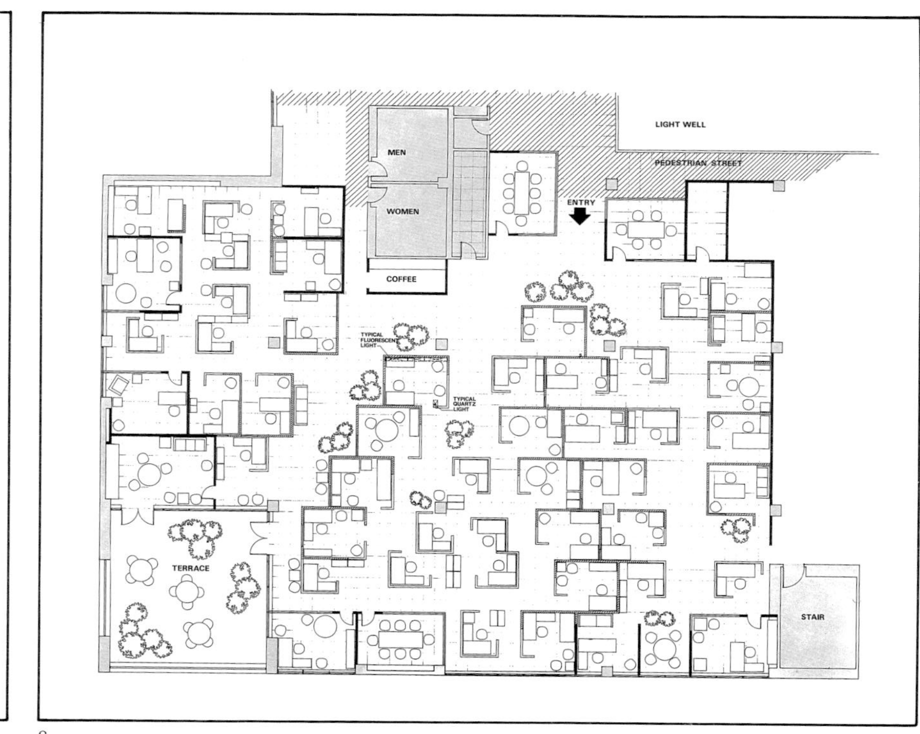
LIGHT WELL
PEDESTRIAN STREET
MEN
WOMEN
COFFEE
ENTRY
TYPICAL FLUORESCENT LIGHT
TYPICAL QUARTZ LIGHT
TERRACE
STAIR

8

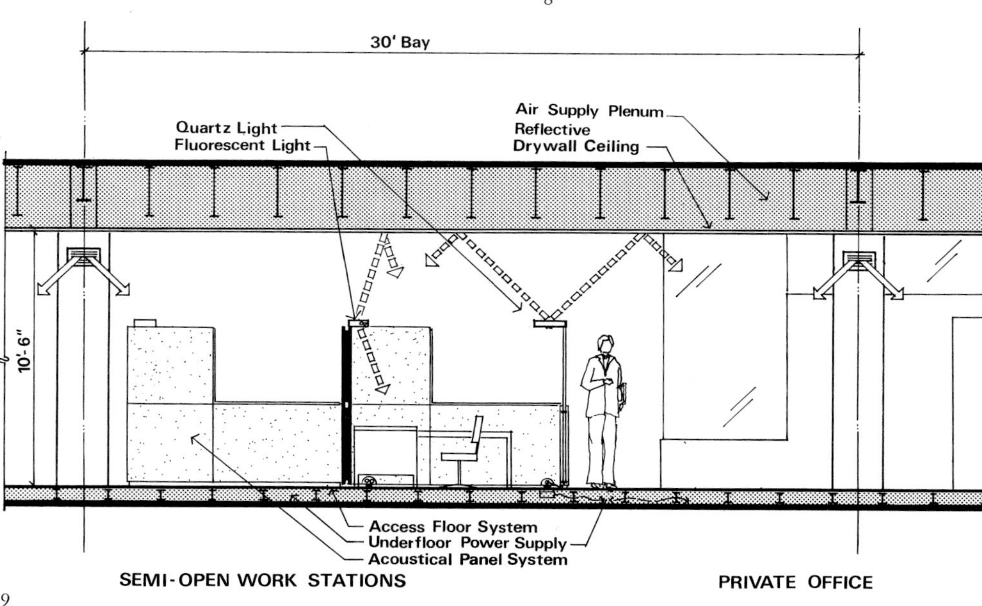
30' Bay
Quartz Light
Fluorescent Light
Air Supply Plenum
Reflective
Drywall Ceiling
10'-6"
Access Floor System
Underfloor Power Supply
Acoustical Panel System
SEMI-OPEN WORK STATIONS
PRIVATE OFFICE

9

1-2.Exterior trellises 3-4.Atrium 5-6.Interiors

1

2

3

4

5

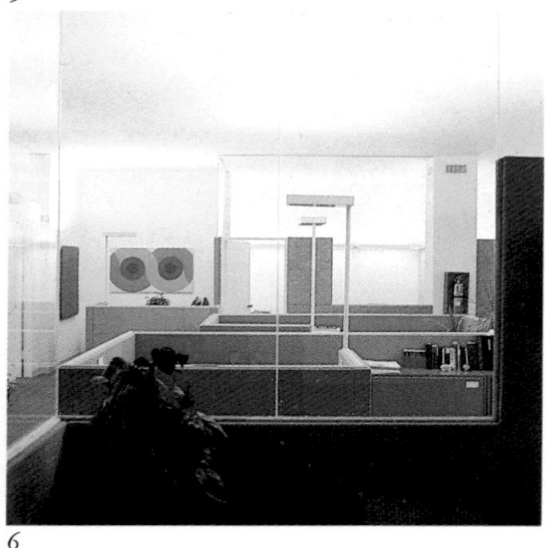

6

Performing Arts Pavilion
Concord, California 1975/77

The site of the Concord Pavilion is rolling countryside at the foothills of Mt. Diablo. A natural bowl in the landscape was further excavated and bermed in an arc to acoustically shield performances from the noise of an adjacent highway, and to conceal the pavilion from view. As Gehry explains it, "I liked the hills around there and didn't want to change them." Upon approach, only the curving berm and its chain-link fence necklace are visible.

Within the bowl an acre of roof—a square form two hundred feet per side and twelve feet in depth—spans between a concrete wall at the rear and two concrete columns opposite. The structural webbing is exposed. As described by critic John Dreyfuss, structural members of the roof "are all painted flat black, so elements of the truss are clearly defined at the edge of the roof, but viewed from the side, they become gradually less 'readable' toward the center, until they fade into each other and a night-like darkness. The effect is mysterious. It's like coming upon a floating, totally foreign creation from the mind of Jules Verne: interesting, exciting, confusing, unsettling." Hung in the structure of the roof are a light and sound booth, three concentric catwalks, lights, speakers, and cylindrical acoustic reflectors.

The pavilion is used for diverse activities and was so designed. A proscenium, thrust stage, arena, or theater-in-the-round can be configured for performances. A portion of the stage is on a hydraulic lift; an orchestra pit understage is surrounded by a device invented by engineer Jaffe for Concord—an acoustical moat. His "assisted resonance" system helps "tune" the pavilion to the requirements of various performances. The earthwork, architecture, and Jaffe's system achieve acoustic success. According to jazz percussionist Louie Bellson, "Every architect and designer of pavilions for the performing arts has a responsibility to go to Concord and experience what has been achieved. . . . For concerts, Concord has no rival."

When called back to Concord to design, among other support facilities, a ticket booth, Gehry decided to build it of the only material visible as one approaches the pavilion—chain-link fencing. Having designed a pavilion for the Long Beach Aquatic Park of chain link, the ticket office became an opportunity to build what he came to call a "shadow structure." The enclosure is trapezoidal in plan with a raking "roof," and is lit at night from below.

1–2.Siting 3.Entrance path 4,6.Views into trusswork 5.Site plan 7.Section toward south 8.Section toward east

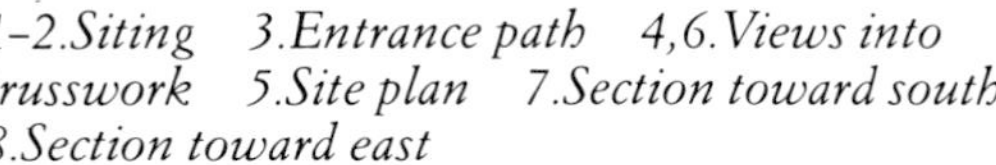

1

2

3

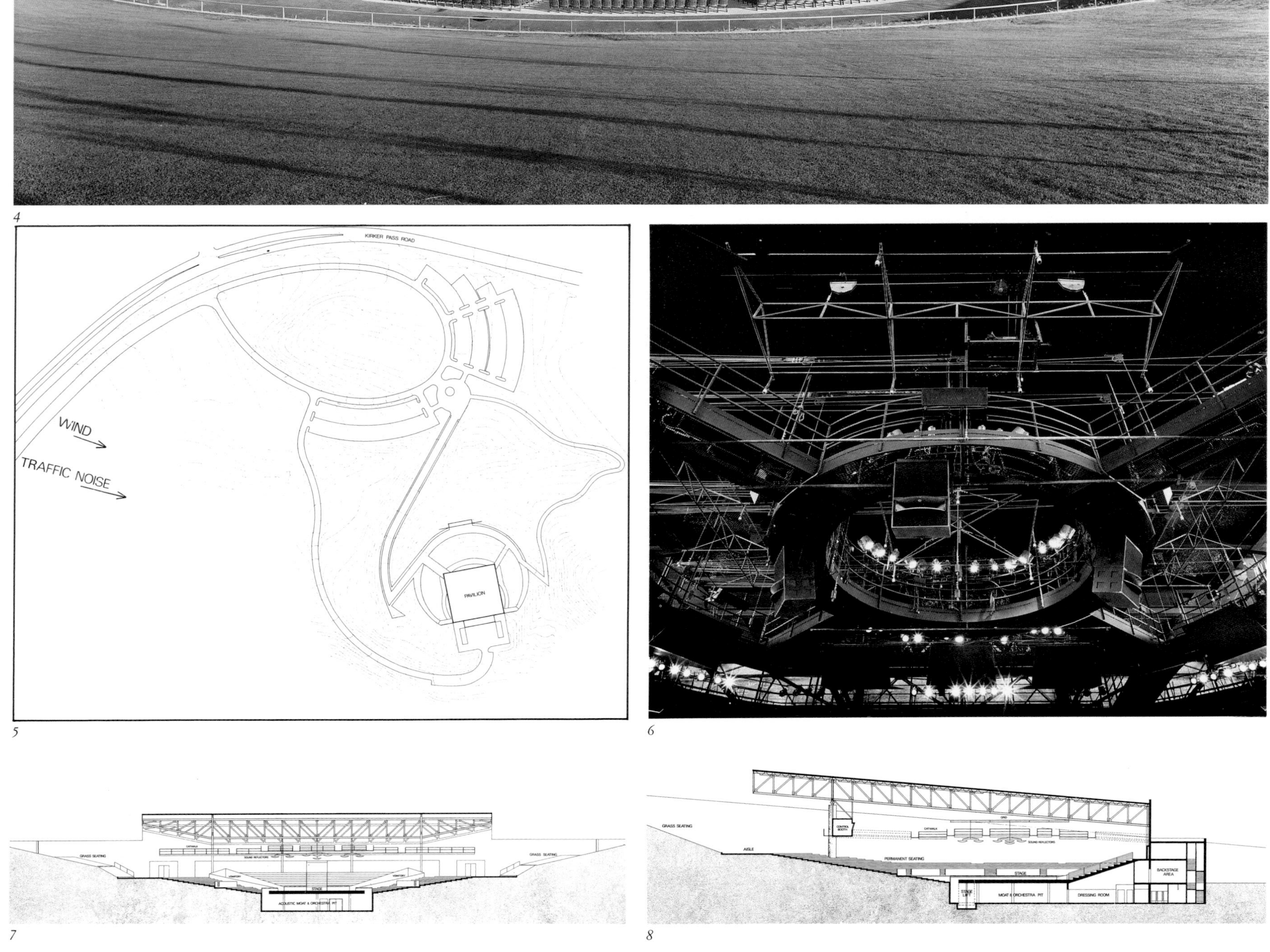
KIRKER PASS ROAD
WIND
TRAFFIC NOISE
PAVILION
GRASS SEATING
CATWALK
SOUND REFLECTORS
STAGE
ACOUSTIC MOAT & ORCHESTRA PIT
CONTROL BOOTH
GRID
AISLE
PERMANENT SEATING
BACKSTAGE AREA
STAGE LIFT
MOAT & ORCHESTRA PIT
DRESSING ROOM

4

5

6

7

8

Gemini G.E.L.
Los Angeles, California 1976–79

Gehry has designed two projects for the studio and gallery complex of a company which produces fine arts graphics. The site is along Melrose Avenue, the same heavily trafficked street of low-scale commercial buildings on which Gehry's Danziger Studio is located. Gemini G.E.L. initially had two small buildings, which Gehry remodeled and bound with a new facade. The facade is a gray stucco plane, the openings of which bear a syncopated relationship to those of the buildings it links, intermittently revealing details of the original buildings. A tall central opening, for example, provides access to a driveway but also reveals a portion of the original building behind. A gap in the facade, and a raking angle it takes at its western end, draws a street lamp, the roof of an apartment building to the rear, an enormous billboard above, and the spotlights lighting the latter into collaborative compositions. The raking angle also responds to a bend in a road approaching opposite, creating the curious illusion of a bent building.

Several years later, Gehry added a 5,000-square-foot, two-story workshop and exhibition space to the eastern end of the complex. The building is essentially open loft space. Its siting creates a court on two sides. The main entrance, through a plywood-sheathed screen wall linking the new and existing buildings, opens onto the court.

A simple stucco box—like those of the Danziger Studio and the Faith Plating Company—is the primary form of the building, elaborated with ideas explored in projects such as the Familian and Gehry houses. The wood frame of the stucco building is intermittently exposed; the studs continuing uninterrupted behind window glazing and skylights. This revealed framing retains, in the completed building, some of the freshness and interest of the building under construction, lends the beauty of its qualities as a material, a sun filter, and decorative fretwork to the otherwise ascetic finishes, and reveals the startling contrast between the apparent mass of the cube and its frame's rhythm and lightness. Trellises continue the framing outside the building. Pursuing the visual excitement of apparent distortions to simple forms studied at the Davis House, a pair of stairs—one open, the other enclosed—conform to a different set of orthogonal coordinates than that of the cube. Both within the enclosed stair, which "breaks free" from the volume of the cube, and also at the rear corner where a studio wall conforms to the stairs' geometry, the implied perimeter of the cube is reasserted by stuccoed framing members. The chain-link fenced parking lot to the east of the workshop building is now the site of Gehry's third project in the area: a restaurant.

1st project: 10.Original building and new facade 13.Exterior
2nd project: 1–3.Model 4.1st floor 5.2nd floor 6–8.Construction 9.Side view 11–14.Junction between 1st and 2nd projects 12.Stair in rear court

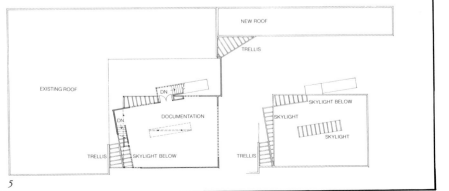

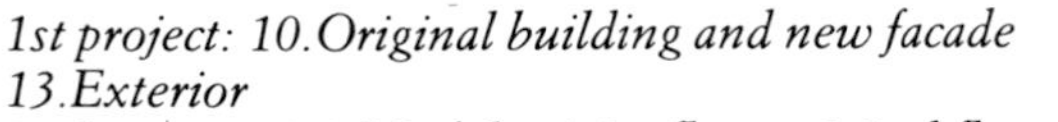

1

2

3

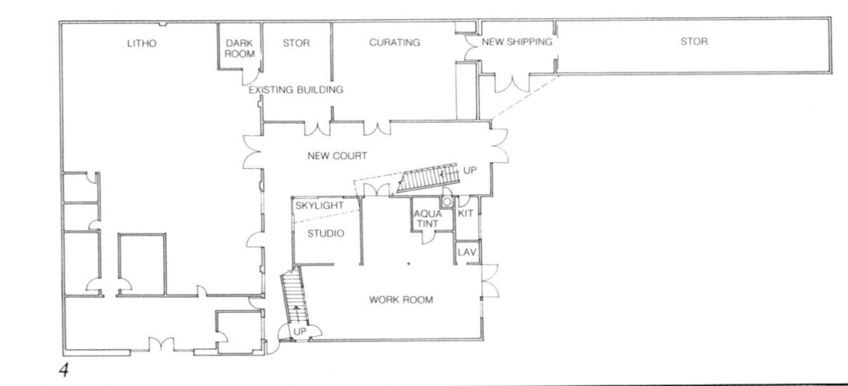

4

NEW ROOF
TRELLIS
EXISTING ROOF
DN
DOCUMENTATION
DN
TRELLIS
SKYLIGHT BELOW
SKYLIGHT BELOW
SKYLIGHT
SKYLIGHT
TRELLIS

5

6

7

11

8

9

10

12

13

14

2nd project: 1.Rear corner 2-3.Entrance stair

1

7

3

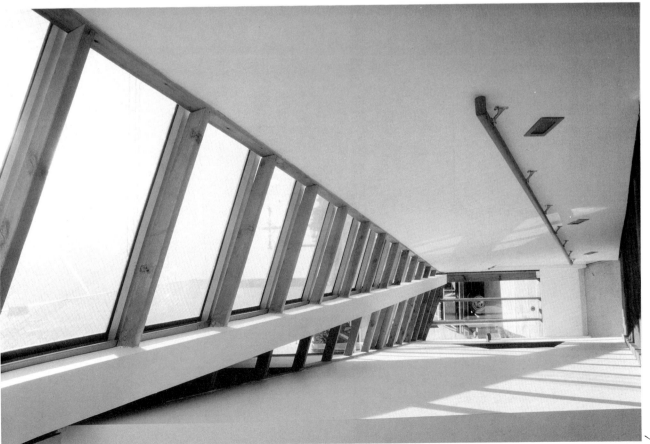

Norton Simon Guest House and Gallery

Malibu, California 1976

The remodeling of an oceanfront house posed a few ticklish questions of style. The clients had purchased a house adjacent to their residence to serve as a guest house, a place for entertaining, and a repository for part of their art collection. The subject house suggests Spanish Colonial genealogy; the art is primarily Oriental; the site is along a Los Angeles beach. A further challenge lay in creating appropriate flexible space and technical support for gallery functions in the context of a residence.

Much of the exterior, particularly at the street, was left unaltered or moderately amended. The interior was gutted and essentially rebuilt. On the top floors are guest quarters: those on the second floor now open onto a large roof terrace; the third floor has been given an uninterrupted, 180-degree view of the ocean. On the ground floor are an office for the owner, a curatorial room, and the major space of the building: a large entertainment and exhibition area, with a glass wall to the beach.

Several means were used to suggest, within the envelope of a Spanish house in 20th century Los Angeles backdrops against which the art was originally seen. First, forms and details recalling each of the relevant architectures were used: wood framing and bracketing, and unadorned plaster planes punctuated with small unframed openings.

During the process of renovation, it was found that a source for evoking some of the spatial and material qualities of Asian temples was already in the house—in its framing. In the main ground floor area, the flat ceiling was removed, joists replaced with trusses, and the wood framing thus exposed was sandblasted. The warmth of rough wood garnered from typical framing members suggested the use of lath strips as a finished wall surface as well as ideas and potential pursued in the Gehry House.

The use of commonplace materials in unorthodox ways is visible in other details. To insure flexibility as a gallery space, brick floors were laid ungrouted on a sand bed in a herringbone pattern for easy rewiring. Relocatable theatrical lighting was positioned along the rafters; ambient light is reflected off the wood ceiling. Rather more startling evidence of the renovator's intervention at work is to be seen in the two unshorn tree trunks which replaced structural columns in the gallery, and in the bracketed trellis which appears to be sliding off the roof.

1-2.Views from beach 3.Living room/gallery 4.Terrace and trellis

1

2

3

4

1.Lath strip panelling at stair   2-4.Interiors

1

2

3

4

Harper House
Baltimore, Maryland 1976

The Village of Cross Keys is a planned community in Baltimore. As at the neighboring Roland Park development designed by Frederick Law Olmstead, attempts have been made in site planning to preserve natural terrain and landscaping. Most of the buildings are small in scale, sited and designed with an eye to visual variety. At the development's center are a shopping area, an inn, and Harper House, a fifteen-story building of condominiums. Harper House is at the edge of a major open area dedicated as community park land. Care was taken in siting and design to preserve existing planting and to minimize intrusion in the park. Taking advantage of a sloping site, parking is beneath the building, partially subterranean. Those levels of the garage above the grade of the park are developed as terraces; the upper terrace is developed as a promontory-like plaza overlooking the park below. Set-backs, balconies, terraces, and a group of two-story penthouses at the top create an irregular skyline and reinstate the small scale of adjacent two-to-five story townhouse ranges.

1.Section 2.Typical floor 3-4.Exteriors

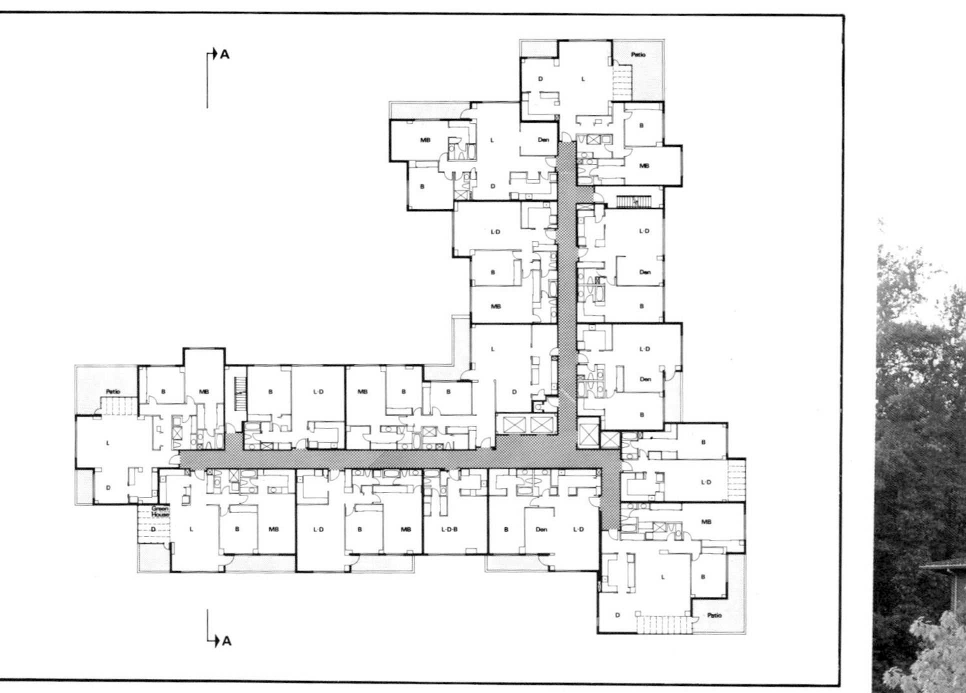

1

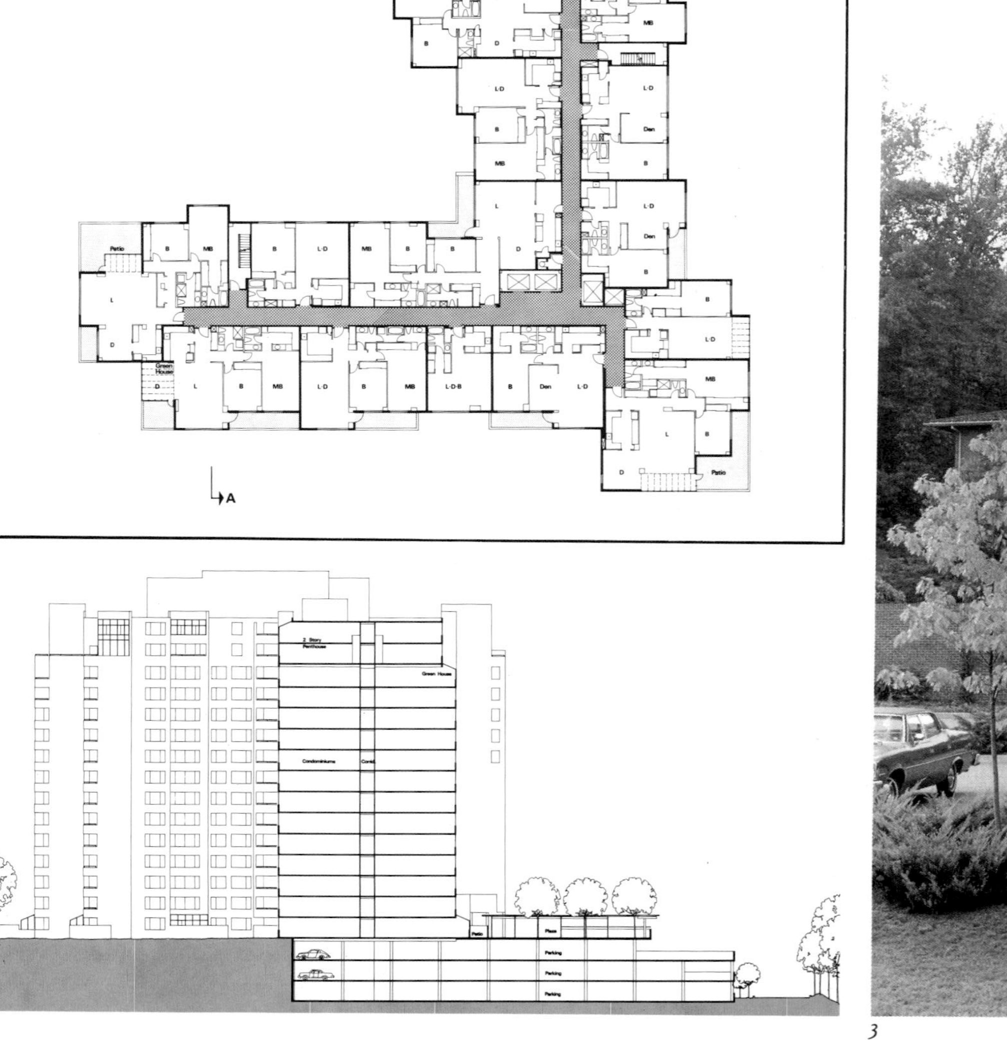

2

3

4

Placement and Career Planning Center
University of California at Los Angeles 1976

The placement department required two kinds of spaces: small offices for counseling, and areas for information boards and bureaus, lounges, and work stations—areas which attract large numbers of students. The building, designed with Eugene Kupper, is wood frame and stucco, an economy allowing spatial aggrandizement of the public areas: they are developed as a series of concourses twenty feet high oriented to either a major cross-campus path to the south or a semiprivate garden to the east. The offices face quiet courts. Many in number and small in size, the offices are given some illusion of openness by wall-to-wall strip windows and interior clerestory windows. Two of the exterior screen walls which define garden areas are of brick, a budget genuflection to the surrounding campus architecture. Inside, the wood framing, window mullions, ductwork, light, and shadows are relied upon to create the decor—described by the architect as "architectural sculpture silhouetted against windows and neutral wall surfaces."

1.Model 2,4.Exterior 3.Interior 5.Rear

1

2

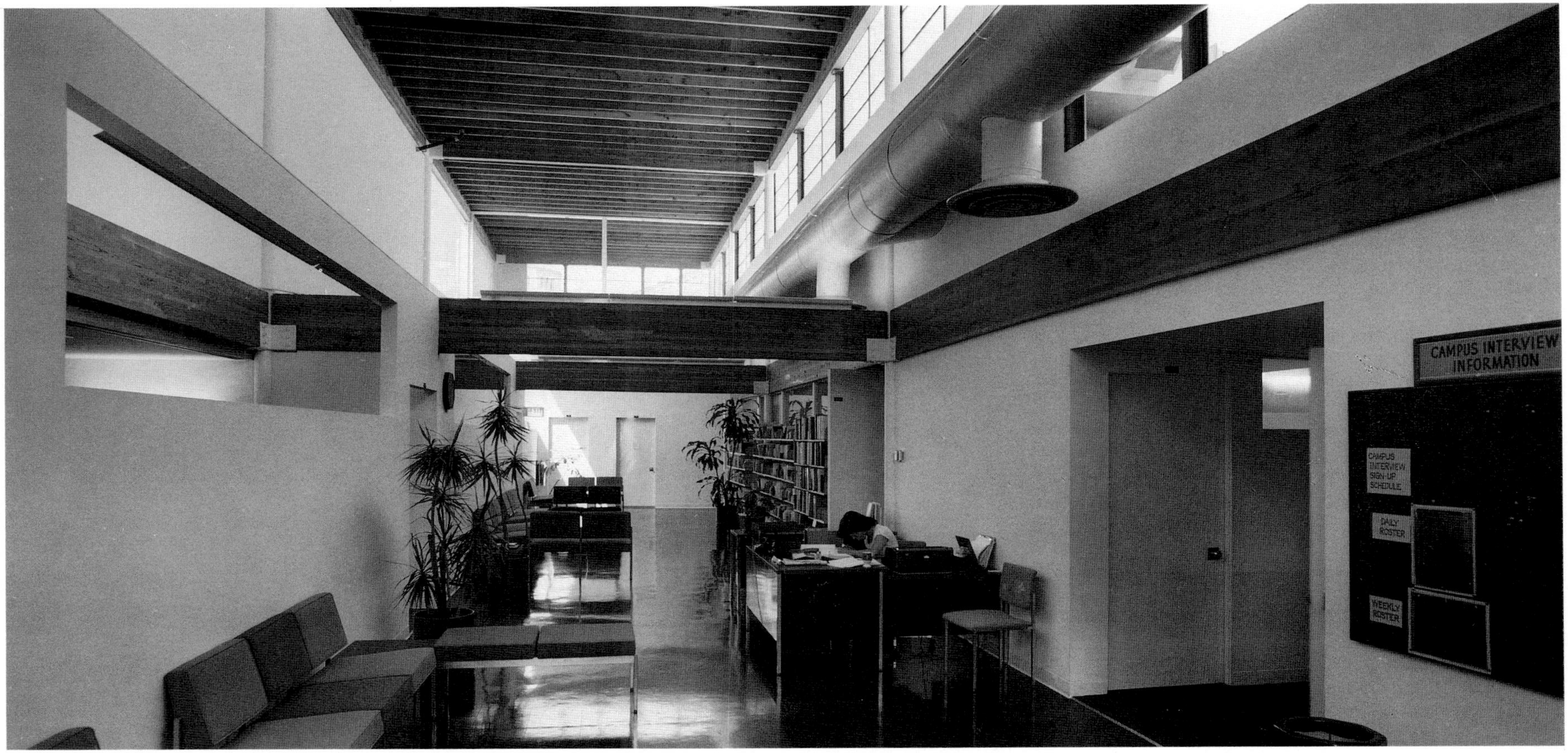

3

4

5

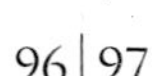

Shoreline Aquatic Park Pavilions
Long Beach, California 1976

The large regional park on the coast at Long Beach was planned by Sasaki, Walker & Associates, a landscape architecture firm, which hired Gehry to design several structures for the park including a boathouse, a lighthouse, and a recreation pavilion. The latter was designed as an open space, within a building describing a three dimensional curve, planned for a variety of recreation activities. Facilities planned include a demountable stage and dance floor, film projection booth, and a mezzanine-level meeting room. Lighting was to be indirect, reflected off "clouds" suspended within the volume. Walls and roof were to be of white, baked enamel panels.

One of the pavilions commissioned was to provide an additional "experience" in and of the park. The landscape firm originally suggested a mirrored cube sixty feet above ground to reflect the surrounding trees. However, according to Gehry, "The budget for it was terrifying, it was so costly." An alternate solution was found in chain link fencing. This was the first project where Gehry used the material as a design medium. The proposal grew out of a discussion with a principal of the landscape firm, Pete Walker. As Gehry describes it, "At the time, both he and I had kids at Cal Arts, and we would drive them from Los Angeles to Valencia. On the trip, you pass that power station with the big chain-link fence covering. I kept looking at it and thinking about it. I liked it. I had thought about playing with chain-link before because every building I do has a chain-link fence around it, like Concord, so it seemed like I should try to deal with it in some way. Pete came to the office one day after he had just driven through there and said, 'Have you ever thought of doing this in chain-link?' And I said, 'Funny you asked.' The structure was designed as a trapezoidal skin of chain-link over steel trusses, enclosing a stand of trees, a winding path, and grassy slopes. The ghost-like presence of the chain-link structure seems, on the one hand, to have been deposited upon and to have arbitrarily cordonned off part of the continuum of the park, and on the other, to demarcate a small independent park within its confines. Like the mirrored structure originally suggested, the design provides an element which both contrasts with and provides a different "take" on the natural elements of the park.

1-2.Recreation building 3.Chain-link pavilion

1

2

3

Jung Institute
Los Angeles, California 1976

He who speaks in primordial images speaks with a thousand voices; he enthralls and overpowers, while at the same time he lifts the idea he is trying to express out of the occasional and the transitory into the realm of the ever-enduring. He transmutes our personal destiny into the destiny of mankind, thereby evoking in us all those beneficient forces that have always enabled mankind to find a refuge from every peril and to outlive the longest night. That is the secret of effective art.
—C.G. Jung "On the Relation of Analytical Psychology to Poetic Art"

While working on the Cochiti Town Center, Gehry "got involved with the sky." The screen walls, built to block out wind and sun, "cut out all the peripheral environment so there was only an intimacy with the sky." When the Jung Institute, through the agent of painter Sam Francis, asked Gehry to design a new facility on a site in an industrial area, he thought again of Cochiti. A walled compound was planned, screening off the unappealing neighborhood and provoking that special concentration on, and appreciation of, the sky. Within the compound, a number of individual structures of distinct sculptural form were designed. The interiors were to be taken and inhabited by the doctors as "found objects." The site was to be asphalt paved, hot mopped for impermeability, and filled with a shallow pool of water. Ironically, Gehry was then unaware that water is the Jungian symbol of the unconscious. Nonetheless, what he designed is a Jungian dream—a compound in which all that is visible is the sky, and a collection of archetypal images reflected in the unconscious.
Gehry later realized that he had worked through the frustration over the project's abandonment by reworking some of the ideas in two later projects—the Berger, Berger, Kahn, Shafton & Moss law offices and the Mid-Atlantic Toyota offices. The frustration, however, was not unexpected: "I knew it was never going to be built. I knew it was a kind of dream on their part..."

1.Sketch 2-4.Model

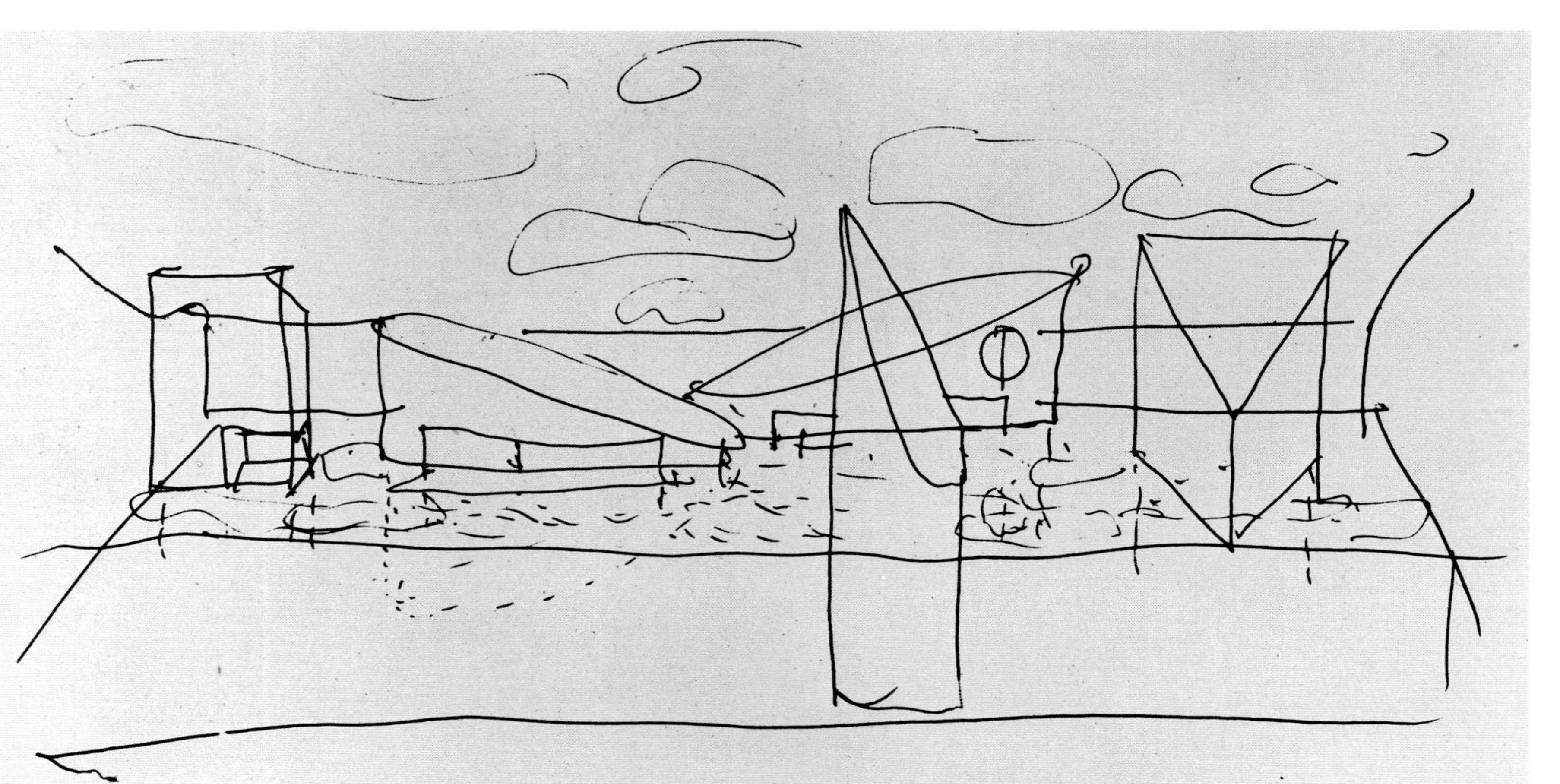

1

2

3

4

Thornwood Mall
Park Forest South, Illinois 1976

Park Forest South is a new town near Chicago under phased construction. Gehry was commissioned to design a regional shopping mall in the area planned as the town center, a project later reduced in scope to a 110,000-square-foot convenience shopping center—to contain shops, restaurants, and a major market. Ultimately, when government, financial, commercial, and cultural facilities are built and the open plain becomes a functioning town center, shopping facilities oriented to the street will be appropriate. Gehry recognized, however, that for the foreseeable future, the shopping center would serve as the interim town center—a place of meetings and events, providing a focus of civic identity in a young and growing town. For that reason, the design was developed as a mall rather than a commercial strip. Stores open onto a clerestory-lit pedestrian "street," 34 feet high. The mall was designed to be built of sandblasted gray aggregate concrete block. Wrapping the concrete block wall, an element was designed to reassert the image and function of a commercial strip: a corrugated aluminum screen wall around the three street fronts of the project incorporates signage and shopping center entries, and screens loading and service areas. The project was taken through working drawings, but was not built.

1.Interior street 2.Site model

The Atrium
Lincoln, Nebraska 1977

Built in 1921 as a department store, the Rudge and Guenzel Building changed hands and uses over the years. With landmark status and proximity to a major downtown redevelopment project, the building was recycled, with restoration and new construction work, into a 250,000-square-foot office and shopping complex. The building's exterior, its marquee, and details of its entry and main public areas were restored. With these features as a framework, new construction was designed to be distinct yet compatible with the dignity of the old building. The complex is organized around a skylit atrium. An adjacent department store was extended as part of the shopping mall which constitutes the lower three floors of the complex. Office space and a health club are above, their interiors overlooking the main atrium. Rooftoops were developed as landscaped terraces for dining and recreation.

3.Section 4.Atrium

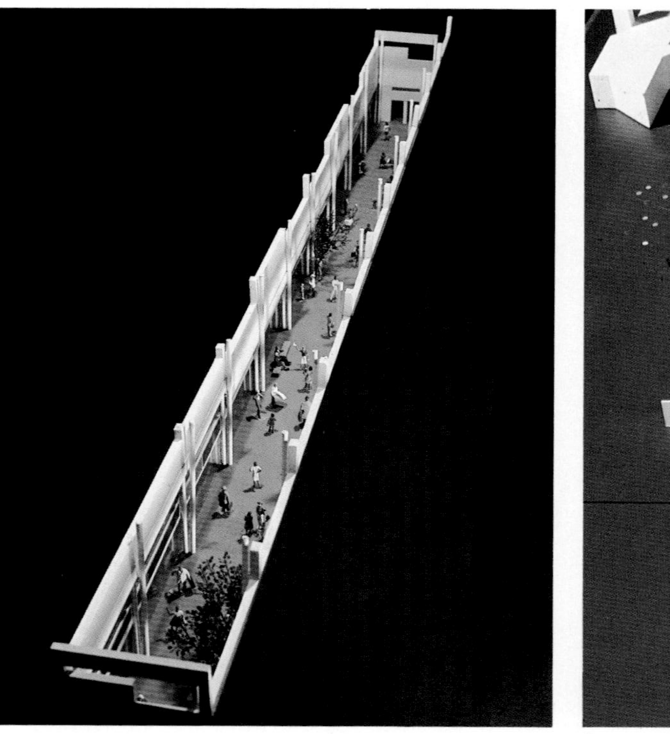

1

2

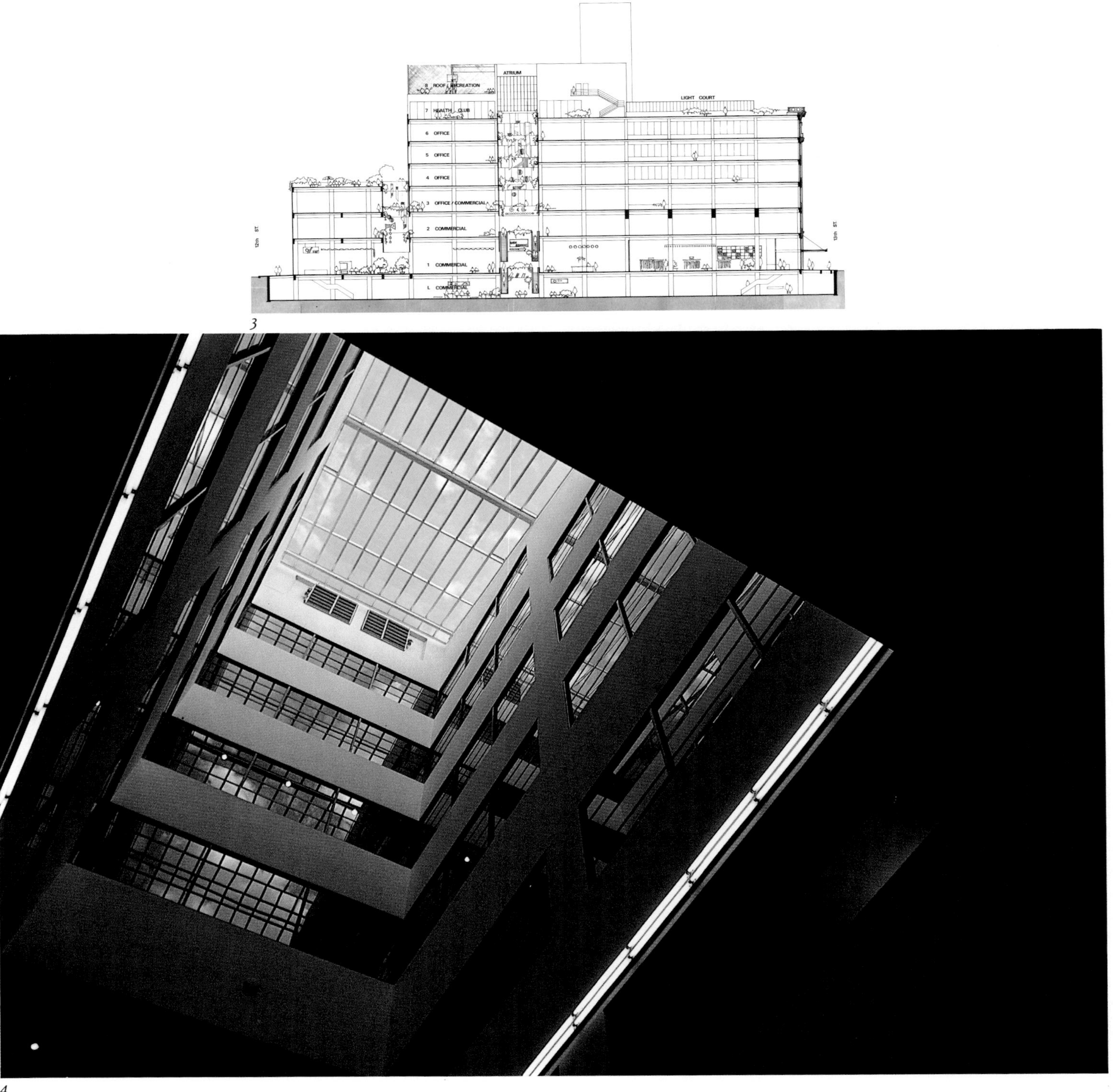
ATRIUM
LIGHT COURT
8 ROOF RECREATION
7 HEALTH CLUB
6 OFFICE
5 OFFICE
4 OFFICE
3 OFFICE / COMMERCIAL
2 COMMERCIAL
1 COMMERCIAL
L COMMERCIAL
12th ST.
13th ST.

3

4

Berger, Berger, Kahn, Shafton & Moss Law Offices

Los Angeles, California 1978

Q: If I go in those offices, what happens to me?
A: You meet a young lawyer who asks you about your legal problems.
Interview with Frank Gehry, 1979

While a "free" plan was recognized early on as one of the opportunities offered by steel and concrete frame construction, it took Frank Gehry to develop the libertine plan. For the Rouse Company Headquarters, he had designed a neutral shell in which the model of village streets could be followed, with the diversity of work and workers providing visual and experiential variety; for these law offices, he took a semifinished floor in a new speculatively-built office building as a shell, in which *he* created a village like no other. Partners' offices, for example, were designed to reflect their individual interests: for the outdoorsman, a log cabin was planned; for the sailing enthusiast's office, a kind of ship's bridge was built. Other incidents include an elaborate, bent, pedimented screen wall, serving to make a kind of porch in front of a pair of glazed doors which open directly onto the exterior window wall; suspended lighting troughs and ductwork zig-zagging down corridors; interior strip windows and portholes; the ubiquitous plant-filled reception area fitted out with park benches and an interior skylight.
The interior windows, doors, and skylights allow daylight into interior spaces and reinforce the suggestion that from the "streets" one is looking into separate buildings. The most particularized "buildings"—the partners' offices—have distinctive forms and were intended to have different materials as well: logs for the cabin, and corrugated metal for another. After the offices were built, Gehry found that there was something familiar about the project: "I realized afterward that it was the Jung project. These discreet little objects set in this environment [were] separated not by water but by sets of space." Asked how two different sets of clients could inspire similar designs, he outlined his criteria: "You've done the job as long as it works and as long as you create something that is exciting, that has some feeling, that has some spirit, that has something that is believable, that clients will interact with."

1.Interior street 2.Conference 3.Partner's office 4.Perspective projection of plan

1

2

3

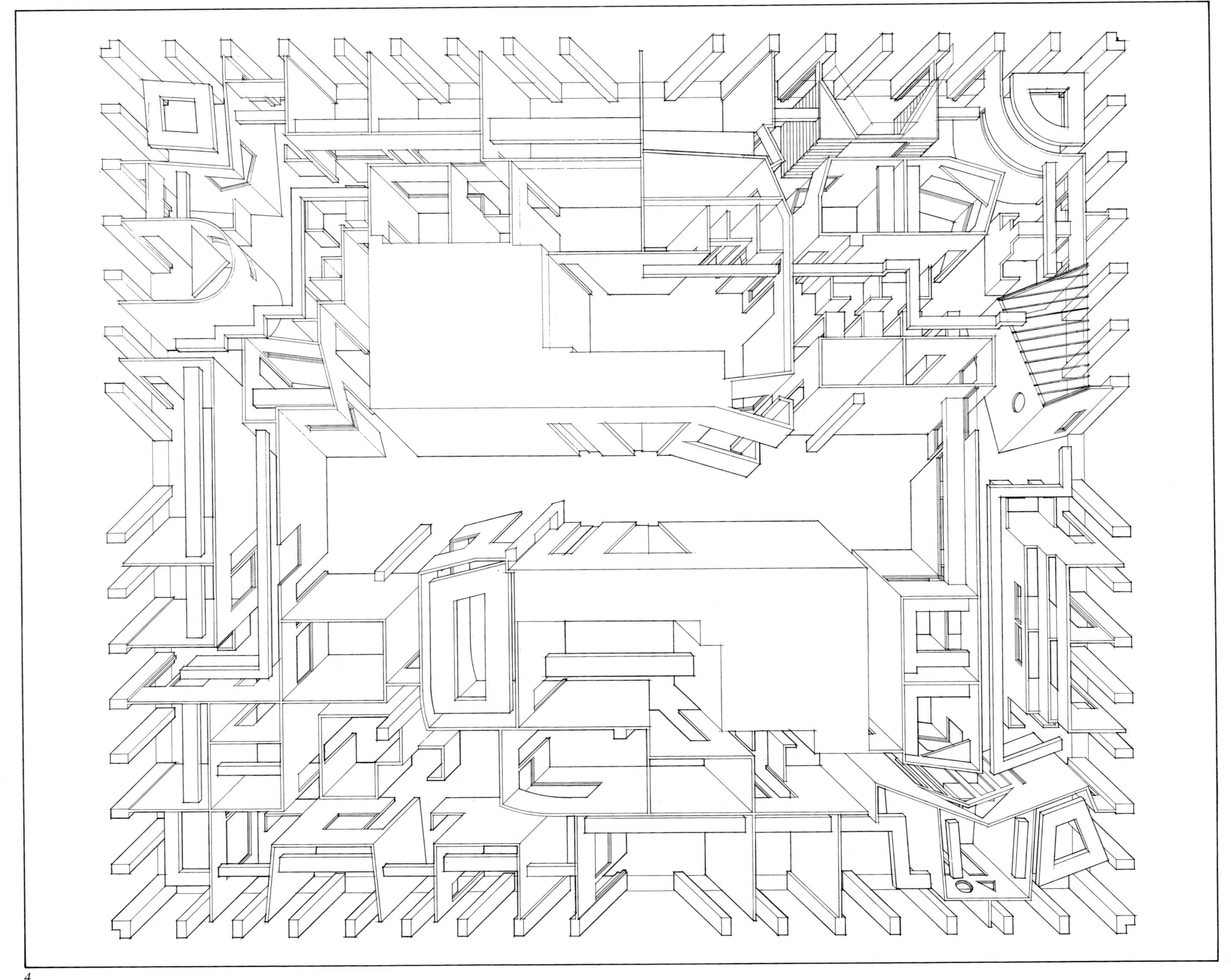

4

Reinforced concrete is the new means to allow the realization of the free plan! Floors are no longer superimposed by partitions. They are free... One is no longer paralyzed.
—Le Corbusier

1

2

3

4

5

6

1,3.Entrances, adjacent to the building's curtain wall, to perimeter offices 2.Lighting system: designed for a lay-in acoustical tile ceiling and downlighting grid, Gehry preferred to use the space's maximum height. Fixtures in suspended troughs reflect off the painted but otherwise undisguised concrete slab ceiling 4.Maritime partner's office 5.Corridor 6.Context: the typical and an alternative.

1.Plan 2.Light trough 3.Reception area with upholstered park benches

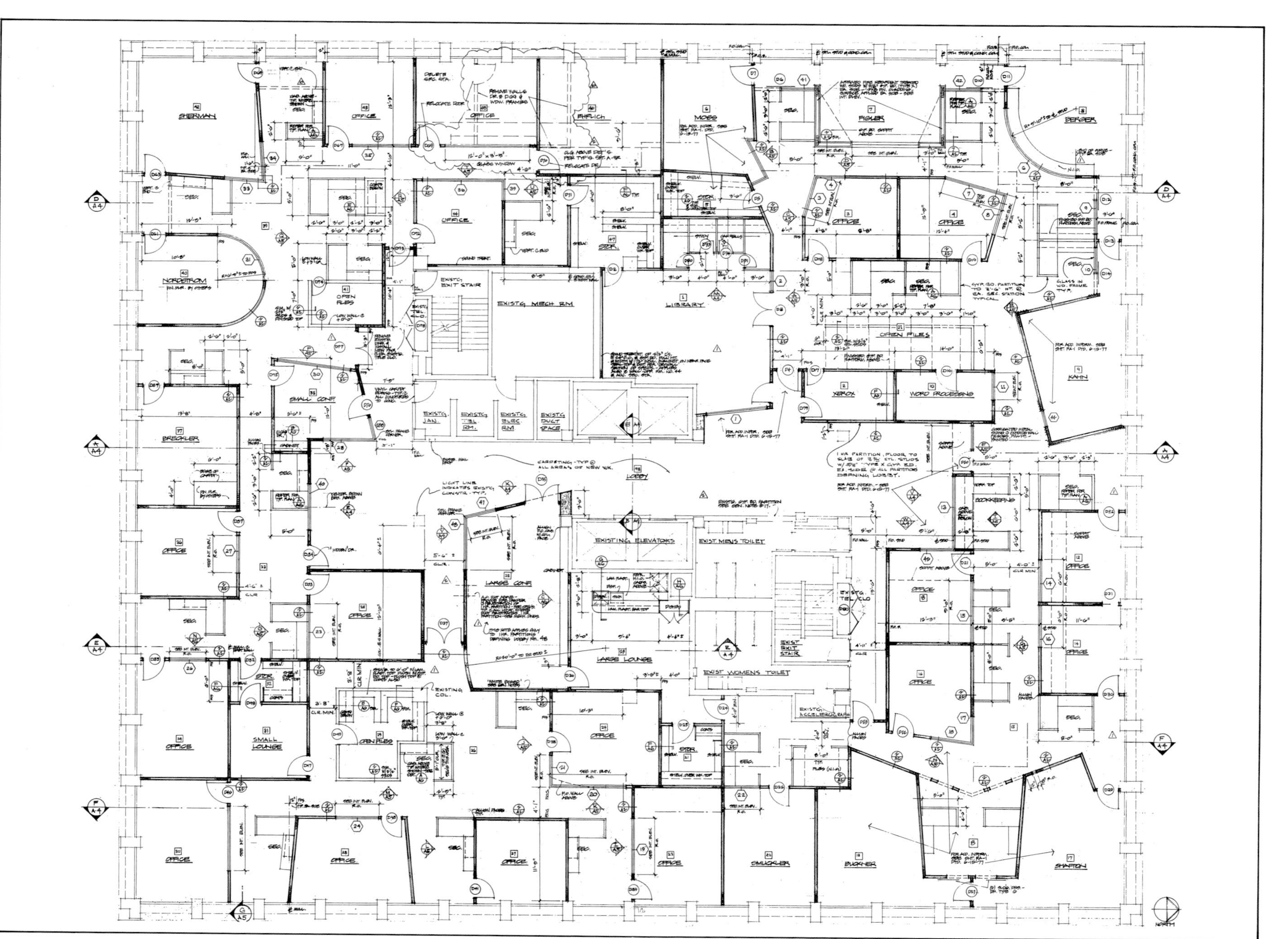

1

2

3

Cheviot Hills House
Los Angeles, California 1978

Like the Norton Simon Guest House, the project in Cheviot Hills was a remodeling of an existing building in which some suggestion of oriental architecture seemed appropriate. The house was remodeled to serve as a guest house for a corporation's guests and out-of-town personnel. The firm sells a Japanese product, and its principal has an interest in that country's culture as well as a collection of its art. Strategies similar to those of the Simon house were used on the three thousand-square-foot, 1940s vintage, ordinary suburban house. Its low ceilings were cut away to reveal the framing of the roof, most notably in the area of a large skylight over the living room. As in the Simon house, log posts, native to Japanese architectural tradition, were used as columns. Also included in the remodeling were a window converted to a traditional katomado, a Japanese-style garden, a wooden trellis at the entry, and a black tiled jacuzzi. Interior partitions were removed where possible. Colors and furniture were designed by Sarah Binder and Lenny Steinberg. The exercise in selectively exposing framing led to the more adventurous "renovation" of Gehry's own house, and projects for new construction like the Spiller House.

1,3.Sketches 2.Living room

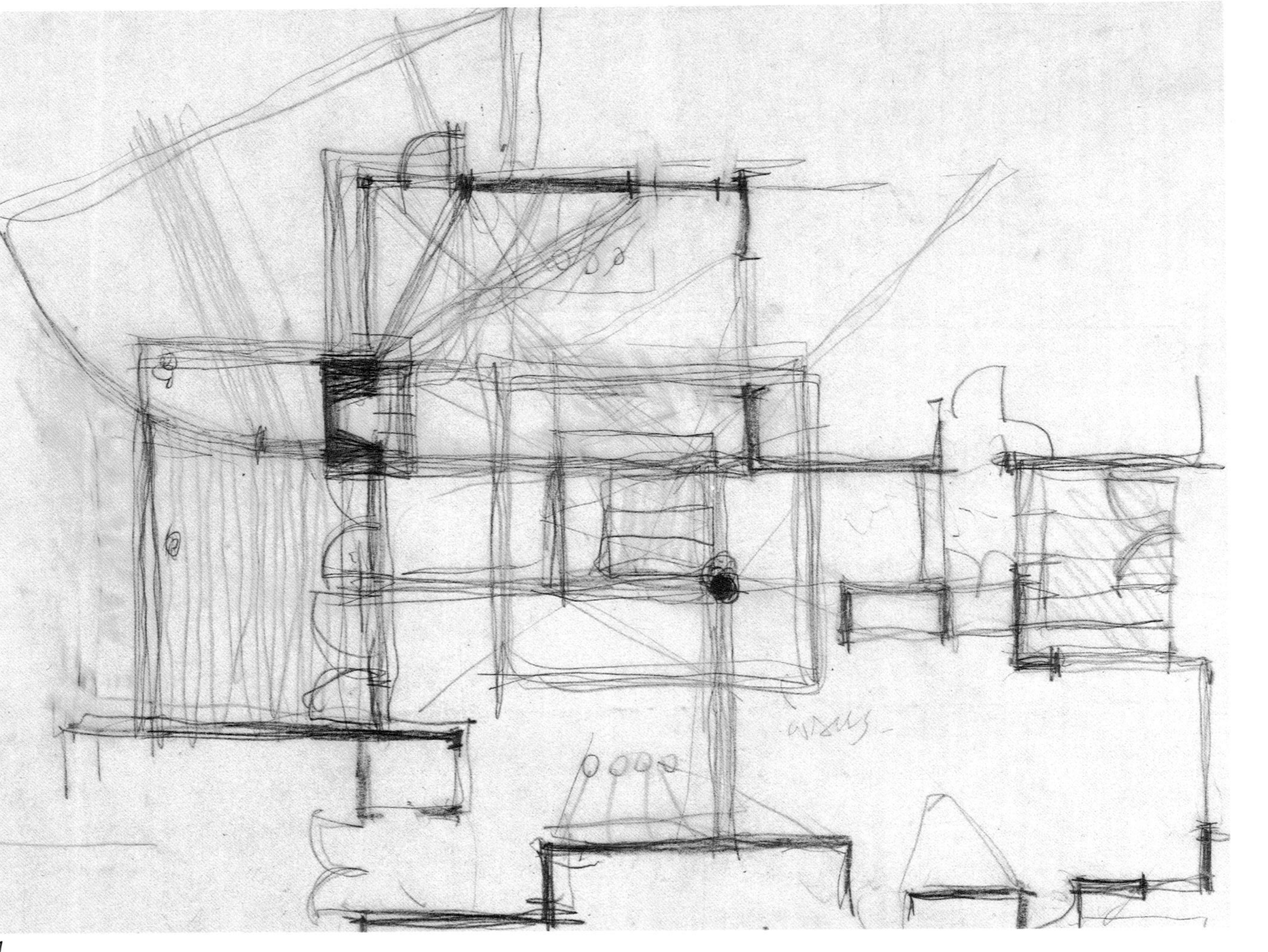

1

2

3

Mid-Atlantic Toyota Distributors

Glen Burnie, Maryland 1978

If you try to understand my work on the basis of fugal order, structural integrity and formalized definitions of beauty, you are apt to be totally confused. I approach each building as a sculptural object, a spatial container.... The manipulation of the inside of the container is for me an independent, sculptural problem and no less interesting than the design of the container itself.
—Frank Gehry, 1978

A contractor supplied the container—a warehouse with a thirty-foot-high interior. Gehry had some involvement with the appearance of the exterior, but in essence he was given, quite literally, a shell within which to work. His participation in the project was commissioned by the company's president, Frederick Weisman, who had several ideas for the project: He hoped to replicate the demonstrably increased productivity of Japanese companies whose open offices seem to make all employees feel they are active partners in the organization. In addition, he wanted to inspire understanding of, and pride in, the culture of the country whose product the company marketed. The warehouse was built of concrete blocks enclosing a single space. Gehry's amendments to its exterior design were limited to the addition of strip windows for the offices, three projecting bays of corrugated metal, and the design and location of the sign. A second floor was added within. The interiors were built, and permits granted, on the basis of the architect's study model rather than drawings. A straightforward arrangement of reception and service areas occupies the ground floor, its most prominent feature being the flood of light on the stairs from the skylit floor above. The second floor, within its shell of concrete block walls and corrugated metal ceilings, holds a kind of architectural landscape, conceived in part as an evocation of Japan's Inland Sea. Angular partitions, narrowing passages between partitions, and suspended trapezoidal panels of chain-link fence can be seen as, respectively, mountains, inlets, and clouds. Office areas, open to each other, lie on either side of a funnel-shaped hall. Along the hall, partition colors increase the perspective illusion of the hall's length with their progressively deepening hues. Particularized shapes and colors—a curved interior window, or a cutout in the shape of an arch, give local landmarks to the landscape. Overhead, among the chain-link clouds, ductwork and troughs containing fluorescent light fixtures (which provide even, indirect lighting) and skylights are, according to Gehry, "thrashing around in a somewhat humorous composition." A conference room, at the head of the funnel-hall, is in the central bay of the three projecting at the front of the building. Gehry has said frequently that his goal as an architect is to make each project something more than simply an inexpensive solution to functional requirements: "I like people to have a sort of dialogue with what I do. So even though I often put as much detail work into what I do as anyone, it always appears casual. That's the edge I'm after. For people to see what I wanted them to see, but for them to not be quite sure if it was designed or if it just happened." His criteria are met in the Toyota building: said one secretary, "I've worked here for two and a half years and I still see things that I've never seen before."

1.Exterior 2-5.Interiors

1

2

3

4

5

1.Exterior 2–5.7.Interiors 6.Axonometric

1

2

3

4

5

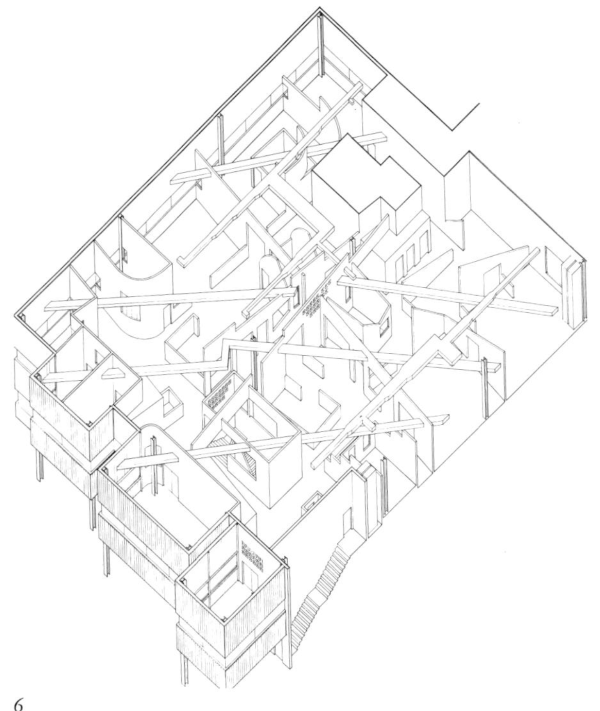
6

7

Nelson House

Los Angeles, California 1979

During the time Gehry was transforming his pink asbestos-shingled bungalow in Santa Monica, his sister, Doreen Nelson, bought a Spanish-style house in West Los Angeles which had been built in the 1930's. Most of the house was left untouched save the kitchen/dining wings, which Gehry was commissioned to remodel. Using surgical techniques, similar to those he was practicing on his own house, Gehry removed walls and finished surfaces to reveal underlying structure. Having used lath strips as a wall surface in the Norton Simon beach house, some of those discovered in his own house and the Nelson House under the plaster were left in place and recycled, as it were, as a warm, rich wall surface. One piece of the original plaster was left in place, providing an interesting contrast in texture and a kind of archeological reference. When the plaster ceiling under a tiled cupola was removed, the structure revealed was an almost baroque pile-up of wood framing members. As at the Norton Simon beach house, lighting—in this case exposed, garden-variety, light bulbs—was located among the exposed framing members to highlight their beauty and complexity.

1.Dining room

St. Ives House

West Hollywood, California 1978

An addition to an existing house took the form of a shell wrapping three of its sides. The addition holds the stairs, entrance, and expanded kitchen. The new construction is built to be stylistically compatible with the existing, 1950s-vintage suburban house. However, within the zone of the new shell, the proportions of openings in the original wall and the tie rods further emphasize that an original building has been subsequently re-wrapped, an idea pursued in the Gehry House.

2.Before 3.After 4.New interior

1

2

3

4

Gunther House

Encinal Bluffs, California 1978

The site on which the Gunther house was to be built is a narrow lot on a bluff overlooking the Pacific. The thirty-five hundred-square-foot house was designed as three levels which are spatially interrelated by means of decks, balconies, and stairs. The weather-sealed part of the building has a fairly irregular massing, providing rooftop decks for second and third floor rooms. The building *appears* from the south to be a more regular volume by virtue of chain-link enclosures. These "shadow structures" suggest, to a certain extent, one of Gehry's spatial containers (like those of the Davis House and the Mid-Atlantic Toyota building). In this case the container is partially dematerialized; the bays and decks of the house itself constitute its interior landscaping. Alternately, the shadow structures create a kind of ephemeral version of a building wrapped in a new container, as at the St. Ives house. A kind of guessing game is thus set up, encouraged by changes in siding—what part of what one sees is the "real" building? The redwood siding suggests that the exterior wall of the house could be an interior wall; outside the chain-link enclosure, its dark color disappearing in shadows, creates the illusion that the fencing is the exterior wall of the building. Alternately, walls rendered in white stucco appear in high contrast to the chain-link, making the latter seem a fragile screen. The shadows cast by the fencing are made richer by means of angled panels of chain-link hung within the cage of the shadow structure.

1.Northwest view 2.South view

1

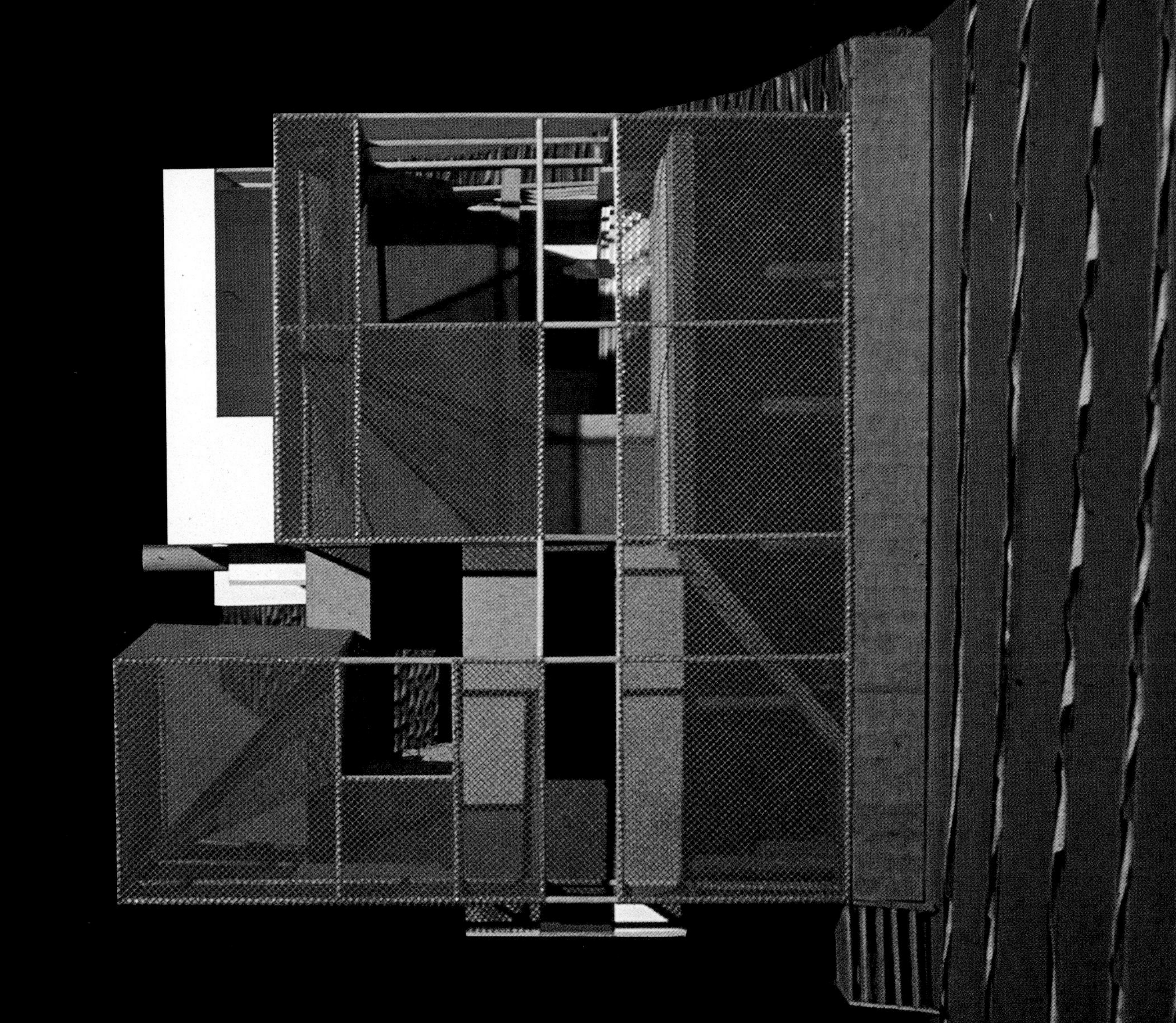

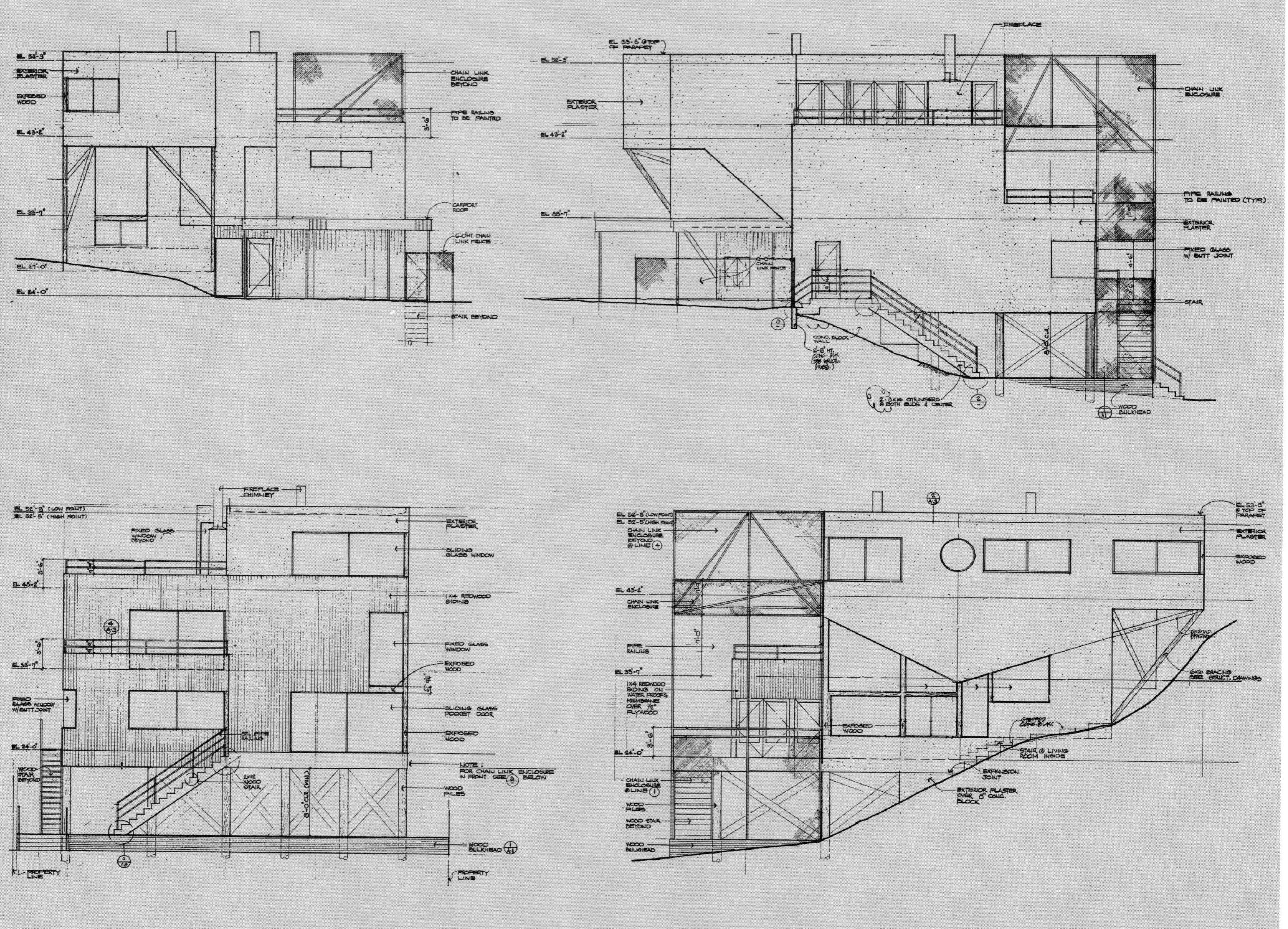
EL 52'-3"
EXTERIOR PLASTER
EXPOSED WOOD
EL 43'-2"
EL 35'-7"
EL 27'-0"
EL 24'-0"
CHAIN LINK ENCLOSURE BEYOND
PIPE RAILING TO BE PAINTED
CARPORT ROOF
6'-0" HT. CHAIN LINK FENCE
STAIR BEYOND
FIREPLACE
EL 53'-5" @ TOP OF PARAPET
EL 52'-5"
EXTERIOR PLASTER
EL 43'-2"
EL 35'-7"
CHAIN LINK ENCLOSURE
PIPE RAILING TO BE PAINTED (TYP.)
EXTERIOR PLASTER
FIXED GLASS W/ BUTT JOINT
STAIR
CONC. BLOCK WALL
2-3X14 STRINGERS @ BOTH ENDS & CENTER
WOOD BULKHEAD
FIREPLACE CHIMNEY
EL 52'-2" (LOW POINT)
EL 52'-5" (HIGH POINT)
FIXED GLASS WINDOW BEYOND
EXTERIOR PLASTER
SLIDING GLASS WINDOW
EL 43'-2"
1X4 REDWOOD SIDING
FIXED GLASS WINDOW
EL 35'-7"
EXPOSED WOOD
FIXED GLASS WINDOW W/BUTT JOINT
SLIDING GLASS POCKET DOOR
EXPOSED WOOD
EL 24'-0"
NOTE: FOR CHAIN LINK ENCLOSURE IN FRONT SEE BELOW
WOOD STAIR BEYOND
2X12 WOOD STAIR
WOOD PILES
WOOD BULKHEAD
PROPERTY LINE
PROPERTY LINE
EL 52'-5" (LOW POINT)
EL 52'-5" (HIGH POINT)
CHAIN LINK ENCLOSURE BEYOND @ LINE 4
EL 53'-5" @ TOP OF PARAPET
EXTERIOR PLASTER
EXPOSED WOOD
EL 43'-2"
CHAIN LINK ENCLOSURE
PIPE RAILING
EL 35'-7"
1X4 REDWOOD SIDING ON WATER PROOFG MEMBRANE OVER 1/2" PLYWOOD
6X10 BRACING SEE STRUCT. DRAWINGS
EXPOSED WOOD
EL 24'-0"
STAIR @ LIVING ROOM INSIDE
EXPANSION JOINT
EXTERIOR PLASTER OVER 8" CONC. BLOCK
CHAIN LINK ENCLOSURE @ LINE 1
WOOD PILES
WOOD STAIR BEYOND
WOOD BULKHEAD

1-4

5

1.North elevation 2.West elevation 3.South elevation 4.East elevation 5.Site plan

Wagner House
Malibu, California 1978

The walls of the canyons that lace the hills around Los Angeles are the improbable avenues of suburban expansion. The architecture of the houses clinging to their slopes generally exhibits a pretension to immutability, periodically undermined, so to speak, by mud slides and earthquakes. Gehry's design for such a site appears both to accept and expect the instability of human intervention on inhospitable and fragile territory.

From below, and as one approaches its entrance, it is designed to look "like a shoe box with the verticals perpendicular to the land slope (which they are not) and appears ready to slide down the hill."

The forms contain accommodation for a single family and a psychiatrist's office. Low cost and minimum disturbance to the land were primary concerns, met by creating a rigid frame of timber pilings, driven deep in the ground and bound above by the shell of the house. Most of the building is held above ground level on the pilings. The "shoe box" is essentially a single volume on three levels under a sloping roof. The master bedroom projects from it at the rear. The doctor's office and carport are under the house on ground level to the south. Pilings were to be driven during construction to support an additional bedroom and deck to be completed at a later date.

The sides of the house toward which the intrepid visitor or patient approaches are designed to appear a complete composition (in distinction to the uphill "backyard") bent toward evoking the precipitous descent of house and lot. The cut-out openings of the corrugated metal walls are biased alternately to the real and to the suggested perpendicular—that of the hill's slope and of the canted clerestory superstructure. Glazing behind the openings is recessed and angles out to the metal walls. The roof, also of corrugated metal, extending beyond the downhill wall as a sunshade, the sculpted asphalt parking pad, the chain-link "shadow structure"—a permeable *porte cochere*—and the extruded entrance stair are "intended as a surrealistic composition to reinforce the imminent slide."

To the rear, "the living side," the composition is "open-ended . . . and unfinished," accentuated by a change to plywood sheathing. Its choreographer describes the scene as follows: "Floating around this side on their own poles are bedrooms and decks which appear as floating satellites in orbit, with a mother ship, bumping into each other, not quite touching"—a sort of zero-gravity inversion of a composition honoring Newtonian physics.

1.Sketch 2-6.Studies of massing and perspective 7.Dining room 8.Plan

1

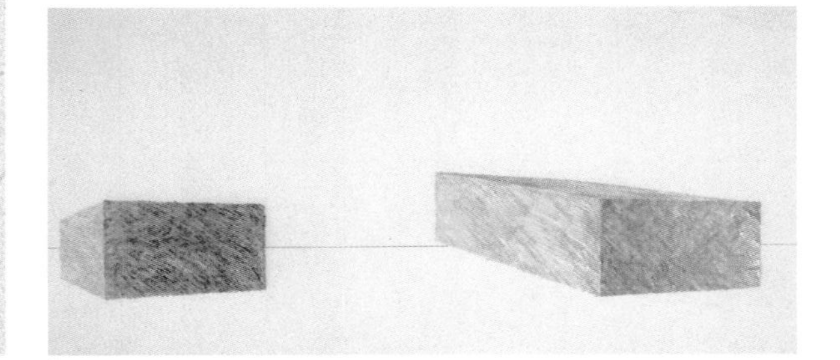

2

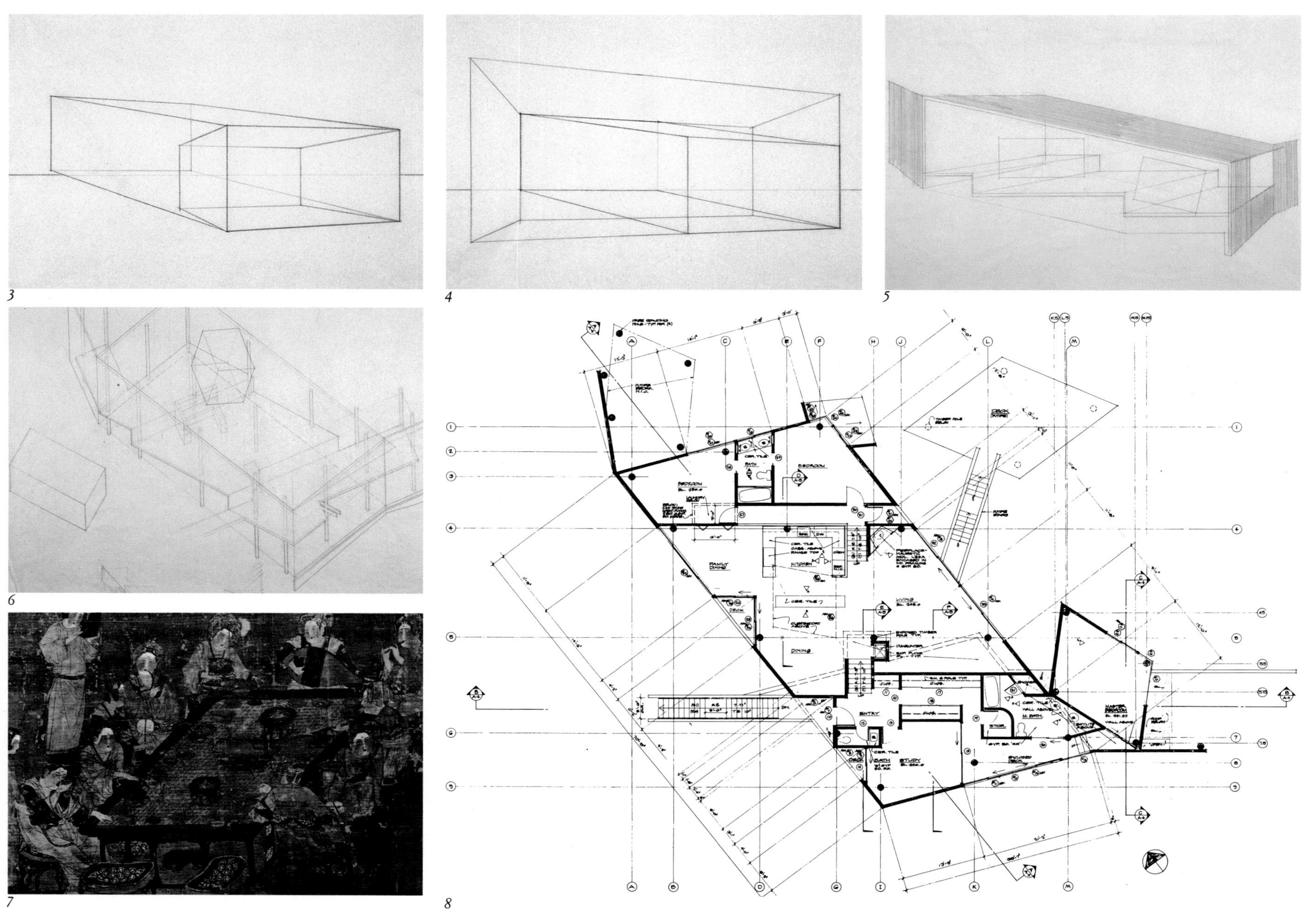

1.West elevation 2.South elevation 3-4.Sections

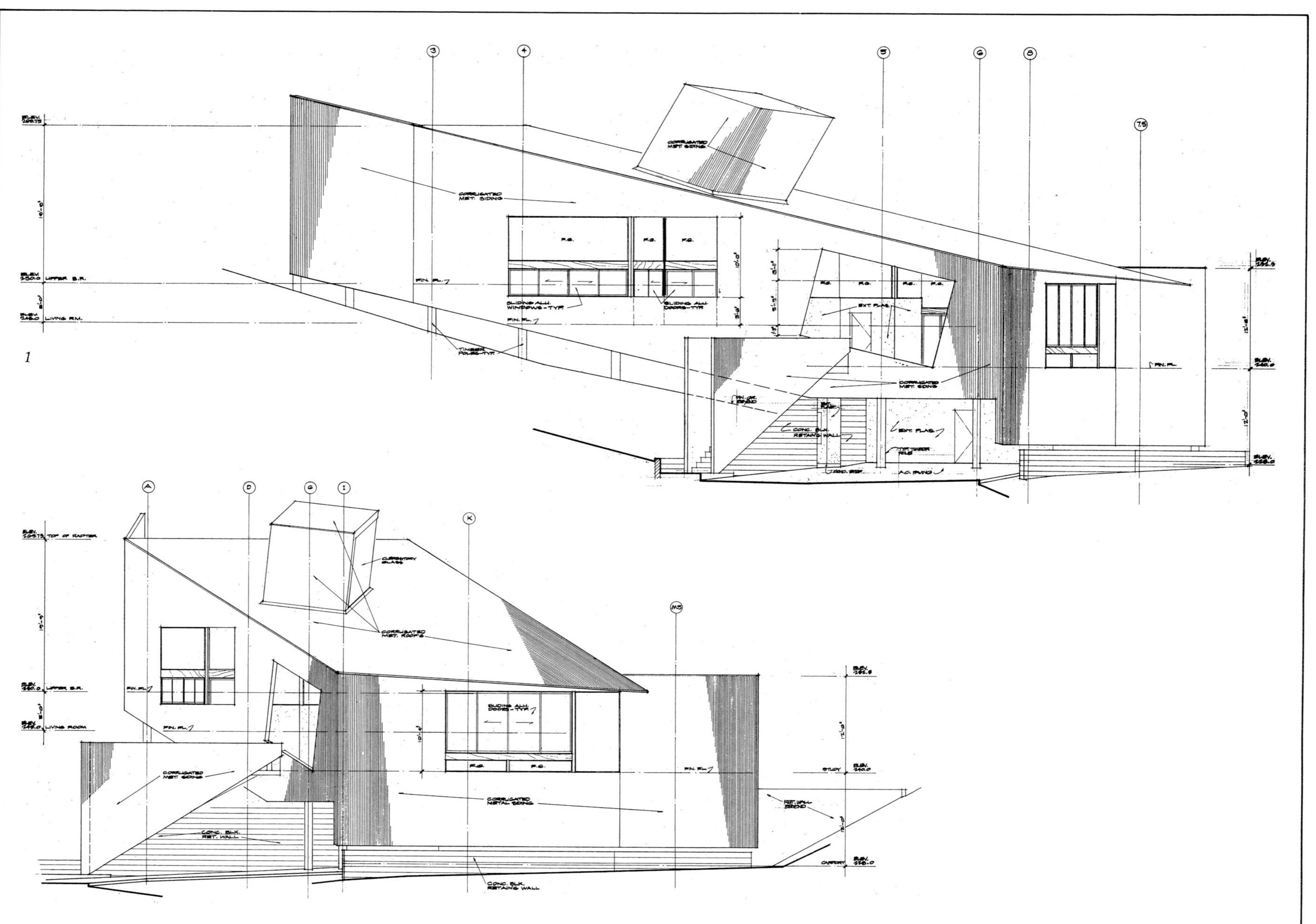

1

2

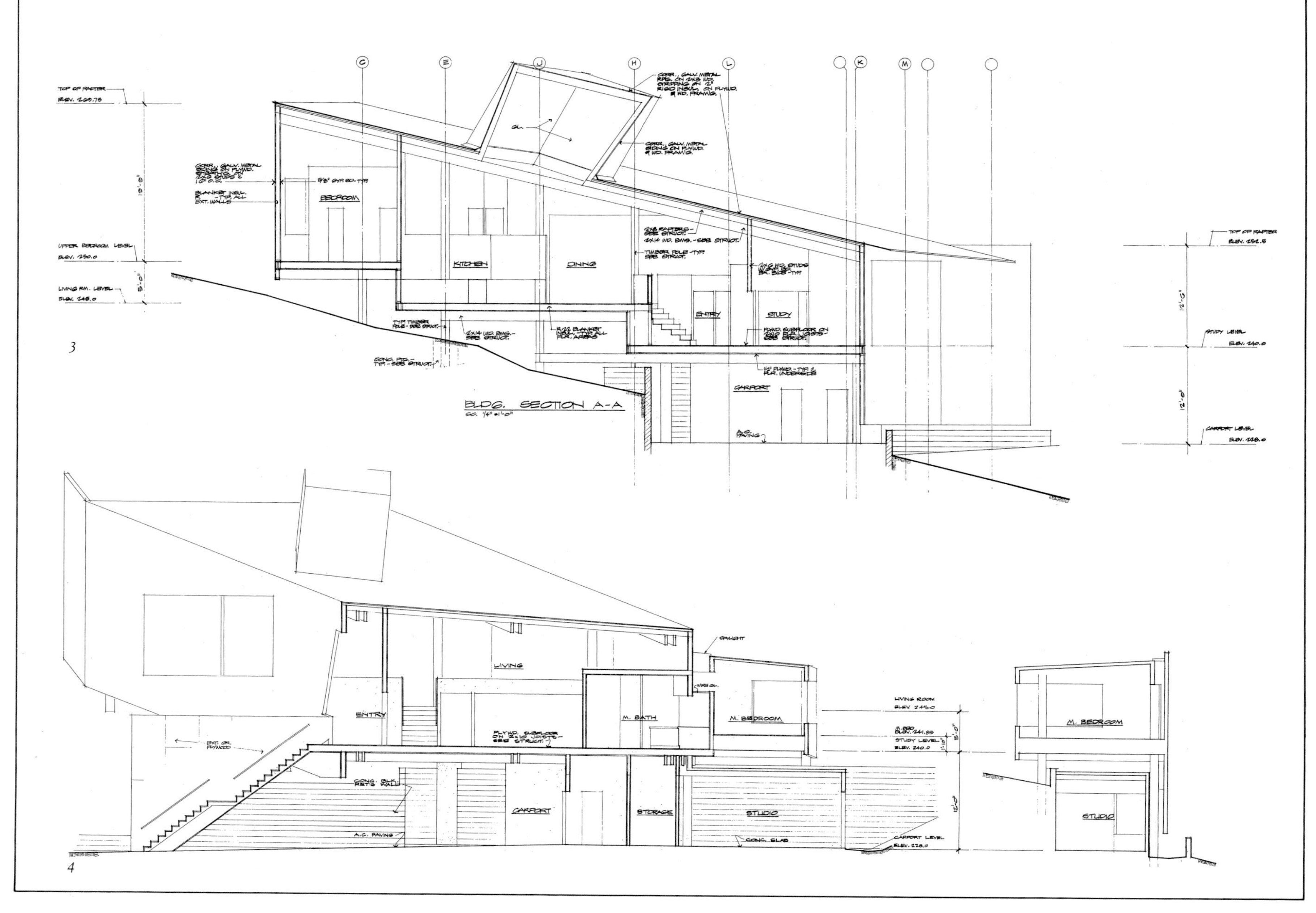
BLDG. SECTION A-A
TOP OF RAFTER
UPPER BEDROOM LEVEL
LIVING RM. LEVEL
BEDROOM
KITCHEN
DINING
ENTRY
STUDY
CARPORT
STUDY LEVEL
CARPORT LEVEL
3
LIVING
M. BATH
M. BEDROOM
STORAGE
STUDIO
CONC. SLAB
A.C. PAVING
4

1-3. Model

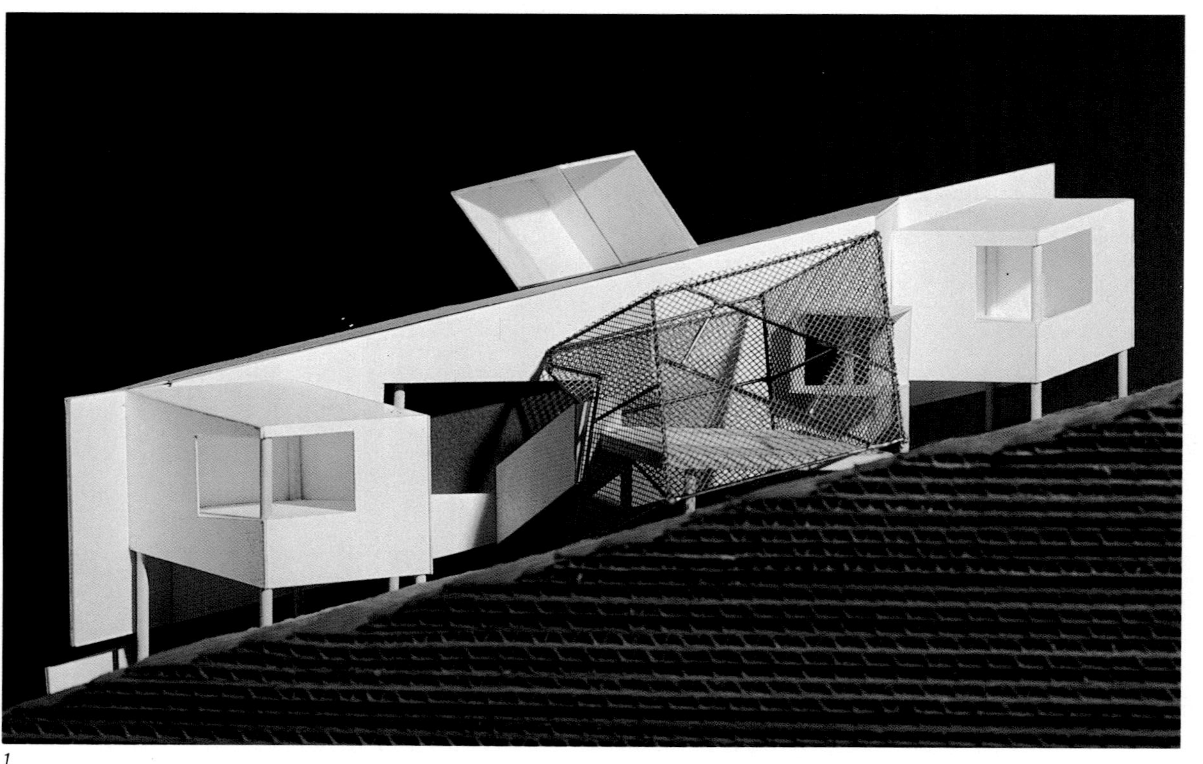

1

2

3

Familian House
Santa Monica, California 1978

American architecture is the art of covering one thing with another thing to imitate a third thing, which if genuine would not be desirable.
—Leopold Edilitz

Balloon frame construction—the ease with which forms can be made from it and surfaces applied to it—has allowed any man's tract house to be made his castle, or chalet, or mission, or "contemporized colonial." The frames themselves, before the application of a cover, hold a visual interest for many. Says Gehry, "We all like buildings in construction better than we do finished—I think most of us agree on that. The structure is always so much more poetic than the finished thing." Having recovered some of the visual excitement of construction by exposing framing in the Simon and Cheviot Hills houses, Gehry began, in projects like the Familian House, to explore "the distortion of the rough wood butcher tract house technology . . . into a tool for sketching with wood. . . . I guess I was interested in the unfinished—or the quality you find in paintings by Jackson Pollock, for instance, or de Kooning, or Cézanne, that look like the paint was just applied. The very finished, polished, every-detail-perfect kind of architecture seemed to me not to have that quality. I wanted to try that out in a building."

The site is a narrow lot which drops off sharply at the rear and opens to a view of the Santa Monica mountains. The main house was designed as two pieces—a 40-by-40-foot cube containing living and entertaining areas, and a 20-by-110-foot structure for the family's bedrooms and private quarters. The two are primarily stucco-sheathed, but are linked with bridges of wood framing. Wood studs are also the material of trellises, skylight monitors, bay windows and an evocative window adornment as they continue uninterrupted behind glazing.

1.Design sketches 2.Ground floor plan

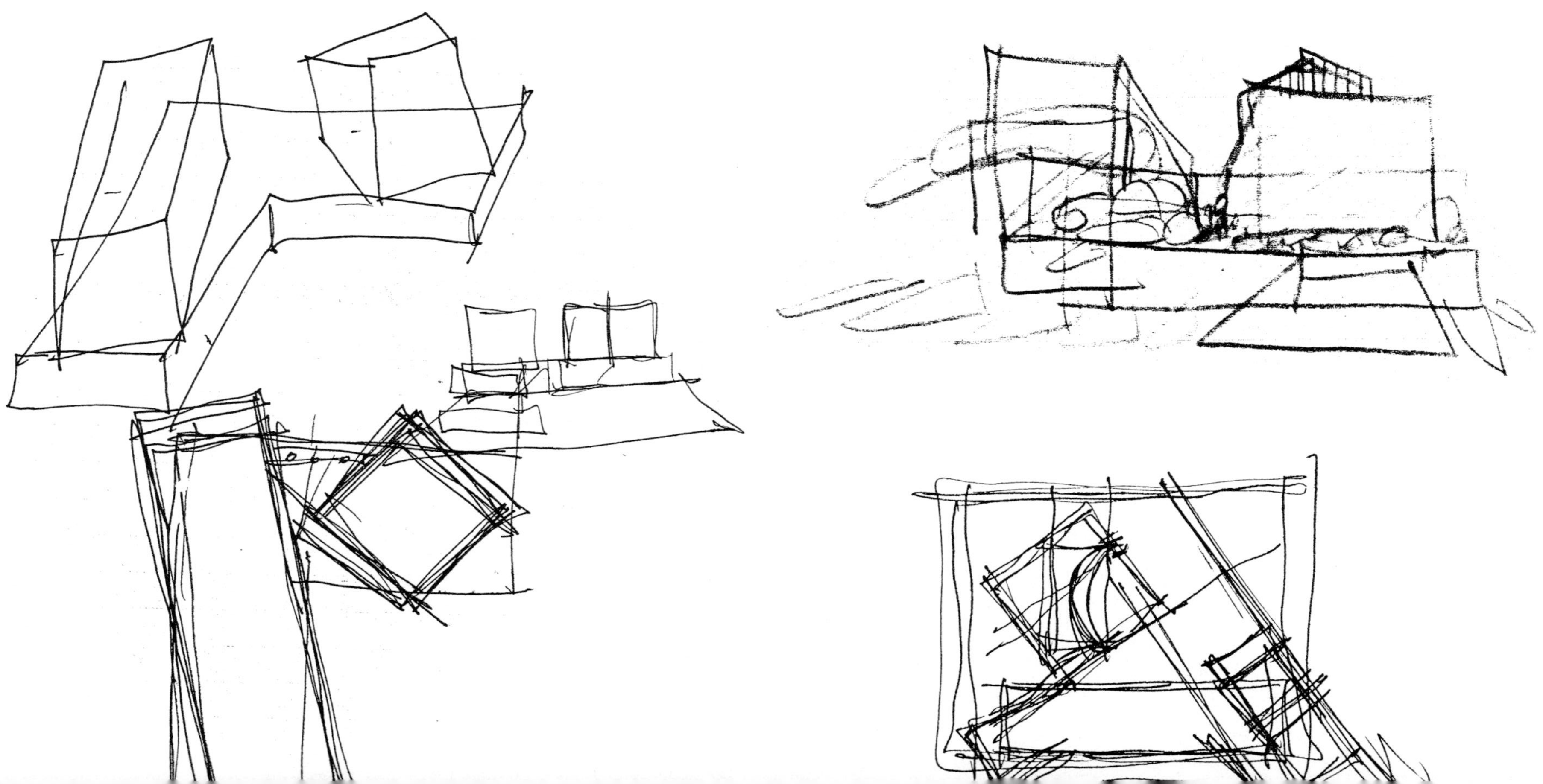

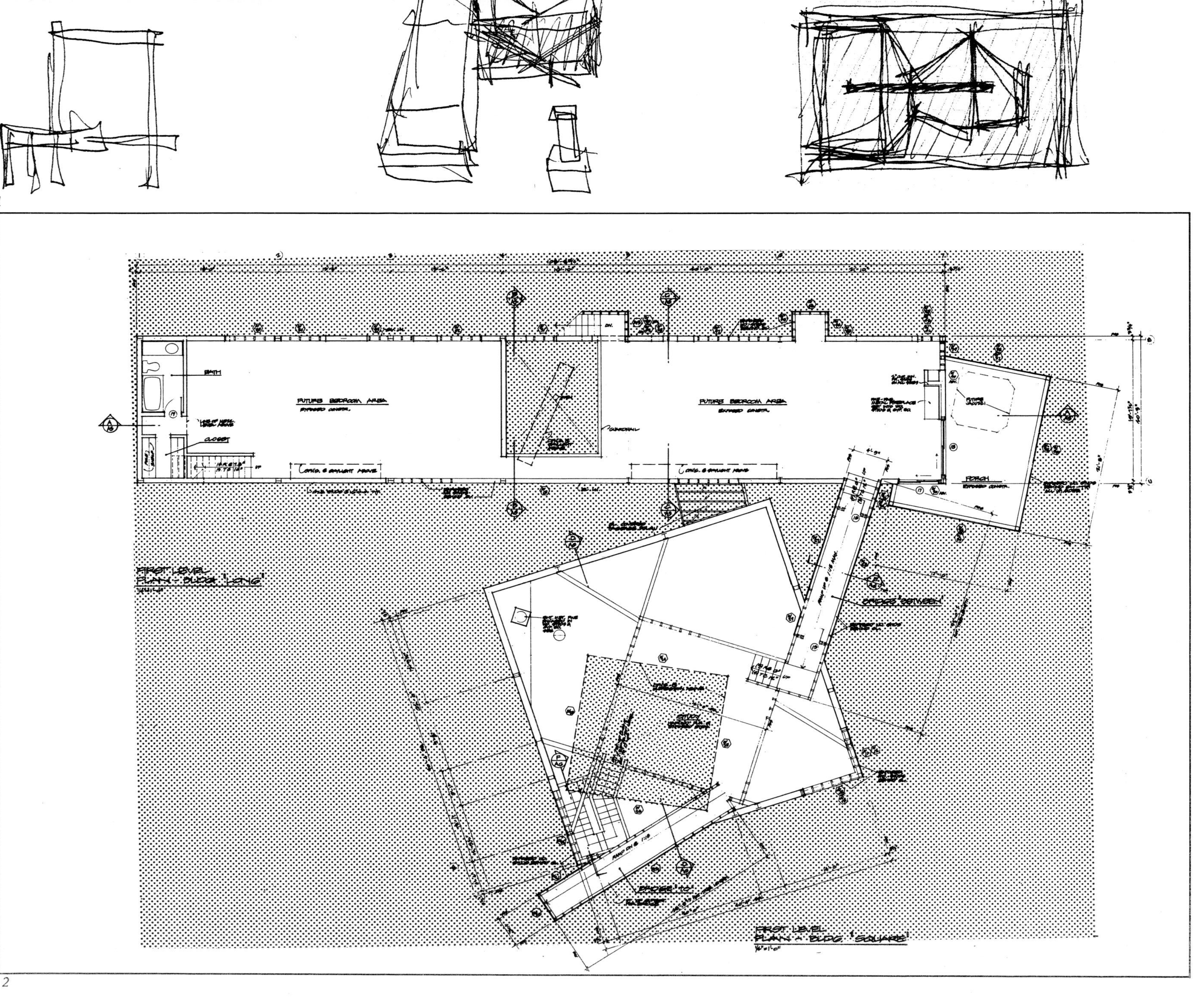
FUTURE BEDROOM AREA
EXPOSED CONSTR.
FUTURE BEDROOM AREA
EXPOSED CONSTR.
BATH
CLOSET
PORCH
EXPOSED CONSTR.
GUARDRAIL
BRIDGE BETWEEN
BRIDGE TO
FIRST LEVEL
PLAN - BLDG 'LONG'
FIRST LEVEL
PLAN - BLDG 'SQUARE'

1

2

1.Tract houses under construction   2-5.Model

1

2

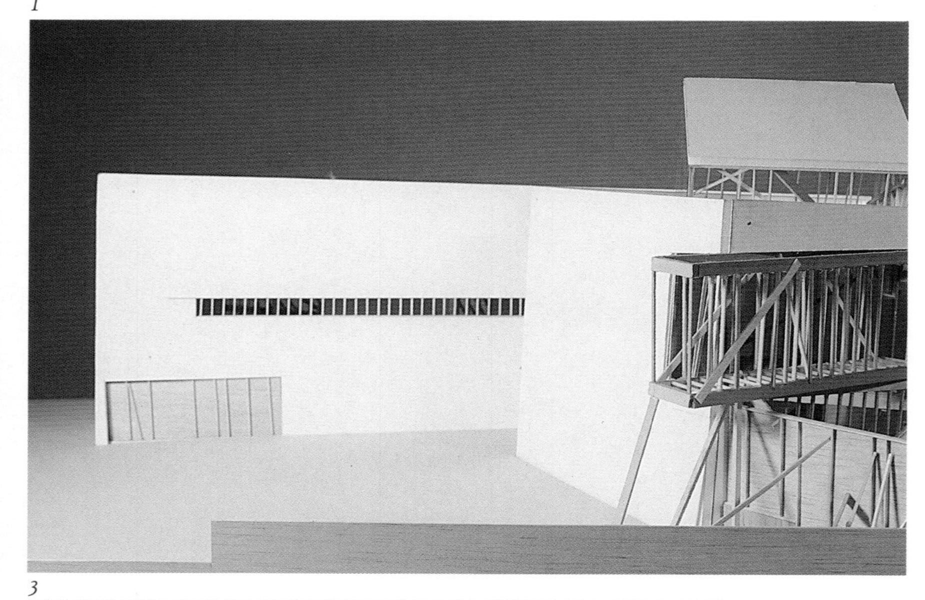

3

4

5

1.South elevation 2.North elevation 3.Projection: "Exterior Circulation Components" 4.Section through square building

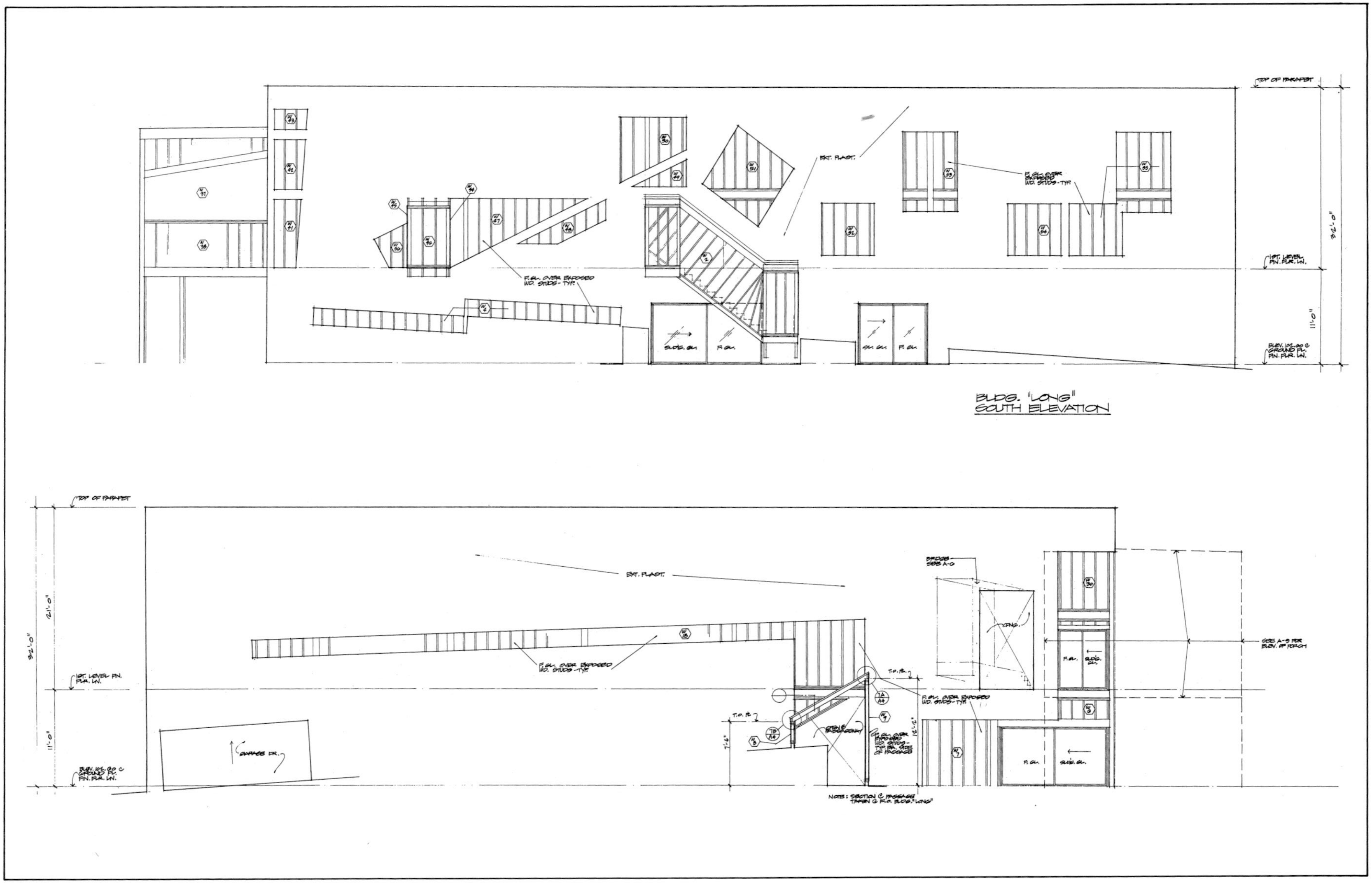

BLDG. "LONG"
SOUTH ELEVATION

1–2

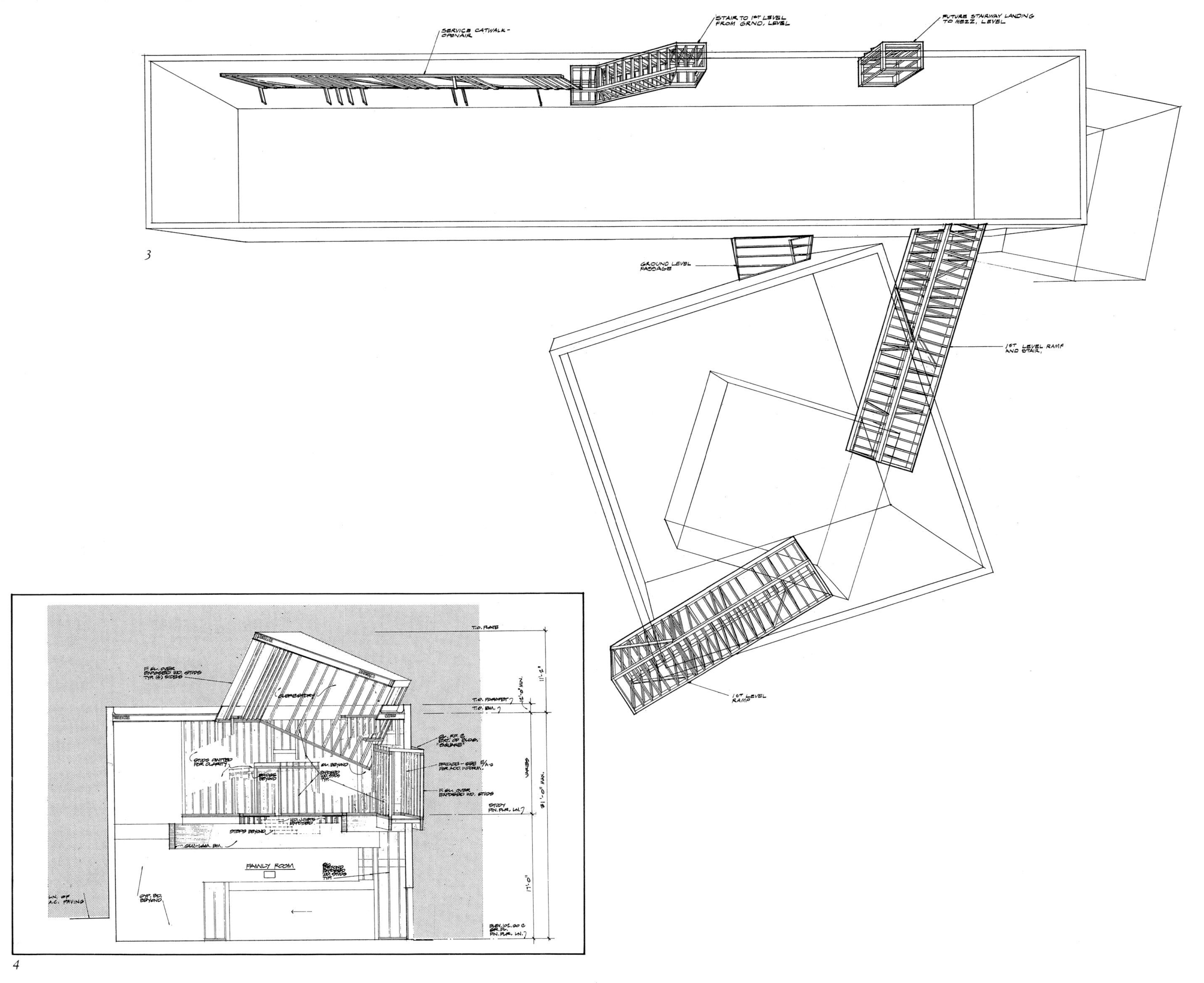
SERVICE CATWALK - OPENAIR
STAIR TO 1ST LEVEL FROM GRND. LEVEL
FUTURE STAIRWAY LANDING TO MEZZ. LEVEL
GROUND LEVEL PASSAGE
1ST LEVEL RAMP AND STAIR.
1ST LEVEL RAMP
T.O. PLATE
T.O. PARAPET
T.O. BM.
11'-2"
31'-0" MAX.
VARIES
17'-0"
STUDY FIN. FLR. LN.
FAMILY ROOM

3

4

Gehry House

Santa Monica, California 1978

I wasn't trying to make a big or precious statement about architecture or trying to do an important work: I was trying to build a lot of ideas.
—Frank Gehry, 1979

Architecture is generally conceived, designed, and discussed as an ordered explication of a single idea, or a compact constellation of ideas, about a program and a site. Those works that weld and translate such ideas into a strong formal order toward which all parts contribute, we have come to understand as our finest achievements. To approach Frank Gehry's house with these critical assumptions in mind is to miss the front door. (In fact, there are two.)

As Duchamp transformed objects of everyday use into "readymades" by "making a new thought for the object," so Gehry took a small pink asbestos-shingled bungalow and "tried to make it more important." A shell—an addition to the first floor—wraps the "dumb little house" on three sides. The effect is to make the old house seem an object *within* a house, a monument on display.

The shell adds about eight hundred square feet to the first floor. To the northeast, an elaborated entry vestibule leads either into the old house or down to an asphalt pad on grade. On the latter, along the longer, northwest street frontage, are a dining area, kitchen, and breakfast area. To the southwest, the zone of new construction is a sort of loggia opening onto the enclosed backyard. The exterior of the original house remains intact, even where enclosed by new construction. Its interior has been revised—stripped to lath and framing in some places, amended or preserved in others.

As one enters, the distinction between the new shell and the old house is underscored by the necessity of passing through a second—the original—front door into the old house. From the dining and kitchen areas on the asphalt pad below, the perception of sitting on a driveway looking at and into the old house gives it a prominence it no doubt had not previously enjoyed—and provides a voyeuristic tickle to boot.

Interior elements of the old house were "edited" for selected prominence: framed, painted windows are elevated to icons on the stripped lath walls. Upstairs, the ceiling was removed and framing exposed to make a big "tree house"—an enormous attic. Fortuitously, the original framing and lath turned out to be redwood, giving the spaces they now define the warmth of local craftsman architecture.

The "memories" of the old house are also honored. In gutting much of the interior and in opening it into the new spaces, Gehry proposed that he had trapped "ghosts" of the original cubic volumes. The window in the kitchen and its chain-link "shadow structure" above were meant "to read as a cube falling out of a box—as if it was trying to escape from the enclosure that was put around the old house."

The distinction between new and old is not made insistently. Explains Gehry, "I wanted to blur the edge between old finishes and new finishes . . . between real and surreal." Similarly, the corrugated metal wall that surrounds the entry and kitchen does not wrap the third side of the new shell; rather, it continues as a screen wall. A window-like opening provides a view into the backyard. From the street, those in the backyard are on stage; however, from the yard the impression is of being backstage looking out through props: both the screen wall and the cactus in midyard are apparently supported by two-by-four-inch bracing.

These "stages" provide a clue to some of the other ideas explored in the house. They follow a line of reasoning, or unreasoning, promoted by Duchamp and explored by a line of twentieth-century artists whom Gehry cites as influences. Duchamp argued that in life one knows and deals only with change and motion, not absolutes and fixity; and that that which is art is equally volatile and amorphous —what he called "something like electricity" between the maker and the observer through the medium of the art work. What Robert Rauschenberg has said of his field—"Painting relates to both life and art. Neither can be made. I try to act in the gap between the two."—Gehry has brought to architecture. Thus the house is made for the people moving through it and living in it, its insights and incidents taking precedence over the strengthening of a formal parti. And, as Duchamp's "Large Glass" offers a frequently changing view of itself by virtue of people seen through and reflected by its surface, so the "stage sets" in Gehry's house are enlivened and changed with the life it houses.

Glazing is used throughout because of its changing reflections, refractions, and shadows. Wire glass was used in conjunction with chain-link panels to intensify those effects. The kitchen and some of the bedroom windows frame the movements and shadows of a stand of Cedars of Lebanon. Other bedroom windows look through the slats, openings, and chain-link screens of the rear loggia. The reflections off the windows of the old house, left intact between interior spaces, are particularly evocative; the old window reglazed with mirror and installed as a medicine cabinet is its endgame. One of the vaguely perpendicular panes making up the dining room window at the front corner slides by, unframed, that which it might have abutted. The result of looking through two sheets of glass set at different angles is a refraction of things seen through it, giving them the sort of kinetic torque Gehry identifies as that of Duchamp's "Nude Descending a Staircase." The angling of the window was one of Gehry's most calculated endeavors. As he describes it, "That slight angle allows the window to be perpendicular to a streetlight that's across the road. In the evening one looks out that window and all the interior lights in the house are reflected in that window and point toward that streetlight. The illusion is that the house is tilted toward the streetlight and it is one of the reflections I did plan. Most of the others are either intuitive or accidental, but they work equally well."

To extend the capacity of the house to surprise, and to allow the observer as much speculation and intrigue as possible, Gehry chose his rough materials and the "deconstruction" of the old house. As he explains it, "I was concerned with maintaining a 'freshness' in the house. Often this freshness is lost—in over-finishing them, their vitality is lost. I wanted to avoid this by emphasizing the feeling that the details are still in the process: that the building hasn't stopped. The very finished building has security and it's predictable. I wanted to try something different. I like playing at the edge of disaster."

1.Kitchen window

1

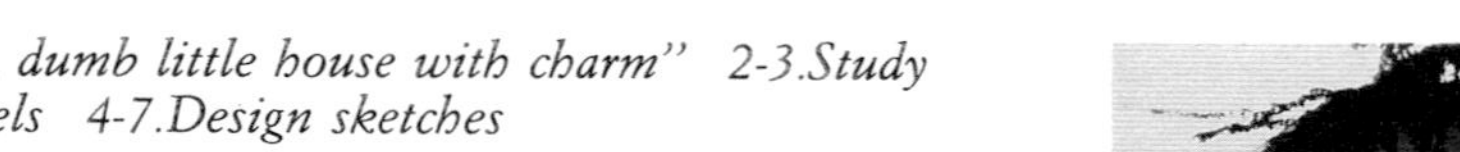
1.“A dumb little house with charm” 2-3.Study models 4-7.Design sketches

1

2

3

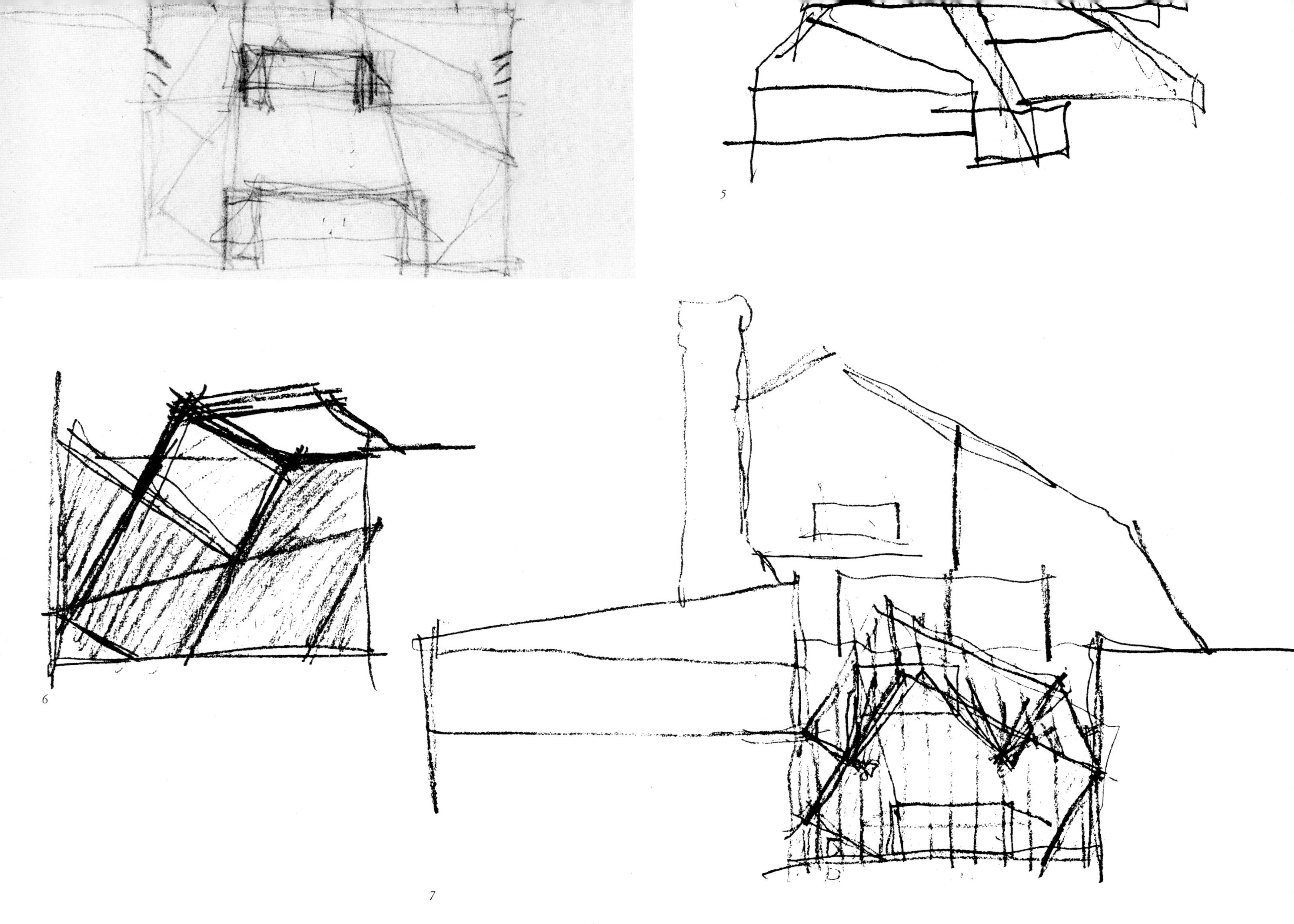

5

6

7

1

2

3

1.Neighborhood 2.Entrance 3.View from backyard

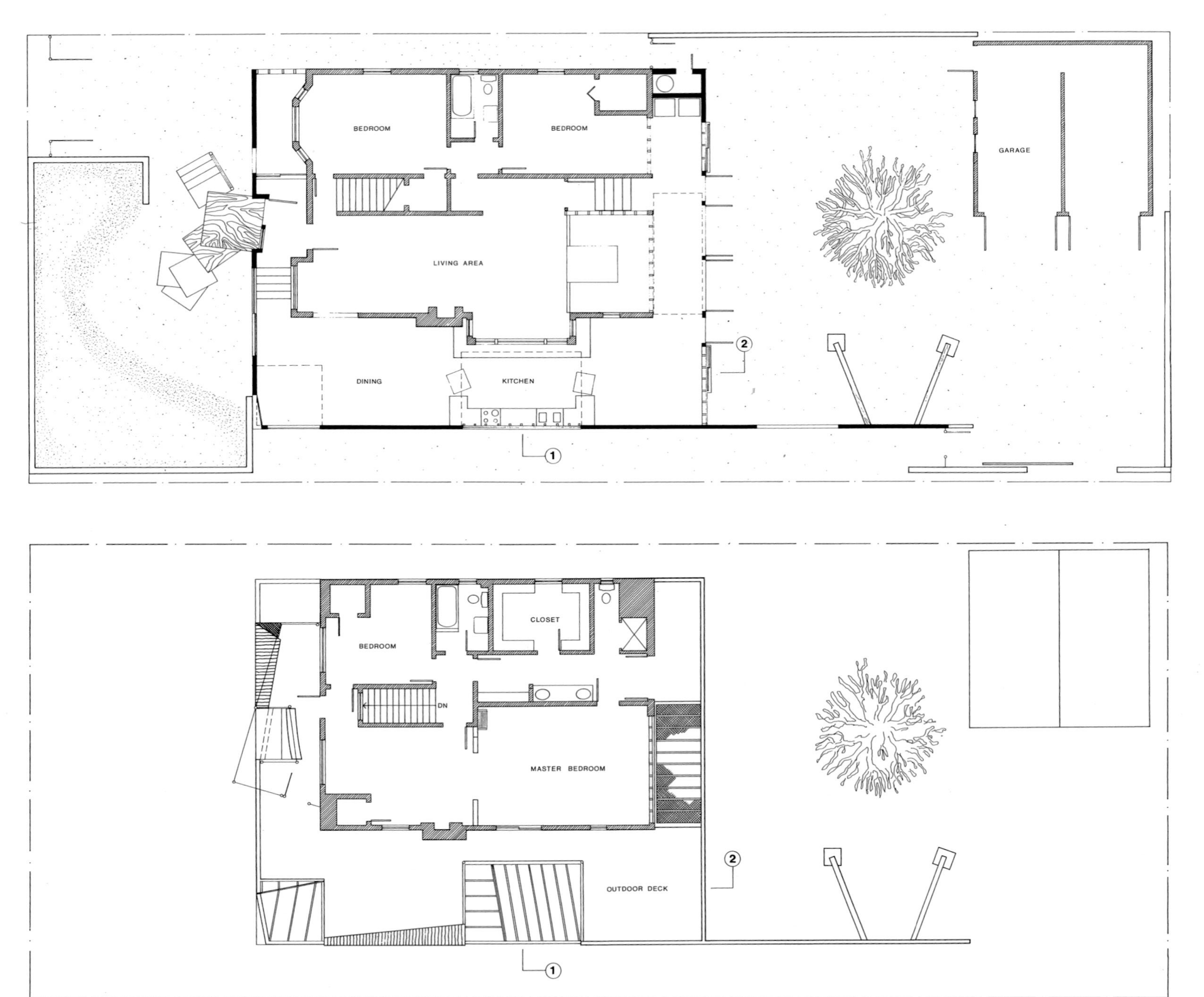
BEDROOM
BEDROOM
GARAGE
LIVING AREA
DINING
KITCHEN
2
1
BEDROOM
CLOSET
DN
MASTER BEDROOM
OUTDOOR DECK
2
1

2

3

4

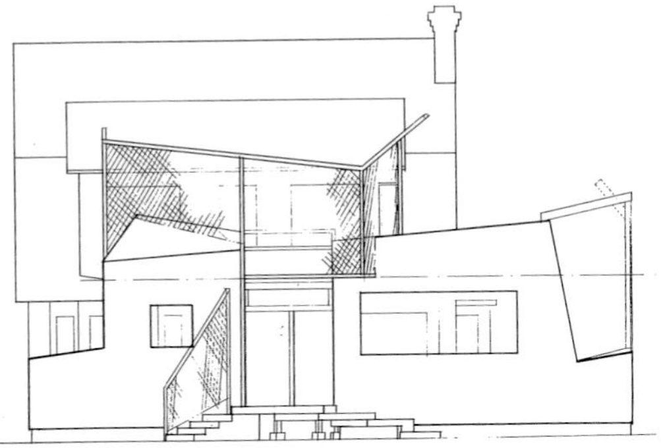

5

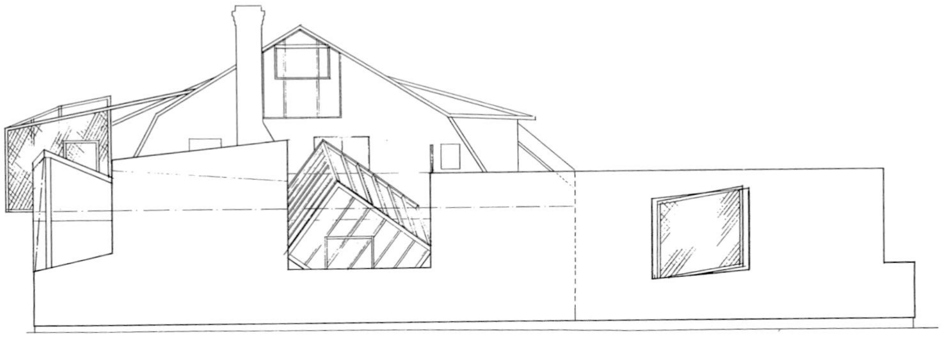

6

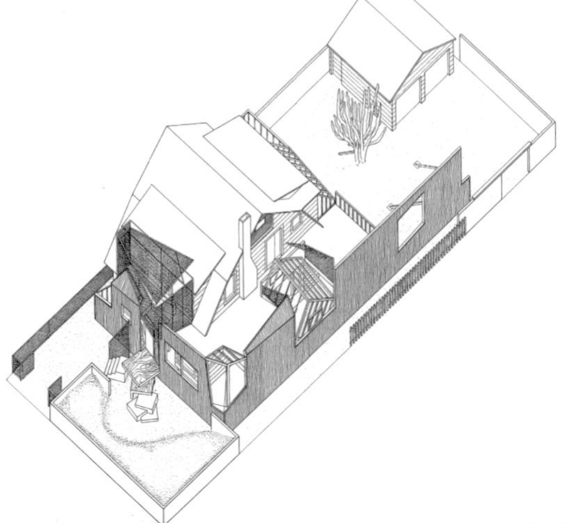

1.1st floor 2.2nd floor 3.West elevation 4.South elevation 5.East elevation 6.North elevation 7.Axonometric

1.Living room, toward backyard 2.Master bedroom 3.Living room wall 4.Medicine cabinet 5.Window upstairs 6."Loggia" roof 7.Kitchen, toward backyard 8.View toward entrance from dining room 9.Door 10.Kitchen, toward dining room

1

2

3

4

5

6

7

8

9

10

1.View into backyard from street 2.View of rear elevation from street 3.Roofscape

1

2

3

Carriage House

New York, New York 1978

Having in his own house wrapped an existing building with another, in this Manhattan project new houses were built within the shell of an old. The client requested "sculpture" in which she and her daughter could live either independently or communally, as desired. The design called for the turn-of-the-century building to be essentially gutted. The two new "houses" rise from a podium of two stories built within the shell of the original. On the ground floor, the existing garages are retained, and a new kitchen, guest quarters, studio space, and sixty-by-eight-foot swimming pool are added. Staff quarters are at the rear on a mezzanine level. The second floor is the main living, dining, and entertaining floor. In a series of broad steps it rises a full eight feet from front to back. At its rear a metal catwalk wraps a skylight which lights the ground floor.

The first two floors are built within existing walls and retain the original glazing. Above the second floor, the two two-story houses are built free of the existing building. They are designed as simple geometric shapes, twisted slightly off the orthogonal to emphasize their independence as sculptural objects and "to create eccentricities with the vertical and horizontal spatial organization." The top third of the facade is left open and freestanding, revealing the independent objects behind and above it in a manner reminiscent of The Atrium in Lincoln. Separate entrances and stairs serve the two houses. Each contains a living room on its first (the building's third) floor with bedroom and bath above. Between the buildings is a tall glass-roofed space crossed by bridges connecting the two on both floors.

1.5.Sketches 2.1st floor 3.2nd floor. 4.3rd floor 6.Section

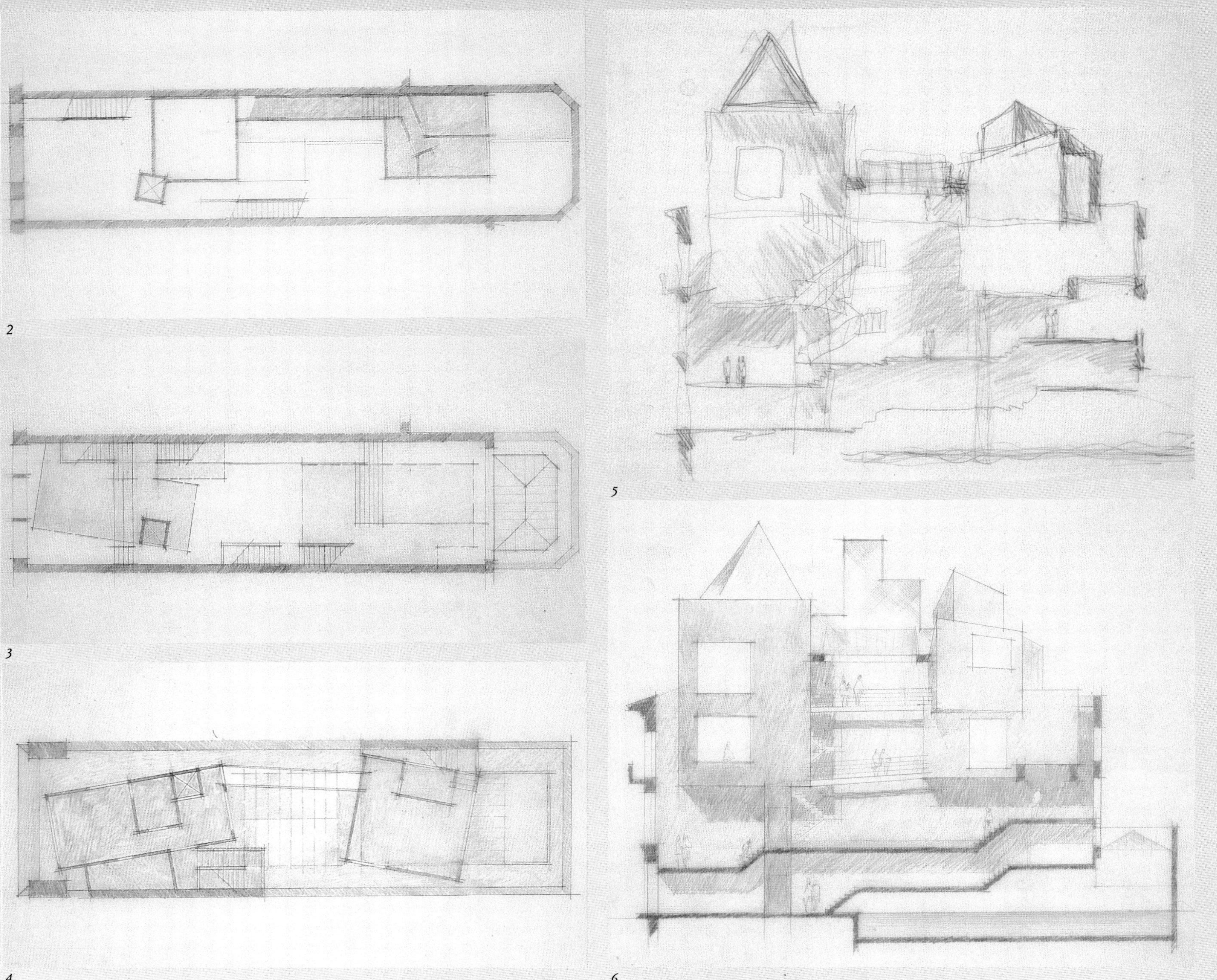

2

3

4

5

6

1. View from above 2. View from street 3. View from rear

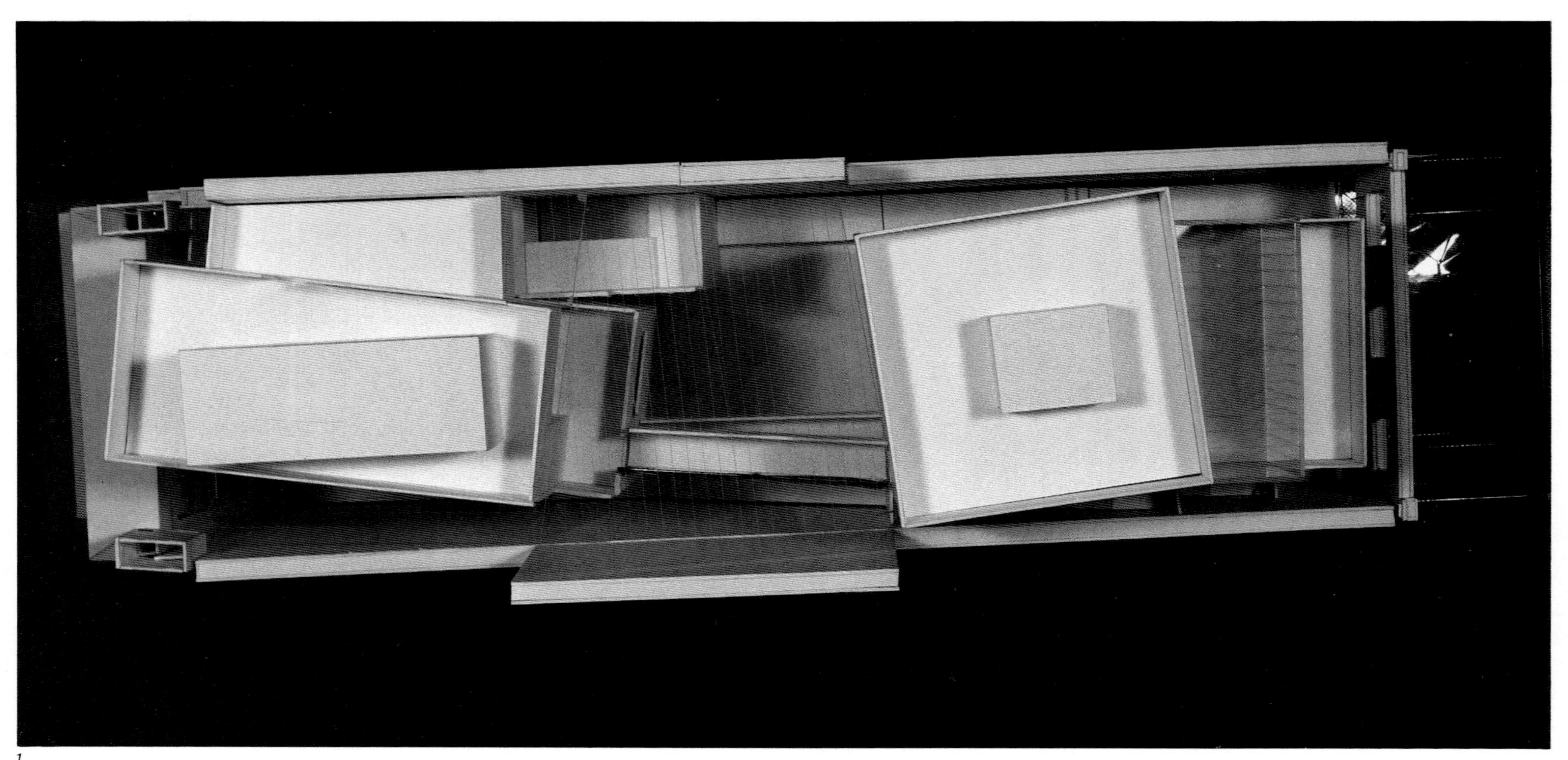

1

2

3

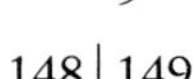

1."House" at rear 2."House" at front 3.Detail of house within house 4-5.Bridge connecting "houses" 6.View of ground floor with catwalk and skylight at rear 7-8.View through party wall 9.Carriage house

1

2

3

4

5

6

7

8

9

Arts Park
San Fernando Valley, California 1978

The San Fernando Valley Arts Council commissioned Gehry and Lawrence Halprin to design a facility that would bring area artists from different disciplines together with each other and with the general public. As important in the program as the facilities for the performance and exhibition of work were means of encouraging group collaboration and providing the public with an opportunity to see artists at work and in rehearsal. The physical facilities—studios, classrooms, shops, open-air sheds and a twenty-five hundred seat theater—are designed as a series of pavilions. A series of bridges and decks lace the buildings together. A park visitor on a stroll along the bridges would wind his way through studios and workshops with open-air views of the surrounding landscape. Buildings and bridges are stilted, as it were, to protect them from the flooding to which the park is occasionally subject. Also incorporated in the design are a chain-link gazebo offering a vista of surrounding parkland and, for those remaining at ground level, a zig-zagging rainbow of solar reflectors in which slices of the sky and landscape may be seen.

1.General view 2.Site plan 3.View from lake 4.Reflective rainbow 5.Observation tower

1

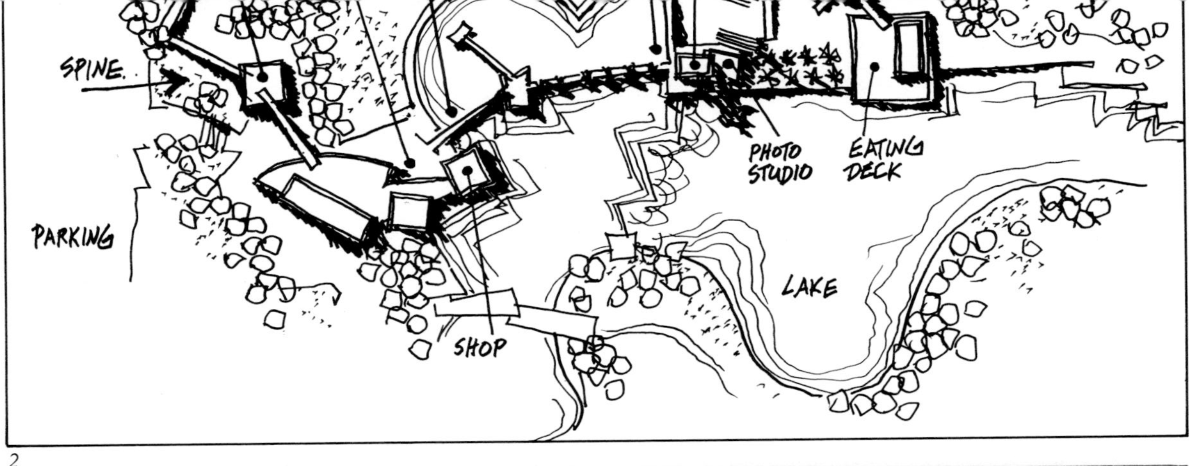

2

3

4

5

Cabrillo Marine Museum
San Pedro, California 1979

The site was a parking lot. The fort above it has chain-link fences, industrial-type buildings and big water tanks. In front are lots of large ships and many industrial buildings. I'm a very traditional architect in the sense that I am interested in context.
—Frank Gehry, 1981

The Cabrillo Marine Museum is devoted to research into, and education about, the marine life along the California coast. It attracts many school children, a group the administration particularly wanted to accommodate in their new facility on a site near an industrial harbor. The museum is a 20,000-square-foot compound of buildings laced together with chain-link fence "shadow structures." These structures bind the parts of the museum into an entity with major circulation routes outdoors, and provide space for outdoor exhibitions (a full-scale fiberglass model of a killer whale is now hung from the chain-link just behind the entrance canopy). The disposition of each pavilion on the site and the articulation of parts of each achieves a small-scale, village-like quality. The administration building, mirror-clad on one side, defines two courtyard areas, and directs visitors from the entrance toward the exhibition building. The 287-seat auditorium, the loading dock at the rear of which can be used as a stage for outdoor performances, is in a building clad in white stucco. The exhibit building is of stucco as well, with an office/control area clad in corrugated metal projecting from it. Adjoining the exhibit building are the labs into which one can look from the court—part of the didactic strategy of the museum. As with Arts Park, the intent behind the design of the museum is to familiarize visitors with the processes involved in the work displayed. Inside the exhibit hall are two major exhibit routes: The aquaria are seen from a tunnel-like route which winds through the interior. A daylit route along the periphery allows views of their mechanics and maintenance. The workings of the aquaria, laboratories, even the pipes for sea water, are bound into the architecture and its invitation to explore.

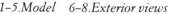

1–5.Model 6–8.Exterior views

1

2

3

4

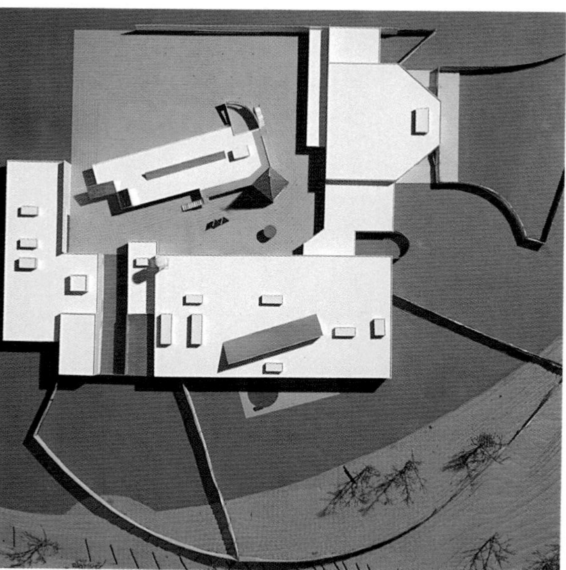

5

6

7

8

1.Plan 2.North elevation 3.West elevation 4.Section 5.Court

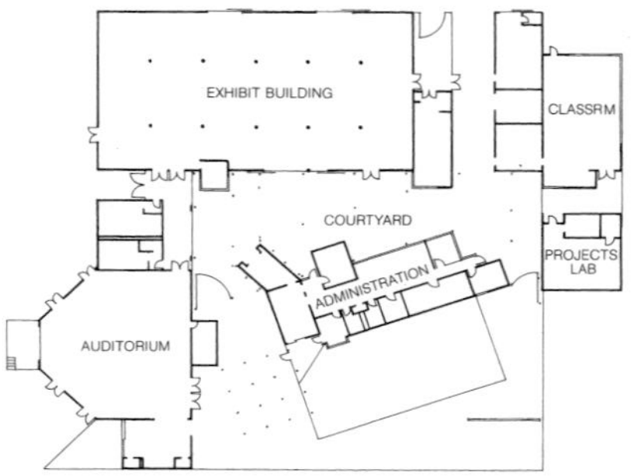

1

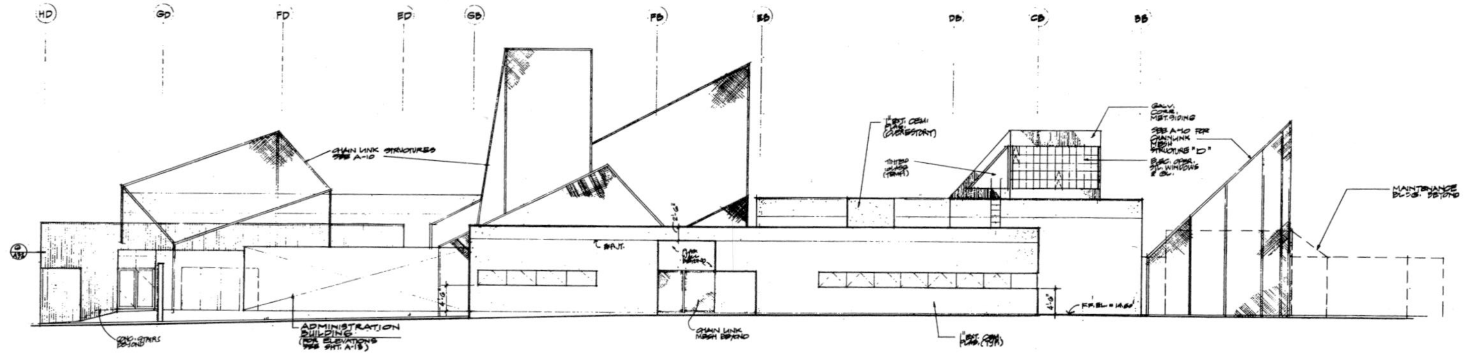

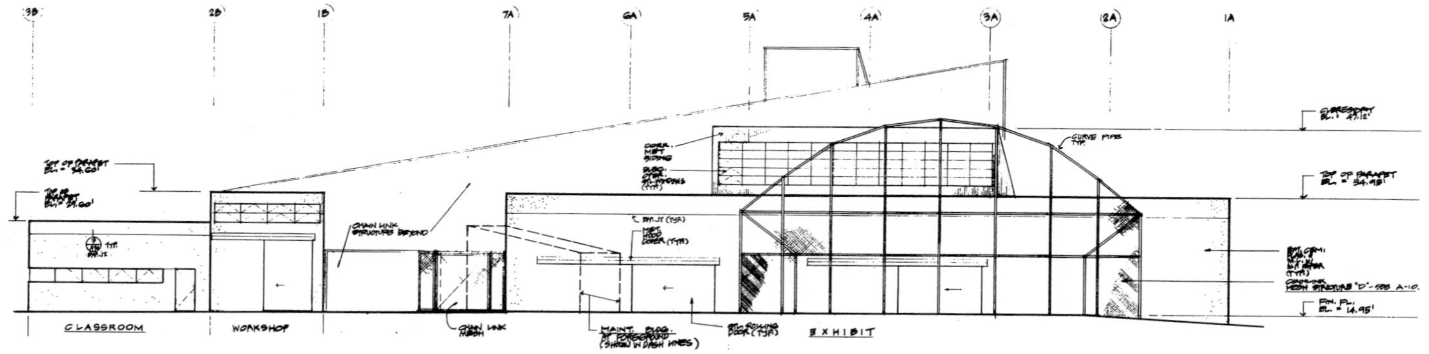

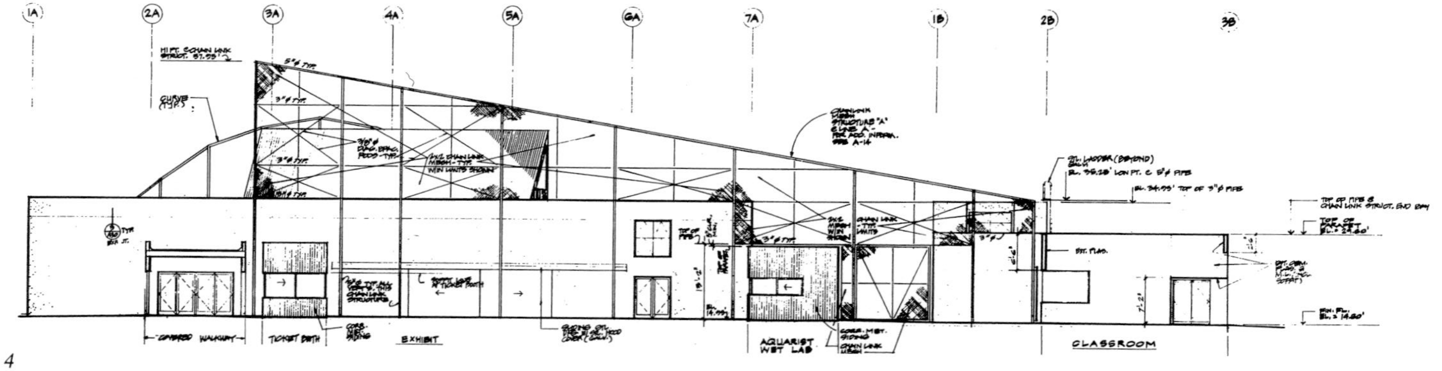

4

5

1.Entrance 2.View past administration building 3.View from above 4.View toward exhibits 5.Court near entrance 6.Exhibit building 7.Isometric of winding interior exhibit route and perimeter "backstage" exhibit route 8-10.Exhibits 11-12.Court lit at night

1

2

3

4

5

6

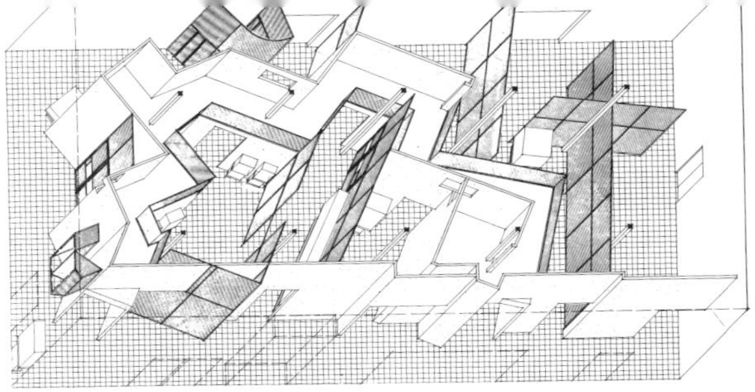

7

8

9

10

11

12

Experimental Edges
1979–82

Gehry's work with cardboard and with furniture design has been ongoing. Felt and chain-link furniture has been designed as well as new developments in the Easy Edges line. Interest on the part of original retailers, like Bloomingdale's, in marketing Easy Edges again spurred further design work. While Easy Edges is made from jigsawed stacks of cross-laminated corrugated cardboard, the sheets of cardboard forming the stacks from which the Experimental Edges line is made are formed by laminating sheets with the corrugations parallel. The surfaces thus exposed are more irregular than those of Easy Edges. The irregularities and the sort of shaggy, "broken-in" appearance they present are emphasized in the fabrication: sections of laminated cardboard are bonded to each other somewhat out of alignment or with slightly different sections, throwing individual stacks of corrugation into relief. The use of different scales of corrugation in the same piece has also been explored. Experimental Edges has been exhibited widely, although public interest remains focused on Easy Edges.

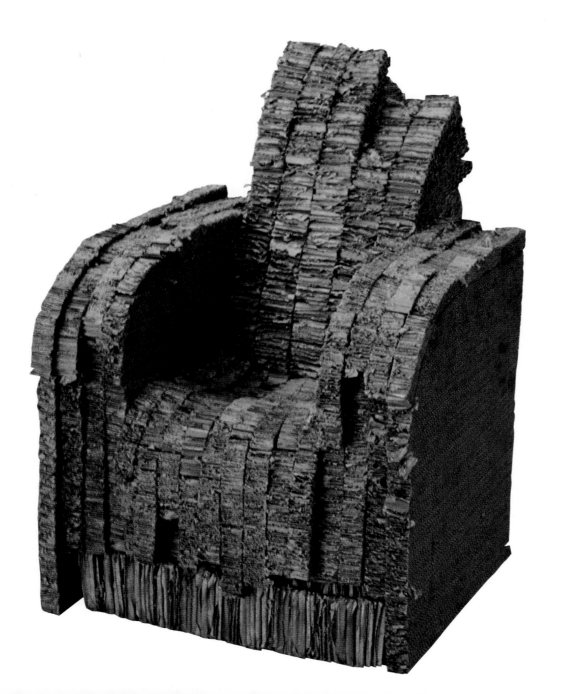

1,2.Experimental easy chairs 3.Coffee table 4.Paper chaise

Angels' Place

Los Angeles, California 1980

The characteristic townscape created [on the hills of nineteenth-century Los Angeles] has almost entirely vanished—though the steeply-terraced rooming houses on either side of the Angels' Flight funicular railway will be lovingly recalled by all fanciers of old private detective movies. But that old high density development of the hillsides belonged to a primarily pedestrian concept of cities and their workings . . .
Reyner Banham, *Los Angeles*

It is a universally acknowledged truth—at least in this decade—that a downtown in possession of a redevelopment program must be in want of a pedestrian precinct. The demise of the latter is generally attributed to the rise of automobile use and a concurrent decline in public transportation and in urban environments convivial to pedestrians. Los Angeles, the freeway capital, is frequently taken as the model of these phenomena. As a counter to them, Bunker Hill, an area adjacent to that part of Los Angeles known as downtown, was the subject of a large-scale redevelopment plan. A cultural center, housing, offices, and retail facilities were designed by a number of architects in concert to establish an "urban park" promoting use by pedestrians. The plan sought to encourage and benefit from use of a downtown-area "people mover"—a public elevated rail circuit—and a planned city rapid-transit system. Gehry's site was that of an earlier and memorable example of public transportation in the city center: Angels' Flight, a short-run funicular railway carrying passengers to the top of Bunker Hill.

Gehry's project for Maguire Partners, called Angels' Place, proposed rebuilding the old funicular, including restoration of its original entrance arch. Angels' Place was designed as a gateway to the transition between "old" downtown and the planned spaces and buildings of Bunker Hill. In the design, a sort of facade is made of the trestle of the people-mover; it is sheathed in reflective material and describes a series of arches of diminishing scale. Behind this facade-in-motion is the restored Angels' Flight entrance arch, the funicular adorned with lighted arches resembling the original, and a series of courts and terraces. These public spaces are planned as more informal than those of the "new" Bunker Hill and are "intended for chance encounters and small-scale events." Below street level, at the foot of the funicular, is a court surrounded by artists' studios, its light filtered through the arches and trestles of the funicular. Studios are also located in pavilions on surrounding street- and upper-level terraces. The pavilions, building facades, and roofscapes are "over-scaled sculptural elements based on fragments of the elegant old structures once found on Bunker Hill." Mixed with the studios on these levels are fifteen thousand square feet of retail space and a museum devoted to the history of Angels' Flight and Bunker Hill.

According to Gehry, "The designers view Angels' Place as schizophrenic in nature, meaning this in a very healthy sense. All too often, modern architecture polarizes qualities that may seem to conflict with each other, but which are really equally important. The new must be built, but elements of the old can be retained. Bigness and formality can be appropriate, but intimacy and informality are also needed. In planning Angels' Place, the qualities usually found in newer urban developments have not been denied, but some of the more elusive qualities have also been provided. The spaces have been designed to be cordial but quite distinctive neighbors to their surroundings."

1. Site model

Lafayette Square

New Orleans, Louisiana 1980

The long-term development plan for downtown New Orleans calls for the transformation of Lafayette Street, which runs through the heart of the central busines district, into a pedestrian mall linking the waterfront with the offices and hotels around the Superdome. Lafayette Park is at present a bit seedy; it is hoped that its historic significance and its position as a focal point along a successful mall will revive it. Gehry was asked to develop a schematic design for the park to include outdoor performance and exhibit facilities. Since the facilities are intended for intermittent use, it is important that each be aesthetically and functionally viable as an open park pavilion. The exhibit areas are designed as three separate open structures. One of them is planned as chain-link, its straightforward gabled form echoing the neoclassical building across the street. The walks will be slightly realigned to provide a grass seating area for 2,500 to 5,000 people around a new stage. Backstage facilities are designed as two thin buildings at the park's edge. Also planned is an area for children's activities, with its own stage, opposite the amphitheater. At the park's corners will be food kiosks, an outdoor dining terrace, and a crafts building. The project will be built in phases, the first of which was planned as the construction of the stage and its two backstage buildings. Its canopy will be translucent, exposing a roof reminiscent of a small-scale version of the Merriweather Post Pavilion. The roof spans between two columns at the front of the stage and four at the rear. When the pavilion is not in use, the four columns at the rear of the open pavilion will appear as a sort of portico on the street, flanked by the wings of the backstage service and storage wings, each sixty feet in length. An amphitheater and stage pavilion is now being developed for construction.

2. Site plan 3. Pavilions from above, showing theater at bottom

1

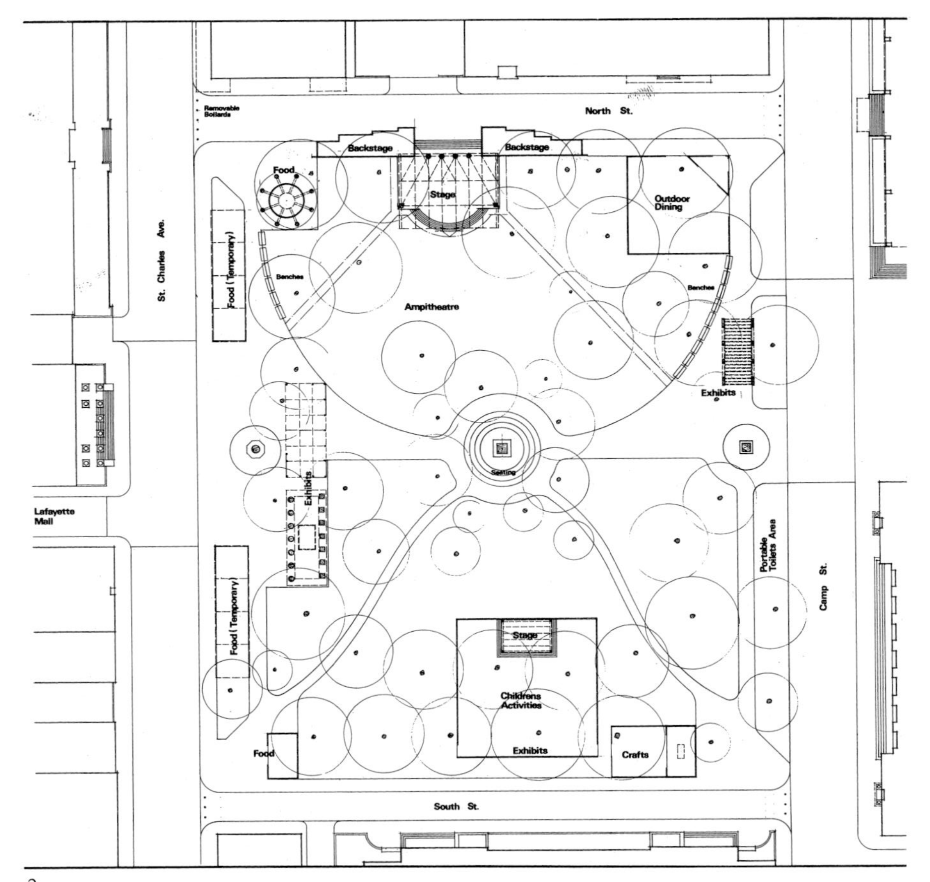

Removable Bollards
North St.
Backstage
Backstage
Food
Stage
Outdoor Dining
St. Charles Ave.
Food (Temporary)
Benches
Ampitheatre
Benches
Exhibits
Seating
Lafayette Mall
Exhibits
Portable Toilets Area
Camp St.
Food (Temporary)
Stage
Childrens Activities
Food
Exhibits
Crafts
South St.

2

3

Children's Museum

Los Angeles, California 1980

The Los Angeles Children's Museum is intended to be both didactic about the way things work and to spur imaginative supposition about how they might work. From a temporary installation in commercial space at the downtown Los Angeles Civic Center mall, the facility has been built in phases as a series of rooms, special exhibits, and constructions through which a system of ramps, stairs, and a crawl-through pipe wind. Gehry has been involved in the museum's educational and policy programing as well as the phased construction and a number of special exhibits and projects. The museum is designed to be explored, touched, climbed upon, and crawled through. The original exhibit, the nucleus of the present museum, is based loosely on the structure of a city. Exhibits and the ramps are designed to provide changing perspectives and scale relationships between parts of the exhibit and the shell of the museum itself. All of the mechanical and support systems of the museum are exposed, making it part of the exhibit about how things work.

The museum design promotes a "hands-on" approach to involving the imagination and participation of children in the built environment. Gehry used a similar idea in a successful city-planning program for inner city children his sister Doreen Nelson created in the late 1960s. Working with his sister's classes, he oversaw the creation of cities in model form and the imaginative resolution of problems of urban form and policy raised as these cities of cardboard and tape grew. Re-running the program in Washington under the auspices of the Smithsonian, Gehry began the course with the admonition, "Remember, you're future people. You're not here-and-now people. You may not want to build a city as you know it today." As he explains it, "Kids don't think that they are allowed to criticize grown-up things, but they should ask questions and have opinions. Our program lets them get involved. I make them all city planners. . . . Doing this has to be fun for them, so that they will associate planning and design with a good experience. What is fun and good is easy to remember."

The Children's Museum, like the Kid City program, represents something more than a museum design and an extracurricular activity. They constitute an effort toward meeting the challenge Gehry outlined as that of improving America's cities by involving early on the interested imaginations of the next generation: "I don't want to impose preconceived notions of cars or parking lots or green space on the kids," explains Gehry. "They are already given too many predigested ideas. Trying to teach them from our experiences is not only useless but detrimental. After all, it's our notions which have created the present chaos."

Plans for the museum's continued expansion include a performing arts facility and a space technology exhibit. At present, the museum is nearly as popular with adults as children. That phenomenon was explained, as is, perhaps, the success of the designer in creating the place, by a twelve-year-old critic who decided, "When you grow up you want to be small again."

Children's Museum: 1.Model 2.Exhibit 6.Plan 7.Axonometric
Kid City: 3–5.Urban design

1

2

3

4

5

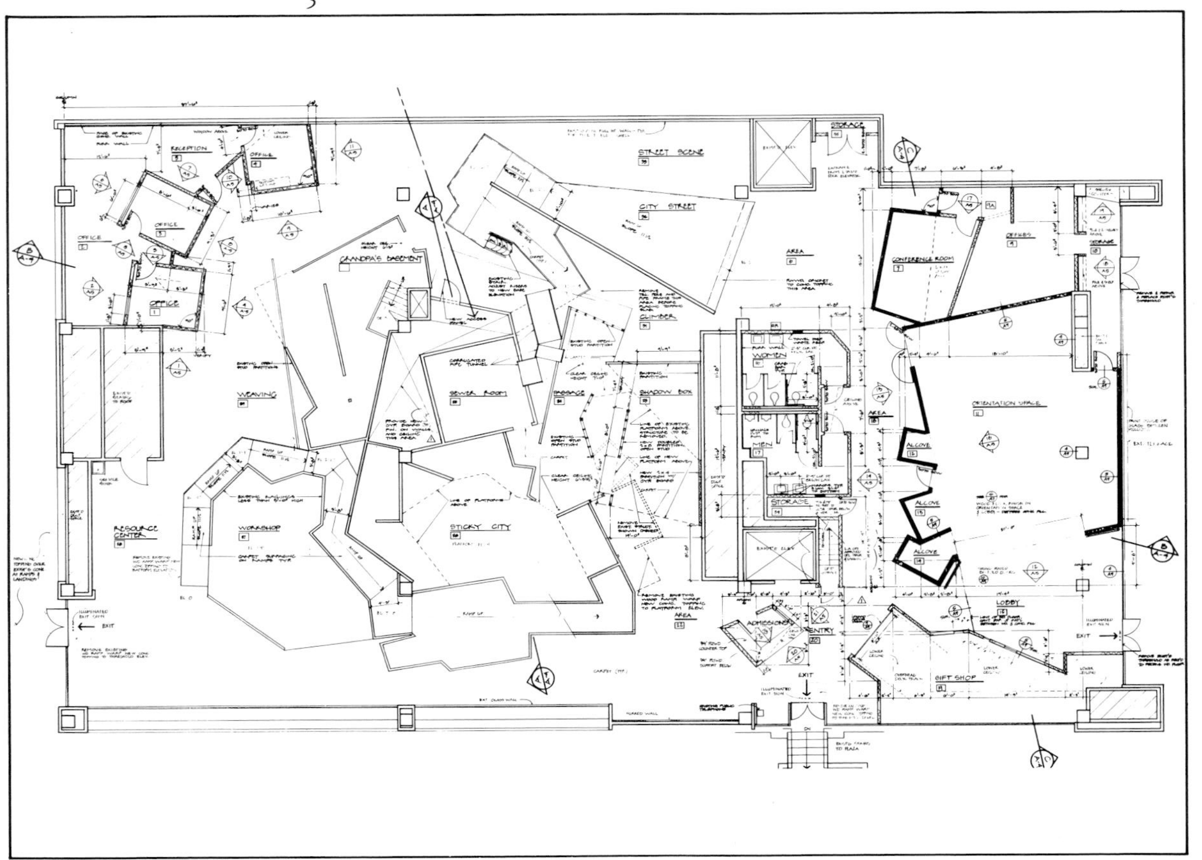
RECEPTION
OFFICE
OFFICE
OFFICE
GRANDPA'S BASEMENT
STREET SCENE
CITY STREET
AREA
CONFERENCE ROOM
OFFICES
STORAGE
WOMEN
MEN
SHADOW BOX
SEWER ROOM
WEAVING
ORIENTATION SPACE
ALCOVE
ALCOVE
ALCOVE
STICKY CITY
WORKSHOP
RESOURCE CENTER
ADMISSIONS
ENTRY
LOBBY
GIFT SHOP
EXIT
EXIT
EXIT

6

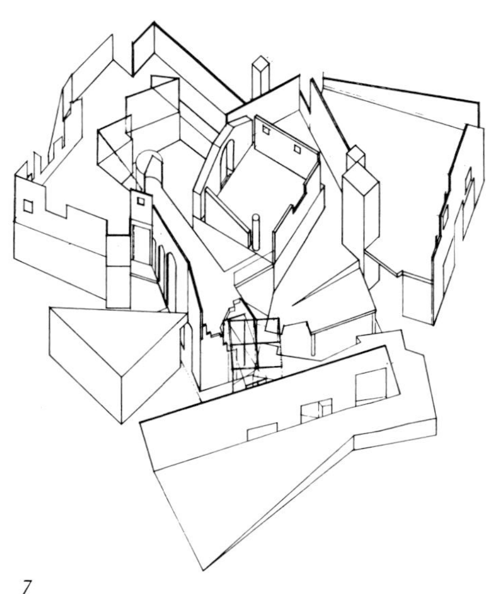

7

Late Entry: Chicago Tribune Tower Competition

1980

In 1922, the Chicago Tribune held a competition for the design of its headquarters, the stated intent being "to erect the most beautiful and distinctive office building in the world." Entries were submitted from around the world. The range of designs has long been considered a useful record of diverse architectural ideas in an age of transition.

Seventy-five years later, on the other side of an era grown skeptical about the utopia prophesied by advocates of the skyscraper, a second competition was held as a sort of poll to gauge current architectural ideas. Most entrants proposed monumental sculptural objects; some took up the banner of reasserting the human scale in a large, urban structure. Gehry's entry addressed both problems forthrightly: It was supposed, in his submission, that technology has reduced the amount of space required for the dissemination of news, but he finds other urban functions for a tower. It is uninhabitable solid concrete. Its top—in the shape of an eagle—contains a computer capable of sending out the news. From wings attached to the side of the building is a hoist-type ride. It is imagined that patrons of the ride concession would pitch tents around the base of the building.

1.Entry 2-3.Hypotheses about the form of other, presumably postmodernist, entries

1

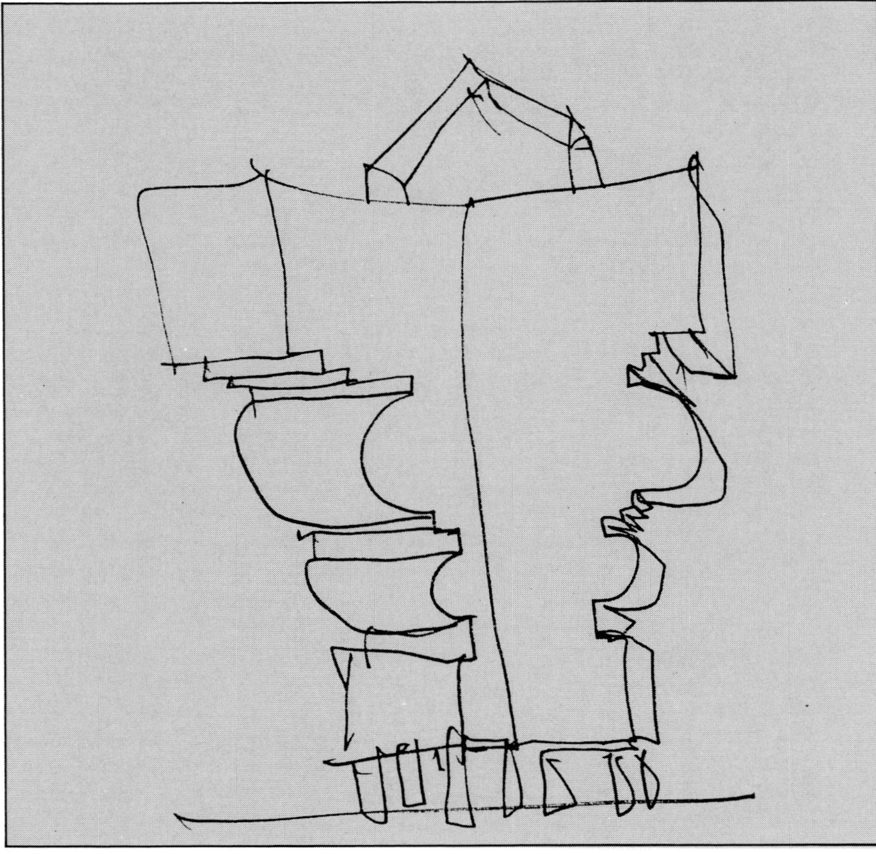

2

3

Spiller House
Venice, California 1980

On a tiny lot in Venice, one block from the ocean, stands a house that is actually two houses—a two-story rental unit toward the ocean with a four-story house for the owner at the rear. Given the extremely tight site size, the strict zoning stipulations governing the allowable floor area to site area ratio, and the attraction of the ocean nearby, the planning and form tend toward a kind of vertical expansiveness. In the words of one critic, "The interior spaces aspire to their skylights." But as with a corset cinched against too ample corpulence, mass and gravity seem to resist and reassert themselves. A bay window, solar panels, and skylights seem to have popped through the walls of the houses. Other elements seem wracked by forces resisting orthogonal trussing: stairs twist and cascade, a trellis sprays up over an angled screen wall.

Pursuing ideas explored with the Familian House and Gemini G.E.L's workshop building, sheathing—in this case corrugated metal as well as glass, plywood, and sheetrock—does not entirely cover the wood framing of which the building is constructed. Rather, the framing is exposed in order to exploit its warmth as a material, the sculptural modulation of its serial elements, and the geometric richness of shadows thrown from it. The complexity and frequency of exposed frame elements, and their appearance inside and outside, creates a kind of layered latticework which subverts a definitive understanding of the physical limits of the house: the interiors of the small houses profit by the ambiguity, and appear more expansive.

The guest house is accessible from the adjacent ocean-side street. Its living and dining area is on the ground floor, which is open near the center to the skylight story above. Above the second-story bedrooms and light well is a roof deck populated by solar panels and the skylight monitor, the latter truncated by a privacy wall shielding the roof deck from the owner's house behind. Panels, monitor, and wall obey different geometries.

The owner's house has, at ground level, a garage and entrance court. The small court is dominated by a large wooden entrance stair. Access to the master bedroom is at the first landing, at the second level. The second run of the stair lands at a trellis-covered area on the roof of the guest house from which a bridge leads back to the main entrance of the house. This third-floor front door opens onto the two-story living, dining, and kitchen area. By the door, an angular, glass-roofed, plywood-clad "bay window" breaks out beyond the metal box of the house. The internal stair of the house winds up through the volume of the living area to a roof deck around the glass light monitor. Having arrived at this uppermost reach of the compound, a view is available of solar panels, glass-and-frame roofs, trellises and stairs, spilling, as it were, down toward the ocean.

1.Venice 2.Sketches 3.From guest house toward main house

1

2

3

1.North elevation 2.West elevation 3.South elevation 4.East elevation 5.3rd floor 6.2nd floor 7.Ground floor 8.Roof deck 9.Upper living room

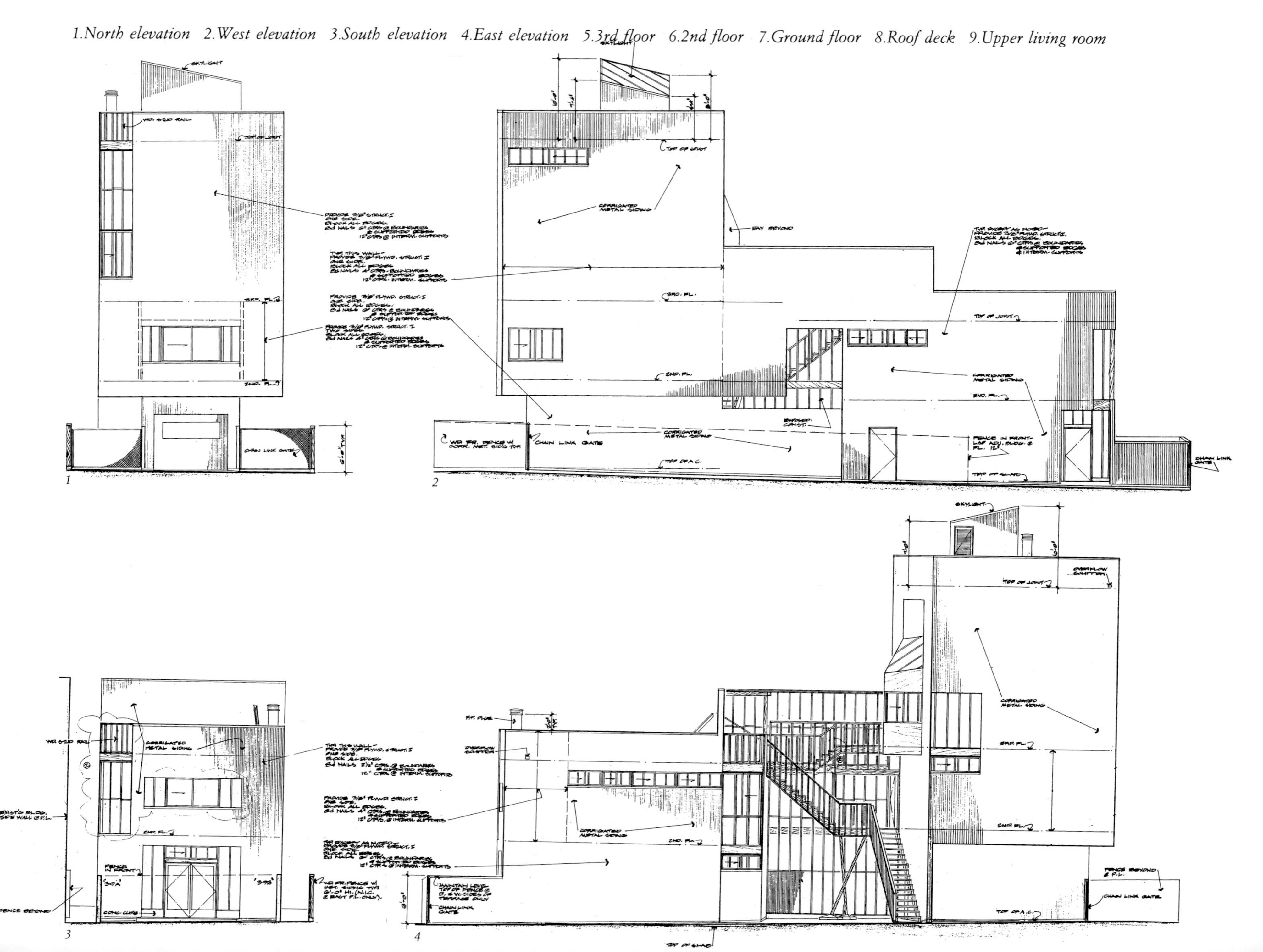

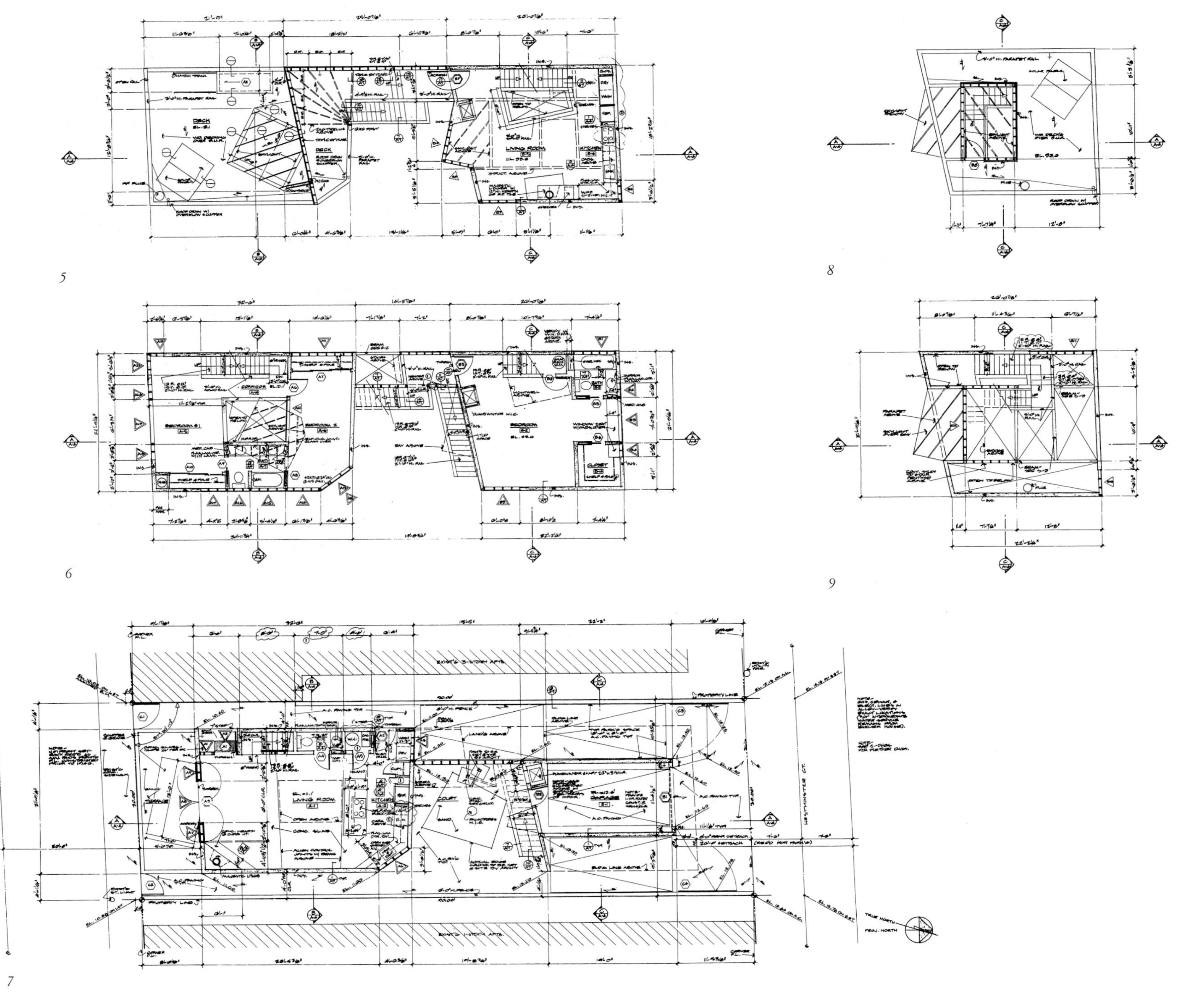
DECK
LIVING ROOM
KITCHEN
BEDROOM #1
CLOSET
COURT
GARAGE
EXIST'G 3-STORY APTS.
HORIZON AVE.
WESTMINSTER CT.
TRUE NORTH
PROJ. NORTH

5

6

7

8

9

1,5.Bay Window projection 2.Entrance from street 3.Livingroom 4.Master bedroom 6.Skylight, main house 7-8.Living room, main house

1

2

3

4

5

6

7

8

United States Chancellery

Damascus, Syria 1980

On the site of the American Embassy in Damascus are the Embassy proper, a chancellery, and the Damascus Community School. More office and classroom space was required. Gehry and Associates' site analysis showed that, given the neighboring buildings and the requirements of privacy and security, the preferred location for a larger chancellery was that occupied by the existing school. Phased construction was recommended, with a new twelve thousand-square-foot school building to be built first. Subsequently, the new sixty-one thousand-square-foot chancellery was to be built.

Several designs for the chancellery were studied, the final of which is a slightly assymmetrical office block cut out at the center to form an entrance court. The office block is treated as a simple volume with an assortment of large openings cut through its surfaces. The partially trellis-covered entrance court is composed of smaller-scaled elements: an entrance pavilion reached by bridge, and the windows and doors of the office block, which in this area are much smaller than on its other facades. The intent was to both relate to neighboring buildings and to create an entrance of appropriately scaled decorum. The whole is conceived as a composition of objects, man-made and natural: the building, its related bridge, plaza, pavilions, trellises and groves of trees are conceived as individual entities contributing to an overall composition—a recurring strategy in later work.

1,2.Sketches 3,4.Model

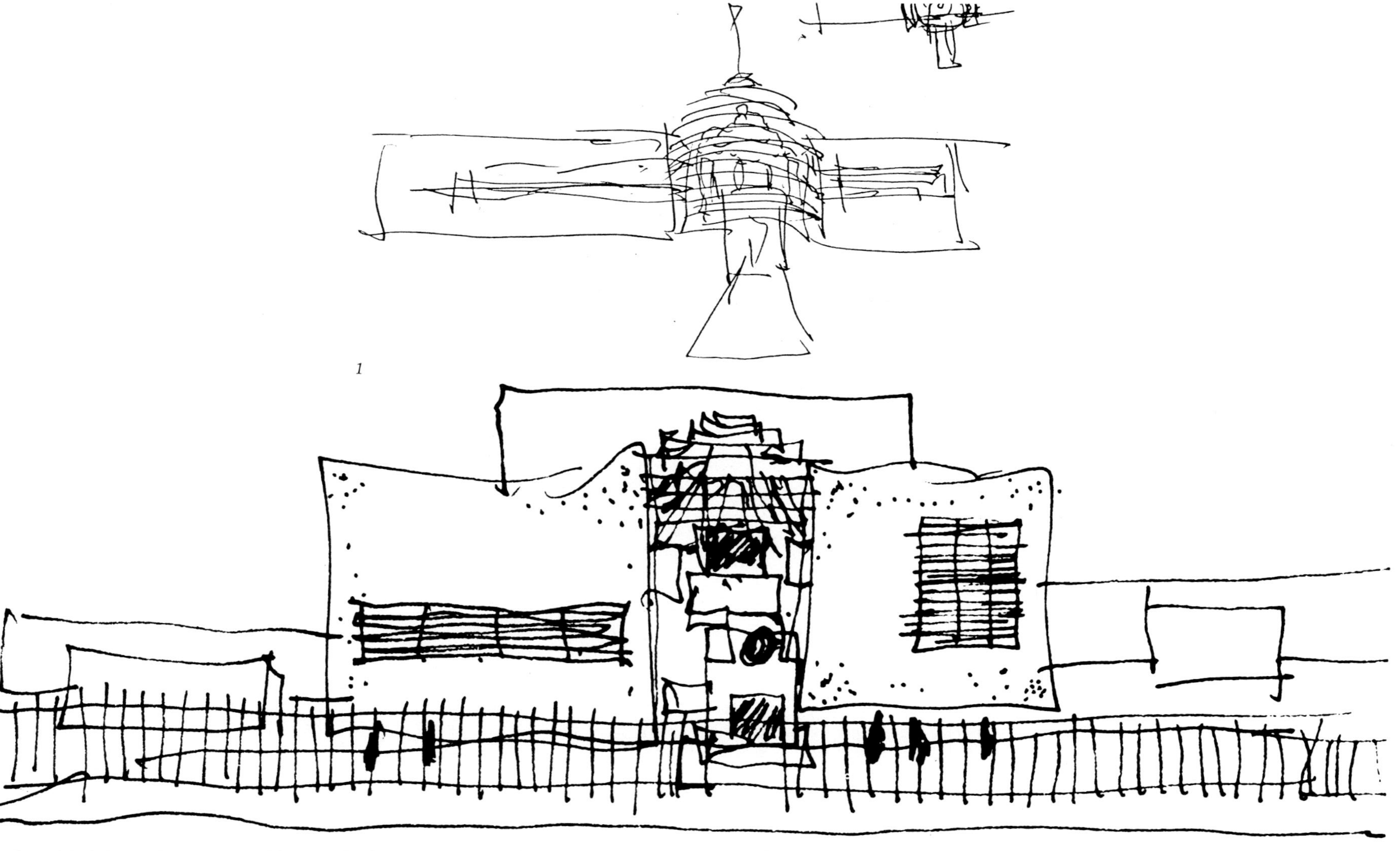

1

2

3

4

The Avant-Garde in Russia 1910–1930

Los Angeles County Museum of Art 1980

The exhibit of Russian avant-garde art was the largest and most comprehensive collection ever assembled in the United States. More than 450 objects were displayed, including paintings, sculpture, constructions, architectural models, books, periodicals, costumes, and stage furniture. The show was organized primarily by movements, rather than chronologically. To define display groupings, partitions were painted red, white, black, gray, or yellow, colors dominant in the paintings and graphics of the period. To open spaces to each other and to lower the perceived wall height to a scale appropriate to the generally small objects, partitions were kept to a height of ten feet, their framing continuing unsheathed to the ceiling recalling the stage sets of the period. Views between spaces were also opened in places by lowering partition heights further.

Special-exhibit events included a recreation of a 1915 Malevich installation, a reconstruction of Tatlin's Monument, aggrandized to a somewhat larger scale by a shadow thrown on a wall behind, and a full-scale recreation of El Lizzitsky's "Proun" room. That Gehry should design the exhibit of a body of work in which exposed framing, and the and the collision and overlapping of forms are part of an accepted aesthetic was both appropriate and fruitful. The particular resonance of his own work with that of the Russian avant-garde was described to an interviewer, who was trying to find a key to Gehry's aesthetic in his background: "I'm working on a show at the Los Angeles County Museum of . . . constructivist paintings and structures. And I decided that that work feels so much like home that maybe my Polish-Russian background is coming out. That might be more of me than the truckdriver. Maybe it's in the genes."

1-6. General views

1

2

3

4

5

6

Décor is above all an independent creation, supportive of a work's spirit, an autonomous art form with its own problems and subject to its own laws.
—Goncharova and Lariotiov *Les Ballets Russe: Serge Diaghilev et la Décoration Theatrical*

1.General view. 2.Furniture and costumes from Stepanova's "Tarlekin's Death" 3.Costume exhibit

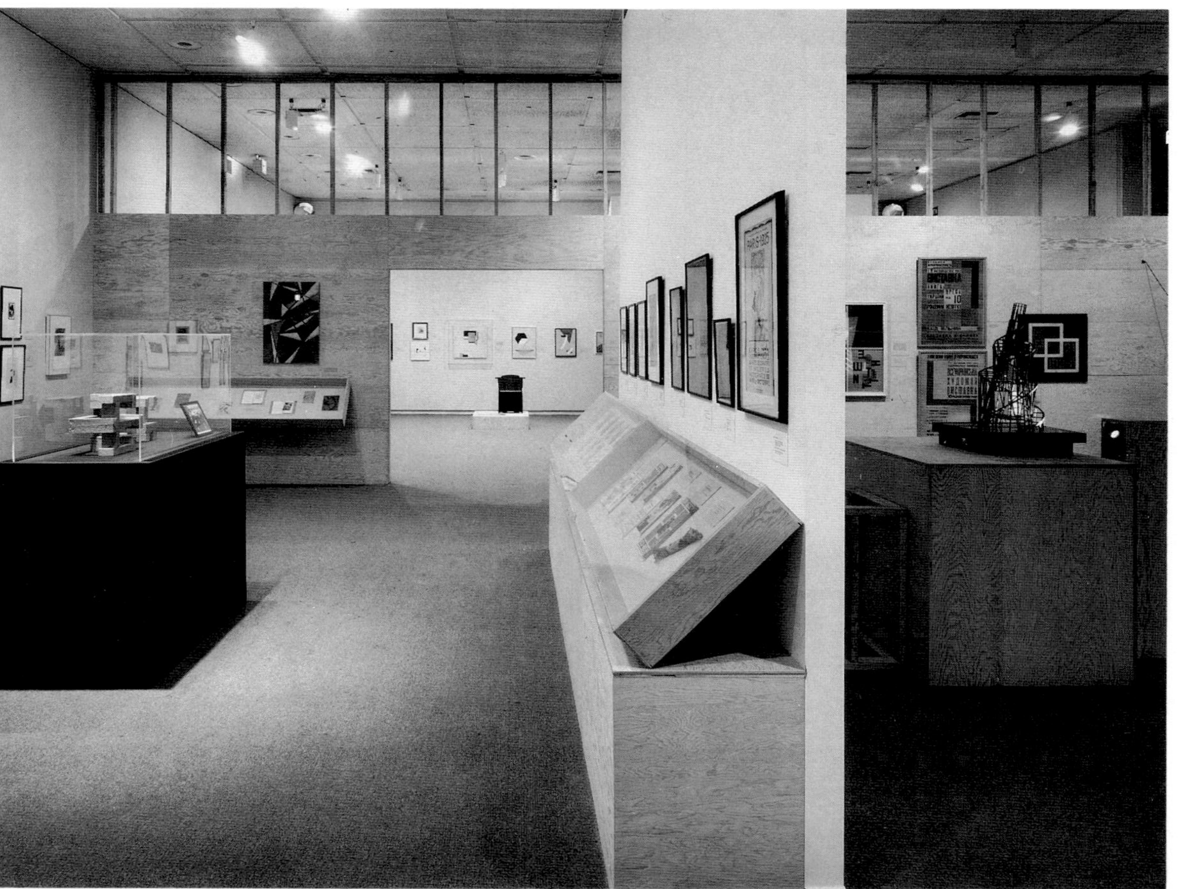
1

2

3

Biennale Exhibit
Venice, Italy 1980

It's like being asked to do a parody of yourself.
—Michael Graves on the 1980 Biennale

The organizers of the biennial architectural exposition in Venice arranged as the centerpiece of the 1980 Biennale the *Strada Novissima.* Within the volume of the arsenal in which the exhibit was held, a zone was reserved as a street; "lots" along the street were assigned to a select number of prominent architects who were asked to design a facade opening onto an area in which their recent work was to be exhibited.

Three screens of two-by-fours, slightly behind one another, constituted the facade and the entrance to Gehry's exhibit area. The foremost, aligned with the other facades along the *Strada Novissima,* was a large square extending from the ceiling to a distance one-third the height of the installation from the floor. Set back from it slightly was another screen in which an opening was left at the center for entrance to the exhibit. A third screen deflected visitors to the right or left, forcing some direct confrontation with the materials of the project. The offset spacing of the two lower screens' studs created a visually denser base for the larger square screen above.

Unlike most of the exhibits, Gehry's did not aim to suggest the idea of a complete building. Rather, the installation was a framework of two-by-fours, transparent to both Gehry's exhibit, delimited by lower screens of two-by-fours, and to the exhibit hall itself beyond. To underscore the position of the work as a temporary stageset within a complete building, the centerpiece, which was the focus of the design, was a window of the exhibit hall in a wall behind the area alloted to Gehry.

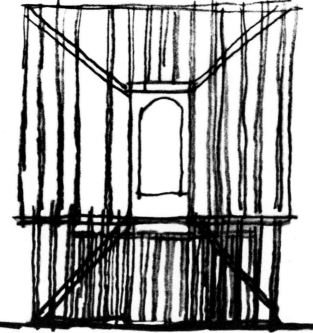

The diagonal bracing of the two-by-fours, on and between the three screens of the facade, suggests a perspective recession of the facade toward the window, simultaneously exploring the illusionism possible with minimal mass, and underscoring the ephemeral and limited nature of the intervention within a real building. Germano Celant's review of the exhibit concludes: "In the end the most radical intervention is decidedly that of Frank Gehry, the California architect who has refuted monumentalizations and imitations by proposing a woodframe skeleton through which to view the sixteenth-century architecture of the arsenal 'in perspective' thus turning this post-modernist rebirth into what might be called a 'renaissance of the Renaissance.' "

1.Design 2.Installation

1

2

Santa Monica Place

Santa Monica, California 1973/80

A few aspects of shopping-center theory do in fact remain impenetrable to me. I have no idea why the Community Builders' Council ranks "Restaurant" as deserving a Number One (or "Hot Spot") location but exiles "Chinese Restaurant" to a Number Three, out there with "Power and Light Office" and "Christian Science Reading Room." Nor do I know why the council approves of enlivening a mall with "small animals" but specifically, vehemently, and with no further explanation, excludes "monkeys." If I had a center I would have monkeys, and Chinese restaurants, and mylar kites and bands of small girls playing tamborines.
—Joan Didion, *On the Mall*

Gehry's client in the design of Santa Monica Place was the Rouse Company, relative innovators in the field, who dare to and usually succeed at tampering with accepted "shopping mall theory." The project represented a major portion of a rejuvenation program for the business district of Santa Monica and, as such, called for the modification of suburban shopping planning for an urban setting. Original plans for the area, proposed by Gehry and the Rouse Company in a 1972–73 study, called for a mixed-use development on the site, including hotel and residential development. Emphasized in the planning were a mix of residential and commercial uses, low massing of buildings along street fronts, and strategies to bind the development to existing city areas—in particular the old, open-air shopping mall to the north, and the beach, a block to the west. The program of the project for the site was simplified to a shopping mall, but other planning ideals were carried through from the original study to the final project completed in association with Victor Gruen Associates.

In what is, in terms of conventional shopping-mall wisdom, a radical departure, the two large department store "anchors" are located diagonally opposite one another. Two six-story parking structures, also designed by Gehry, are located at the other two corners of the site. Although the anchors were designed by the stores' own architects, those areas under the architects' and the developer's control were designed in response to the scale and opportunities of the surrounding town. As a terminus to, and an invitation from, the old open-air mall to the north, an enormous gable-roofed greenhouse marks the principal entrance. The parking garage to the north sports a superimposed grid to relate its bulk a bit more sympathetically to the older, smaller buildings across the street. To the west is a series of large outdoor terraces and stairs held in stucco frames with views out to the ocean; its blue awnings relate to the nearby Santa Monica Pier. Adjacent, the west front of the second parking garage is screened with chain-link fence, juxtaposed with a white concrete panel throwing a cluster of palms into sculptural relief. The east entrance is an exuberant gate and frame; its geometries and collisions serve as a sign for the diagonally planned mall inside. The most remarkable sign, however, is that seen on the south side of the same garage, the major approach route by cars: to the blue chain-link-fence sheathing of the south parking garage are affixed enormous letters of white chain-link. They are simultaneously transparent and unmistakably legible. The entrance adjacent carries through the large-scale panache with a huge diagonal opening in the stucco wall. The three-story interior galleries, under continuous skylights, connect the four entrances. That the entrances are offset from one another is visible in the shifted geometries of its columns, beams, and central atrium. The three galleries step back terrace-like; "sidewalks" in front of the shopfronts are defined by the regularly spaced column structure. Gehry considers Santa Monica Place a collaboration between the community, shopkeepers, developer, and architect. The role of the architect in the collaboration was to respond architecturally to the conditions of the surrounding community and to develop a framework in which each individual shop could determine its own identity. One such shop, Bubar's Jewelers, determined its identity with the help of the mall's architect.

1–2,4–5,7.Study model 3.Conceptual diagram 6.Mall level plan

1

2

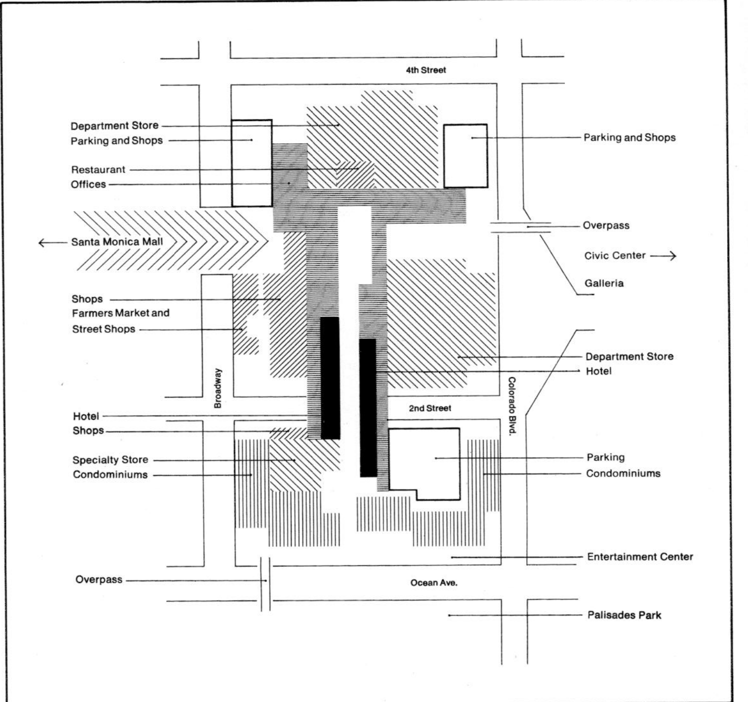
4th Street
Department Store
Parking and Shops
Restaurant
Offices
Santa Monica Mall
Shops
Farmers Market and
Street Shops
Broadway
Hotel
Shops
Specialty Store
Condominiums
Overpass
Parking and Shops
Overpass
Civic Center
Galleria
Department Store
Hotel
2nd Street
Colorado Blvd.
Parking
Condominiums
Entertainment Center
Ocean Ave.
Palisades Park

3

4

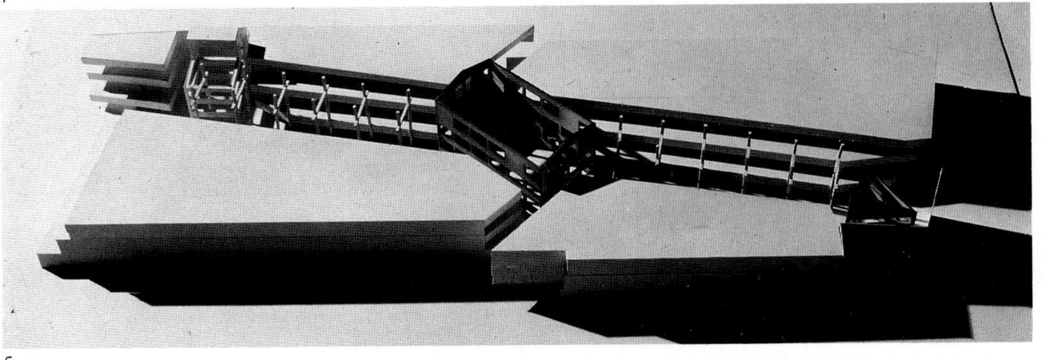

5

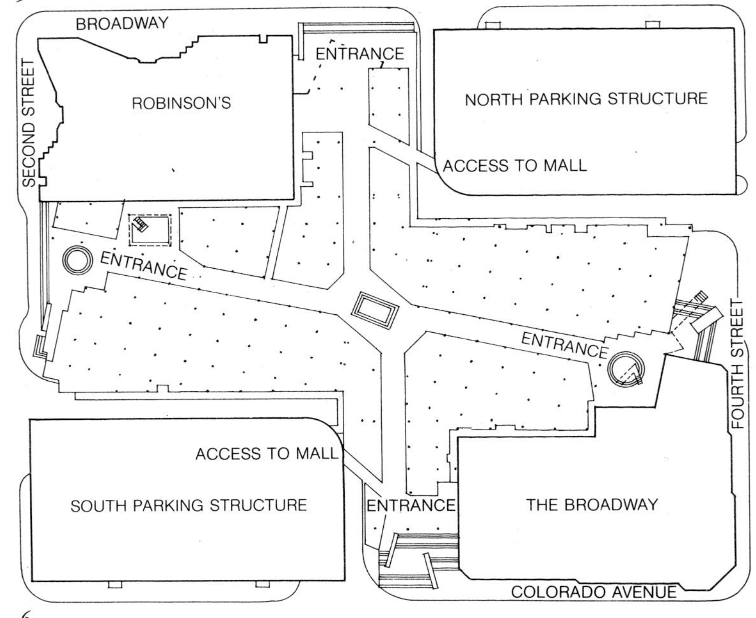
BROADWAY
ENTRANCE
ROBINSON'S
NORTH PARKING STRUCTURE
ACCESS TO MALL
SECOND STREET
ENTRANCE
ENTRANCE
FOURTH STREET
ACCESS TO MALL
SOUTH PARKING STRUCTURE
ENTRANCE
THE BROADWAY
COLORADO AVENUE

6

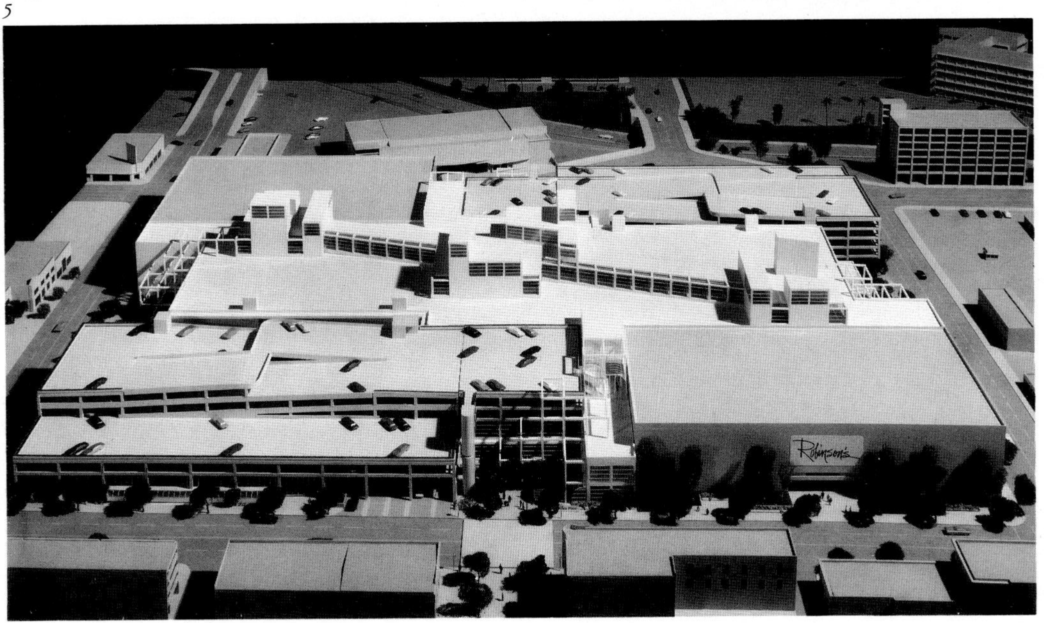

7

1.Approach from freeway 2–3.Oceanside entrance
4.Aerial view 5.Exterior stair 6.Mall interior

1

2

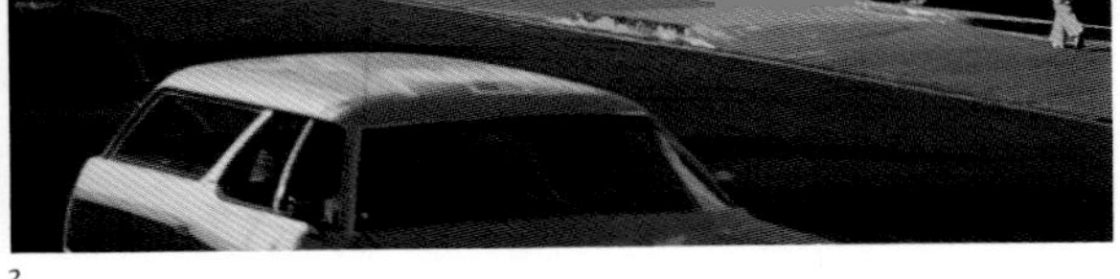

3

4

5

6

Bubar's Jewelers
Santa Monica, California 1980

When filled with individual businesses, the regular bays of shopping malls exhibit an extraordinarily dense and intense eclecticism. For a shop in Santa Monica Place, the design not only contributes to the heterogeneity of the mall, but also comes close to replicating it at smaller scale within the shell of one tenant's space. Various types of the jeweler's merchandise were organized into individual display cabinets designed as distinct pavilions arranged along an interior "street." The eighteen-by-one hundred-foot leasehold space was treated as a shell containing the pavilions; the typical dropped ceiling was not installed, leaving the container at its full height for the freestanding display pavilions. The pavilions are arranged in nonorthogonal, seemingly casual, relation to each other and the shell of the store. A nearly-centered pediment is glued to the glass of the storefront; under it, in something like symmetry, a marble-tiled bay stands opposite a slightly askew pavilion with a truncated hipped roof. Belying the formal organization these elements might suggest, the scattering of the elements inside transforms a march up the nave to a stroll through the casbah.

1.Site 2.Entrance 3.Interior 4.Section 5.Plan

1

Jewelers
BUBAR'S
Since 1945
2

3

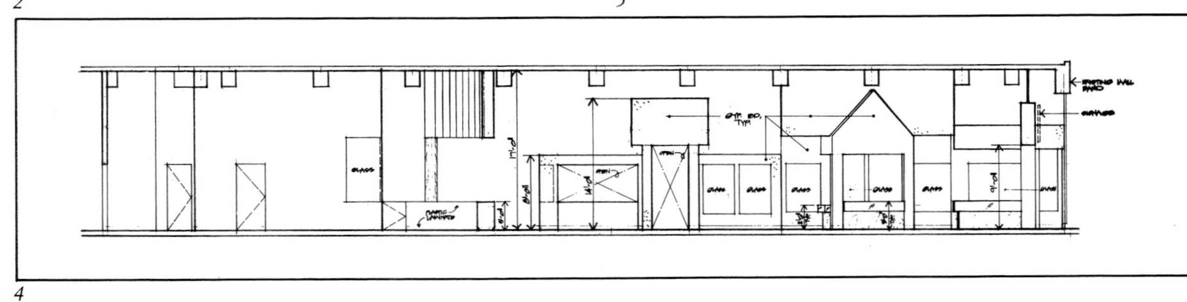
4

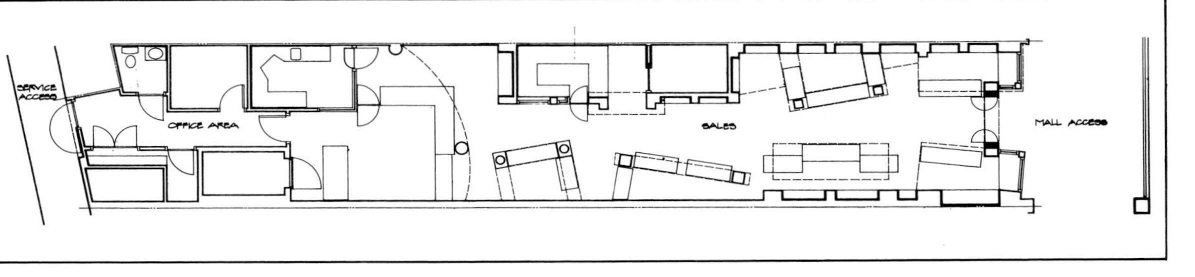
SERVICE ACCESS
OFFICE AREA
SALES
MALL ACCESS
5

World Savings Bank

North Hollywood, California 1980

The little bank has a big name. To avoid appearing a parodic annex to its sign, the small branch had to achieve a scale at least equal to the neighboring Radio Shack and Marie Callender's Pies franchises. Further, as most customers enter the bank from the parking lot at its rear, suggestions of scale befitting the name needed to extend beyond the street front.

The original design created a play of images as well as of scale. A stucco box, compatible with the architecture of the commercial strip in which the bank is located, was proposed. It was to have its center drawn up to an adequately imposing height. Behind a glazed front wall, a three-story pedimented form, complete with windows on its second and third "floors" was to be seen. Mullions in the glazing and two small structures in the entrance vestibule were designed to force a perspective perception of a deep recession toward the pedimented form. The effect would be that of a grand old bank which had been engulfed in a vast new shed, more appropriate to the neighborhood's architecture and more commodious for a growing institution. Within the space, the pedimented form, in fact a plane, was to be one of several freestanding forms. A conference room was to hang above the banking space, held back from the pedimented plane, but affording a view through its windows. At the rear of the bank, layers would be reversed: a second pedimented plane, of transparent material, would be within the space, marking the entrance to the banking room from the parking lot; the rear elevation would be stucco with rectangular windows.

As the design evolved, the budget shrank. A second design was developed in which the high central space was excised save those places where it was most needed—at the street and at the parking lot. The building, as built, is the leanest version. At the street elevation, the perspective distortion of the glazing mullions somewhat aggrandizes the high entrance foyer. Its rear wall is repeated at the back of the building as a freestanding wall rising above the parking lot.

The implied grandeur of a three-story bank with a high central banking room is undercut by the interior organization. In the bank, as in its preceding stages of development, doors and the banking room are set to one side of the implied central volume. The implied perspective recession of the mullions acknowledges the shift by respecting a vanishing point three feet to the left of center. This distortion also defers to the perspective of those passing in automobiles, the vantage point from which the bank is most commonly seen. The wood framing of the ceiling is left exposed. A skylight, with framing members continued through as baffles, marks, at a slightly cockeyed angle, the off-center of the banking room.

1–3,5.Study sketches 4.Model 6–7.Exterior views 8.Interior

1

2

3

4

WORLD
SAVINGS

5

7

WORLD
SAVINGS
1006
INTEREST
BEARING
CHECKING
ACCOUNTS

6

8

Connections
Architectural League, New York 1981

Sculptor Richard Serra has expressed his admiration for Gehry's work on several occasions—for its inventiveness and its understanding and exploration of context scale. Gehry describes their mutual admiration as follows: "I am a great admirer of his work and have learned much from him. He, in turn, has seemed curious about my work and occasionally appears to be making gestures of approval as he wanders through my spaces." Their mutual interests led to the idea of working on a project together. Serra had finished a film on bridges and proposed the subject for their collaboration. The interest was in the nature of bridges as both objects and connections. After research and discussion, "we realized that everything was a bridge." Conveniently, the Architectural League of New York sponsored a group exhibit for which pairs of architects and artists collaborated on a project of each pair's choosing. Gehry and Serra's collaboration, already under discussion, became their contribution to the show. Narrowing the scope of the project from "everything" proved difficult. The solution presented itself, as it were, during discussion at Serra's New York studio: "Richard's studio window faces the World Trade Center. As we thrashed about looking for something upon which to focus, we decided on a project that joined two unlikely architectural objects: the World Trade Center and the Chrysler Building. That certainly poses problems, both philosophical and pragmatic." An intuitive understanding of pragmatic problems led to the element which most explicitly makes the bridge a representation of a connection between the two artists: to stabilize the span and assume some of its structural load, two pylons beyond the buildings were designed. One in the East River is a canted monumental Serra pylon. Beyond the World Trade Center, a Gehry fish of monumental scale rears from the Hudson. Between the fish and pylon the cables are held in tension, a bridge connecting two sensibilities.

Gehry's fish, ubiquitous in his design studies of the early eighties, made its public debut in the project. It first appeared in an early study sketch of a Smith House colonnade, as a companion to a column surmounted by an eagle. Since then it has appeared as a hotel in Kalamazoo, the Loyola Law School Chapel belfry, an electric lamp, a prison, and a tract house. In sketches, the fish seems a shorthand notation for a building mass or sculpture of startling singularity, but of symbolic content and form yet undetermined. Gehry concurs this premise is "sort of right—I've had chances to build it and never have, if that tells you anything."

1.Design exhibit 2,6,8.Studies 3.Detail, World Trade Center 4.Detail, fish scales (building skin over structural frame) 5.Detail, Chrysler Building 7.Detail, Serra pylon

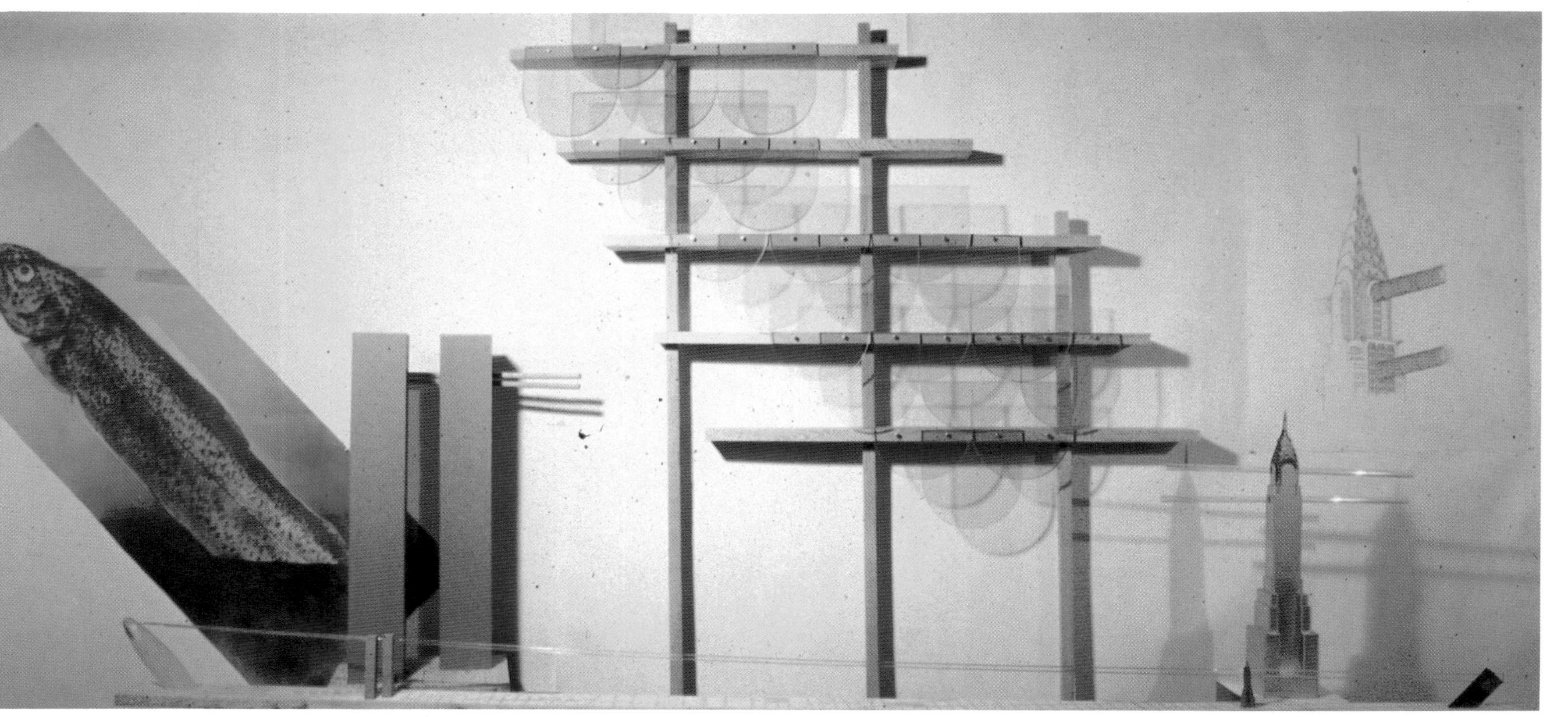

1

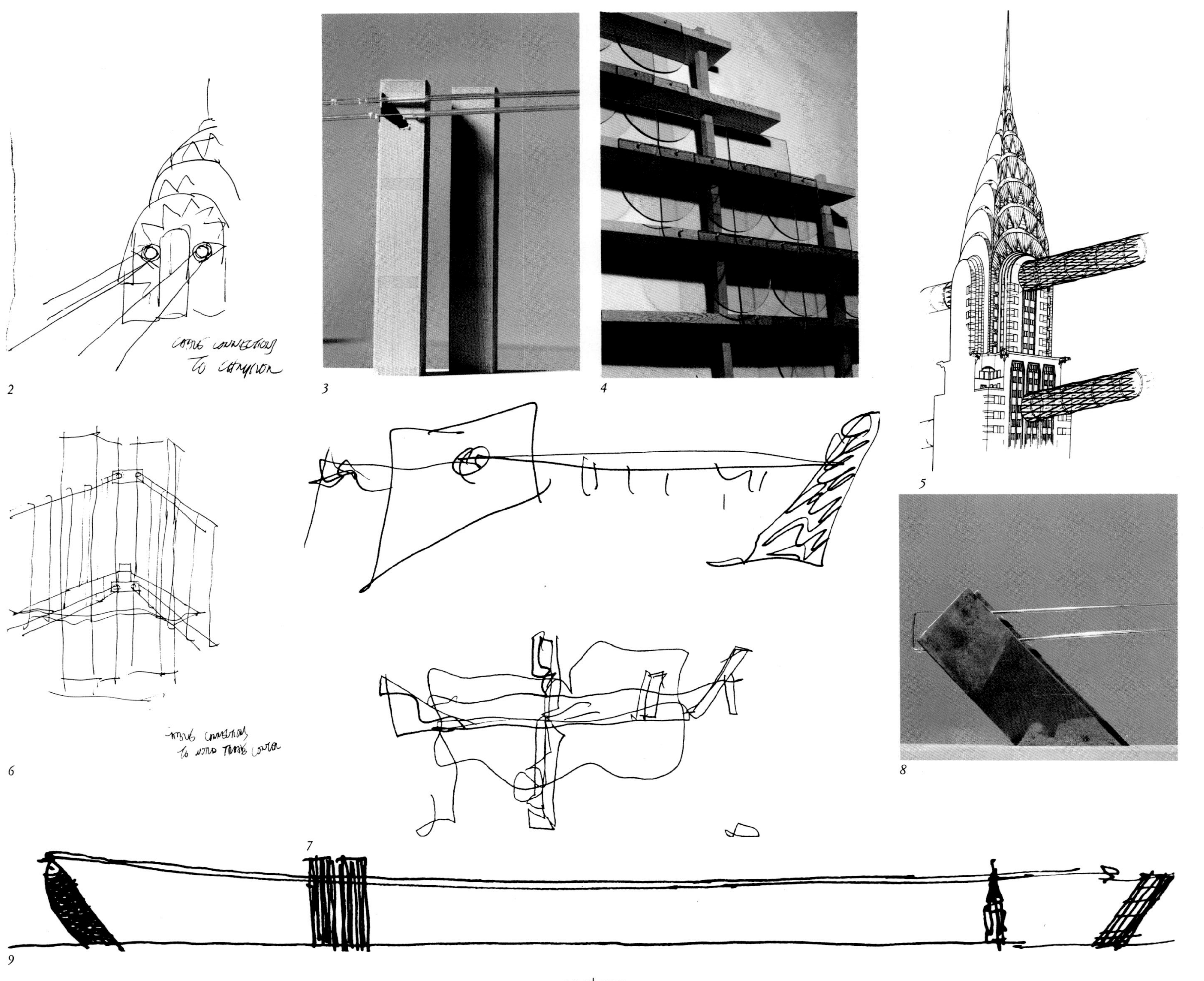
CABLE CONNECTIONS
TO CHRYSLER
CABLE CONNECTIONS
TO WORLD TRADE CENTER
2
3
4
5
6
7
8
9

Lafayette Street Lofts

New York, New York 1981

As large canvases and the installations of conceptual art became standard during the sixties, numbers of artists in Manhattan found sufficient space to live and work on loft floors of the vast, old industrial buildings of the Soho district. As more loft spaces were converted to studio and residential use—and zoning laws passed to protect the homesteaders—galleries, boutiques, and the nonpainting population followed. The handsome loft buildings now have a powerful, nearly iconic cachet which evokes, to space-starved New Yorkers, the luxury of large spaces and the borrowed glamour of pioneering artists.

Both because of his work for Los Angeles' artists and his interest in making "spatial containers," Gehry has been involved in designing loft spaces and their interiors since his work on the Davis House before 1970. To secure a New York base and as a development project, Gehry planned to rehabilitate two loft buildings in Soho. One of the buildings has six stories, the other two, with an open court between them.

In design studies, miniature freestanding "loft buildings" were proposed in, adjacent to, or over the court. The idea basic to the design development studies involves cutting away, from the ground floor of the taller of the existing buildings, three enlarged niches for three new small loft buildings. The three relate sculpturally to three other objects—more small loft buildings, temples, or fish—in the court, on a truss over the court, or on poles above the court.

1-6.Studies of courtyard development

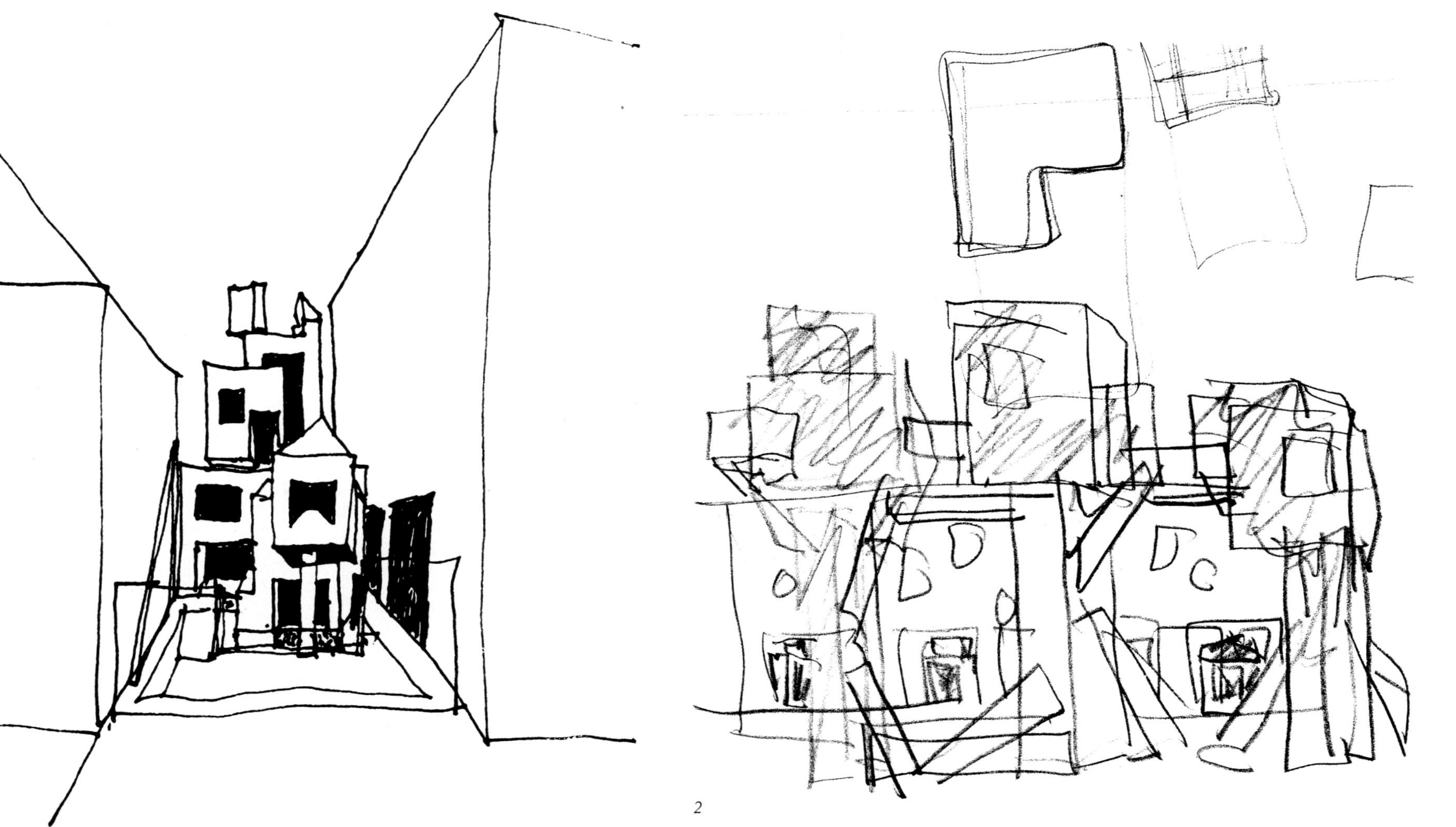

1

2

3

4

5

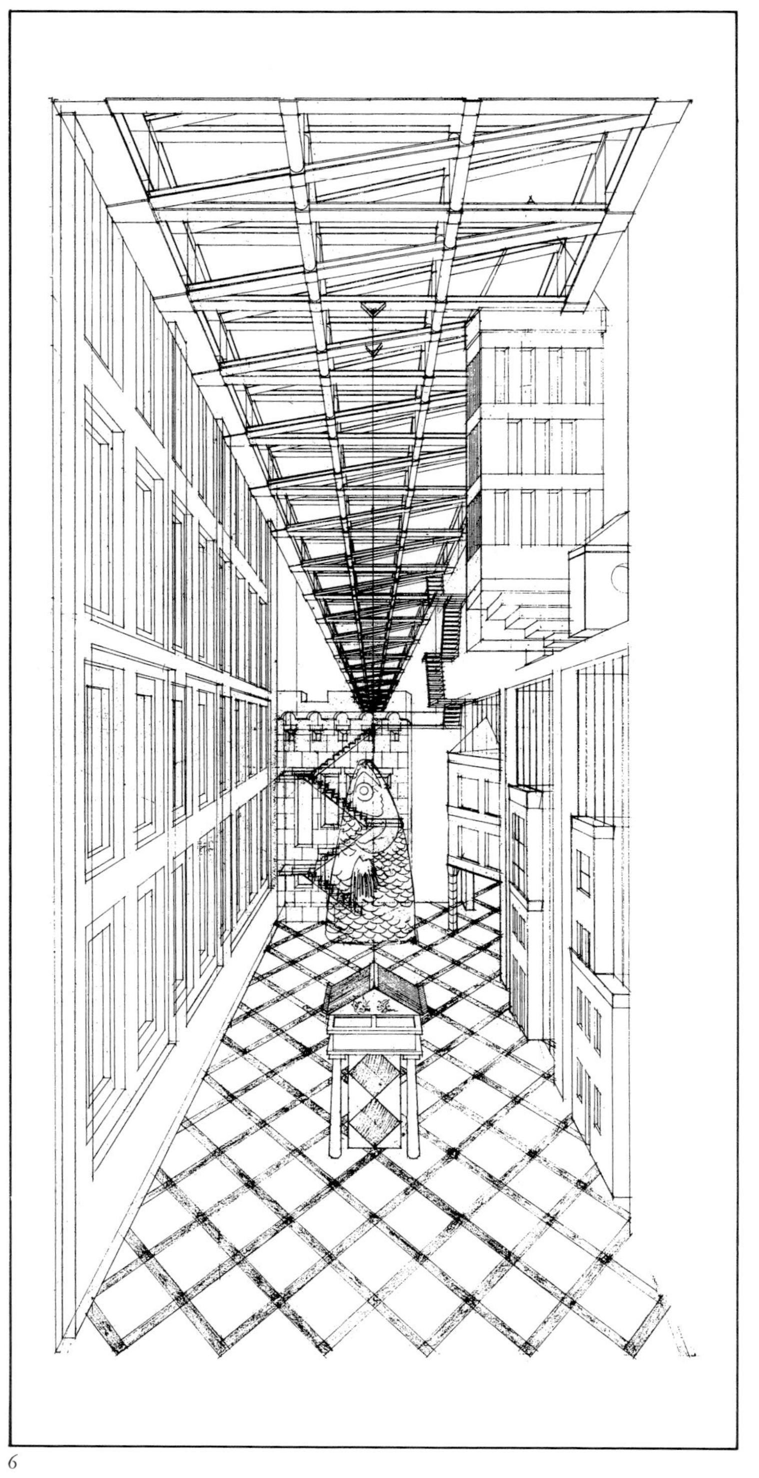
6

14th Street Housing
Atlanta, Georgia 1981

For a development in midtown Atlanta, several innovative approaches were employed to achieve attractive, reasonably priced, in-town housing. Units were scaled down in size from typical speculatively-built apartments, with some of the cost savings thus garnered allocated to locations like the kitchens, in which built-in amenities were designed to assure especially well-functioning, efficient, attractive—and marketable—work areas. At a larger scale, problems of scale and identity were addressed with diligence and economy. The multi-story buildings, for example, were conceived as "bare-bones," cost-efficient structures; out of its simple frames were to grow architectural elements located where they would have the most impact, and provide a reduction in the perceived scale of the building and an image of their dwelling place for individual owners—at the roof line and at ground level.

These same ideas and strategies were applied to the detached housing units which form a street edge at the perimeter of the site. These buildings not only use small-scale architectural elements to create a sense of the residential and of individual identity, their very diversity was designed to suggest a typical city street, the fabric of which has been created over time and in different architectural forms. Further, their scale helps moderate the over-all perceptual scale of the project and also suggests a hierarchical order not usually seen in projects of this sort. In a sense, this walled complex, fitted out so carefully with urban character, becomes in and of itself a microcosm of the city.

1.Studies for tower 2.Tower model 3.Site 4.Model

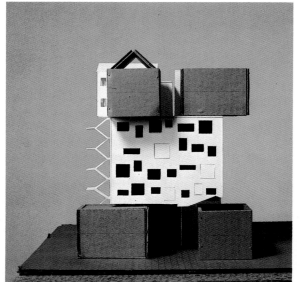

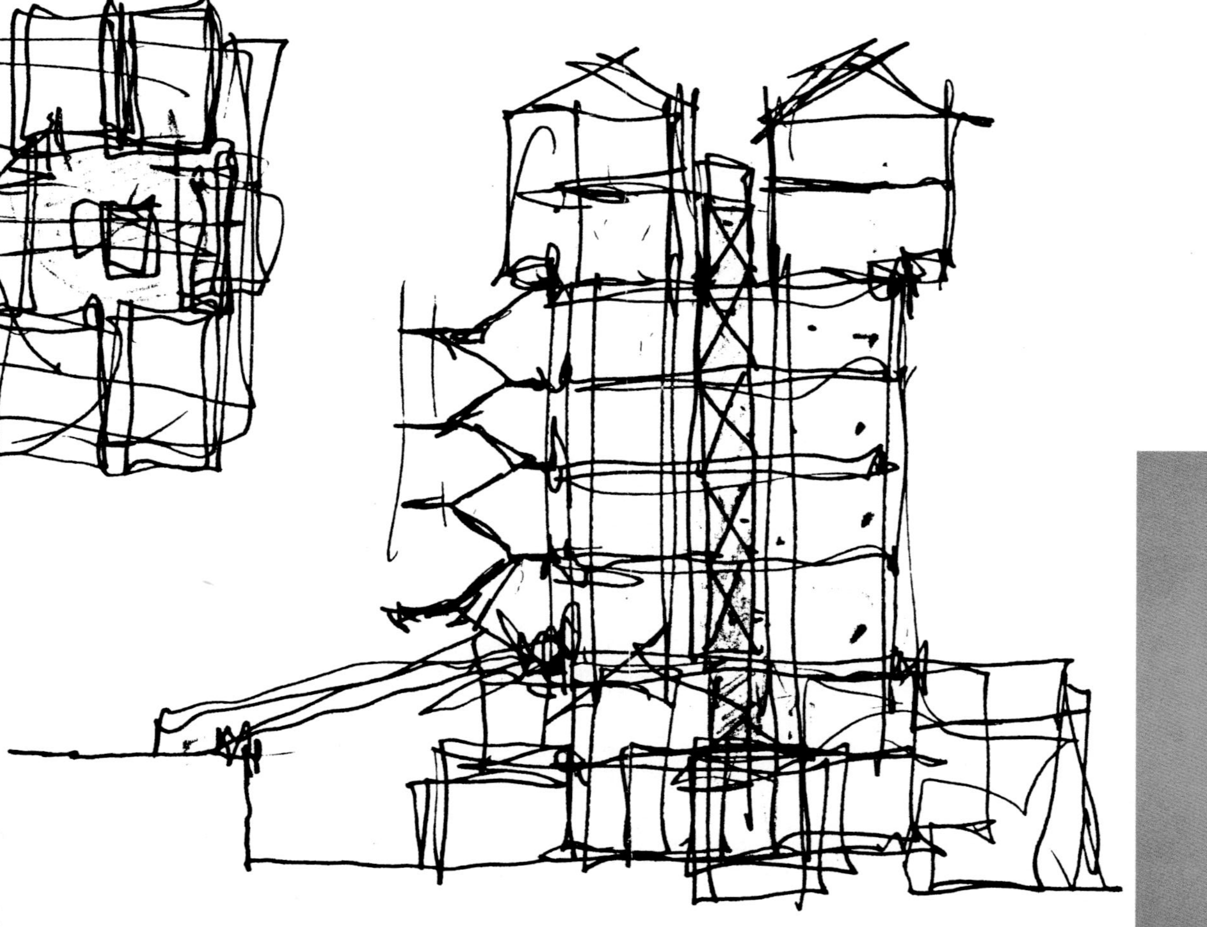

1

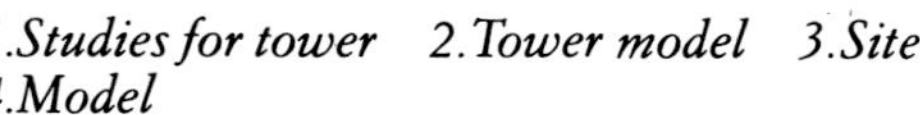

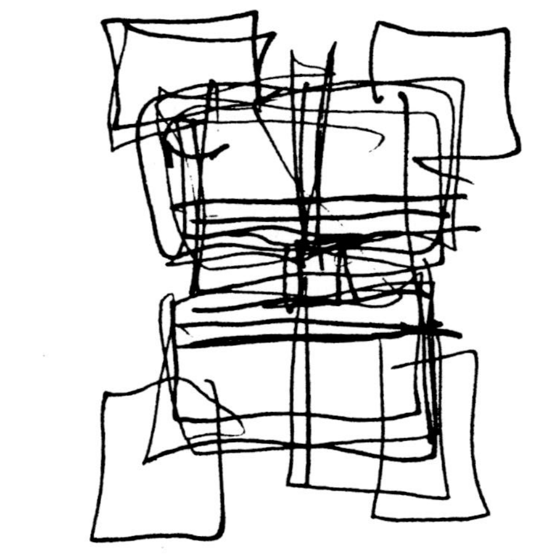

2

4

Benson House
Los Angeles, California 1981

"A man's house is his castle."
—Sir Edward Coke, 1644

Approaching the Benson House along the crest of the hill on which it is located, one's first view is of an apparently one-room box sheathed in brown asbestos shingles. To one side, two small plywood boxes are visible, one of vertical proportions, one horizontal. The boxes—a chimney, and skylight monitor—offer a preview of the larger composition of the house visible upon closer inspection. A sort of negative plinth is made by cutting into the face of the hill. Within this area, edged by retaining walls, is a box from which the chimney and skylight protrude, containing living and dining room, and a bedroom tower, the top of which is seen on approach.

The Benson children were also consulted as clients in the design process, and images of drawbridges and a tower-top fort developed with their direction. The areas between the two building parts and the retaining walls make a kind of moat. Bridges across the moat and stairways lace the two buildings together. In addition to the two primary forms, a carport was planned, originally seen as "a roof element in the shape of a cloud."

1.Sketch 2.East elevation tower 3.South elevation tower 4.West elevation tower 5.North elevation tower 6.1st floor 7.2nd floor 8.Mezzanine 9.Roof 10.East elevation, living box 11.West elevation, living box 12.North elevation, living box 13.South elevation, living box

1

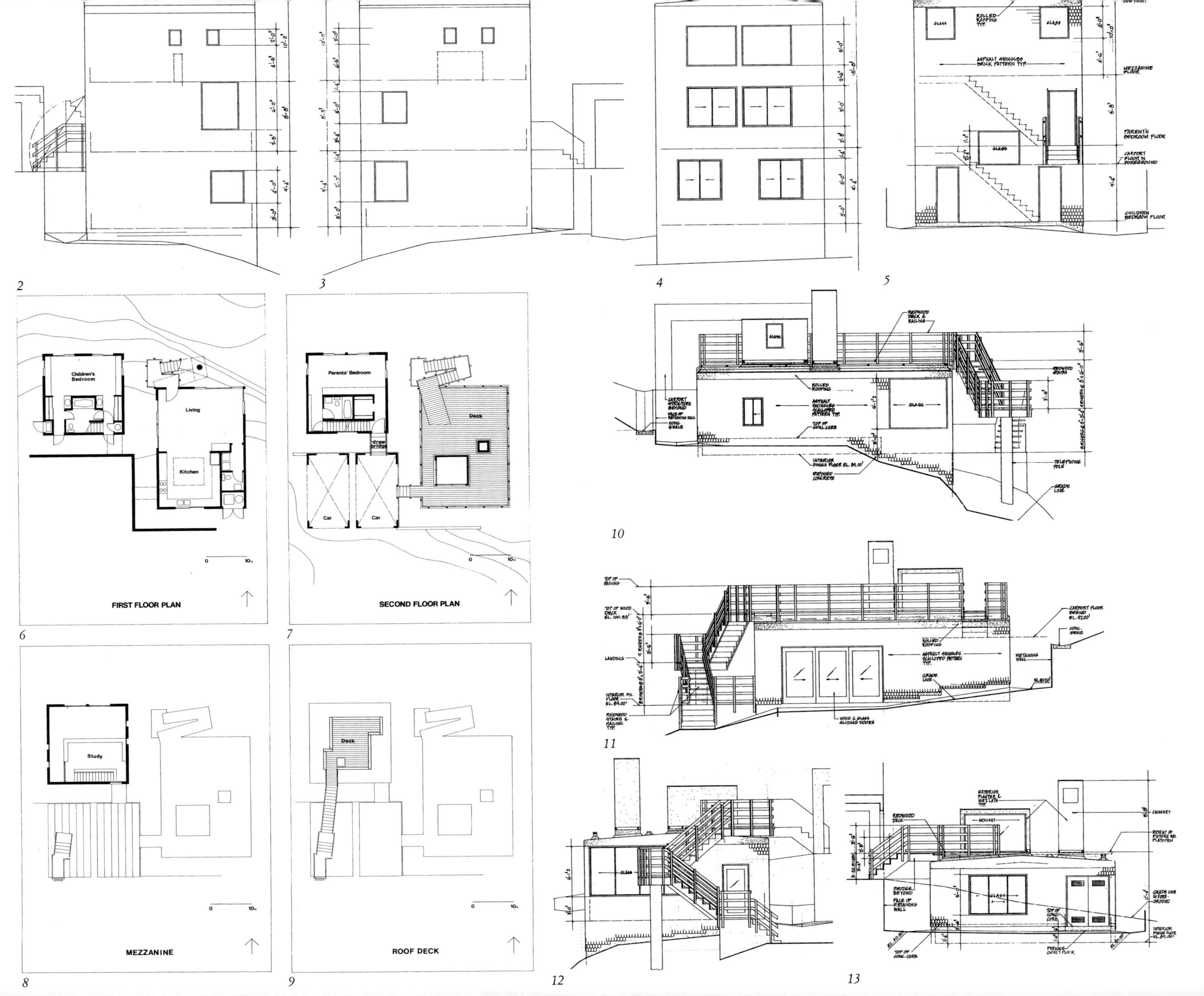

2 3 4 5 6 7 8 9 10 11 12 13

104.Model 5–6. Living box with tower beyond 7.Moat

1

2

3

4

5

6

8

9

Screen Actors Guild
Studio City, California 1981

Ventura Boulevard winds along the feet of the Santa Monica Mountains. Development along it is generally suburban in scale and density—small buildings set on the slope of the mountains which rise dramatically behind them. For one such sloping site, a private developer and the Screen Actors Guild planned, as a joint venture, an office building of 140,000 square feet. The latter group was to be the chief tenant, assuming one-third of the planned office space; retail commercial space and a parking structure were also to be built.
The scale of the proposed project was of a bulk which, if built as a monolithic block, would appear disturbingly large from the boulevard and obscure the rise of the mountains behind. Accordingly, in the design, the office space is separated into three blocks. Between them, atria are developed with small retail outlets on paths and plazas winding up from street level. The uppermost plazas are above the parking structure built into the hillside at the rear of the building. The back walls of the atria screen buildings to the rear, but are cut away above, along a line replicating that of the mountains behind, to admit south light.
The retail "hill towns" within the atria re-establish the scale of neighboring buildings and suggest an idealized alternate vision of buildings in an undulating landscape. The scenographic revision would, it seems, have been an appropriate setting for part of an industry devoted to fabricating illusions.

1.Preliminary sketch 2.Preliminary model 3-4.Atria 5.Model 6.Plaza level plan

1

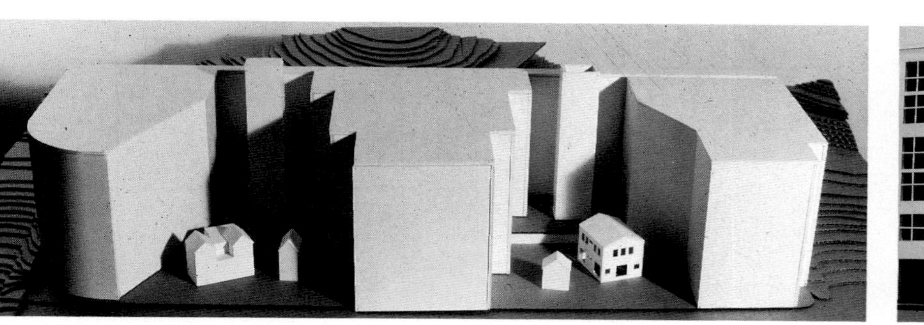

2

3

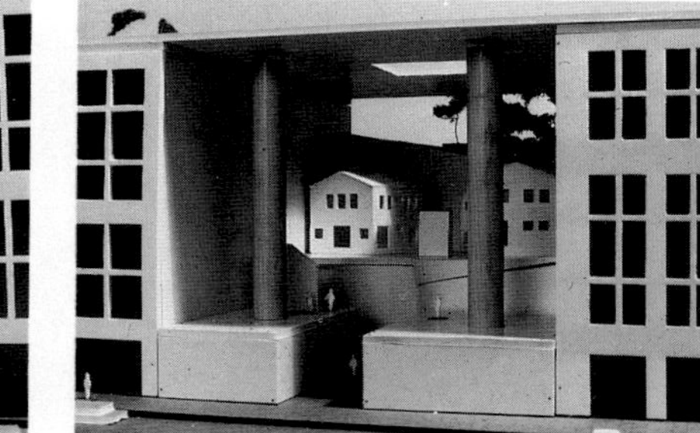

4

5

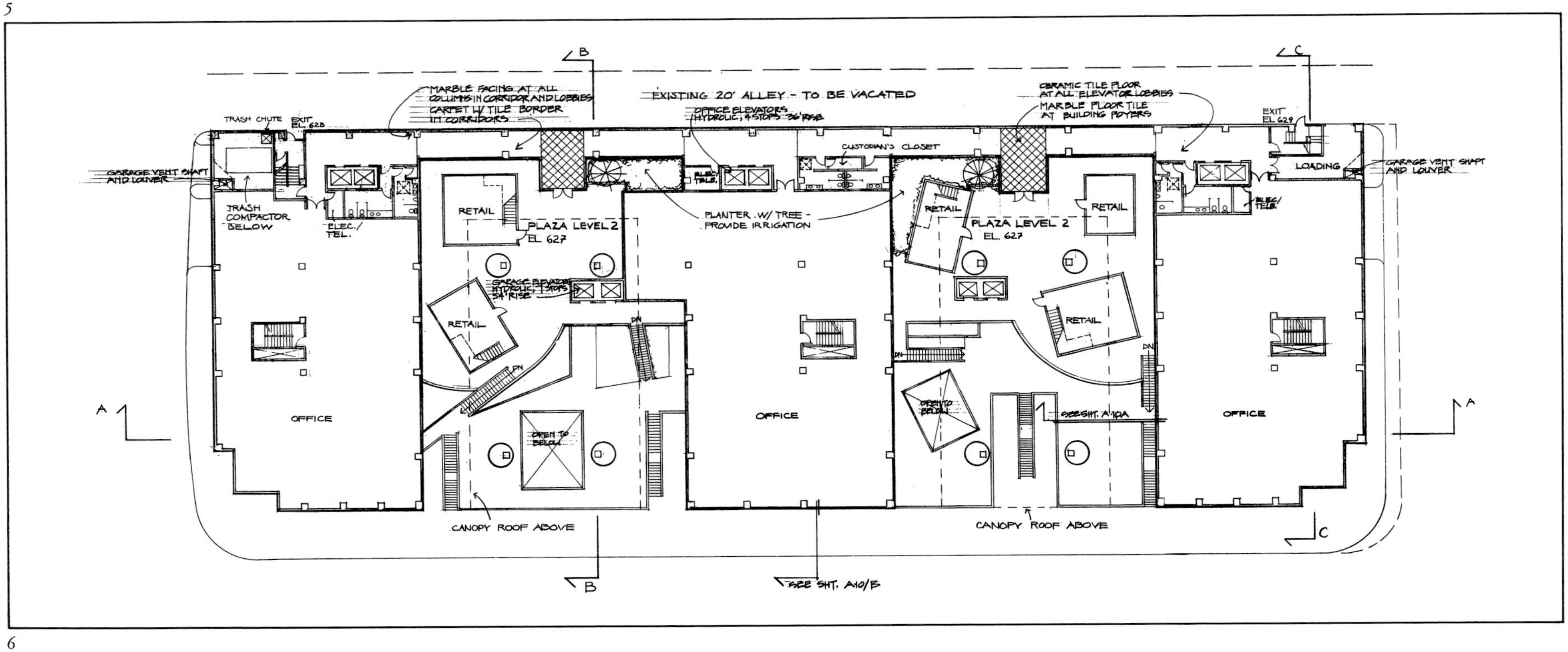

6

EXISTING 20' ALLEY - TO BE VACATED

MARBLE FACING AT ALL COLUMNS IN CORRIDOR AND LOBBIES
CARPET W/ TILE BORDER IN CORRIDORS

OFFICE ELEVATORS HYDROLIC, 4 STOPS 36' RISE

CUSTODIAN'S CLOSET

CERAMIC TILE FLOOR AT ALL ELEVATOR LOBBIES
MARBLE FLOOR TILE AT BUILDING FOYERS

TRASH CHUTE

EXIT EL. 628

EXIT EL. 629

GARAGE VENT SHAFT AND LOUVER

TRASH COMPACTOR BELOW

ELEC./TEL.

LOADING

RETAIL

PLAZA LEVEL 2
EL. 627

GARAGE ELEVATOR HYDROLIC, 1 STOPS 34' RISE

PLANTER W/ TREE - PROVIDE IRRIGATION

OPEN TO BELOW

OFFICE

CANOPY ROOF ABOVE

SEE SHT. A10/A

SEE SHT. A10/B

House for a Film Maker

Los Angeles, California 1981

The bachelor's quarters are a compound of individual buildings rather than a single house. The site is a densely vegetated canyon floor which slopes from a steep hillside at the east toward a stream to the west. There are a number of components, originally meant to be relatively interchangeable functionally—a living room, master bedroom, garage, and guest house/study. Also designed are a pool, and a few site embellishments like a low, stucco-covered wall. Each component is designed as a different shape and surface material. Thus far three parts have been built: a red garage (designed as fiberglass, built of plywood), a concrete block living and dining pavilion, and a two-story master bedroom suite sheathed in natural finish plywood panels bounded and held in place with extruded aluminum "reglet" sections. The plywood panels of the master bedroom have been detailed as shutters and rolling panels to allow the box to be opened to the court and stream. Views across the canyon and upstream can be seen from its private roof deck. The south wall of the living room and kitchen opens to the court with views of the canyon ridges through its skylights. Its floors are stone. One bay of the garage is used as office and studio space, opening to the yard as well as the driveway. Planned are a glass-over-wood-stud wall, greenhouse/sitting room, and a pink stucco guest house. The west wall of the latter is to serve as an outdoor movie projection screen.

In the ongoing exploration of the composition of disparate architectural "pieces" which has characterized much of the work in the seventies, the film maker's house is something of a watershed. The "spatial container" associated with such projects—from the literal one of the Berger, Berger, Kahn Shafton and Moss law offices through the sort of earthworks suggestion of a container at the Benson House—is here reduced to implication by topography and one disjunct low wall. "The halls of the house," according to Gehry, "are disconnected from the house and placed in the yard."

1-3.Studies 4.Model 5.Garage, living room, bedroom 6.Plywood with riglets 7.Computer projection 8.Garage

1

2

3

4

5

6

7

8

Indiana Avenue Houses
Venice, California 1981

The three big boxes on Indiana Avenue were designed as artists' studios and houses. The scale of the houses in Venice characteristically borders on the miniature, with their standard-size windows and doors seeming oddly over-scaled. Gehry's program—fifteen hundred-square-foot houses, with double-story studio spaces and a garage at the rear—made physical prominence in the neighborhood inevitable. Adapting the peculiarities of the perceptual scale of the neighborhood buildings, elements on the three studio buildings have been oversized, giving the paradoxical impression that the comparatively large buildings are somehow rather small. These overscaled elements—a bay window in one house, a form pretending to be a chimney in another, and a flamboyantly fictional stair in the third, were intended as well to "become abstract sculptures." The project is essentially three wood-framed boxes differentiated by sheathing—green asphalt shingles on one, unpainted plywood on another, and sky-blue stucco on a third—and by the various large elements and distensions by which their composer has sculpted them. Early project sketches show explorations in excising and twisting the boxes in some concert one to another. Thus the skew of the "chimney" and of an over-scaled window in the middle house can be seen, if one so chooses, as responsible for the curious angle at which the improbable "stair" leans against the adjacent house. On the other hand, as in much of Gehry's work, one may choose to abandon all search for formal relationships and retreat to the comfort of enjoying the composition while scratching one's head—the pleasurably mysterious results of careful, meticulous composition.
As with the house for Ron Davis, it was intended that the architecture provide only the building shell, so that each artist, in response to the shell and his own needs and sensibilities, would participate in creating unforeseeable collaborative works. The interiors of the three wooden boxes, then, were left as open loft space with exposed wood framing, to be finished and furnished by the artists.

1.Studies 2-4.Model 5.South elevation 6.Roof plan

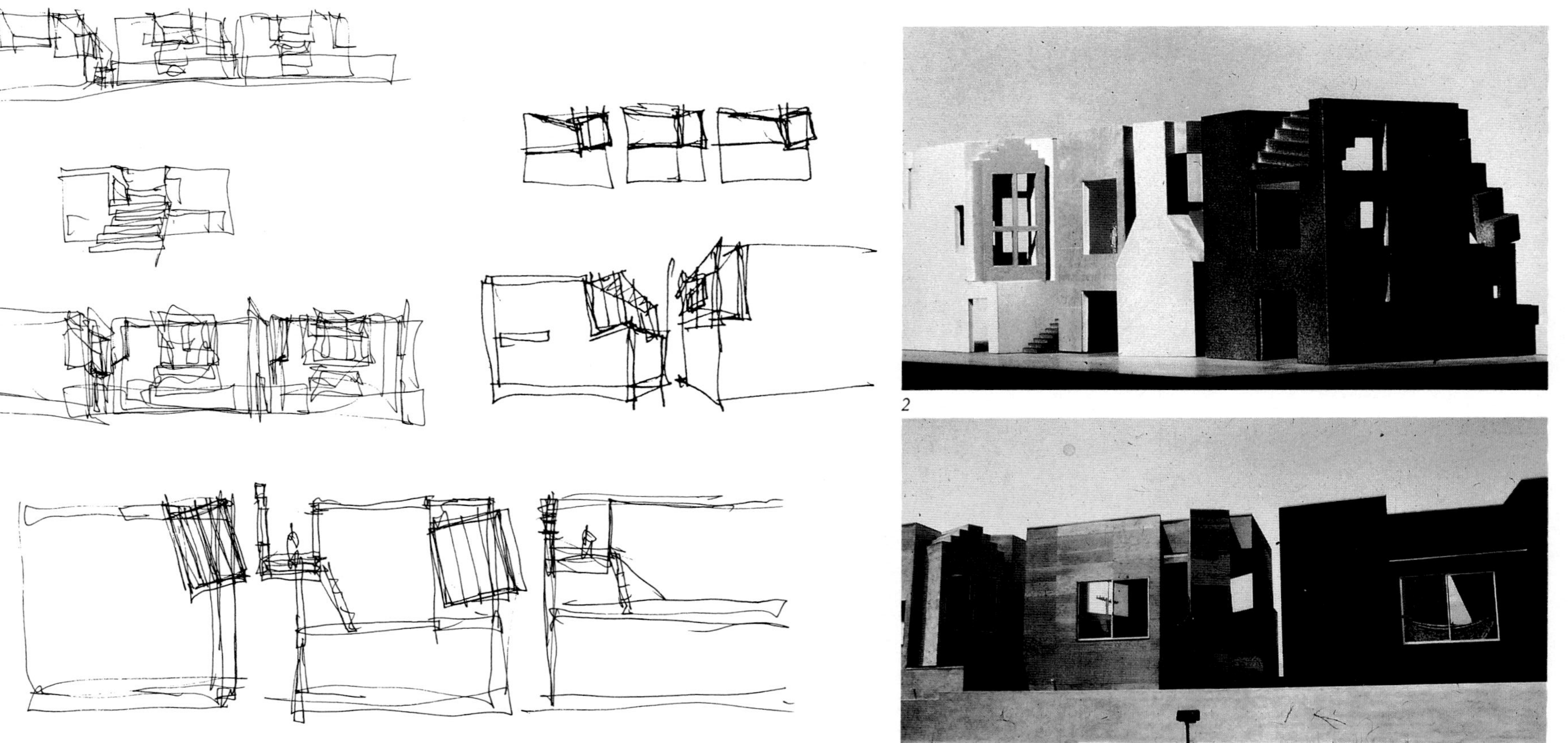

1

2

3

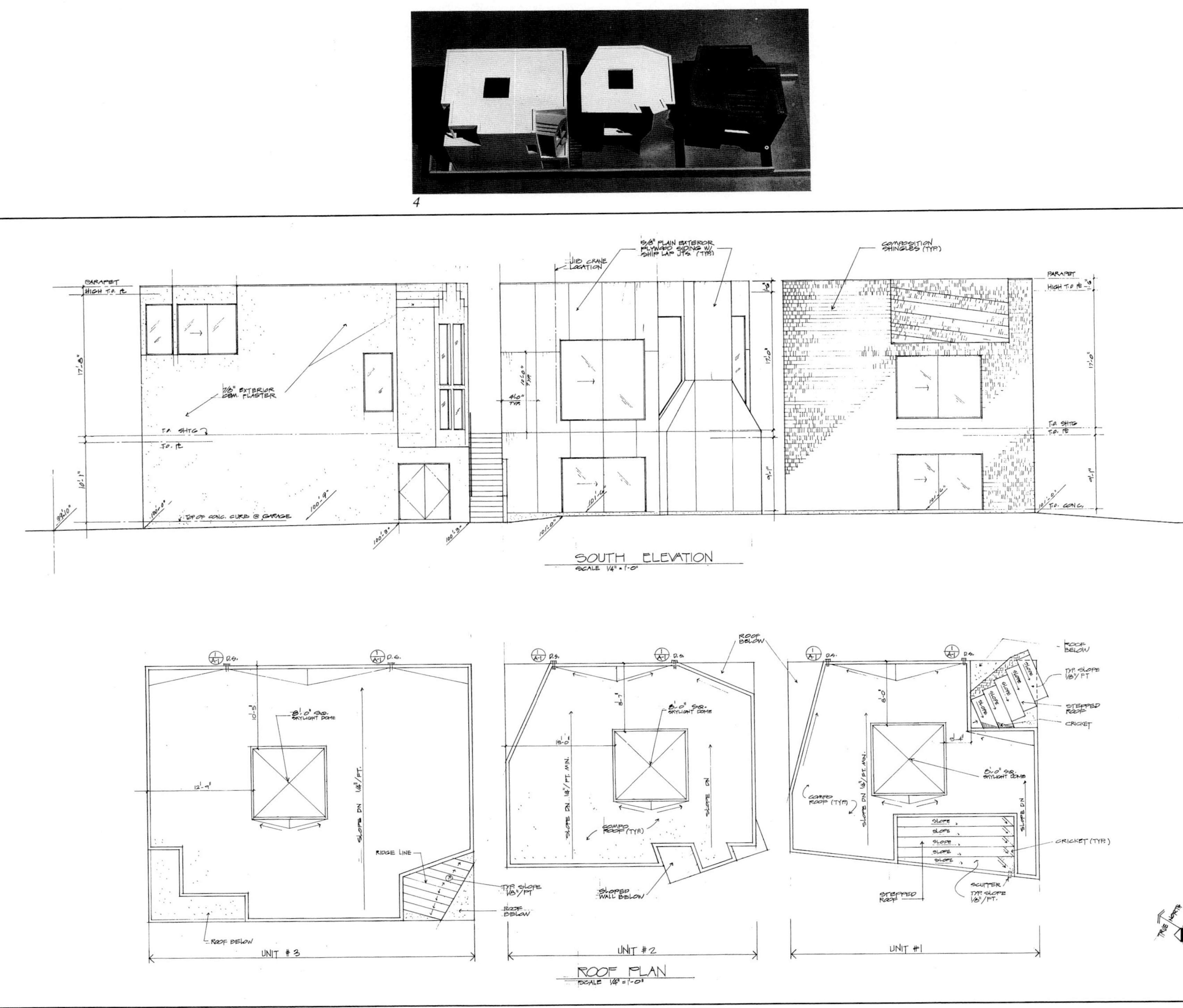
SOUTH ELEVATION
SCALE 1/4" = 1'-0"
ROOF PLAN
SCALE 1/4" = 1'-0"
UNIT #3
UNIT #2
UNIT #1
COMPOSITION SHINGLES (TYP)
5/8" PLAIN EXTERIOR PLYWOOD SIDING W/ SHIP LAP JTS. (TYP)
JIB CRANE LOCATION
7/8" EXTERIOR CEM. PLASTER
PARAPET
HIGH T.O. PL.
T.O. SHTG
T.O. PL.
T.O. CONC.
TOP OF CONC. CURB @ GARAGE
8'-0" SQ. SKYLIGHT DOME
SLOPE DN 1/4"/FT.
SLOPE DN 1/8"/FT. MIN.
COMPO ROOF (TYP)
RIDGE LINE
TYP. SLOPE 1/8"/FT
ROOF BELOW
SLOPED WALL BELOW
STEPPED ROOF
CRICKET
CRICKET (TYP)
SCUTTER
TRUE NORTH

4

5-6

1,2.Venice 3.Exterior view
4."Stair" 5."Chimney" 6."Bay window"
7-9.Interiors

1

2

3

4 *5* *6*

7 *8* *9*

Paramount Theatre Shell

Oakland, California 1981

The Paramount Theatre has an opulent art deco interior and landmark status, but acoustics less than ideal for symphony performances. In a design for, and dedicated to, Calvin Simmons, a demountable orchestra shell is hung within the theater for Oakland Symphony performances. Walls of undulating hardwood are designed to be surmounted by a canopy resembling nesting scallop shells. The doubly curving hardwood surfaces would help mix sounds on stage and reflect them into the theater.

1.Interior 2.Shell

1

2

Binder House

Los Angeles, California 1981

The site on which the Binder House was to be built is on a hillside in a Beverly Hills canyon. A house already existed on the site, but it was too small for the clients' program and too close to the street (there is little level land between the street and the hill). Gehry designed a structure with five thousand square feet on three levels. The ground floor was to be garage and studio space, providing a base on which the living quarters would be raised to a height allowing views out of the canyon. Four distinct, two-story building forms and volumes were proposed, one containing the living room, another the dining room and kitchen, the third the guest, children's and recreation rooms, and the fourth the master bedroom suite. The latter was to be salvaged from the existing house and supported on stilts above a new pool. A long two-story wall was to be built as a buffer to the street, with the circulation spine of the house directly behind it. The project will not be built.

1.Sketches

4

5

Seventeen Artists in the Sixties
Los Angeles County Museum of Art 1981

The exhibition reviewed work done in the 1960s by seventeen artists, most of whom work in Los Angeles. Included were Bengston, Bell, Moses, Kienholz, Irwin, Kaufmann, Hockney, Francis, McLaughlin, Berman, Naumann, Ruscha, Price, Voulkos, Goode, Diebenkorn, and Davis. Unlike the Russian Avant-Garde and German Expressionists shows in which a great deal of unfamiliar material had to be organized with a certain didactic intent, the sixties show was organized as a series of individual retrospectives. Individual galleries were designed for each artist, tailored to the scale and spirit of his work. The galleries were arranged along a central spine allowing comprehensive views of many artists' work simultaneously. Sparing use of color—yellows, mauve, grays, and browns—were used with predominate white to draw one's attention through the exhibit. Portraits of the artists and contemporary photographs were integrated into the show.

1.Installation mock-up 2-5.Views along corridor

1

2

3

4

5

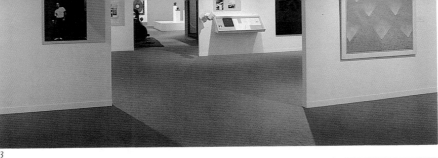

Smith House

Brentwood, California 1981

So long, Frank Lloyd Wright.
—Simon and Garfunkel

When the Steeves house, the first project illustrated in this volume, was built in 1959, the site was in a relatively undeveloped neighborhood. The house's two intersecting rectilinear forms, reminiscent in composition and detail of the work of Frank Lloyd Wright and Richard Neutra, follow the level area of a promontory. Twenty years later, when Gehry was asked to design an addition to the house for new owners, the neighborhood had become densely developed with a heterogeneous mix of relatively small houses. Given the changes in the neighborhood, the configuration of the slope of the site, the scale and compositional completeness of the original house, and the changes in the architect's interests during the intervening years, a mimetic extension of the existing house was not designed. Instead, it was decided to develop the new facilities as a series of attached but discreet building elements in a more informal arrangement. Despite the architect's sensitivity to context, the design was denied approval by the Bel Air Fine Arts Commission.

The site plan suggests that the "truncated" wing of the original house grew, twisting to find level ground. The spine of the axis is slightly askew; the elements along it are more so. The link between the original house and the new facilities was to be a sort of loggia, made of glazing over two-by-eight stud framing; it is set four degrees off the geometry of the original house. To its east are a new entry, a small, metal-clad, pedimented service area, a cruciform kitchen clad in ceramic tile with clerestory lighting, a brick bathhouse and a pergola made of a brick screen wall, wood columns, and trellis. Off the family room, a screened porch edges the swimming pool planned at the other end of the loggia. To the west of the loggia are the master bedroom and bath. The plywood sheathing of the former is designed to suggest a deeper volume perspectively. Earlier studies show an interest in developing variations on the theme of cross-axial planning which characterize the composition of the original house. Two cruciform shaped "buildings" descending in scale with the descent of the site elevation, define the splay of the addition from the original building. A major diagonal cross axis is developed along a cross contour of the site: emphasized by a hipped roof on the family room, two bay windows are developed at the corners along the diagonal. Where the diagonal axis crosses that of the house (slightly skewed by the loggia) a sort of clearing is made with the pool "bumped" into alignment with the diagonal. A gazebo further down the slope marks the continuance of that axis. Wright, the progenitor of the aesthetic represented by the original house, devoted himself to "the destruction of the box"—of static enclosure. Gehry has followed the argument a step further, destroying the container of individual spaces. A system of screen walls, colonnades, retaining walls, and a moat-like ditch are the remaining fragments of a box exploded.

1.Study: eagle and fish colonnade 2-3.Studies 4.Site plan 5.East elevation 6.South elevation

1

3

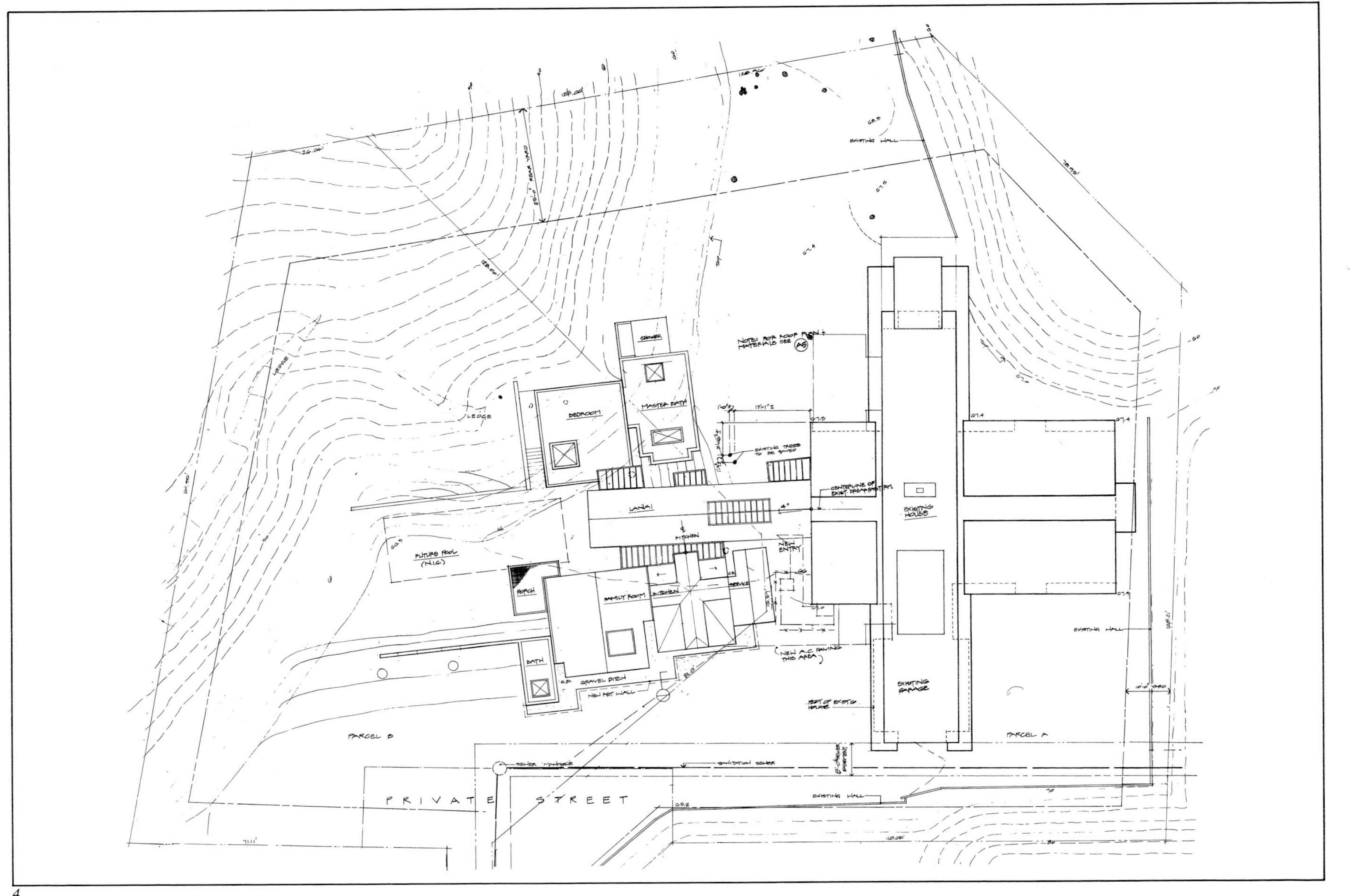
PRIVATE STREET
PARCEL A
PARCEL B
EXISTING HOUSE
EXISTING GARAGE
LANAI
KITCHEN
NEW ENTRY
BEDROOM
MASTER BATH
SHOWER
FAMILY ROOM
SERVICE
PORCH
BATH
FUTURE POOL (N.I.C.)
LEDGE
EXISTING WALL
GRAVEL DITCH
NEW RET. WALL
SANITATION SEWER
(NEW A.C. PAVING THIS AREA)
PERGOLA
OPEN
FAMILY ROOM
KITCHEN
SERVICE
ENTRY

4

5

6

1. View from south 2. View from northwest 3. Kitchen utility room with lanai beyond 4. View along east wall

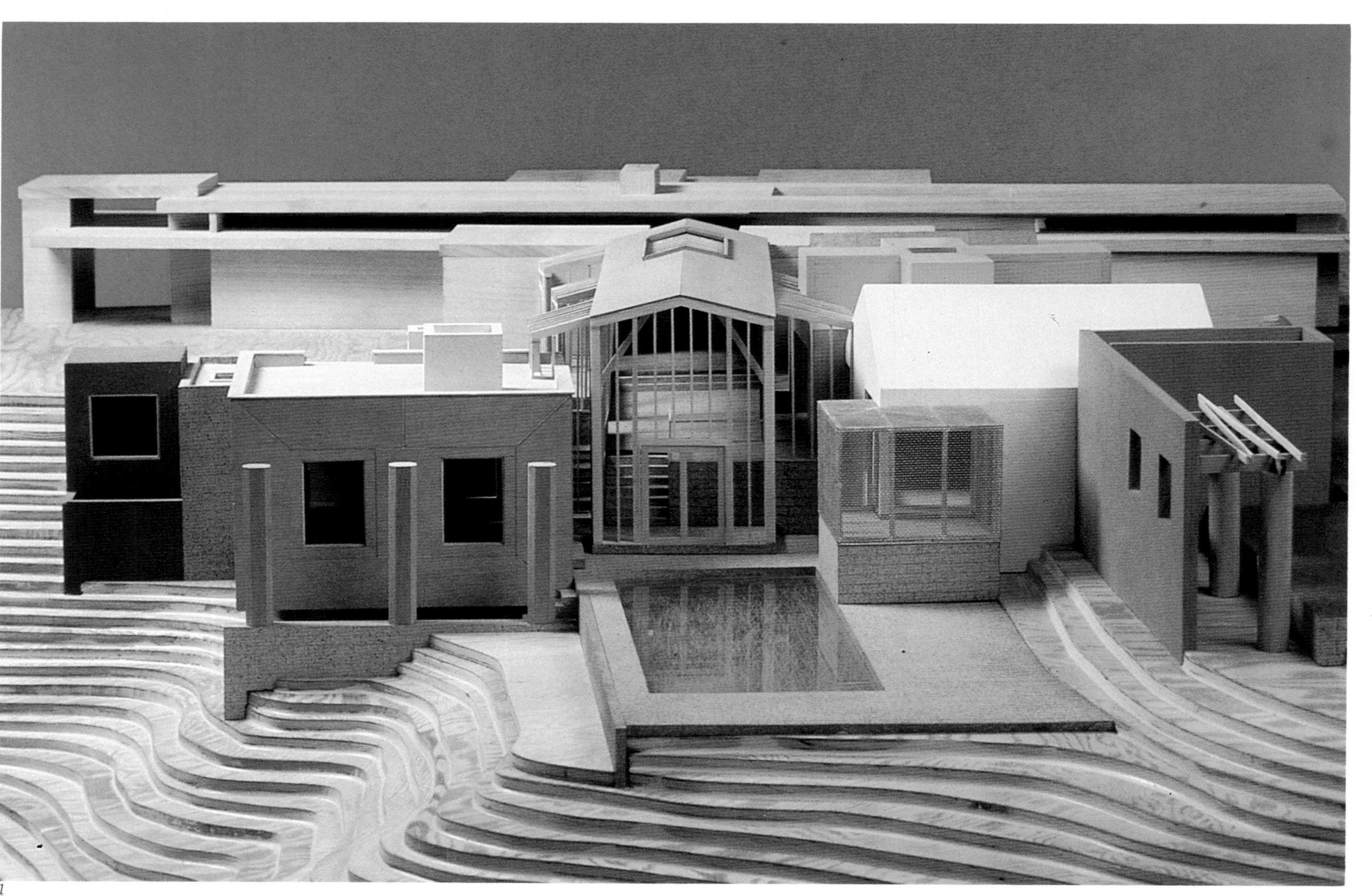

1

2

3

4

Loyola Law School

Los Angeles, California 1981–84

The common plan followed in this country of making one large expensive building, I consider as unfortunately erroneous. It is infinitely better to . . . make it what it should be in fact, an academical village.
Thomas Jefferson, of his design for a university

Loyola Marymount University's Law School is located in an area outside downtown Los Angeles which can best be described as gray. Large undistinguished commercial buildings line Olympic Boulevard. Along the side streets are slightly smaller undistinguished run-down buildings, which in turn give way to poor housing. Sensitive to context, the law school's original buildings are large, gray and bland. Gehry and associated architects Brooks-Collier's commission involved not only an expansion of facilities (fifty-five thousand square feet of new construction and an additional fifty-five thousand square feet of renovation) but also the creation of a real campus. The faculty believed the quality of education was impaired because the existing facilities offered neither inducement to remain at the school between classes nor places for casual meeting. As a result, students rarely enjoyed the profits of extracurricular discussions with the faculty or other students. Architecture and context were thus conspiring, the faculty feared, to render an already high-pressure course of study inhumane. Faculty members also spoke of their hope that a sense of permanence and symbolic reference to the history and traditions of law could be evoked in the new construction.
Gehry worked with the faculty and university administration to develop a building program to achieve these desired ends. To introduce a more human scale and to promote cross-campus traffic, it was decided to build small individual buildings to house some of the elements of the program.
This planning principle also represents a cost-control strategy, as all special functions requiring atypical structure (e.g., high ceilings, long spans over large open spaces) are taken out of the main building envelope. Against the backdrop of a large classroom, office, and student center building, two small classroom buildings, a moot court, and a chapel are arranged along a spine extending from the north classroom building, next to the school's garage, to the other instructional hall at the south. The placement of buildings, building parts, and objects along the spine is seemingly casual, which—with the human traffic moving among them—creates a more lively environment. This composition of casualness—with its layering of objects, buildings, columns, stairs and landscape elements that creates changes in scale relationships and a modulation of open spaces—is, according to Gehry, in part learned from Oriental compositions like the Zen garden of Ryoanji—made simply of rocks, raked sand, a wall, a veranda, and trees behind a wall. Despite the punster's temptation to call the area thus created a court, is in character and intent a forum: It is a public area where a number of civic and religious buildings are located and in which public gathering and debate are fostered. The model of the Roman Forum had been suggested in discussions with the faculty. When other business took Gehry near Rome during the design phase, he stopped for a tour—but of the work of Borromini: "I only went to seen Borromini buildings that I had seen before; I just wanted to reinforce what I already knew."
That cross-pollination of the Roman Forum with Borromini is perhaps most evident in the first part of the project to be built—the Burns Building, a large classroom and office structure. Toward the neighborhood it presents a quiet gray face. Toward the forum is an ochre-colored screen facade intended as a a backdrop for the more animated forms of the smaller buildings in front of it. Its main stair and two fire stairs break through the facade, binding the internal traffic of the building to the forum. The main, central stair sweeps up from the forum at a raked angle, pierces the facade, and reappears for another twisting ascent above the forum. It culminates in a greenhouse area under a glass gabled roof. In the regularity and severity of its openings and in the centrality of its main stair, the building achieves a solemnity enlivened and enriched by the stairs climbing against it. The angle of the main stair also succeeds in turning the campus toward the main boulevard, a route theretofore ignored in the orientation of the campus buildings.
The smaller buildings face the court but are also designed to relate to this adjacent primary street, forming a symbolic gate to the campus from it. The court, classroom, and chapel buildings are designed to suggest classical dignity and monumentality within the means of relatively inexpensive materials. On the chapel, for example, the rich materials of fine furniture are suggested by the use of a Finnish plywood usually used for concrete formwork. The material has a smooth, dark brown, durable, resin-impregnated finish; on the chapel its edges are protected by detailing with the aluminum reglets used in the House for a Film Maker. It is in their scale and proportions that these buildings are lent an impression of monumentality. Similarly, the tower of the chapel and the over-scaled "columns" in front of the court building are composed to evoke, not to attempt imitation of, the vocabulary of classical monuments.

1-2.4.Sketches 3.5.Model 6.Chapel

2

3

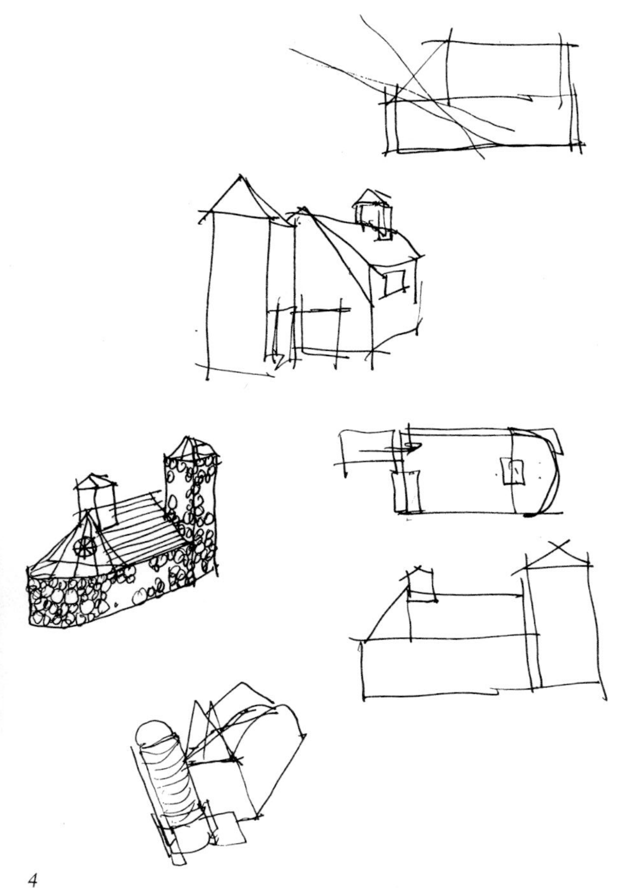

4

5

6

1.Burns Building 2,3.Views past Court House toward South Instructional Hall

1

2

3

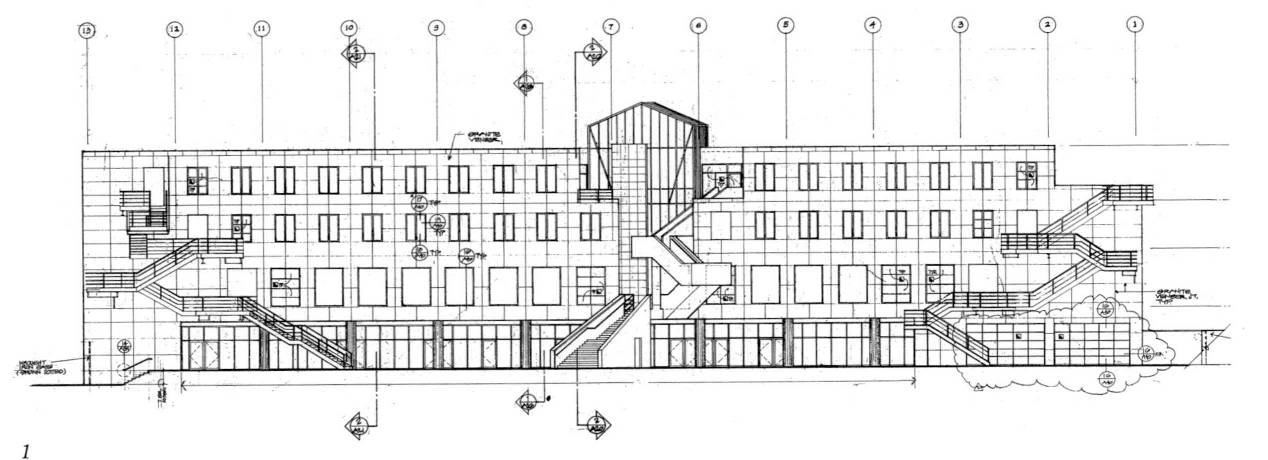

1

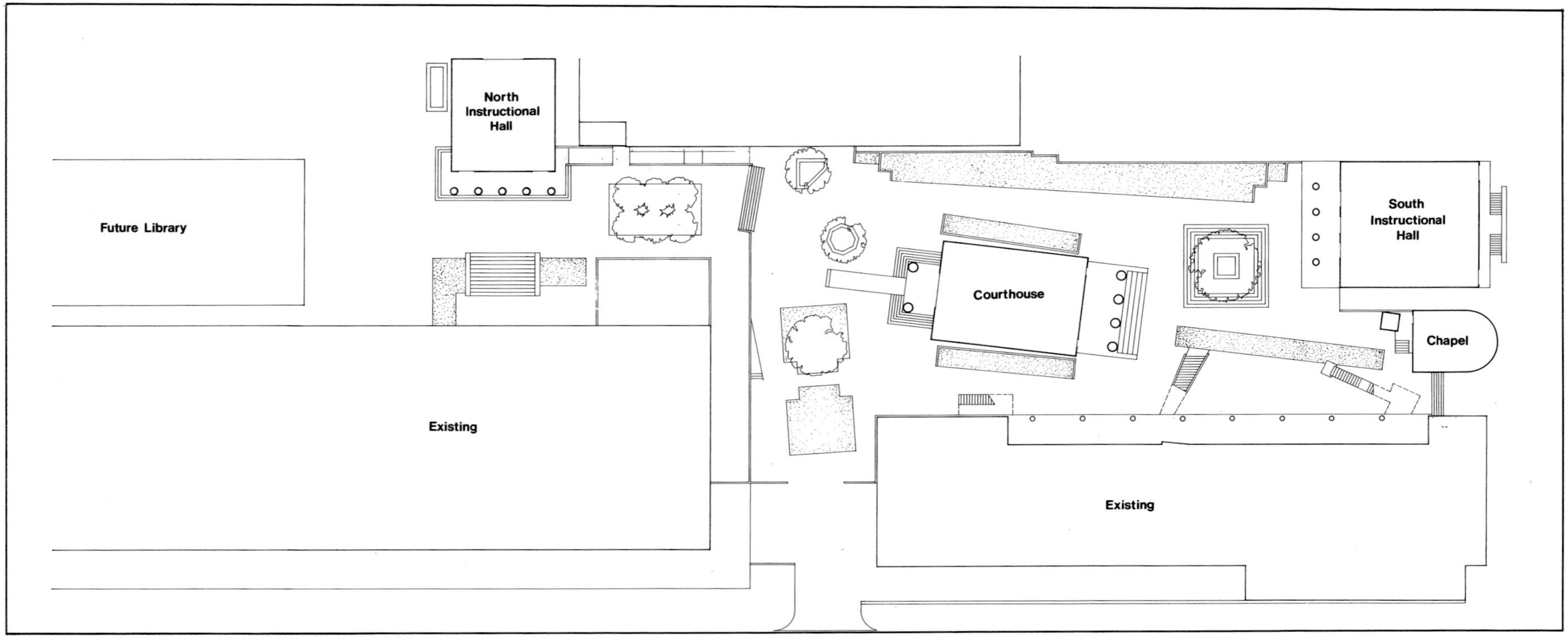

North Instructional Hall

Future Library

Courthouse

South Instructional Hall

Chapel

Existing

Existing

2

3

1.Elevation, Burns Building 2.Site plan 3.View from Olympic Boulevard

1-3. General views

2

3

Central Business District
Kalamazoo, Michigan 1981

The Michigan state chapter of the American Institute of Architects sponsored a week-long intensive design study of downtown Kalamazoo. Four teams of students, each led by a prominent architect, were asked to develop ideas for revitalizing the city's declining central business district. The Gehry team proposed sculpting a new natural and architectural environment sufficiently attractive to draw people back into town from the suburbs and create a viable urban environment. A "tried and true developer strategy" was employed to achieve these ends and in particular to draw residential development: An existing creek was dammed to create perennially attractive waterfront lots. At one side of the newly created lake a parking structure—serving new housing and commercial development—was terraced to create zones for individual buiding lots overlooking the lake—a terraced pedestal for individual houses. New commercial lakefront development backed up to the existing downtown mall. The lake further provided a more striking entrance to the city center—a causeway leading over the lake, punctuated by a new hotel in the shape of a fish. The design of the architectural and urban forms are heterogeneous, a characteristic Gehry sees as basic to American cities. By following his convictions about the importance of diversity and about the power of sculptural forms and spaces in the design of cities, he found that "all the ideas I'd been following in my work up to that point turned up in the same project."

1-2.Study sketches 3-4.Model

1

2

3

4

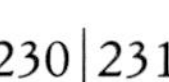

World Savings Bank
Denver, Colorado 1982

The site of the "small bank job in Denver" is a corner of a shopping center on a strip highway. The sketches and models shown below represent the earliest studies for the project. Preliminary and far from the design eventually proposed, they provide some insight into the working methods by which Gehry's designs evolve. The design studies propose a simple box open around three sides with objects denoting the entrances and signage requirements of the buildings. Gehry's design sketches in general show the bank as a one-story neutral volume on, over or around which pavilions of more evocative architectural character rise. In each variation the pavilions add mass and a rather distinctive skyline. Sketches include a temple, fish and tree combo, a dome-with-minarets, miniature modernist skyscrapers, a cathedral with spires and a kind of Carmen Miranda conservatory. In the final scheme parking is at the rear of the building with that of the shopping center. The building's only solid blank wall faces the shopping center. The entrance objects are located at the two sides, the main one being a glass box enclosing the sign.

1–3,6.Study sketches 4–5.Study model

1

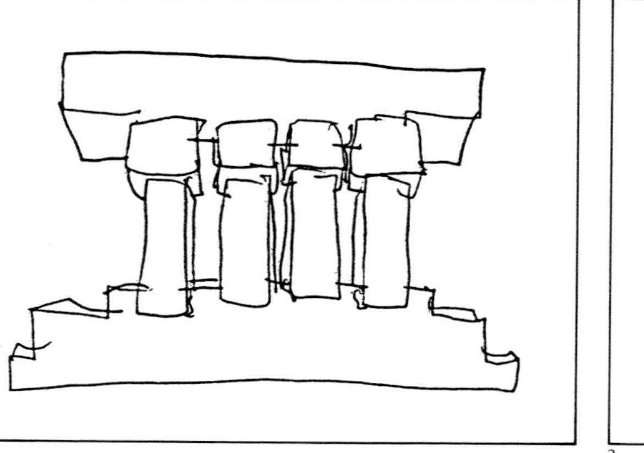

2

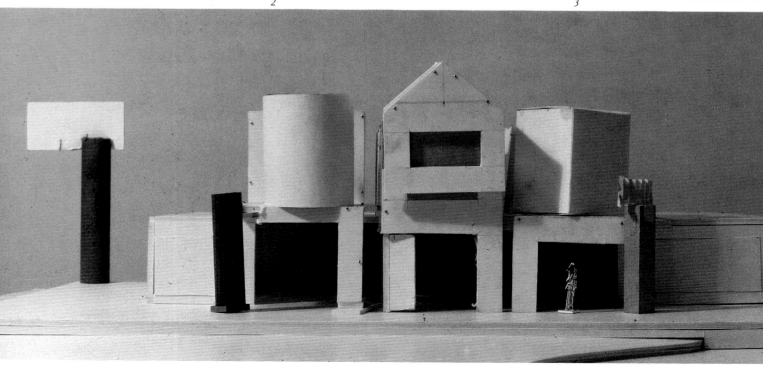

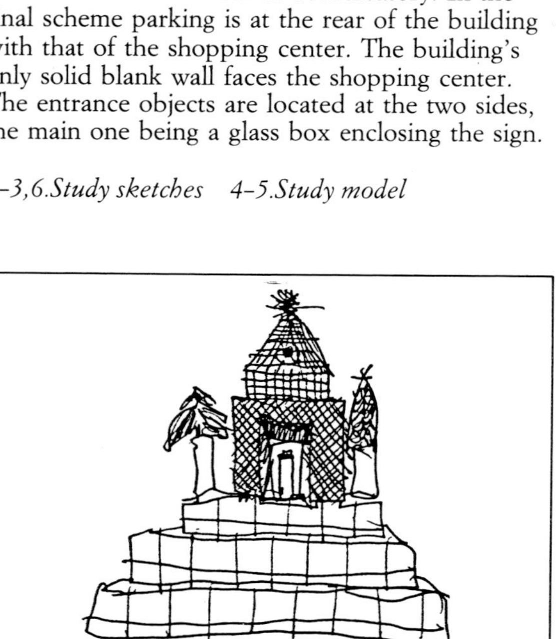

3

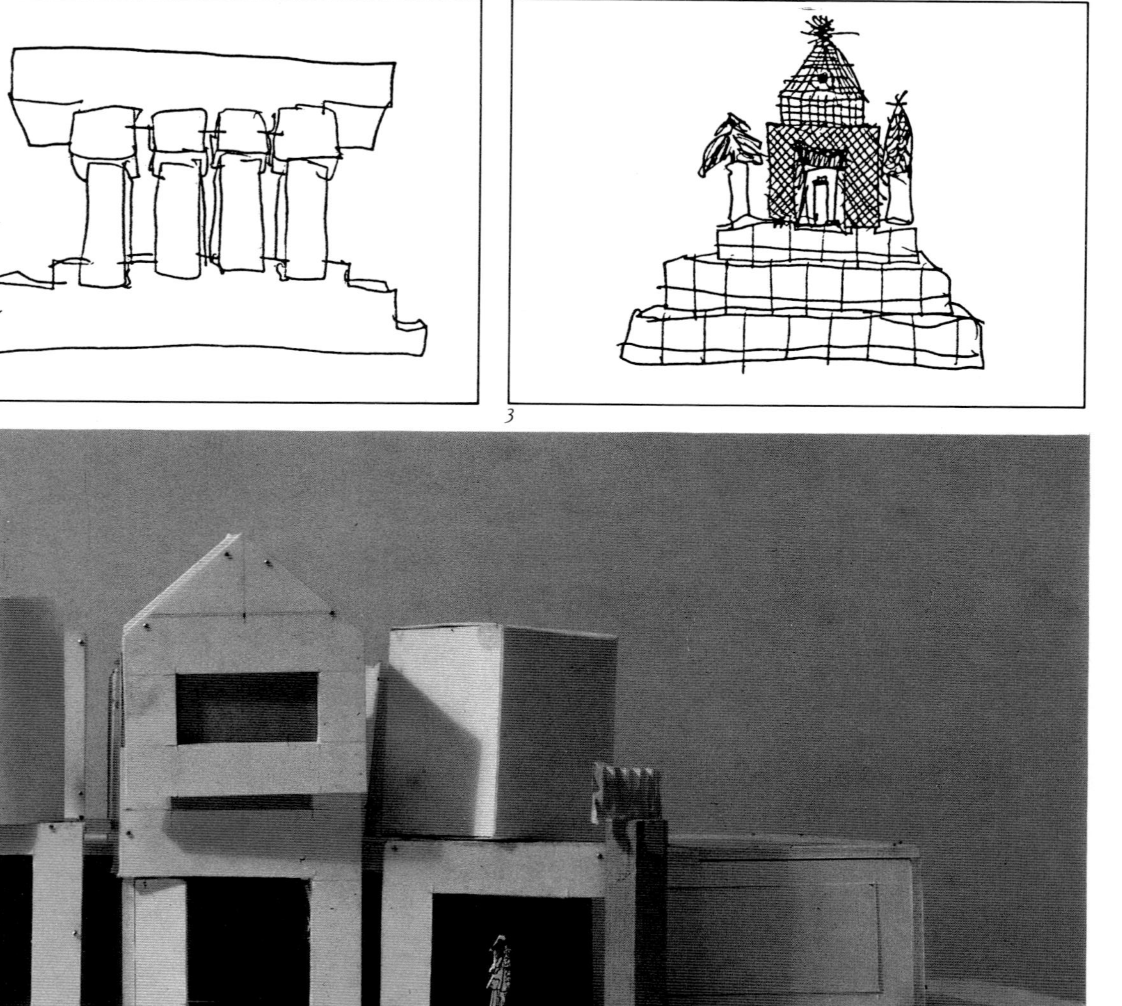

4

5

6

Tract House
1982

As evidenced by his projects for the Smith and Wosk residences, Lafayette Street lofts, and even Bubar's Jewelers, one of Gehry's interests in the early eighties has been in composing stylistically and formally disparate elements. American suburban development, thanks to the adaptibility of balloon-frame construction, has been characterized by eclectic wrappers on large numbers of similarly scaled buildings. In Gehry's studies for a tract house, he explores and exploits the compositional possibilities of that venerable land-use pattern. He composes kits of buildings, walls, and fences, disassembles single houses into separate components, and proposes a solution to the problem of the center in a nine-square configuration (in the center is the ubiquitous fish).

1-5.Studies: "walls and objects"

3

4

5

1

2

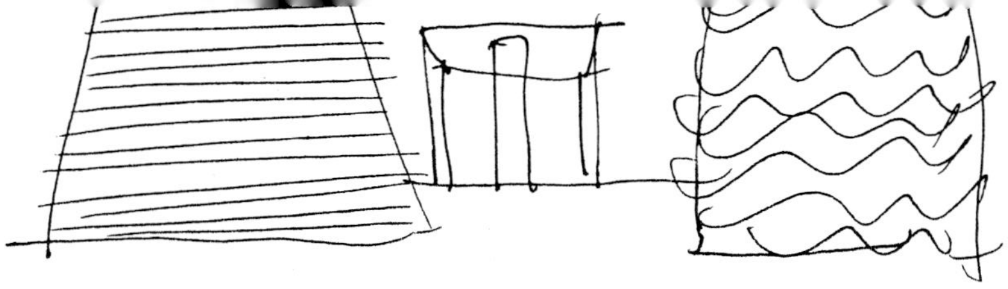

3

4

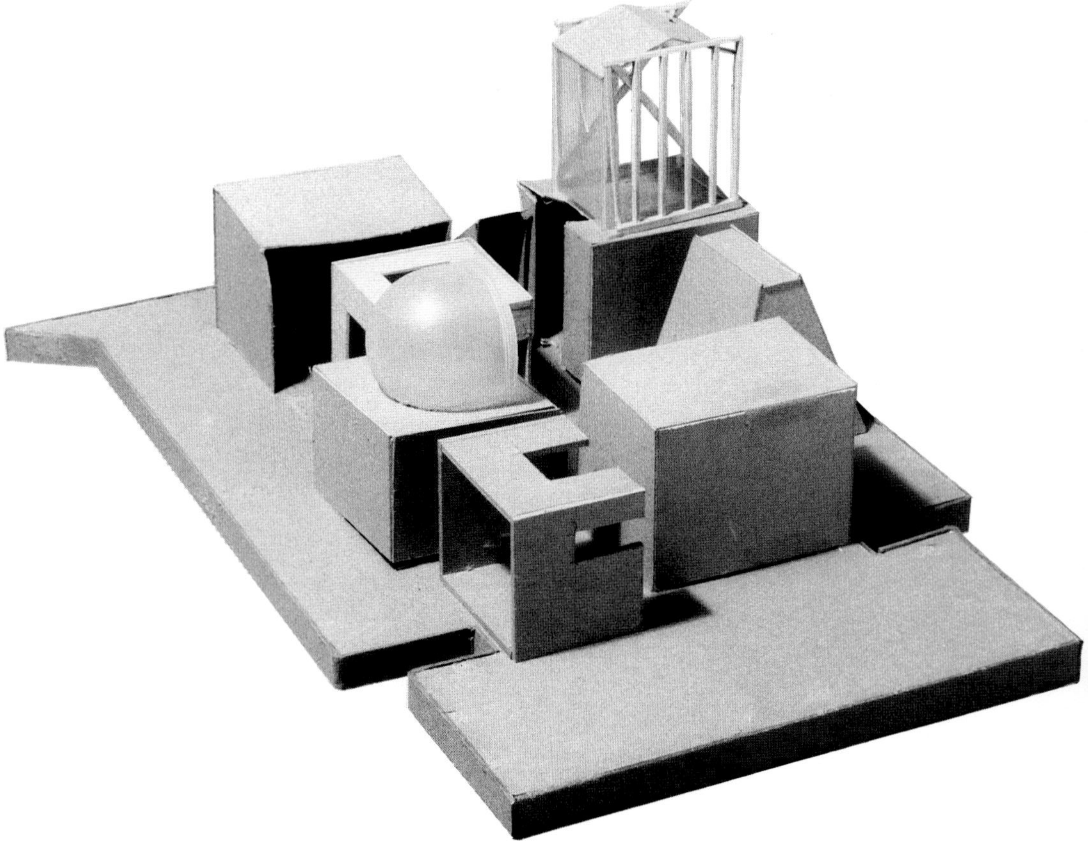

5

World Expo Amphitheater
New Orleans, Louisiana 1982

Fish gotta swim, birds gotta fly.
—Oscar Hammerstein

The Louisiana World Exposition, open from May through November of 1984, sponsored the construction of a five thousand-seat covered amphitheater, for which a variety of free and paid attractions were scheduled. The site is a wharf on the Mississippi River near the Exposition grounds. In his design, completed in association with Perez Associates, Gehry proposed a roof shaped like a large slice of pie, tilted toward the river. The roof spans between columns behind the seating and columns at the stage. The latter makes a proscenium and serves to frame audience's views of events along the river. Integral with the structural system behind the audience is a system of panels serving to screen sun and rain at the rear.

The design called for a translucent "scale-like" shingled roof, to provide diffused light inside and a dramatic effect at night outside the pavilion. Since the facility was intended to be a temporary structure, the shingles were originally designed as canvas around a steel frame sandwiched between wire mesh. Eventually fiberglass was substituted as the shingle's intended material. The biomorphic suggestions are several, described by critic Lindsay Stamm Shapiro as follows: "The overall massing of the theater roof conjures up a transluscent wing in flight. Yet, curiously, instead of simulating plumage, Gehry plans to cover the steel-trussed roof structure with transluscent plastic shingles that allude to a fish-scaled skin." The amphitheater as built differs substantially from the original design.

1-3. Preliminary studies 4-6.Model
7-9.Construction photos

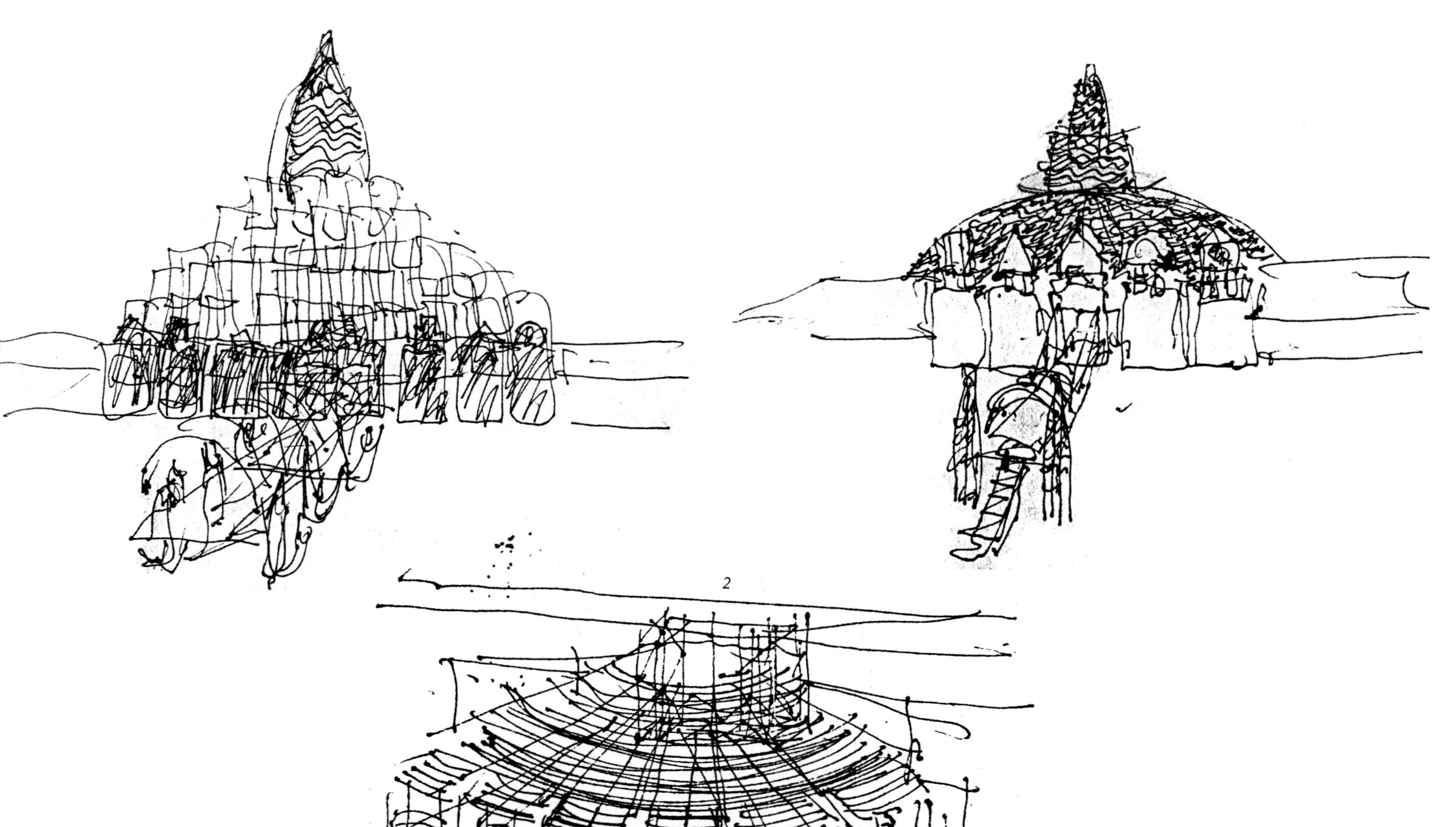

1

2

3

4

5

6

7

8

9

California Aerospace Museum

Los Angeles, California 1984

The coliseum which housed a majority of the events in the 1984 Summer Olympics is in an area called Exposition Park. In anticipation of the Games, site improvements, including the installation of two new museum facilities, were undertaken. The area allotted to the California Aerospace Museum was an old armory building set back slightly from the street. To co-ordinate with preparation for the Games—but in advance of full funding for all planned program elements, exhibits, and conversion of the armory—it was decided to construct a building on the narrow site between the old armory building and the street. The new building was designed to house the first exhibits, to be a gateway to the eventual complex of facilities planned in and around the armory, and to be a kind of exhibit itself—drawing support for, and conveying the spirit and excitment of, the institution's subject and plans. The building rises from its narrow 206-by-65-feet site up—and in places out over the sidewalk—to a height of 75 feet. It consists of two major volumes linked by a glazed wall. Above the latter a sheet metal sphere, which lies over the entry to the complex at the rear of the new building, is visible through a knife-shaped, metal-covered form. One volume is faced in white stucco surmounted by a cruciform skylight monitor. Hanging over the sidewalk is an airplane, suspended in mid-nosedive on a braced armature. The other volume is, above a height of 30 feet, sheet-metal clad, irregularly shaped, seven-sided polygon, part of which cantilevers over the street. A ramp curves up from the sidewalk around the polygonal volume and its attendant exit stair and leads to the museum's entrance. Surmounted by a ziggurat form which contains the building's circulation core, and crowned by the sheet-metal sphere, the entrance serves as a central element connecting the new building to the armory, and—by a walkway continuing between the two buildings—the outdoor exhibit area to the east. Inside, platforms at 12½, 27, and 45 feet overlook the 80-foot high exhibition spaces and the exhibits and furnishings designed by Joseph Wetzel and Associates. The ziggurat shape is reflected in the disposition of the viewing platforms immediately adjacent to the elevator core. The outdoor exhibit area to the east is also populated by an exit stair from the stucco-faced volume, and by an octagonal "IMAX" theater which hosts huge-screen presentations of aerospace film materials. The pylon which marks its entrance is an inexpensive construction of several layers of chain-link fencing. During a second phase of construction, the armory will be renovated for museum use. Gehry describes the building's enduring qualities in a fair assessment of much of his work: "A lot of people will read a lot of things into it—that's what will save it from becoming obsolete." One of the things Gehry himself reads into it is "a fantasy . . . a baroque space shuttle."

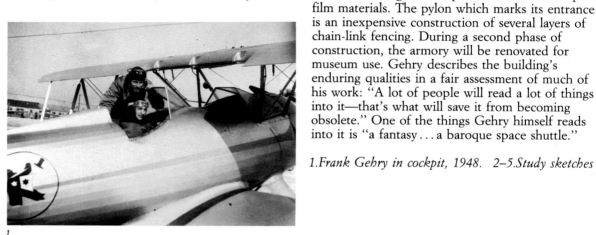

1

1.Frank Gehry in cockpit, 1948. 2–5.Study sketches

2

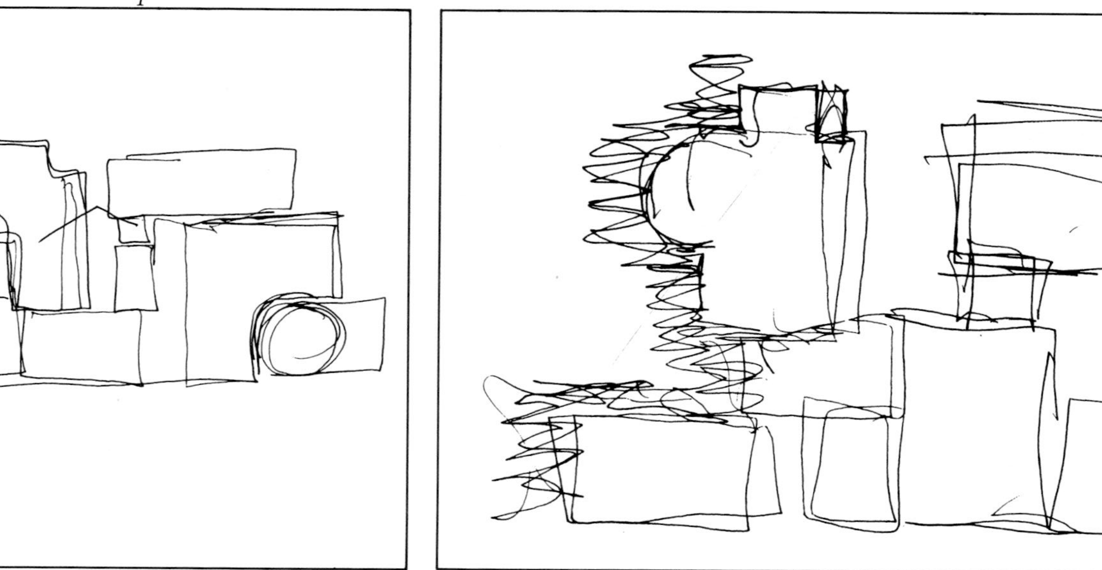

3

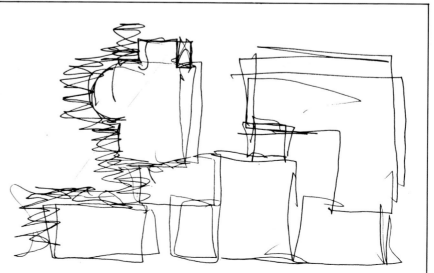

4

5

1.Street front view 2.View from above 3.Sectional model 4.Entrance adjacent to arsenal

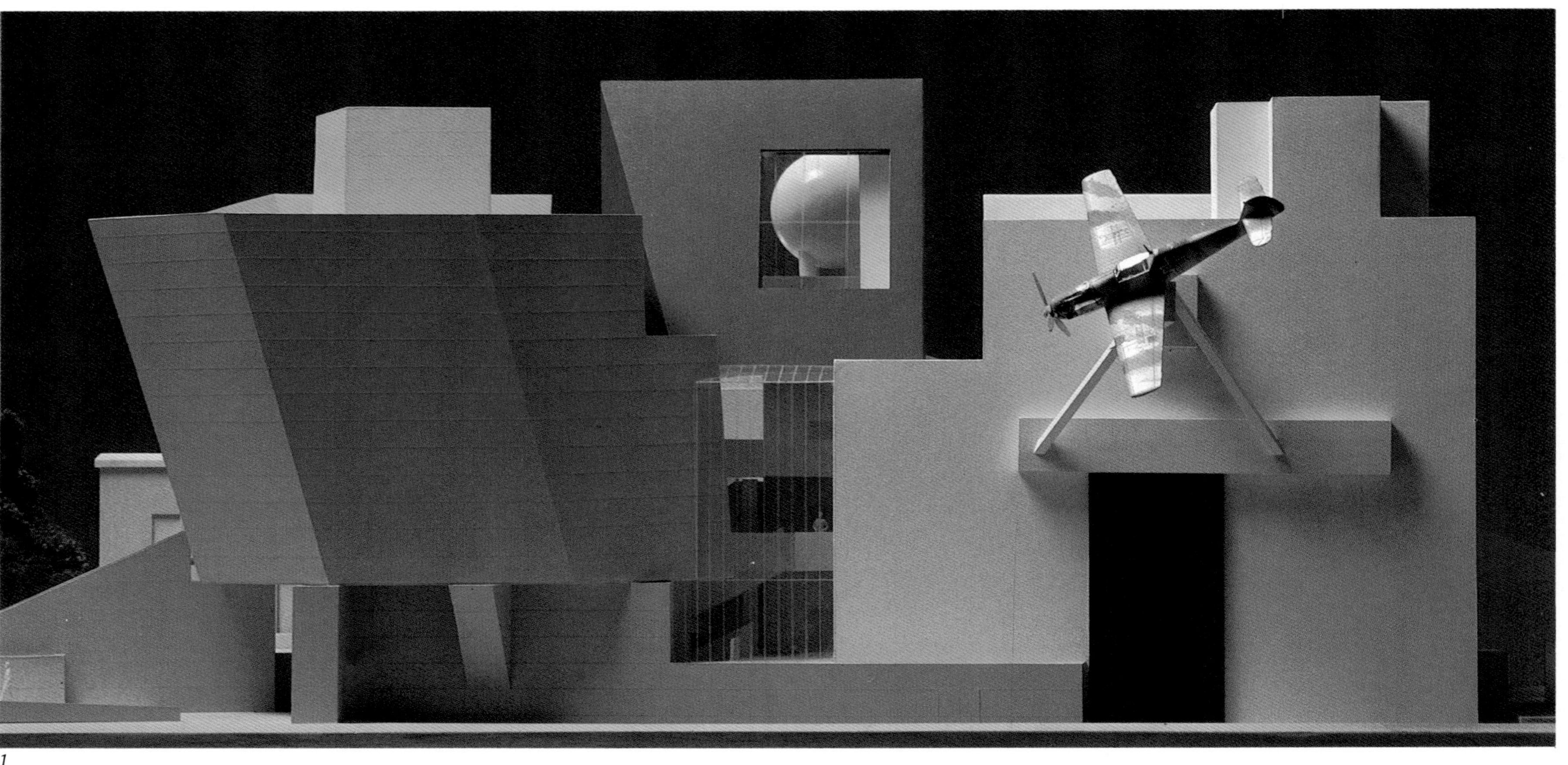

1

2

3

4

1,2.Front facade from sidewalk 3.Section 4.Exit from polygon 5.Entrance, between new building and arsenal 6.Interior 7.Ramp leading around polygon to entrance

1

2

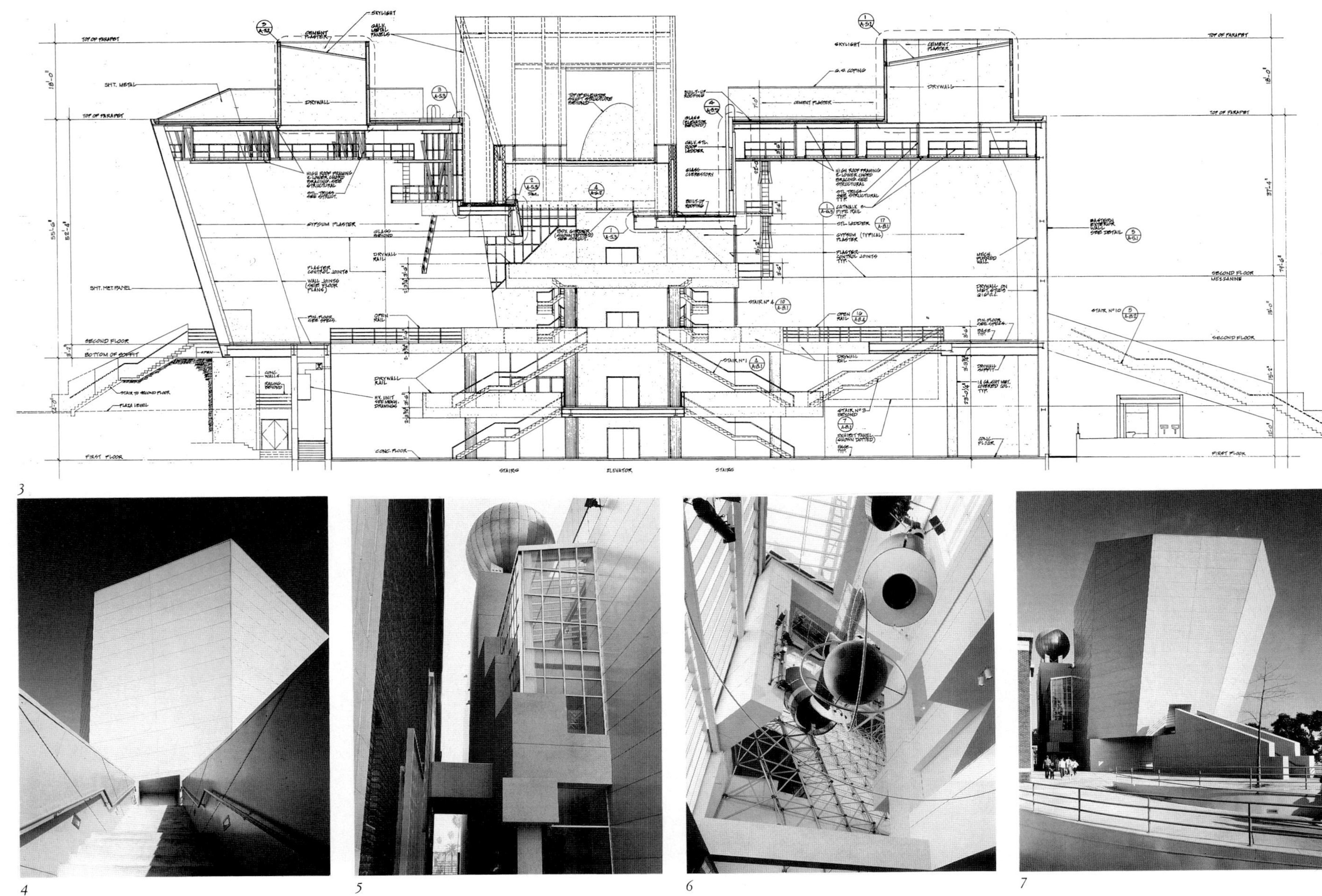

3

4

5

6

7

1,2,4. Views of street front 3. Ramp to entrance between new building and arsenal

1

2

3

4

Civic Center Competition
Beverly Hills, California 1982

The City of Beverly Hills solicited design proposals for a ten-acre, two-block site on which its 1932 "Spanish Baroque" city hall, a fire station, and a public library are located. The program required that the city hall interiors be replanned more efficiently, that the library be expanded, and that a new police station, a headquarters for the fire department, a community cultural resources facility, and parking be added. With his entry, Gehry seeks to aggrandize the prominence of the city hall by building a plinth of terraces for it (covering structured parking) and prominently extending its central axis with a visitors' center at one side and a concert hall at the other. The concert hall spans the street which bisects the site, binding the other block to the city hall grounds. All buildings on the site step up in height toward the city hall, supporting its role as the city's beacon. Further, the lower scale of the buildings toward the perimeter of the site is intended to help knit the civic center into the surrounding city context.

Gehry explains that the project grew out of a very particular "idea about American cities"—specifically, the richness and diversity of the forms and siting of its buildings and spaces. Thus, the concert hall, with its "Spanish Steps" amphitheater roof, in the words of one critic, "out-baroques City Hall by orders of magnitude," while a proposed art gallery is a minimally detailed cube spanning a secondary street. The children's reading room of the renovated library is a turreted castle, while the facade of the original fire station is seen behind a minimally detailed glass wall of the new headquarters. Critic Joseph Giovannini explains how this diversity is orchestrated into something greater than mere eclecticism: "This project . . . is best understood not from a bird's eye view of the model, but with the eye at ground level, where 'it' can walk around the project. The project is an episodic discovery of small buildings, which overlay the site in what is a secondary level of organization, giving the overall scheme a disarming modesty and spontaneity—and even a sense of organic urban growth over time. What reads as disunity from the bird's eye view is in fact a quite reasonable array of different building types, at different sizes. The architect . . . designs with a full lexicon of shapes. The project has to be understood with elements separated by more space and time than an overview implies."

1.Study 2.Plaza level plan

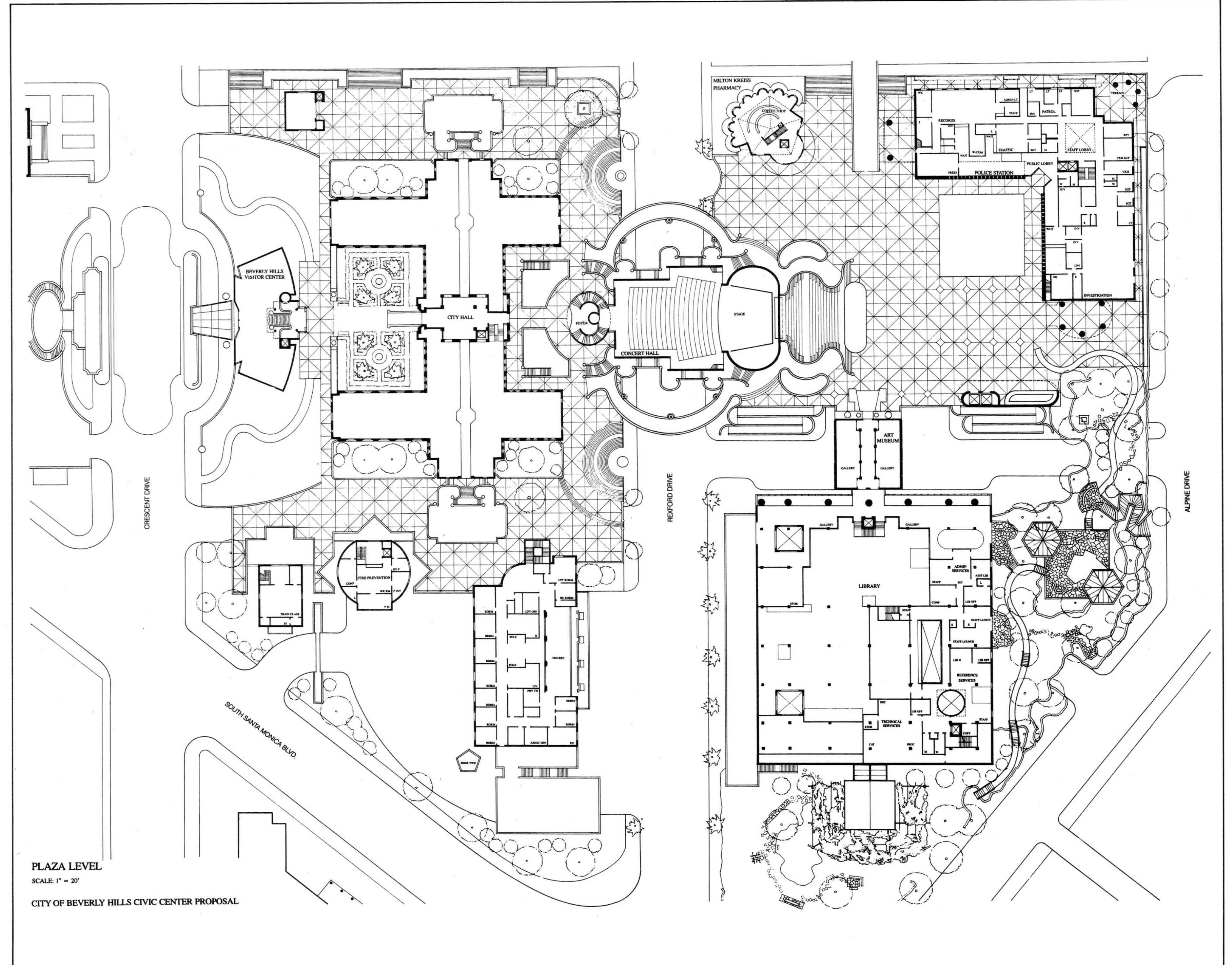

PLAZA LEVEL

SCALE: 1" = 20'

CITY OF BEVERLY HILLS CIVIC CENTER PROPOSAL

2

"I think that in all of its intricacy of detail and form the project comes close to reflecting the essence of Beverly Hills."
—Frank Gehry, 1984

1-3.Aerial views: site and model 2-4.Views from northeast: sketch and model 5.Model 6.City hall and concert hall

1

3

4

5

6

Wosk Residence

Beverly Hills, California 1982–84

On a residential street of small-scaled, relatively richly-detailed houses stood a four-story, stripped-down, speculatively-built, stucco apartment block. Out of scale and out of step with the neighborhood, it was also out of compliance with current Beverly Hills height and set-back regulations. The owners proposed renting the apartments of the first two and a half floors and renovating the top for themselves. Gehry proposed removing the fourth floor (and originally some of the third), building in its place a collection of smaller-scaled pieces—evoking the scale, detail, and eclecticism of the neighborhood—to accommodate the various parts of the clients' program.

In the original design, Gehry proposed substantial revisions to the exterior of the third floor as well as the rebuilding of the fourth. In developing the project, many compositions of colors and forms were explored. Considered were a sort of glazed baldacchino connecting the third and fourth floors, a miniature cathedral facade, and a totem or two.

The present, more restrained, design leaves the exterior of the third floor essentially unaltered and assumes its roof as a platform on which new construction rests. That platform has been extended on brackets slightly beyond the existing building at the front. Interior furnishings were selected by the client, artist Miriam Wosk. The half of the third floor remodeled for the owners includes bedrooms, two rather exotic baths, and a half-oval stair. Above are a vaulted studio, a domed kitchen, a half-ziggurat television room, a greenhouse dining room, and a tiled living room. The once aggressively solipsistic building has, then, been cut down to size literally and figuratively—transformed into a mute pedestal for a composition of objects in the sky.

1–3.Studies 4.3rd floor plan 5.4th floor plan 6.Section

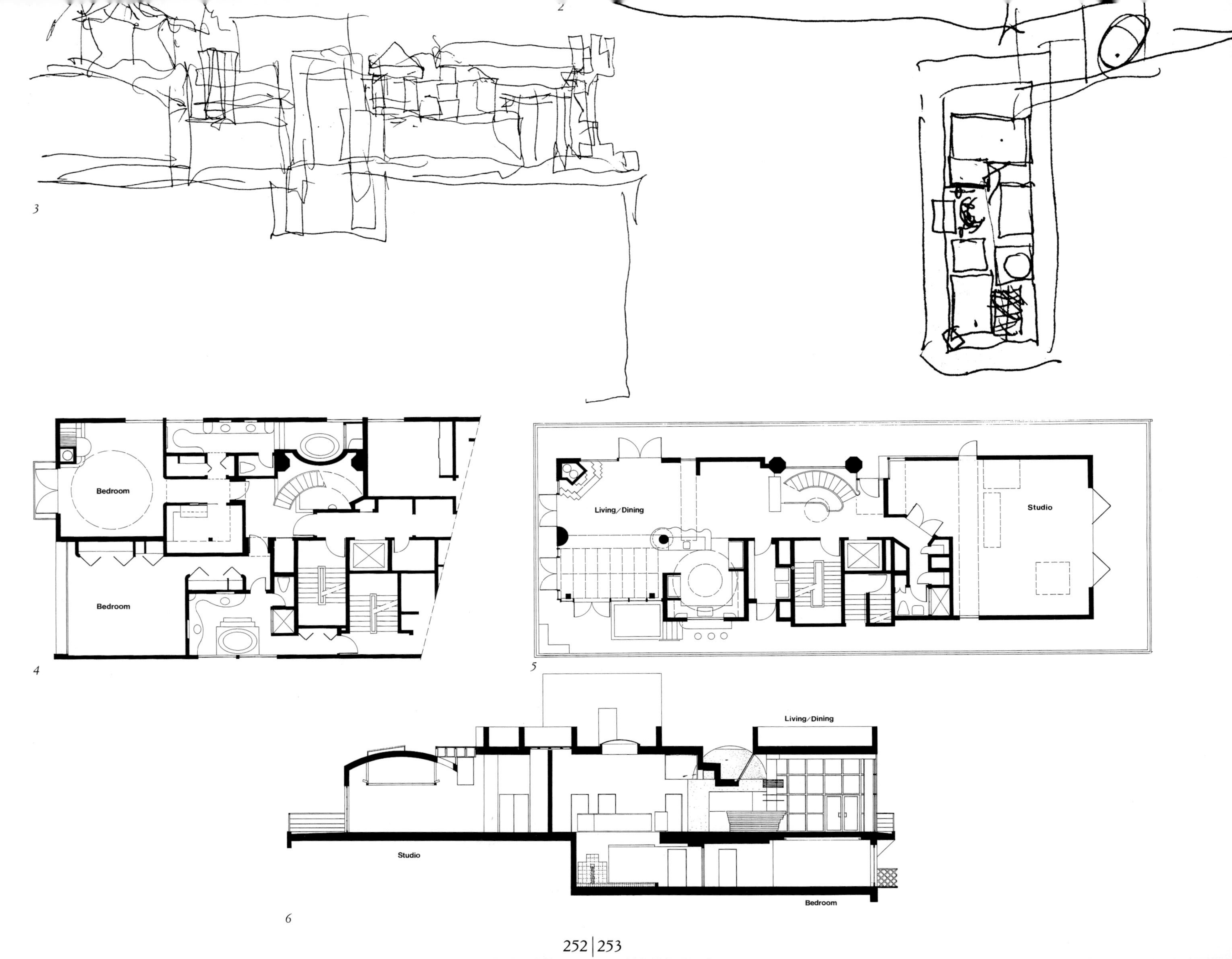
Bedroom
Bedroom
Living/Dining
Studio
Living/Dining
Studio
Bedroom

2

3

4

5

6

1-2.Preliminary study model 3.Model, design development 4-5.Final design model 6,9.Interiors 7,8,10.Exteriors

1

2

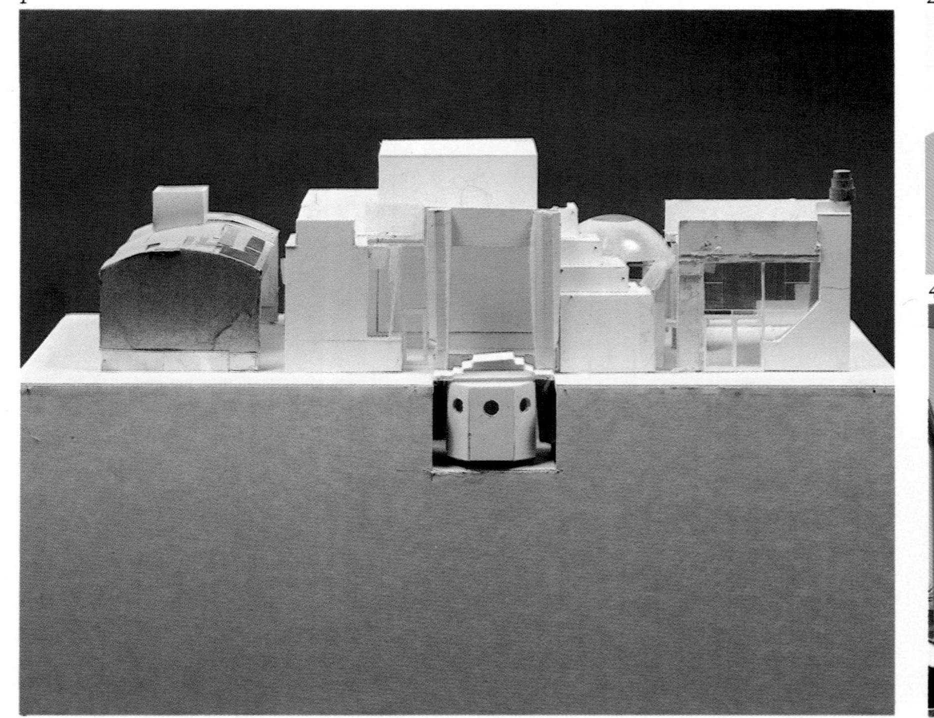
3

4

5

6

8

9

10

The Galleria

Oklahoma City, Oklahoma 1983

The Galleria is being built as a three-level shopping mall housing over 650,000 square feet of retail space, including three new department stores. Parking, the first phase of which is already constructed, will be both in a nine-story garage and in a single level under the mall, connecting directly to adjacent office buildings and hotels. The mall will also serve as the entrance from the adjacent park to the new office buildings being constructed with the Galleria as part of a large-scale urban development project. One of these new office buildings has been designed by Gehry. Conceived as a gateway to the Galleria, it features a glass "campanile" as a corner. The budget and site were both small; by restricting expense in fine finishes to the small area of the campanile, the budget was met while still affording "a human scale and memorable quality." The project is scheduled for completion in 1985.

1.Office tower with campanile in context 2.Site model

1

2

Cricket Inn

Farmington, Connecticut 1983

The Cricket Inn is promoted as representing a new concept in hotel accommodations. Swimming pools, public bars, restaurants, and night clubs are excluded from the program, which is modeled instead on those of European inns. By deleting those high-overhead facilities often provided for guest entertainment, the developers believe that luxury accommodations and services may be offered at a moderate price. It is felt that guests will find sufficient enjoyment in the inn and its park-like setting. Gehry and Associates' design for the Inn is a four-story structure. On each floor, three wings of rooms open onto the atrium of the lobby. The building mass is reduced to a height of three floors at the entrance and the two end pavilions, creating roof gardens for fourth-floor rooms. The chimneys of fourth-floor fireplaces, window boxes, and ground-floor trellises are intended to provide further visual variety. The major materials are stucco and wood.

1.Sketch 2.Model

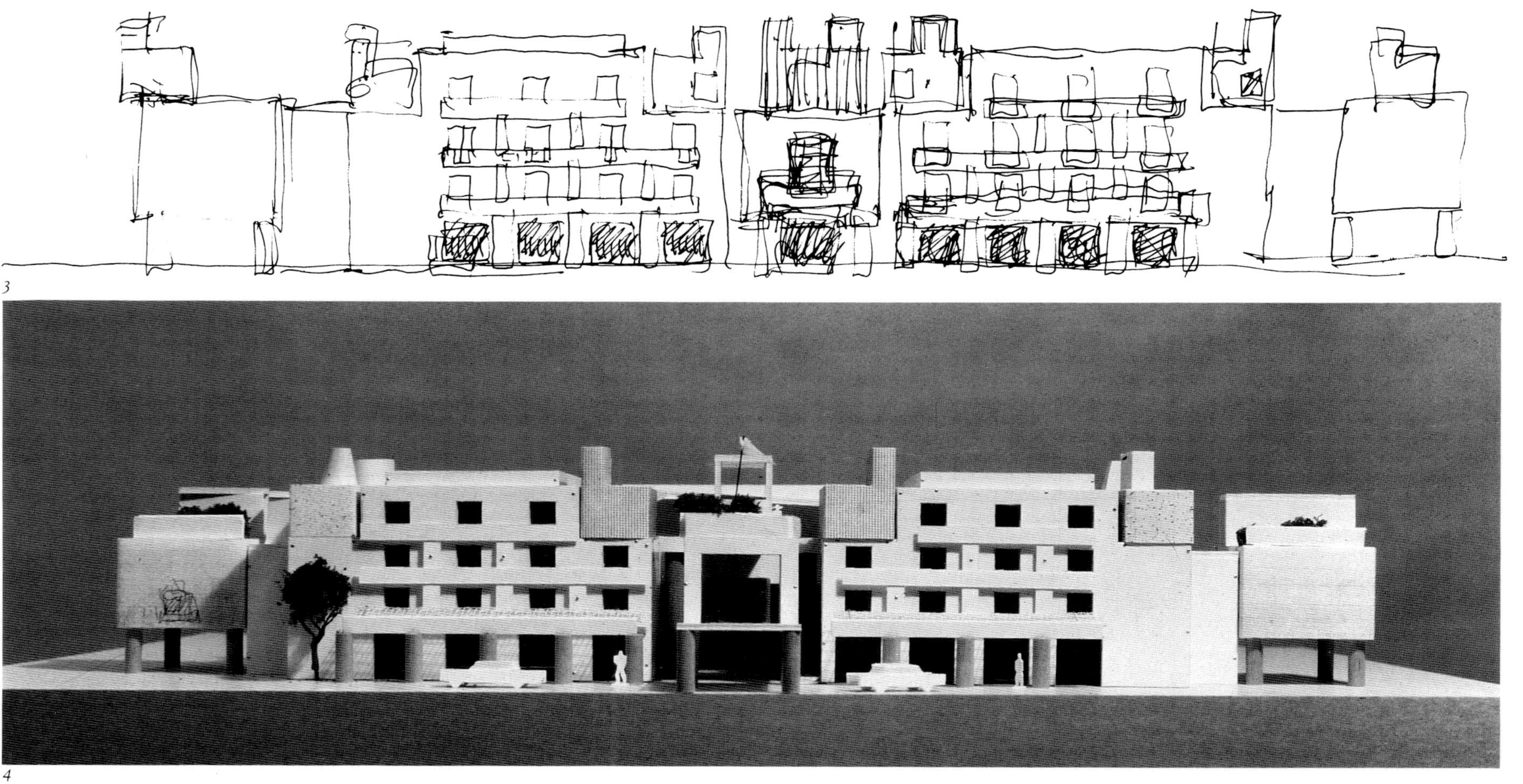

3

4

Winton Guest House

Wayzeta, Minnesota 1983–84

The main Winton House was designed by Phillip Johnson in the early 1950s. In contrast to its refined propriety, the clients referred to their idea for an addition as a potting pit to the main house. It is intended for use by the client's children and grandchildren. The client's metaphoric description of the program, and the intended users, suggested to the architects, respectively, "a certain relaxation in terms of materials and design" and "a certain degree of fantasy."

It is proposed that a line of trees and an existing hedge adjacent to the bedroom wing of the original house separate the Johnson house from the addition. The guest house will be a collection of small differentiated building forms—a rooftop log cabin, a central hall, and several other parts—which follow the contours of the site. While many of the individual parts are reminiscent of the unbuilt Smith House, a stronger order binds this building's parts together. A biaxial arrangement is implied, honoring, after a fashion, the centralized planning of the big house next door. Between eighteen hundred and two thousand square feet have been planned.

1

1.Main house by Philip Johnson, 1952
2.Sketch 3.Model

2

3

Norton House

Venice, California 1983

The client had begun his career as a lifeguard and chose his narrow beachfront lot to recapture some of the occupation's pleasures. Practically, however, the adjacency to the beach posed problems of privacy, especially given the boxy new buildings next door which were shouldering their way to the beachfront. The house was designed for privacy, to mediate between the scale of the new three-story buildings on one side and the two typically tiny Venice houses on the other, to open most rooms to ocean air and light, and to provide a large outdoor terrace/observation deck. The placement of the fireplace, stairways, and the beachfront screen wall was also determined with privacy in mind. The client, in addition to beach-watching, is also interested in the colorful artifacts of Mexican culture, and in the artists' community in which his house is located. These interests influenced the forms and finishes of the project. The house is essentially boxes of graduated height laced together by stairs. The lowest beachfront volume contains Lyn Norton's studio, with a trellised terrace to the beach; the remainder of the ground floor houses service and garage space. Above, the partially high-ceilinged living, dining and kitchen area opens on to a deck over the studio. A light which penetrates the top two floors brings light into the kitchen and the bedrooms on the top floor. Bedrooms, like the living area below, also have views out to the ocean. The roof of this volume is an observation deck linked to the other decks and the beach by a long, straight-run stairway. A major compositional element, it is developed in its uppermost run with a series of tiled pedestals on which several sculptural objects are to be installed. Another stair leads from the living room deck over the studio to an observation tower, denominated the "breakfast nook" on plans and now called a study, in which the form and prospect of the Venice lifeguard stands are recreated.

1.Study sketch 2–3. Study model 4.West elevation 5.East elevation 6.South elevation 7.1st floor plan 8.2nd floor plan 9.3rd floor plan

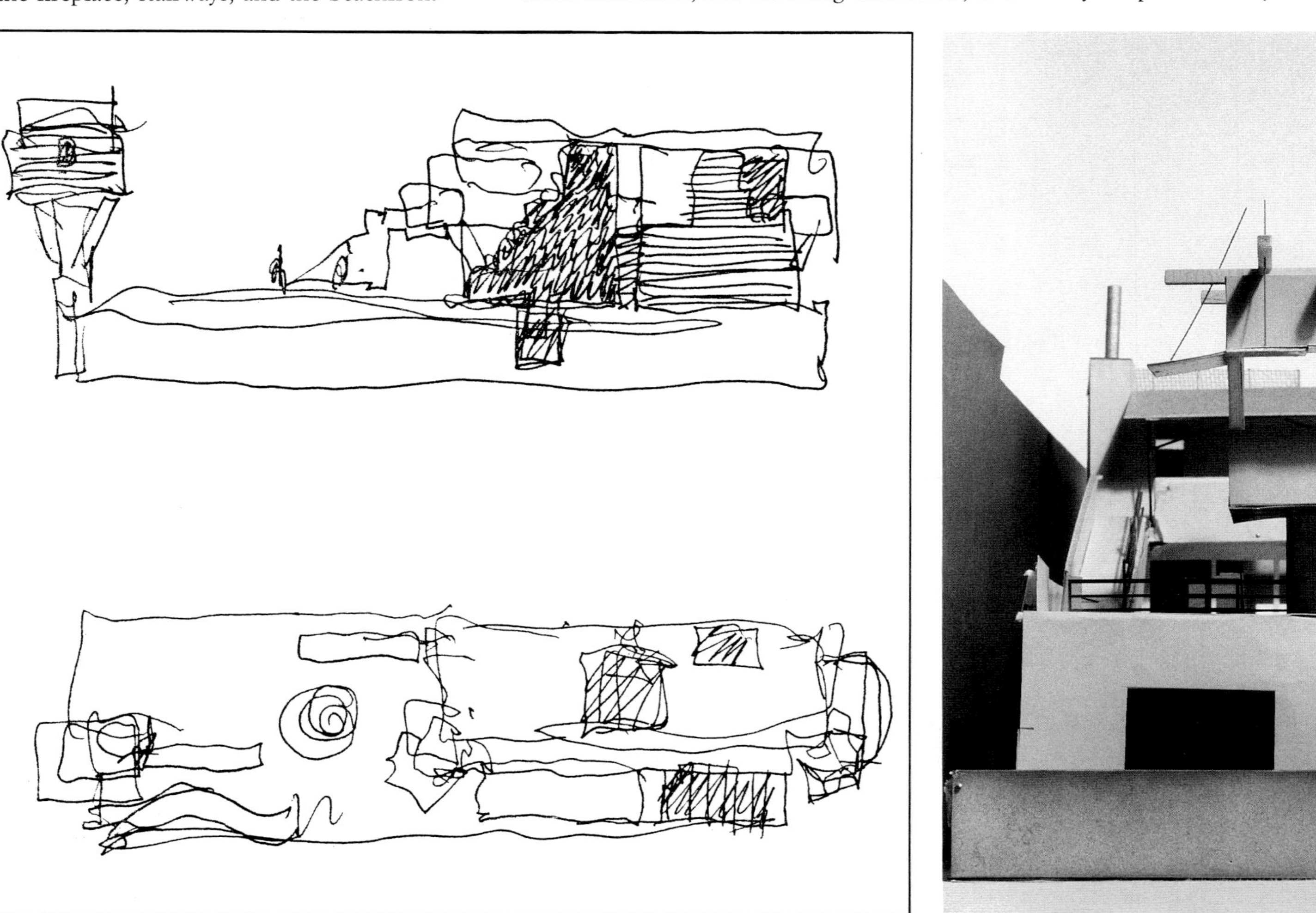

1

2

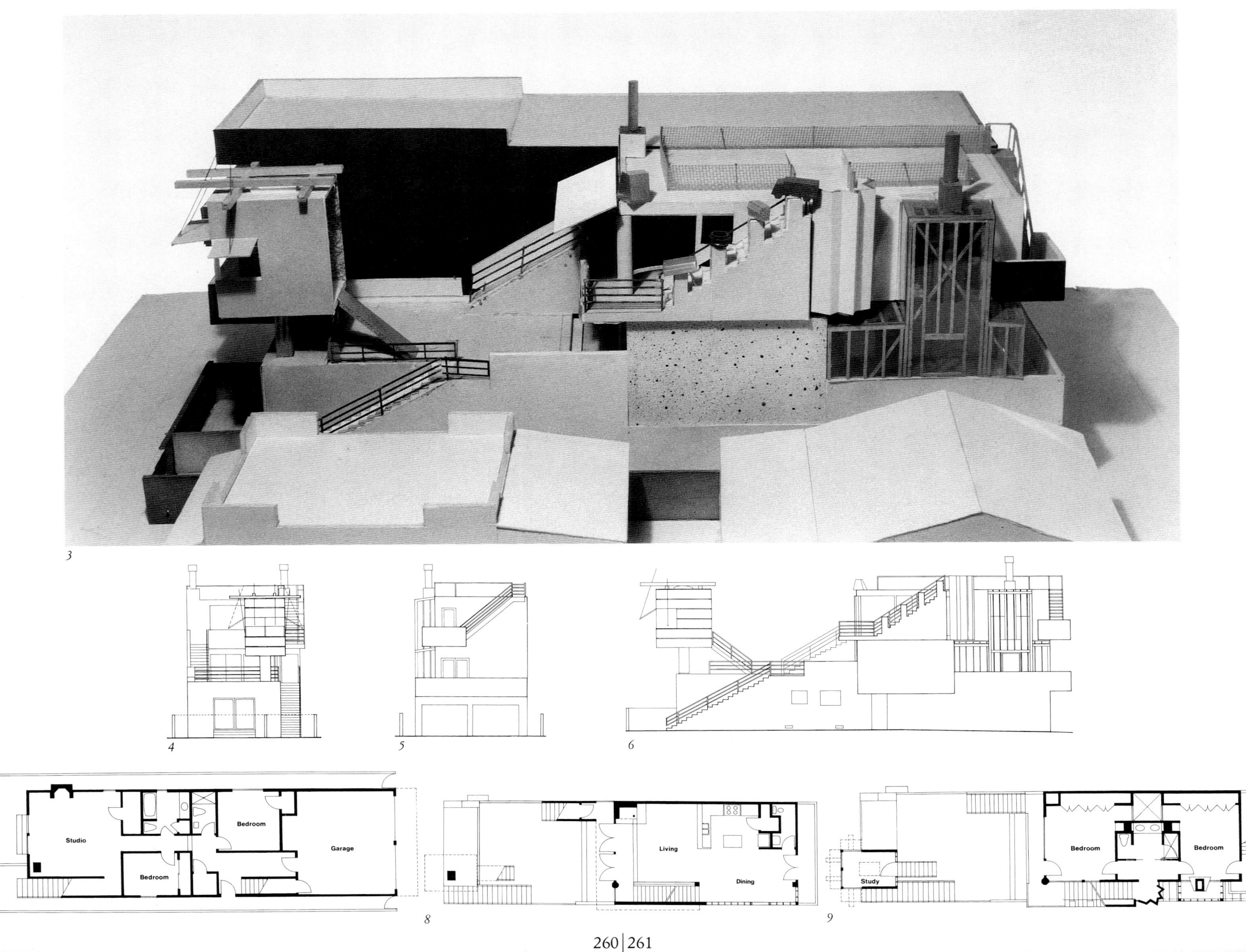
3
4
5
6
7
Studio
Bedroom
Bedroom
Garage
8
Living
Dining
9
Study
Bedroom
Bedroom

1.Site on the beach 2.Venice lifeguard stand 3.View from beach 4.Side view over adjacent rooftops 5,6.Observation room/study

1

2

3

4

5

6

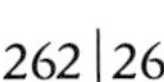

Hauserman Work Station
1983

For the 1983 Neocon, the annual interior furnishing exposition, Gehry was asked to design an exhibition demonstrating an application of a new Hauserman Company product, a wall panel system for open-office planning. The product is composed of two metal panels with a raceway between them for utility circuitry. Gehry's design involved cutting vertical openings in typical panel sections into which strips of panel were inserted. A trellis-like enclosure was thus made. In the raceway between the two panels, operable roll-up window shades were inserted, allowing use as an open, semi-enclosed, or private office area. Behind the work station, which had panels painted white, a wall of panels, painted red, was erected. The desk was constructed from two slabs of marble set on a base made of panels painted black. The project not only suggests a way of exploiting a new product, but as a gazebo, suggests the possibility of designing, literally, the trade's cliché—an office landscape.

1.Model 2.Installation

Jencks' Front Porch
1983

While it fell to God to name the creatures of the earth, critic Charles Jencks has undertaken the task of labeling contemporary architecture, with particular attention to phylum and genus. Gehry's assemblage finds the critic trapped in a world not of his own making. The creatures and chimeras, however, respectfully dispose themselves in some symmetrical relation to a pedimented structure, clearly identifying themselves and the critic as postmodernists. The small maquette was made as a Christmas present for his friends Charles and Maggie Jencks.

3.Assemblage

1

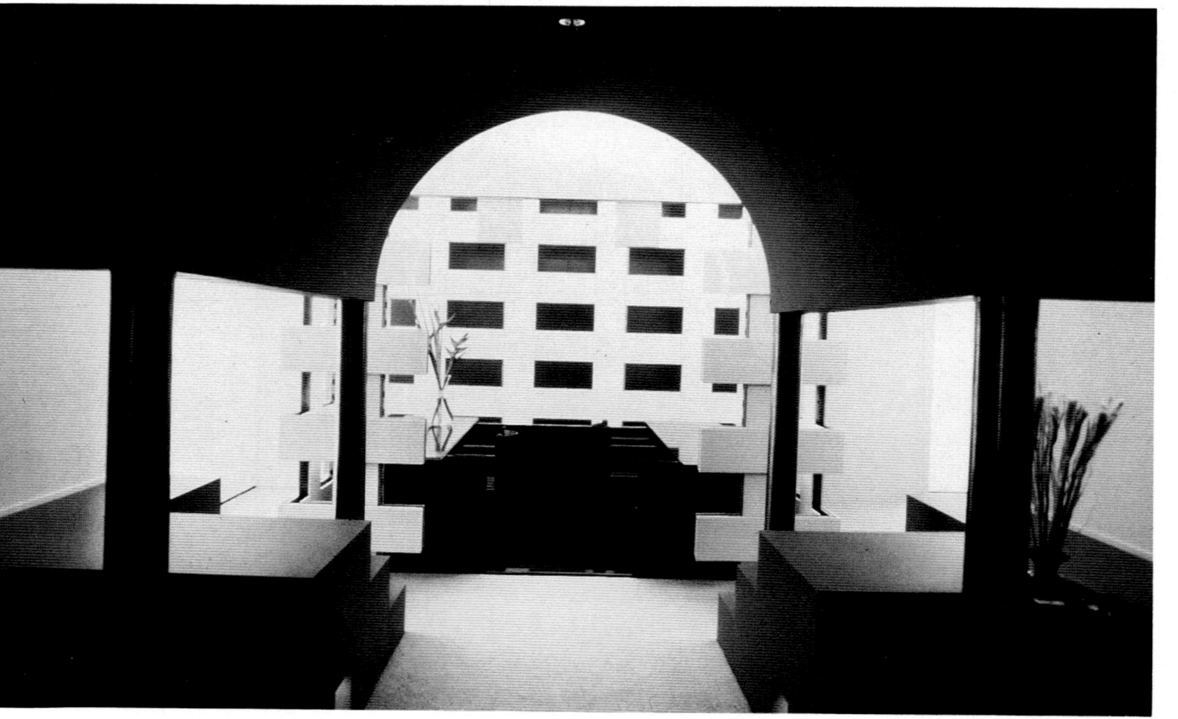

2

3

Fish and Snake Lamps
1983

Warning: Do not immerse appliance in water.
—Underwriters Laboratories

To promote a new product, The Formica Corporation commissioned a number of architects to create designs illustrating possible applications. The product, a plastic laminate with color integral through its depth (conventional laminates have only a thin surface layer of color), eliminates the visible seams which make laminate coverings so clearly identifiable as veneers. Most commissioned designs exploited the product's potential to appear part of a sculpted solid. Gehry, ever interested in "hands-on" design, took samples and broke them. The small chips were then used as scales to create luminous fish and snakes. Also planned is a scale-covered "fish chair." Gehry says working with the product is nearly as satisfying as working with cardboard: "I can design something in the morning and have it finished by the end of the day."

1–2.Sketches 3–6.Lamps

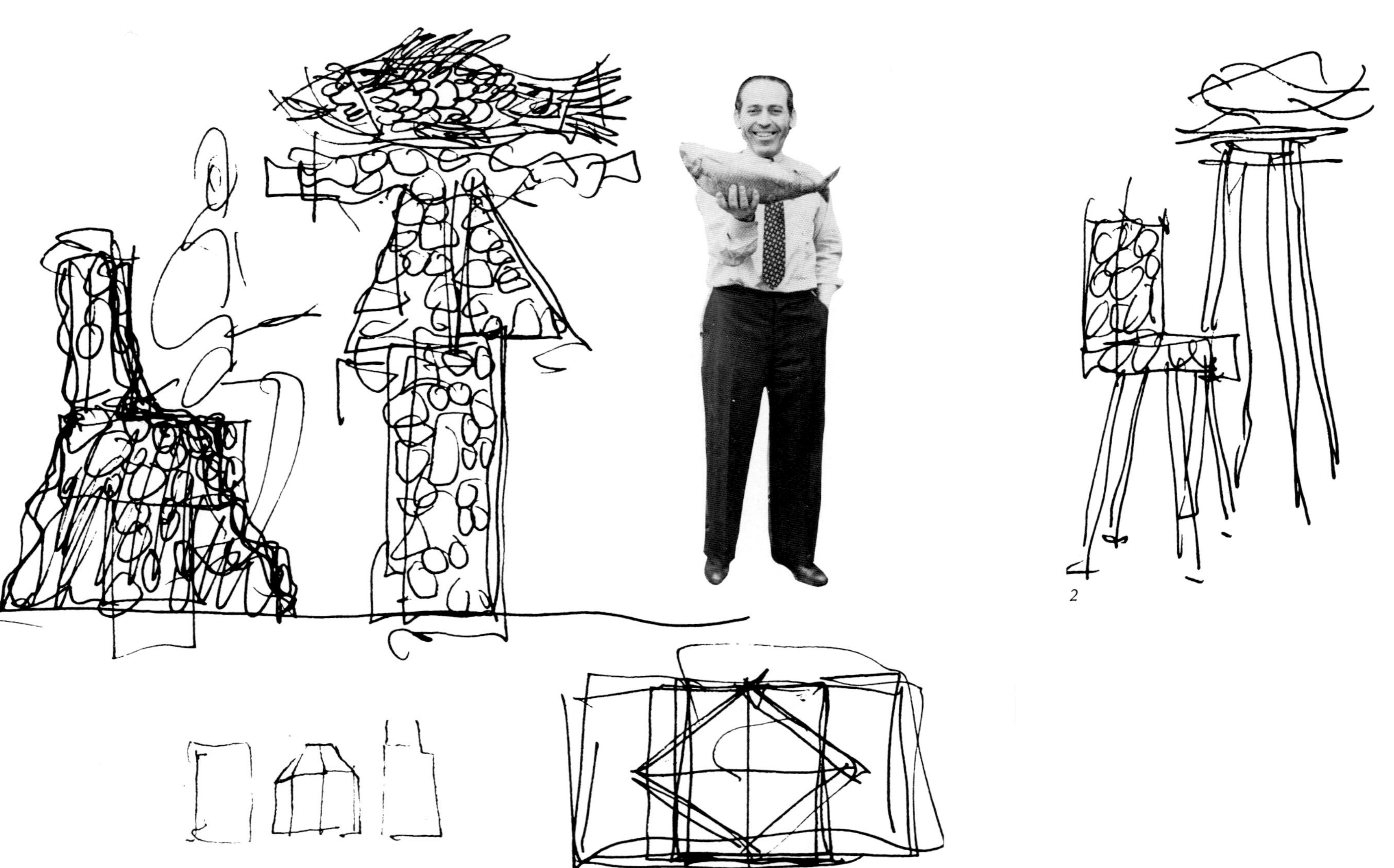

1

2

3

4

5

6

Folly: The Prison
1983

Architectural structures of no discernible function other than improving the decor of an estate's landscaped park have been dubbed "follies" since the eighteenth century. In the twentieth, two art galleries invited a group of prominent architects to design follies for exhibition. Ever practical, Gehry's folly is designed to fulfill a function—that of park prison. His description of the project entitled "The Prison," follows:

To enhance the security of the estate, we propose a prison. As a warning signal to prospective burglars, it declares that the owner is serious. The prison also functions as a holding place for the apprehended burglar until the police arrive. There may be other potential uses of the prison, depending upon the eccentricity of the wealthy owner.

The prison is to be shaped like a snake and constructed of brick, giving it the physical solidity associated with the word 'prison.' The form of the snake is used because it symbolizes hostility and invokes fear. The use of animate forms allows for a great deal of flexibility in adjusting the scale of the folly to the specific location and budget.

It is proposed that the apprehended criminal be placed in a cage under a light-well in the center of the coiled snake. The cage can be transported to an adjoining transparent pavilion, in the shape of a fish. The form of the fish has the symbolic meaning of that famous prisoner Jonah who lived inside the whale. And then there was Pinocchio. At the owner's discretion, a mechanism can be activated which moves a car holding the cage (which in turn holds the prisoner) through an underground tunnel and into the center of the glass fish pavilion. When situated in the fish, the prisoner would be visible from the house.

1.Sketch 2-4. Model

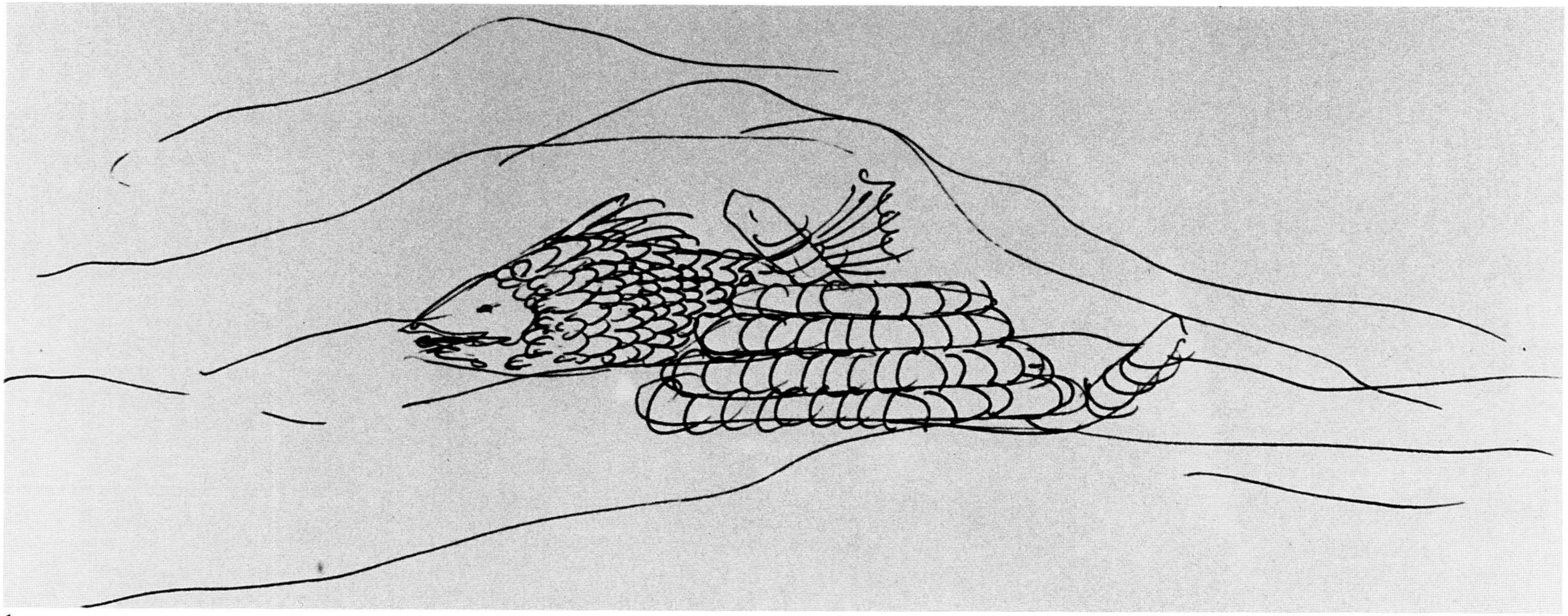

1

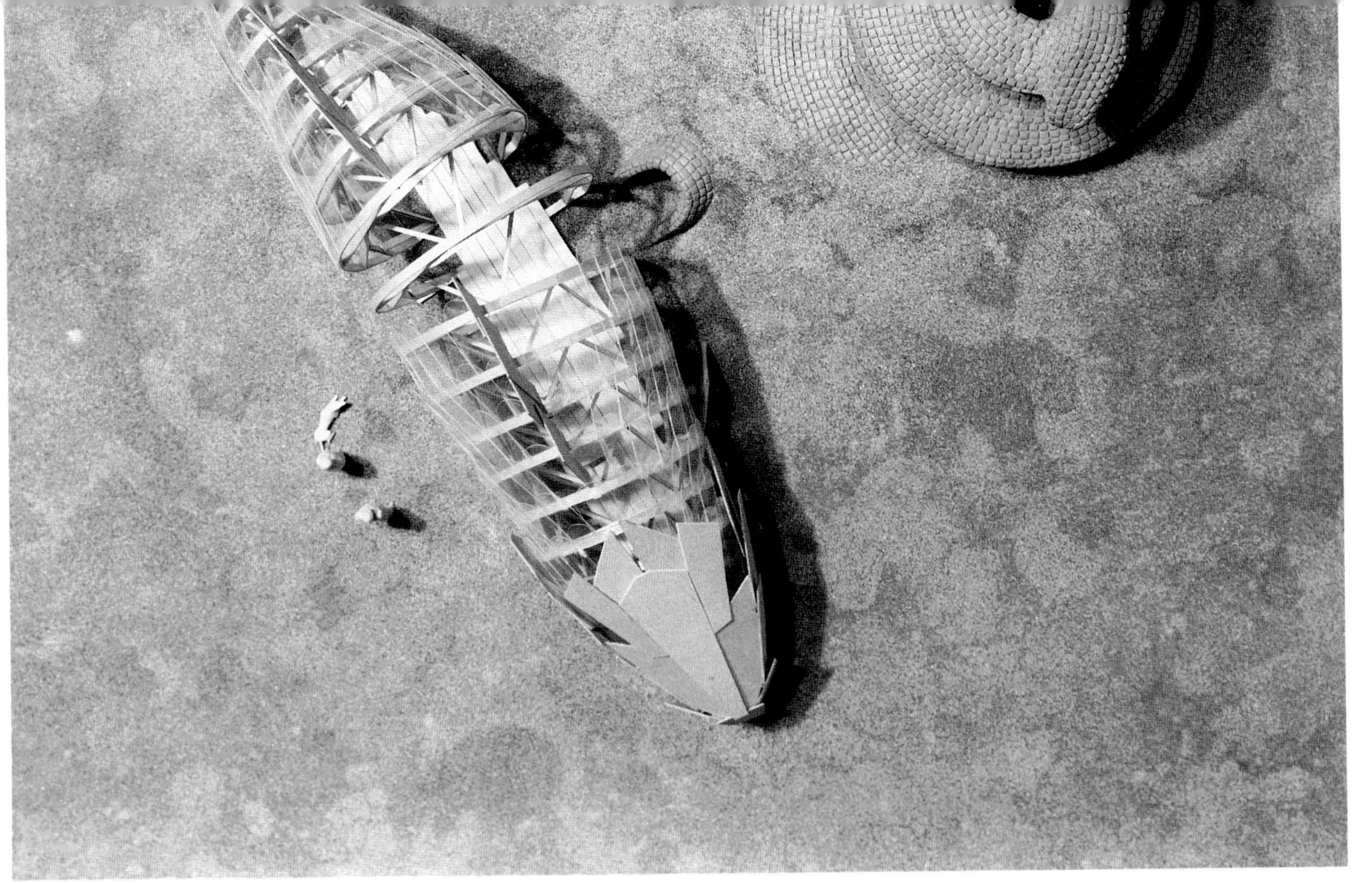

2

3

4

Available Light

1983

The new Los Angeles Museum of Contemporary Art sponsored a series of collaborations to bring artists in different media together. The first such commissioned work brought together dancer/choreographer Lucinda Childs, composer John Adams, and Gehry. None of the artists knew each other previously, although Childs was sufficiently familiar with Gehry's work to request him as a collaborator when MOCA suggested a collaborative project to her. The performance was to innaugurate the Temporary Contemporary, another Gehry project. Gehry's set for the performance took advantage of the refurbished but still empty warehouse space by putting the stage within, rather than at one end, of the warehouse volume. The audience was accommodated in two areas—one group of elevated bleachers looked down on the performance through columns; more seating was located in front of the stage. Gehry's intent was that seats should be exchanged during intermission to give each audience member both perspectives on the performance. The set itself involved two platforms: the stage proper and a second stage at a higher level set at a diagonal to the first. Both were of construction-grade framing. The platform worked with a choreographic interest of Childs', that of "doubling," which has been explained by Susan Sontag as follows: "A recurrent structure in Childs's work: splitting the performer into two versions, the action into two levels, which proceed simultaneously. Having several people doing the same rhythmic thing—side by side, or one in front of another, or one above the other—has always been part of choreographing ensembles, military, ceremonial and balletic. Indeed, doubling is the most basic principle of artifice—of form itself. What Childs has done is to concentrate on and draw out the implications of doubling, as a formal principle, and as the basis of choreographic syntax: the geometrical, or diagrammatic, idealization of movement . . . The adding of decor is never merely decorative but functions to create richer possibilities of doubling. Thus the film that [Sol] LeWitt made as the decor for *Dance,* a film of portions of *Dance* projected on a transparent scrim, creates a perfectly synchronized double set of dancers. For example, the split screen allows the audience to see the dancers in the film, never less than life-size, on top; the live dancers (behind the scrim) on the bottom. What LeWitt supplied for *Dance* with a film Frank Gehry supplies for *Available Light* with an architecture. In *Available Light,* the stage itself has become two-level, allowing other variations on the theme of doubling. Instead of traveling ghosts, there are live trackers: one to three dancers are upstairs echoing, playing off, providing counterpoint to what the dancers are unfolding below."

The dancers on the diagonally located platform danced parallel to the main stage edge, while those on the stage proper danced parallel to the platform. A scrim of chain-link fence was erected at one side.

1.Model 2-3. Performance

1

2

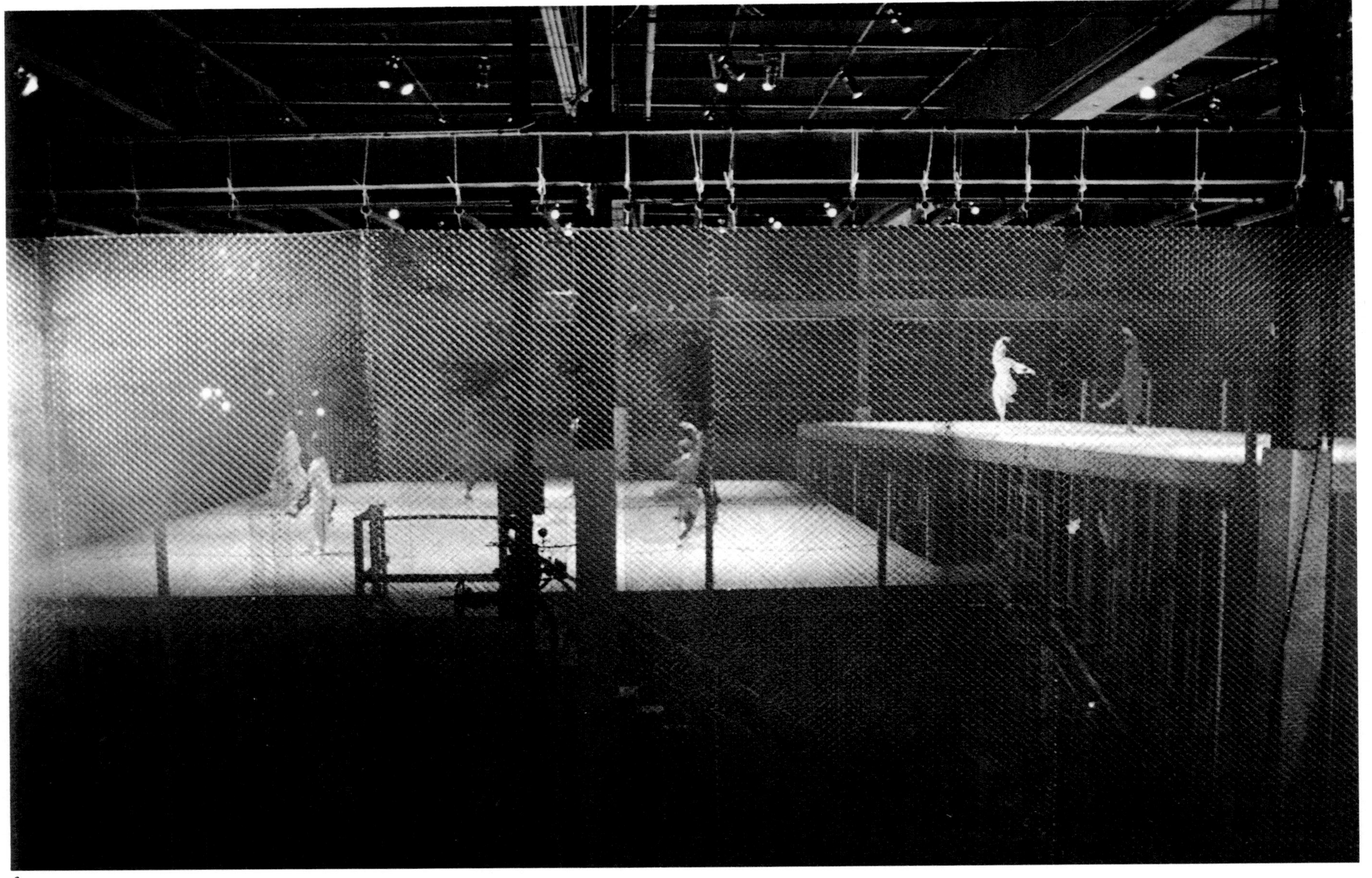

3

Temporary Contemporary

Los Angeles, California 1983

I've never seen a more beautiful installation.
—Robert Rauschenberg

In 1979, a group of Los Angeles civic and cultural leaders began to work towards establishing a museum dedicated to contemporary art.
Gehry was a finalist among architects considered for the museum's permanent building, on Los Angeles's Bunker Hill, a commission which finally went to Arata Isozaki. Pending completion of that building in 1986, a temporary facility has been opened, designed by Gehry. The site of The Temporary Contemporary is near downtown in "Little Tokyo" on the edge of a warehouse district in which many area artists studios are located. It is installed in two adjacent warehouses built in the thirties. Before conversion, one stored hardware, the other a police garage. Gehry's rehabilitation work was based on the conviction that the warehouse space itself was a beautiful and appropriate setting for contemporary art. The existing steel trusses and wood joists were cleaned and the buildings were painted and brought up to code. The buildings open on a to a dead end block of Central Avenue. The street has been covered with chain-link fencing, making it into a foyer for the museum. Planned installations include work from private collections, a history of car design, and performance art. The facility was opened with the Lucinda Childs/Frank Gehry/John Adams collaboration, "Available Light." So successful is the project considered that plans to keep it in use after the main building is completed are under discussion.

1.Sketch 2.Model 3.Exterior entrance hall

1

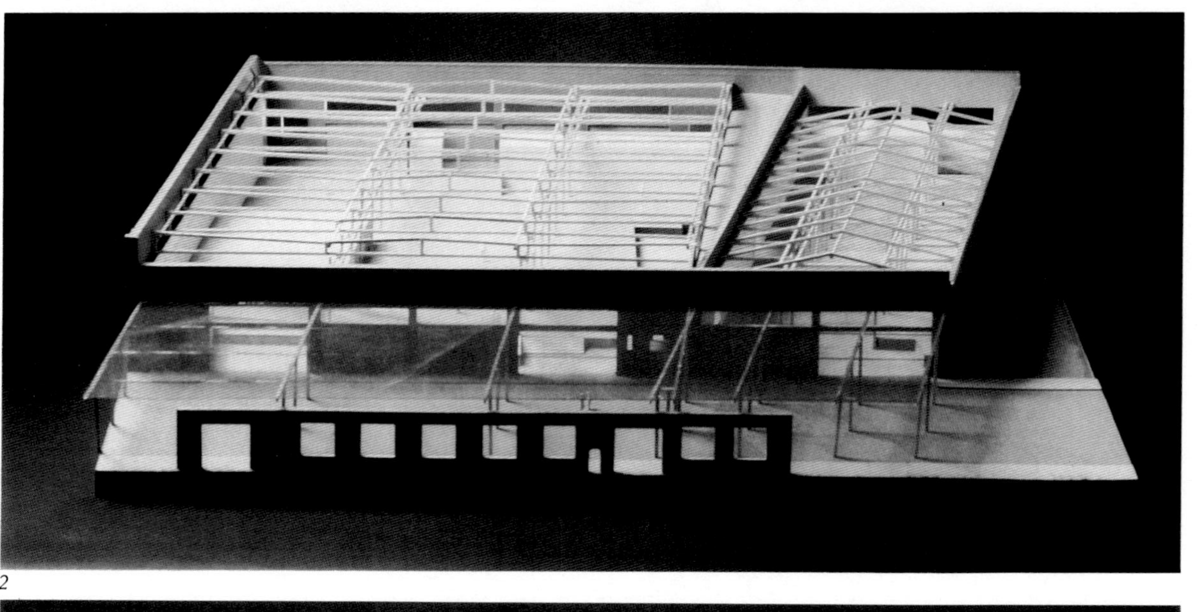

2

3

1–3. Installation

1

2

3

German Expressionist Sculpture
Los Angeles County Museum of Art 1983

The Special Exhibitions Gallery of the Los Angeles County Museum was again transformed by Gehry and Associates, this time for an exhibition of 150 pieces of German expressionist sculpture and related graphic material. The work exhibited was produced between the beginning of the century and the 1930s. Much of the work, and many of the artists who produced it, are unfamiliar, in large part because of an all-too-effective Nazi campaign. In the early thirties, the work was seen by the Nazi party as an example of the degeneracy from which Germany needed to be saved. "Degenerate Art" exhibitions were held, and much of the work of the artists featured in the show was destroyed. Given the tragic history and the emotional content of the work, Gehry sought to place each piece in an appropriately poignant setting. To stress the unique power of each piece, different architectural materials and different display techniques were used. Concrete, natural finish and cabinet-quality plywood, brick, and black and white lacquer created a variety of pedestals, platforms, and walls. A large statue of a beggar by Barlach was set in a niche replicating its original setting in a church facade. Lehmbruck's "Fallen Man" was in a very low niche against a dark crimson wall. Small bronzes were displayed on a workbench. A group of lifesize figures inhabited a maple-floored room seen through plexiglass; it was intended that the viewer feel drawn into the room with the statues. Works by Kirchner were grouped on a dais of boards to suggest the floor of the artist's studio; behind the extant pieces, however, set against a black backdrop, were photographs of his destroyed work.

1.Sculpture group in plexiglass-walled room 2.Works by Kirchner—extant and photographic record of work destroyed

1

2

Frances Howard Goldwyn Regional Branch Library ,
Hollywood, California

The Hollywood Branch Library was destroyed by arson in 1980. A replacement now under construction is being privately funded and will be given to the city. The buildings in the library's neighborhood are relatively large industrial and commercial structures. To make a private, controlled environment for the library, a wall fifteen feet high surrounds the property. The building's massing is symmetrical and monumental, lending the library a civic character at a scale competitive with its surroundings. In the central bay is a two-story entrance and reading hall, flanked by large reading rooms on each floor of the two-story pavilions. On the north side of the central hall's second floor ambulatory is a wall of glass opening the hall to views of the distant hills.

1

The pavilions, or "reading boxes" as they are called by the designer, are lit by clerestories, designed as objects overhanging the roof in part to protect the upper reading rooms from late morning and afternoon glare. The areas between the reading rooms and the site walls are developed as water gardens, on to which the ground floor reading rooms open directly. The proportions of stucco planes to glazing and the relatively small, asymmetrically located clerestory structures suggest a more domesticated scale than implied by the overall massing. Construction is scheduled to be completed by August of 1985.

1.Ground breaking ceremony 2.Elevation 3.Section 4.1st floor plan 5.2nd floor plan 6–9.Model

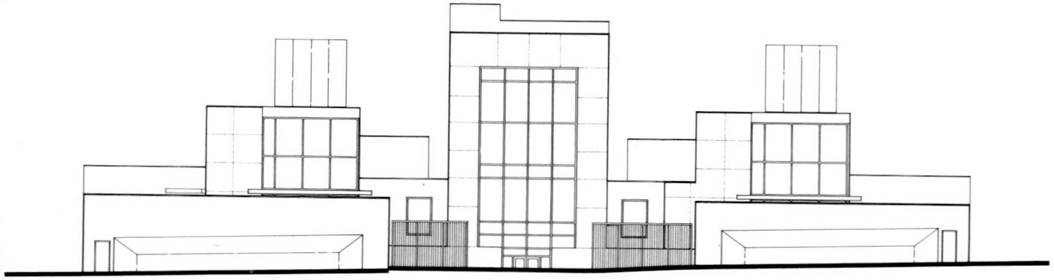

2

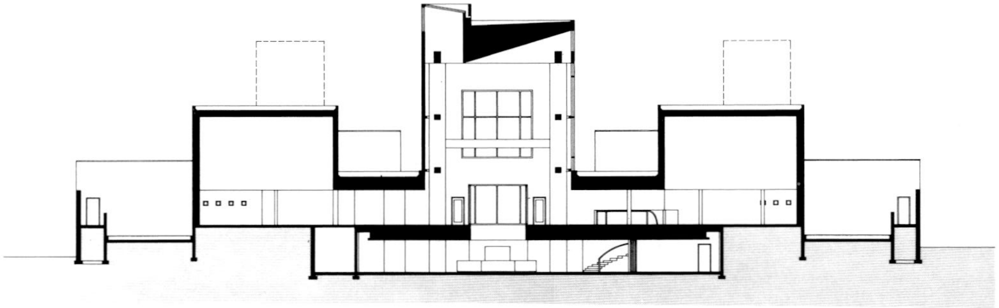

3

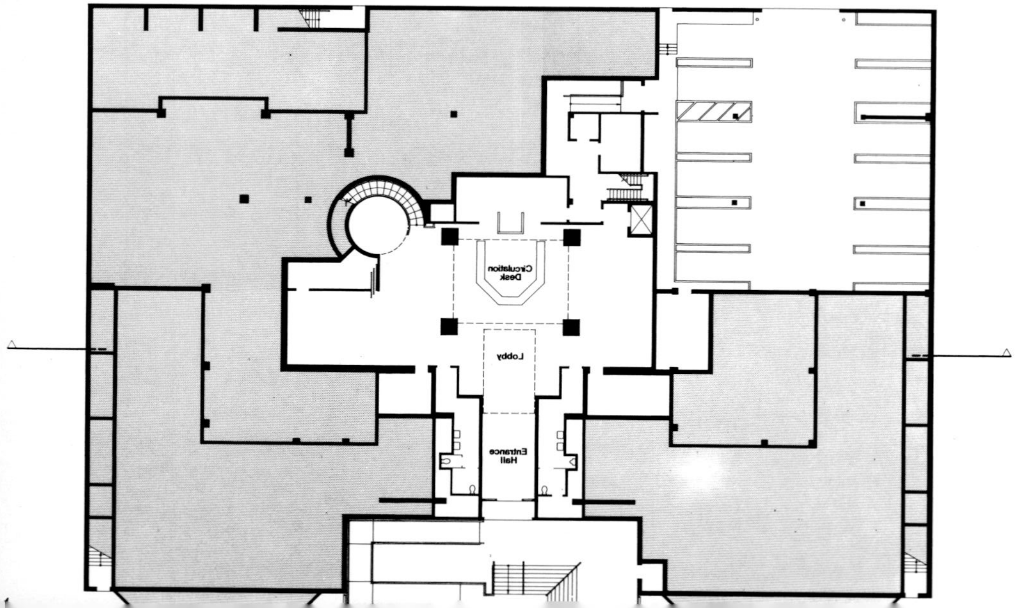

Circulation Desk
Lobby
Entrance Hall

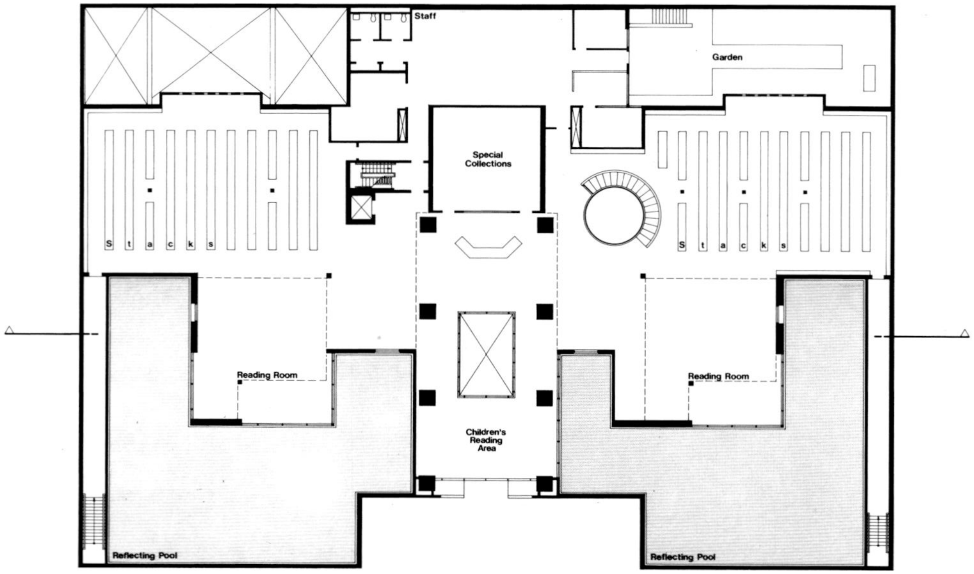

Staff
Garden
Special Collections
Stacks
Stacks
Reading Room
Reading Room
Children's Reading Area
Reflecting Pool
Reflecting Pool

5

6

7

8

9

Sirmai-Peterson House
Thousand Oaks, California 1984

The site on which this three-thousand-square-foot house is being constructed slopes down to a stream and a pond at the floor of a ravine. It is sufficiently large so that the rural character and natural beauty of the site can be maintained if new construction does not disrupt its scale with too monumental an insertion. Toward that end, a collection of small-scaled architectural pieces have been proposed to house program elements—living, dining and kitchen areas, service, den-television room, and two bedroom suites. Continuing exploration of composed relationships between architectural objects—seen in projects like those for the Jung Institute, the Smith House, and the House for a Film Maker—several apparently independent buildings have been arranged so as to underscore their individuality and to accommodate the specificities of view and terrain. As one approaches from the access road, more than twenty feet in elevation above the house, one's first view will be of the roof of the major building form and a tall cruciform element rising from it. From the kitchen/entry court at the north to the living room fireplace at the south, living, dining and kitchen spaces are organized along a central axis which bends slightly in deference to the site's slope and primary views. The cruciform element so visible upon approach is nearly filled, one discovers inside, by a second object—a concrete block shaft in which the kitchen vent stacks and heating flues have been collected to avoid the visual clutter normally found on rooftops. The cruciform shape, which rises an additional eighteen feet above the volume's twelve-foot ceilings, is slightly distorted from the orthogonal, reflecting the similar distortion of the building's axis. The bedrooms are housed in two volumes pulled slightly away from the main building component. One is reached by a bridge, the master bedroom by a semi-submerged tunnel. A wood-slat deck atop the master bedroom pavilion, reached by ascending the slope over the concrete-block "tunnel," clerestories bringing light into the bedroom pavilions and providing ventilation, several roof hatches also designed to channel warm air out of the house, and the cruciform stack element, are the only interruptions of the galvanized metal roof. Seamed metal panels will also be used as a wall surface on the center portion of the house. Other major materials are stucco and concrete block. Interiors are to be of drywall, exposed wood rafters, and unpainted plywood. To the east, the stream will be dammed to create a shallow lake onto which the living area will open. A planned guest house across the lake, a garage, and a swimming pool will complete the compositions of objects on the hillside.

1–4.Studies 5.Roof plan 6.Sections through core 7.Main floor plan

2

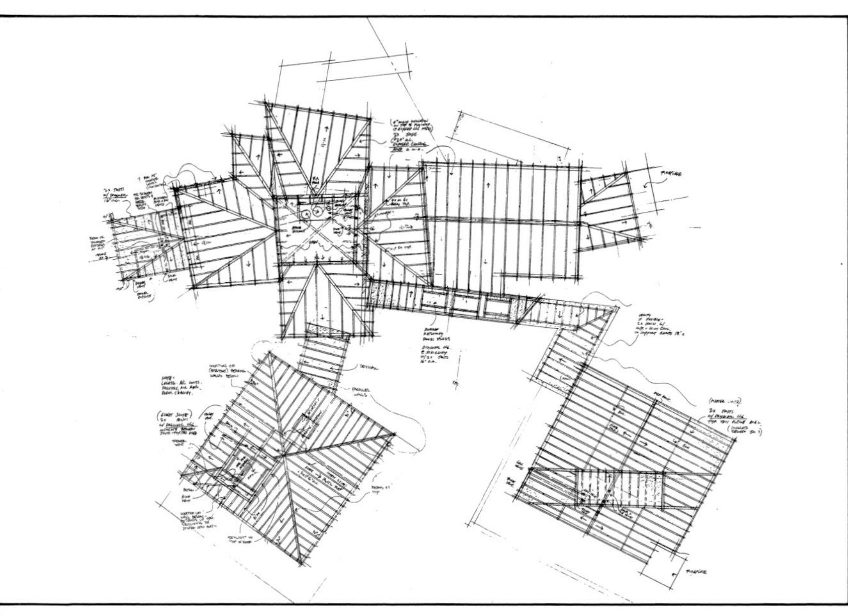

5

4

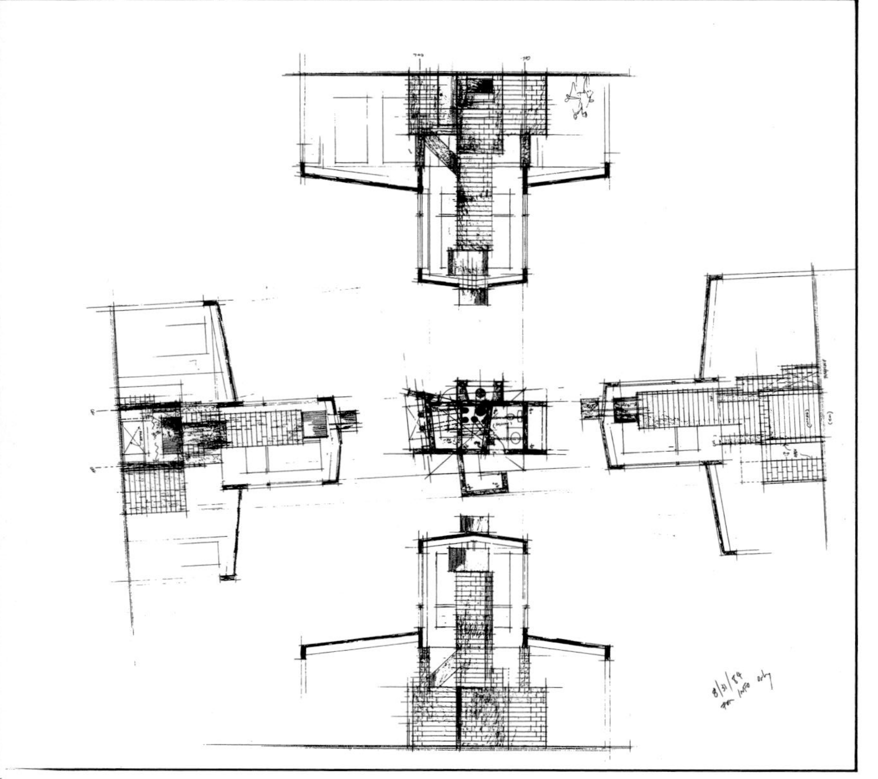

6

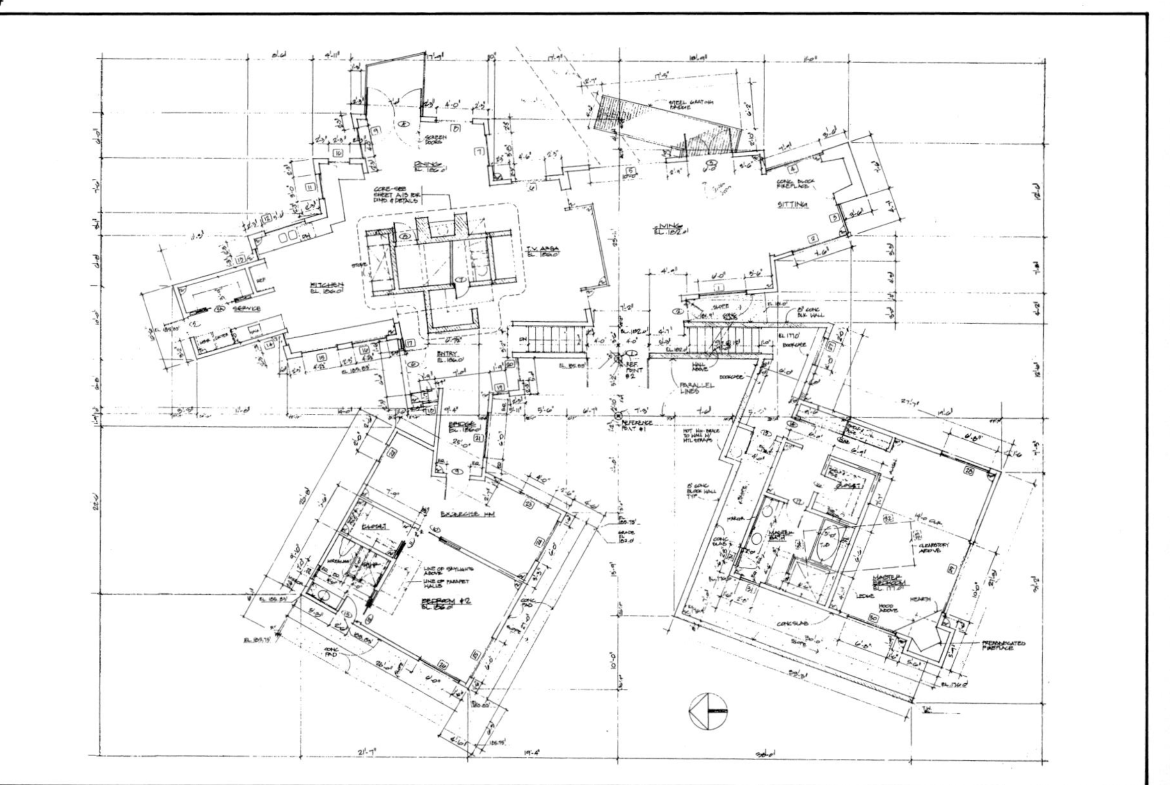

7

1–4. Model

1

2

3

Médiathèque—Centre D'Art Contemporain
Nîmes, France

The city of Nîmes in southern France enshrines one of the finest surviving examples of first century Roman architecture—the Maison Carrée. Built as a temple in the forum of the old Roman town and now a museum displaying ancient artifacts, it has attracted visitors and admirers for nearly two millenia. To further enliven its old town center and in the hope of approximating the tremendous success of the Centre Pompidou the city sponsored an invitational competition for a new contemporary art museum and library to be situated on one of the two adjoining open sites in the area. Contestants were charged to work toward a vision of a complex and site area full of activity, exuberance and excitement and to create a building with its own strong character. Gehry felt that anything "cute, seductive, or background" was contrary to the spirit and intent of the commission. Further, the site area was quite small compared to the program areas to be housed. He set out, therefore, to design a sculptural object distinct from but equally legible to, the Maison Carrée with relationships in scale to its context.
Several sets of design components were employed. First, substantial below-grade facilities serve not only to reduce the perceptible bulk of the project but also, as they extend beyond the site, provide a physical under-street link with the Maison Carrée which sits on a plinth slightly below existing ground level. Second, two distinct entrance pavilions—a spiral form as the main entrance, and a small apsidal building adjacent to the Maison Carrée—provide a transition in scale at street level, and act in concert with the overall sculptural composition of the complex. Third, the major building block corresponds in height to the cornice level of most buildings in the area. Fourth, a collection of smaller-scale pieces surmount the block, their relatively casual arrangement bearing some relationship to the smaller above-cornice building elements characteristic of many buildings in Nîmes and, most importantly, giving a strong sculptural character and identity to the new building. Fifth, lacing the components of the building together are a system of stairs, escalators, terraces and view platforms designed to invite and promote use of the building as an extension of the streets and open areas around it—the building was made to be activated by, and appear to come alive with, people moving through and over its forms.
The three below-grade elements include service, storage and closed stack areas, theaters and galleries. The latter are contained in the middle of these levels and are lit with a system first explored for the Janss House. Light wells rise from the galleries, through the level directly above, to grade. Within these tall shafts light is reflected and re-reflected so that even, ambient indirect daylighting reaches the galleries. The level immediately below grade is designed as an interior "street"—onto which a book store, tea room, theaters and entrance to administrative areas open—linking the complex to the Maison Carrée. A circular, glass-roofed entrance adjacent at the latter rises up from a bridge overlooking the galleries.
Upon entry through the spiral-form pavilion, one would find oneself on a bridge above the galleries holding the permanent collection, down to which escalators lead. Ahead one would find the library entrance with its own series of escalators. The seven levels of the library are designed around a naturally-lit atrium, also open to all museum levels below. Three levels above the entrance contain library reading rooms, including one devoted to the region's history and traditions of bullfighting. Beyond this room's north window, sculpture representing a bull's head would also provide an axial focal point visible from several area streets. The fourth level contains administrative areas, including the Center Director's office, articulated by its non-orthogonal placement and its private terrace. The fifth, sixth and seventh floors contain the children's library and attendant workshops developed with a series of terraces, outdoor stairs, lookout points linked by a sequence of stairs which climb around the spiral form (the top of which forms a lookout facing the Maison Carrée), and zig-zag across the face of the library block.
That the crown and most exuberant portion of the complex is devoted to children's facilities is a carefully considered decision. Gehry cites a policy commitment on the part of the French Government recognizing that the future of French culture lies with her children. An exciting environment for early exposure to reading and art Gehry felt would stimulate positive reactions to learning. He also feels it an expression of optimism about the future, for the French Government's faith in and commitment to children as our hope and greatest resource is a primary tenet of Gehry himself. From his workshops for inner-city school children to his designs for projects like the Los Angeles Children's Museum, Arts Park and the Cabrillo Marine Museum, Gehry has sought in his work to engage the minds and spirits of children in exploring the world around them, in considering how things do work and how they might work. The decision is also appropriate to the complex's function as a museum of contemporary art. For at its best, the gift of contemporary art is that it helps us see parts of the world anew, recaptures the sense of wonder at things seen for the first time which most of us seem to lose after childhood. It is also the gift of Frank Gehry and his architecture.

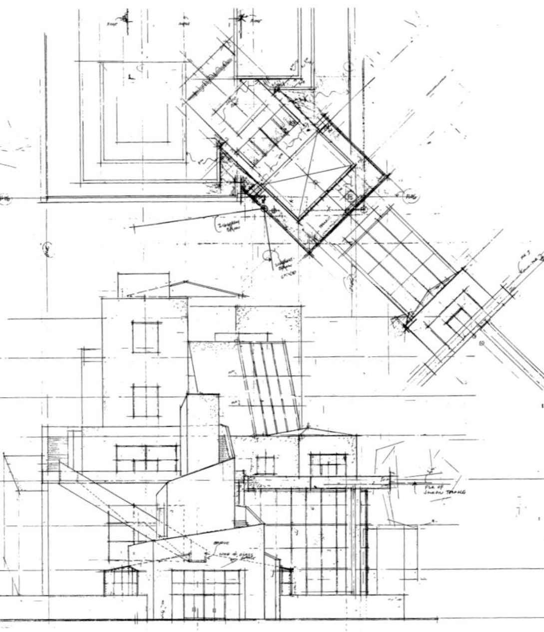

1

1.Study: entrance 2.Plan: 1st level below grade 3.Plan: 2nd level below grade 4.Plan: 3rd level below grade 5.Ground level plan 6.2nd floor plan 7.3rd floor plan 8.4th floor plan 9.5th floor plan 10.6th floor plan 11.Section

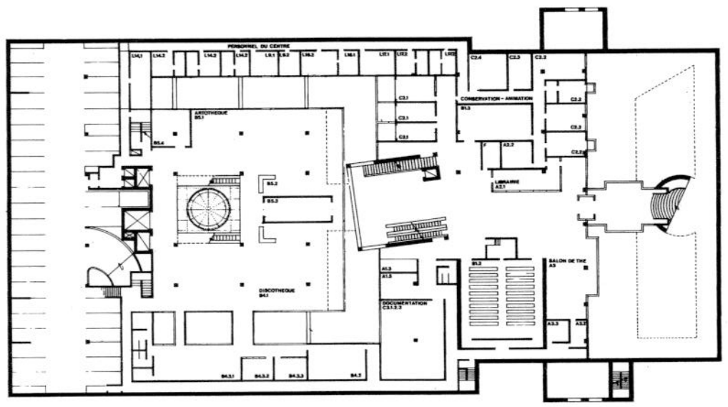

2

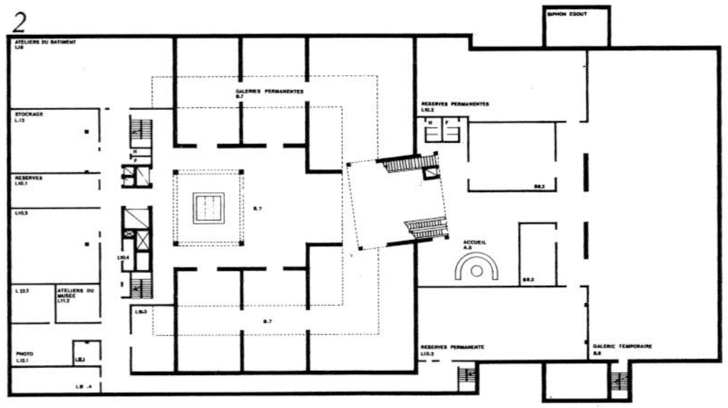

3

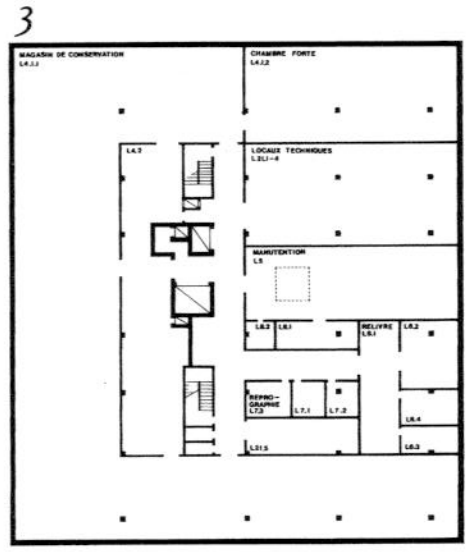

4

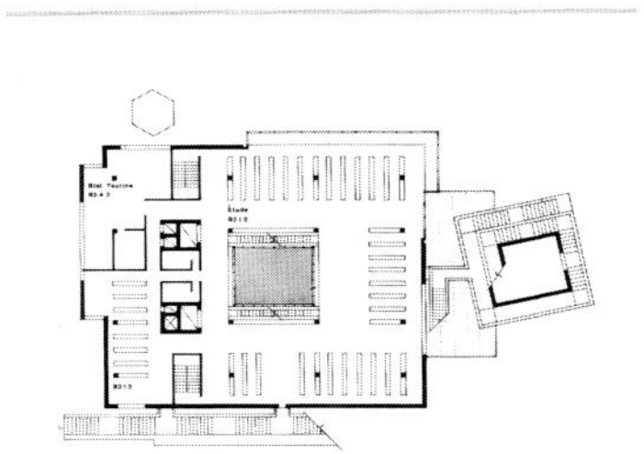

5

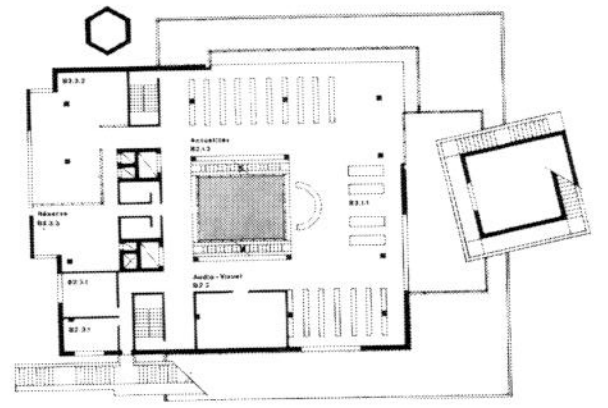

6

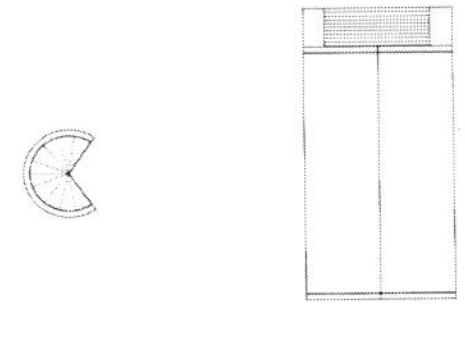

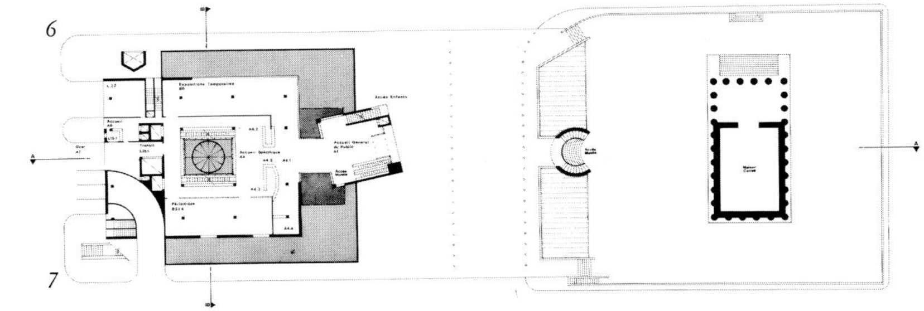

7

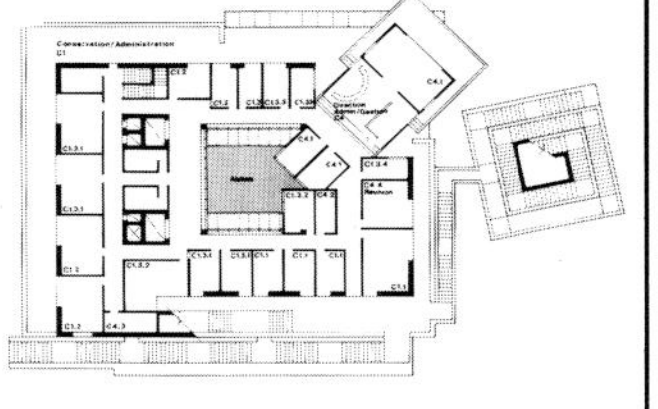

8

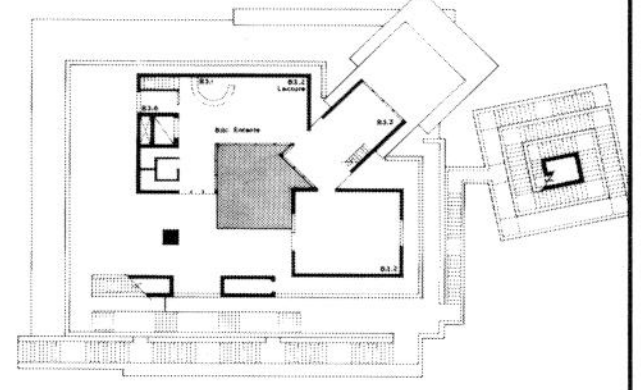

9

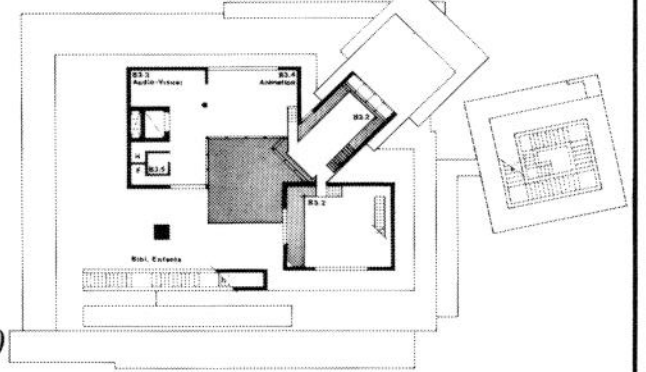

10

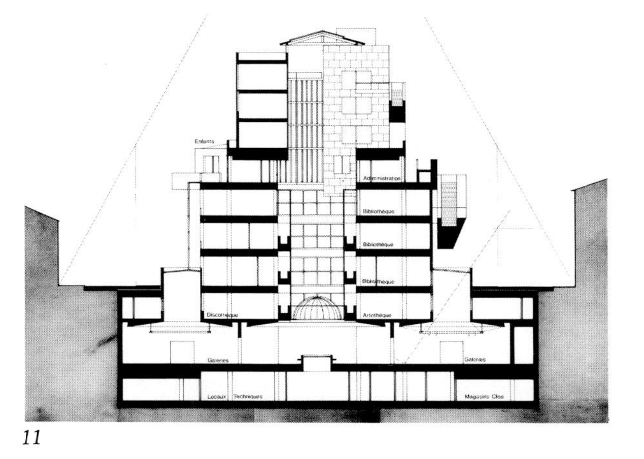

11

1.Section through library and galleries. 2,3.General views

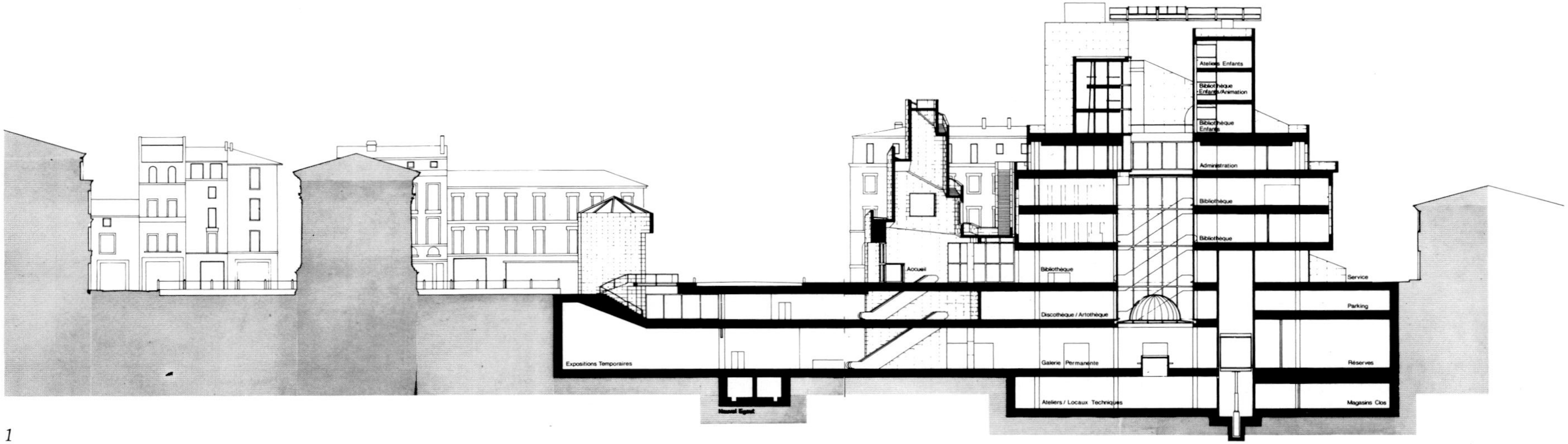

1

2

3

Project Credits

The projects shown in this volume represent the work of the following individuals. We have made every effort to ensure that the names and dates are complete and correct but we apologize for any errors or omissions.

1962–1963
Wesley Bilson
Robert Ford
Frank Gehry
Fereydoon Ghaffari
Virgilio Rodriguez
Richard Snyder
Frederick Usher
Gregory Walsh

1964
Richard Berry
David Brodsley
Elizabeth Doore
Frank Gehry
Katherine Goff
Gere Kavanaugh
David Rosen
Frederick Usher
Gregory Walsh

1965–1966
Elizabeth Doore
Frank Gehry
Alfredo Javier
Gere Kavanaugh
Jerry Sirlin
Deborah Sussman
Alan Tossman
Frederick Usher
Gregory Walsh
Peter Wurzburger

1967
Robert Beauchamp
Elizabeth Doore
Alfredo Javier
Frank Gehry
David O'Malley
Radoslav Sutnar
Alan Tossman
Gregory Walsh

1968
Roberta Altoon
Robert Beauchamp
Frank Gehry
Alfredo Javier
David O'Malley
Alan Tossman
Gregory Walsh

1969
Xavier Aboitiz
Roberta Altoon
Laurie Anderson
Madeline Banchik
Robert Beauchamp
Jeffrey Bernstein
William Chapman
John Garritson
Frank Gehry
Tahn Hyun
Alfredo Javier
Kenneth Kuss
Maynard Lyndon
Adolpho Ortega
David Reyes
Brent Saville
Sandi Simola
Sharon Singer
Richard Smith
Ernest Tanji
Chitra Techaphaibul
George Terpatsi
Alan Tossman
Frederick Usher
Mark Wagner
Gregory Walsh
Russell Werth
Peter Wurzburger
Joshua Young
Rochelle Young
Ted Zilius

1970
Xavier Aboitiz
Roberta Altoon
Laurie Anderson
Michael Asher
Larry Barrish
Jeffrey Bernstein
William Chapman
Virginia Chesman
Stephen Dane
Christopher Dawson
Veronica Felder
Gary Ferguson
Gabrielle de Ganges
Frank Gehry
Carol Han
Stephen Harger
Ann Hosfeld
Tahn Hyun
Alfredo Javier
Lynda King
William Lester
Robert Maxwell
Adolpho Ortega
David Reyes
Virgilio Rodriguez
Frank Romero
Joan Santagata
Hak Sik Son
Allan Stanton
Alan Tossman
Joseph Toussaint
Frederick Usher
Roderick Usher
Gregory Walsh
Elizabeth Williams
Joshua Young
Rochelle Young

1971
Xavier Aboitiz
Katrin Adams
Michael Asher
George Barnes
Jeffrey Bernstein
Donald Bloom
David Brodsley
Pamela Burton
Donald Burton
Donald Carlson
William Chapman
Virginia Chesman
Clodualdo Crisostomo
Steven Dane
Brina Gehry
Frank Gehry
Leslie Gehry
Arnold Ginsberg
Helen Harris
Tahn Hyun
Rene Ilustre
Alfredo Javier
Ramon Juncal
Gerald Kamitaki
Mark Keiserman
Jerry Kotas
Jeffrey Lentz
Ernesto Leyva
Robert Maxwell
John Morgan
Enrique Navarrete
Adolpho Ortega
Charles Patton
James Porter
Paul Prejza
Ralph Ridgeway
Antonio Rodriguez
Virgilio Rodriguez
Edwin Sankey
Stephen Schuck
Frederick Schwartz
Mark Schwartz
Alexis Smith
Elsie Solvberg
Hak Sik Son
Deborah Sussman
Alan Tossman
Joseph Toussaint
Elliot Tsujiuchi
Wayne Twedell
Frederick Usher
Gregory Walsh
Elizabeth Williams
Karlin Wong
Joshua Young

1972
Xavier Aboitiz
Mary Armstrong
Vaughn Babcock
Donald Carlson
William Chapman
Virginia Chesman
Renato Corzo
John Dash
Alan Erenberg
Frank Gehry
Leslie Gehry
Roy Holman
James Hutton
Douglas Hyun
Tahn Hyun
Rene Ilustre
Mark Keiserman
Gerald Komity
Jerry Kotas
Edward Levine
Ernesto Leyva
Paula Lintz
Brian Maridan
Steven Millington
John New
Adolpho Ortega
James Porter
Ralph Ridgeway
Stephen Schuck
Alexis Smith
Hak Sik Son
Donald Swiers
Naomi Swiers

Tziporah Toubi
Robert Walder
Gregory Walsh
Margaret Watson
Elizabeth Williams
Joshua Young

1973
Ronald Altoon
Marc Appleton
Romeo Asprec
Adelino Bacani
Vaughn Babcock
Wilfredo Burgas
Pamela Burton
Donald Carlson
William Chapman
Virginia Chesman
Timothy Clement
Suzanne Coles
Kathleen Connell
William Daughlash
Jan Dorbritz
Alan Erenberg
Ignacio Garcia
Frank Gehry
Leslie Gehry
Jaime Gesundheit
James Hutton
Rene Ilustre
Reynold Kimura
Eugene Kupper
Ernesto Leyva
Dale Lewis
Jose Luciano
Beverly Meredith
Steven Millington
Adolpho Ortega
Barton Phelps
James Porter
Melchor Reyes
Ricardo Sabella
Ricardo Santiano
Joan Sacks
David Schneider
Hak Sik Son
Alexis Smith
Donald Swiers
Morgan Thomas
Tziporah Toubi
Gregory Walsh

1974
Ronald Altoon
Marc Appleton
Vaughn Babcock
Donald Carlson
Virginia Chesman
James Collimore
Robert Doyle
Frank Gehry
Rene Ilustre
Eugene Kupper
Jean O'Laire
Barton Phelps
Hak Sik Son
Morgan Thomas
Gregory Walsh

1975 Ronald Altoon
Marc Appleton
Vaughn Babcock
Donald Carlson
James Collimore
Joyce Cox
Robert Doyle
Frank Gehry
Thelma Gehry
Rene Ilustre
Richard Orne
Barton Phelps
Claire Pollock
Hak Sik Son
Gregory Walsh

1976
Ronald Altoon
Diane Arnold
Sarah Berwick
Marla Brasius
Jerzy Czerwinski
Jesse Ferguson
Michael Folonis
Berta Gehry
Frank Gehry
Gary Goldsmith
Rene Ilustre
Nancy Michali
Thomas Michali
Marjorie Mix
Ruben Ojeda
Adolpho Ortega
Hak Sik Son
Gregory Walsh

1977
Patricia Belton-Oliver
Rebecca Berwick
Sarah Berwick
Thomas Blaskiewitz
Gerald Chavez
John Clagett
Jesus Corpus
Sheri Eaton
Frederick Fisher
Matthew Fry
Berta Gehry
Frank Gehry
James Gibbs
Rene Ilustre
Donald King
Paul Lubowicki
Jose Luciano
Richard Luke
Albert Pope
Virgilio Rodriguez
Marna Schnabel
Hak Sik Son
Steven Tomko
Bruce Tucker
Clay Tudor
Gregory Walsh

1978
Patricia Belton-Oliver
Rebecca Berwick
John Clagett
Sheri Eaton
Frederick Fisher
Matthew Fry
Berta Gehry
Brina Gehry
Frank Gehry
Andra Georges
James Gibbs
Rene Ilustre
Paul Lubowicki
Erica Millar
Jerry Pomerantz
Hak Sik Son
Steven Tomko
Clay Tudor
Gregory Walsh

1979
Margo Alofsin
Albert Borgo
Rebecca Berwick
John Clagett
Robert Cloud
Jeffrey Daniels
Sheri Eaton
Kenneth Francis
Douglas Gagan
Berta Gehry
Frank Gehry
Elyse Grinstein
Rene Ilustre
Heather Kurze
Paul Lubowicki
Mitzi Montgomery
Shirley Nounan
Sharon Peckinpah
Stephen Porten
Hak Sik Son
Steven Tomko
Gregory Walsh
Kin Wah Yung

1980
Robert Cloud
Jeffrey Daniels
Pamela Donnelly
Kenneth Francis
Kathryn Frankel
Elizabeth Gaskins
Berta Gehry
Frank Gehry
Michael Hargrave
Paula Howard
Rene Ilustre
Joanne Joyce
Daniel Kantor
Kiki Keyser
Heather Kurze
Paul Lubowicki
Adolpho Ortega
Antonio Romano
Hak Sik Son
Maureen Tamuri
Steven Tomko
Rachel Vert
Gregory Walsh
Laurie Weeks
Sharon Williams
Edwin Woll

1981
Michele Andrew
Robert Bernstein
Anna Chin
John Clagett
Pamela Donnelly
Jean de Gastines
Addison Edwards
Irene Frankel
Kathryn Frankel
Berta Gehry
Frank Gehry
Robert Hale
Carla Harary
Rene Ilustre
John Johnston
David Kellen

Paul Krueger
Matthew Larrabee
Paul Lubowicki
Michael Moran
Antonio Romano
Hak Sik Son
Steven Tomko
Rachel Vert
Gregory Walsh
Sharon Williams
Edwin Woll

1982
William Block
Albert Borgo
Nancy Braswell
Claudia Carol
Joshua Chaiken
John Chase
John Clagett
Gregory Cloud
William Cooperman
Addison Edwards
Ian Espinoza
Irene Frankel
Berta Gehry
Frank Gehry
Ralph Gentile
Robert Hale
Carla Harary
Rene Ilustre
John Johnson
Ronald Johnson
David Kellen
Amy Lann
Charles Lowrey
Paul Lubowicki
Michael Moran
Paul Nagashima
Adolpho Ortega
Ewa Osinski
Tomasz Osinski
Dean Perton
Anthony Pleskow
Antonio Romano
Katherine Spitz
Steven Tomko
Kenneth Walker
Gregory Walsh
Diana R. Weinberg
Sharon Williams
Edwin Woll
David Zung

1983
Yuk Chan
Joshua Chaiken
John Clagett
John Davis
Douglas Davis
Douglas Dworsky
Irene Frankel
Berta Gehry
Frank Gehry
Robert Hale
David Hertz
Ruth Higley
Rene Ilustre
Ron Johnson
David Kellen
Mitzi Kubrick
Paul Lubowicki
Michael Moran
Robert Moriarty
Charles Oakley
Eamonn O'Mahony
Adolpho Ortega
Thomas Ochi
Tomasz Osinski
Patricia Owen
Dean Perton
Jerry Radin
Gregory Walsh
Sharon Williams

1984
Peter Becker
Ildiko Choy
Dona Marie
John Clagett
John Davis
Nicholas Eisenman
Irene Frankel
Berta Gehry
Frank Gehry
Diane Gillis
Robert Hale
Rene Ilustre
Ron Johnson
David Kellen
Mitzi Kubrick
Mitchell Lawrence
Michael Lehrer
Paul Lubowicki
Dominique Lyon
Michael Moran
Eamonn O'Mahony
Tomasz Osinski
Patricia Owen
Undine Prohl
Loriah Robinson
Josh Schweitzer
Caroll Stockard
Gregory Walsh
Diana R. Weinberg
Sharon Williams
Sergio Zeballos

Biography

Frank O. Gehry was born in 1929 in Toronto. He attended the University of Southern California, first as Fine Arts major, then as an architecture student, receiving his Bachelor of Architecture in 1954. Subsequently, he worked as a designer in the office of Victor Gruen Associates and served in the Special Services Division of the United States Army. During 1956 and 1957, he studied City Planning at Harvard's Graduate School of Design. In the years following, he worked at the offices of Hideo Sasaki, Pereira & Luckman, Victor Gruen Associates and Andre Remondet. Since 1962 he has been a principal of his own design firm. A corporate member of the American Institute of Architects, Southern California Chapter, Mr. Gehry was elected to the College of Fellows of the American Institute of Architects in 1974 for Achievement in Design.

He has served as a critic and design instructor at the University of Southern California, the Southern California Institute of Architecture, Rice University, the University of California at Los Angeles, Parsons, Yale, and Harvard. He has also worked with the Los Angeles School System, the National Endowment for the Arts and the Smithsonian Institution developing and teaching programs to introduce grade school children to the problems and forms of urban planning.

His work has been published internationally in books and magazines ranging from *Art in America* to *Time.* His drawings and furniture have been exhibited at the Museum of Modern Art, the Cooper-Hewitt museum, and the Louvre. In 1983 the American Academy and Institute of Arts and Letters awarded him its Arnold W. Brunner Prize, given annually to "an architect who has made a significant contribution to architecture as an art."

Books and Catalogs

Banham, Reyner. *Los Angeles: The Architecture of Four Ecologies.* Harmondsworth, England; Baltimore; Ringwood, Australia: Allen Lane/Penguin, 1971.

Hennessey, James, *Nomadic Furniture.* New York: Pantheon, 1973.

La Jolla Museum of Contemporary Art. *Innovations: Contemporary Home Environs.* La Jolla, California: La Jolla Museum of Contemporary Art, 1973.

Gebhard, David and Robert Winter. *A Guide to Architecture in Los Angeles and Southern California.* Santa Barbara and Salt Lake City: Peregrine Smith, 1977.

———, and Deborah Nevins. *200 Years of American Architectural Drawings.* New York: Watson-Guptill, 1977.

San Francisco Museum of Art. *A View of California Architecture: 1960–1976.* San Francisco: San Francisco Museum of Art, 1977.

California Institute of Technology. *Jack Brogan: Projects.* Baxter Art Gallery, California Institute of Technology, 1980.

Diamonstein, Barbaralee. *American Architecture Now.* New York: Rizzoli, 1980.

Gill, Brendan. *The Dream Come True: Great Houses of Los Angeles.* New York: Lippincott & Crowell, 1980.

La Biennale di Venezia. *La Presenza del Passato.* Venice: Edizione La Biennale di Venezia, 1980.

Tigerman, Stanley. *The Chicago Tribune Tower Competition and Late Entries.* New York: Rizzoli International, 1980.

Boissiére, Olivier. *Gehry/Site/Tigerman—Trois Portraits de l'Artiste en Architects.* Paris: Editions du Moniteur, 1981.

Diamonstein, Barbaralee, ed. *Collaborations: Artists and Architects.* New York: Watson-Guptill, 1981.

McCoy, Esther, and Barbara Goldstein. *Guide to U.S. Architecture 1940–1980.* Los Angeles: Art and Architecture Press, 1981.

Williams, Tod, and Ricardo Scofidio. *Window Room Furniture.* New York: Rizzoli, 1981.

Wurman, Richard Saul. *L.A. Access.* Los Angeles: Access Press, January 1981.

Giminez, Carmen, and Juan Munoz. *Correspondences.* Madrid: Ministerio de Obras Publicas y Urbanismo, 1982.

Institute for Architecture and Urban Studies. *California Counterpoint.* New York: Rizzoli, 1982.

Institute for Architecture and Urban Studies. *Indiana Avenue Artists' Studios, Venice California, 1981.* New York: Institute for Architecture and Urban Studies, 1982.

Institute of Contemporary Art. *Frank O. Gehry, An Exhibition of Recent Projects.* Boston: Institute of Contemporary Art, 1982.

La Jolla Museum of Contemporary Art. *The California Condition.* La Jolla, California: La Jolla Museum of Contemporary Art, 1982.

University of Southern California, *Frank Gehry: Selected Works.* Los Angeles: The University of Southern California, The USC Atelier, 1982.

Whitney Museum of American Art. *Shape and Environment: Furniture by American Architects.* New York: Whitney Museum of Art, 1982.

Archer, B. J. *Follies. Architecture for the Late-Twentieth-Century Landscape.* New York: Leo Castelli Gallery, 1983.

Brooklyn Academy of Music. *Next Wave Festival,* New York: Brooklyn Academy of Music, 1983.

Gilbert-Rolfe, Jeremy, Ingram Marshall, and Susan Sontag. *Available Light.* Los Angeles: Museum of Contemporary Art, 1983.

Goldberger, Paul. *On The Rise.* New York: Times Books, 1983.

Institute of Contemporary Arts. *Ten New Buildings.* London: Institute of Contemporary Arts, 1983.

Kardon, Janet. *Connections: Bridges/Ladders/Ramps/Staircases/Tunnels.* Philadelphia: Institute of Contemporary Art, University of Pennsylvania, 1983.

The Metropolitan Museum of Art. *Notable Acquisitions.* New York: The Metropolitan Museum of Art, 1983.

Jencks, Charles, and William Chaitkin. *Architecture Today.* New York: Abrams, 1984.

Newspapers

"After the Kids." *Los Angeles Herald Examiner,* August 18, 1963.

"Picture Preview of Progress in Construction." *Southwest Building and Contractor,* January 24, 1964.

"Apartment Planned." *Los Angeles Times,* April 19, 1964.

"Architect Explains Leisure." *Santa Maria Times,* October 30, 1964.

"Wilde Lake Village Development Begins." *Baltimore Sun,* July 19, 1966.

"D.C. Symphony Pavilion to Be 'Giant Umbrella'." *Washington Evening Star,* June 21, 1967.

"Columbia Seeks to Revive 'Village Life'." *Baltimore Sun,* June 28, 1967.

Galkin, Elliot W. "Music Festivals: Unique...". *Baltimore Sun,* July 9, 1967.

Hill, Frederic B. "Wet Throng Hails Columbia, Rouse, Humphrey, and Music." *Baltimore Sun,* July 15, 1967.

"Music Fete Marred by Mud, Rain." *Baltimore Evening Sun,* July 15, 1967.

MacPherson, Myra. "Symphony Gala Ends as Okefenokee of the Arts." *The New York Times,* July 16, 1967.

Schonberg, Harold C. "Music: Columbia Festival is Baptized." *The New York Times,* July 16, 1967.

"Rain Christens Culture in New Columbia Pavilion." *The Washington Post,* July 16, 1967.

Hume, Paul. "New Symphony Pavilion Has Gay Nineties Aura." *The Washington Post,* July 17, 1967.

"Music Pavilion Opens." *Baltimore Sun,* July 17, 1967.

Schonberg, Harold C. "Music: Hurtling from Famine to Feast." *The New York Times,* July 23, 1967.

MacPherson, Myra. "Maryland Partygoers Refused to Be Rained Out Again." *The New York Times,* August 5, 1967.

James, Hibbard. "Cheer the Pavilion Hear, Hear." *Washington Daily News,* August 11, 1967.

Desser, Lou. "Ponte Vecchio Theme: Architect Envisions Seaside Tourist Spot." *Los Angeles Times,* August 27, 1967.

Aree, Hector, "Things to Come... Now." *Home Furnishings Daily,* July 2, 1968.

" 'Sound Barrier' Solves Noise Problem." *Los Angeles Times,* August 11, 1968.

"Store Openings: Joseph Magnin." *Fashion Week,* November 25, 1968.

"Eye on Architecture." *Home Furnishings Daily,* December 16, 1968.

Schonberg, Harold C. "Acoustician Hits a High Note with His Slide Rule." *The New York Times,* July 19, 1969.

"Architects Win Awards for 12 Building Designs." *Los Angeles Times,* November 16, 1969.

"Guidance by New Towns." *Baltimore Sun,* November 23, 1969.

"Architects Report New Towns Need Public Guidance." *Home Builder News,* December 8, 1969.

Aree, Hector. "Store Packaging: Fashion in Display." *Women's Wear Daily,* January 13, 1970.

Rockwell, John. "A Different Bowl Awaits Summer Concert Goers." *Los Angeles Times,* April 22, 1970.

Scott, Gay. "Bowl Gets Facelifting to Tune of $160,000." *S.C. Citizen News,* April 25, 1970.

Bernheimer, Martin. "A New Look, a New Sound for an Old Bowl." *Los Angeles Times Calendar,* May 24, 1970.

LePage, David, "First Apartments at Irvine Put Focus on Space." *Los Angeles Times,* July 5, 1970.

Turpin, Dick. "Child Planners Build City of Dreams... More Space for Recreation." *Los Angeles Times,* July 5, 1970.

Bernheimer, Martin. "Krips Conducts Opener at the Revamped Bowl." *Los Angeles Times,* July 9, 1970.

Koch, Sharon Fay. "First-Nighter Picnic, Hear Beethoven." *Los Angeles Times,* July 9, 1970.

Mouson, Karen. "Sound Mars Festive Hollywood Bowl Opening." *Los Angeles Herald Examiner,* July 9, 1970.

Pastier, John. "Design Team Makes Notable Contribution to Hollywood Bowl." *Los Angeles Times,* July 19, 1970.

"School Children Build Models to Learn City Problems." *Los Angeles Herald Examiner,* November 15, 1971.

California Institute of the Arts. "Institute Is Host to Young City Builders." *Institute News,* January 5, 1972.

Fried, Alexander. "Concord Readies Pavilion." *San Francisco Examiner,* February 19, 1972.

Murphy, Jean. "From Sand Castles to Cities of Future." *Los Angeles Times,* March 14, 1972.

McCormack, Patricia. "Award Winning Architect Designs New Furniture." *Lexington Leader,* March 25, 1972.

———. "Different Kind of Lib." *Montreal Sunday Express,* March 26, 1972.

———. "Here It Is: Low Cost, No Upkeep Furniture." *Miami Herald,* March 26, 1972.

"Furniture for a Revolution." *San Francisco Examiner,* March 27, 1972.

"Bar, Desk Unit or Perch." *Rocky Mountain News,* April 1, 1972.

"The Squiggly Look." *Baltimore Sun,* April 3, 1972.

"Easy Pieces." *Home Furnishings Daily,* April 7, 1972.

Meyers, Mary. "Bloomingdale's... Living Naturally." *Home Furnishings Daily,* April 12, 1972.

Reif, Rita. "Mediterranean Style Upstaged." *The New York Times,* April 12, 1972.

Rogers, Susan. "That's Right... Cardboard." *New York Post,* April 13, 1972.

"Easy Edges Marks the Next Step in Furniture Design." *Chicago Tribune,* April 17, 1972.

Hoffman, Marilyn. "Liberated Design: Cardboard Moves in on Furniture World." *The Christian Science Monitor,* April 19, 1972.

———. "Cardboard Furniture: Chic and Low Cost." *Baltimore Sun,* April 30 1972.

Hazlett, Judy. "Lifestyle: New Concept Is Easy to Live With." *Long Beach Independent Press-Telelgram,* May 30, 1972.

"The Cardboard Furniture Is Here." *Riverside–San Bernadino Press-Enterprise,* June 4, 1972.

"Fiberboard Furniture: Easy on The Eye, Easy on the Wallet." *Chicago Tribune,* June 11, 1972.

"Paper Chairs? Fashioned Furniture." *Biloxi–Gulfport Daily Herald,* June 12, 1972.

McDermott, Madeline. "It's Different, Curvy and Cardboard." *Houston Chronicle,* June 22, 1972.

Manning, Amy. "The Corrugated Comeback." *Washington Sunday Star,* July 9, 1972.

Sabol, Blair. "Teacher Chauvinism Not Tolerated: The City That 20 Children Build." *Village Voice,* August 31, 1972.

Holmes, Amy. "The Spotlight: New Looks in Now Design." *Houston Chronicle,* December 1, 1972.

Moosbrugger, Ed. "SM Picks Rouse Plan for Center." *Santa Monica Evening Outlook,* May 23, 1973.

Beubis, Seymour. "Firm Named for $100 Million Project in Santa Monica." *Los Angeles Times,* May 24, 1973.

Moosbrugger, Ed. "Imagination Wins in Santa Monica: Openness Counts." *Santa Monica Evening Outlook,* May 25, 1973.

Hollis, Robert. "Proposal May Halt Bay Fill." *San Francisco Examiner and Chronicle,* June 3, 1973.

Pastier, John. "A Vote for Innovation in Santa Monica." *Los Angeles Times,* June 4, 1973.

"Greenbrae Mall Plan to Be Aired." *Los Angeles Times,* June 4, 1973.

Perry, Patricia, "Shopping Center Vote Is Cheered." *San Rafael Independent Journal,* June 6, 1973.

"Shopping Center Action Is Taken." *San Rafael Independent Journal,* June 19, 1973.

"Water Issue Stirs Anger in Marin Country." *Los Angeles Times,* June 20, 1973.

Feather, Leonard. "No Dissonance: Jazz Festival in Concord." *Los Angeles Times,* August 1, 1973.

"Renovation Study of Hollywood Bowl Set."· *Los Angeles Times,* September 26, 1973.

Ingram, Erik M. "Lack of Public Transit for Proposed Center Hit." *San Rafael Independent Journal,* November 15, 1973.

"Santa Monica Officials in High Praise of Redevelopers." *Los Angeles Times,* November 16, 1973.

"Shopping Center Stand Tabled by Town Meeting." *San Rafael Independent Journal,* November 12, 1973.

"Desert Facility." *Los Angeles Times,* December 2, 1973.

"Corte Madera Open Space Plan Element Is Approved." *San Rafael Independent Journal,* January 21, 1974.

"No Commercial Use of Muzzi Marshland." *San Rafael Independent Journal,* January 22, 1974.

Moosbrugger, Ed. "For Redevelopment: Santa Monica Agency Picks Three Consultants." *Santa Monica Evening Outlook,* January 24, 1974.

"Ferry Foes Beaten by Full Board." *San Rafael Independent Journal,* February 5, 1974.

Moosbrugger, Ed. "Environmental Impact: Shopping Center Consultant Picked." *Santa Monica Evening Outlook,* February 15, 1974.

Morgenthaler, Anne. "Santa Monica Development: Shopping Center Faces Obstacles." *Santa Monica Evening Outlook,* February 20, 1974.

Fanucchi, Ken. "Planners Will Tackle Mandate: Improve Quality of Life in Santa Monica." *Los Angeles Times,* February 24, 1974.

Morgenthaler, Anne. "Downtown Center Redesign Weighed." *Santa Monica Evening Outlook,* March 8, 1974.

Moosbruger, Ed. "Rouse Company Report." *Santa Monica Evening Outlook,* March 13, 1974.

"Energy Saving Concepts: SM Center Change Detailed." *S.C. Roberts News,* March 13, 1974.

Moosbruger, Ed. "Shopping Center: Redevelopment Project Development Delayed." *Santa Monica Evening Outlook,* March 27, 1974.

———. "Santa Monica Shopping Center—Hahn, Inc. to Join in Development." *Santa Monica Evening Outlook,* April 5, 1974.

Snyder, Camilla. "New Contemporary Museum Will Open for Los Angeles." *Los Angeles Herald Examiner,* June 13, 1974.

"Concord Pavilion Nears Completion." *Oakland Tribune,* October 27, 1974.

Adams, Bruce. "Concord Pavilion Acoustics Will Aid Concerts, Theater." *Contra Costa Times,* March 19, 1975.

"Editorial: Concord Opening Key to Future." *Contra Costa Times,* May 1, 1975.

Tircuit, Heuwell. "Music World: An Acoustical Reason to Celebrate." San Francisco Chronicle, May 13, 1975.

Dengel, John. "Jazzy Debut for a New Pavilion." *Oakland Tribune,* May 16, 1975.

"Editorial: Concord Pavilion Comes Alive Tonight." *Contra Costa Times,* May 16, 1975.

Glackin, William C. "Arts in Review: A Place for All Reasons." *Sacramento Bee.* May 18, 1975.

"Concord Pavilion: An Exercise in Acoustics." *Berkeley Gazette,* May 19, 1975.

"Pavilion Christened by Jazz." *Oakland Tribune,* May 19, 1975.

"Perfect Weather for the Pavilion." *Oakland Tribune,* May 19, 1975.

"Fiery, Jazzy Dramatics at the Concord Pavilion." *San Francisco Chronicle,* May 20, 1975.

Morgenthaler, Anne. "Facelifting of Santa Monica Pier Approved." *Santa Monica Evening Outlook,* May 28, 1975.

Moosbrugger, Ed. "Indirect System Used—New Light Shed on Offices." *Santa Monica Evening Outlook,* May 30, 1975.

"Santa Monica Architect Wins Awards for Design." *Santa Monica Evening Outlook,* May 30, 1975.

Elwood, Philip. "Tanya Earns a Rave at Concord." *San Francisco Examiner,* June 2, 1975.

Clavan, Benjamin. "Architecture: Sounds from the Hillside." *The Daily Californian,* June 6, 1975.

Turpin, Dick. "Southland AIA Chapter Will Present 20 Awards." *Los Angeles Times,* June 8, 1975.

Lembke, Daryl. "Concord: Start of Something Big?" *Los Angeles Times,* August 21, 1975.

Simpson, Joseph. "The Greening of the Offices." *Baltimore Sun,* September 28, 1975.

Morrison, Pat. "Environmentalist Will Design Museum." *Los Angeles Times,* February 1, 1976.

Seidenbaum, Art. "A Bowlful of Musical Chairs." *Los Angeles Times,* February 20, 1976.

Bernheimer, Martin. "An Overdue Face-Lift for a Musical Landmark." *Los Angeles Times Calendar,* February 22, 1976.

Lewis Bruce. "Councilmen Plan Look at Speaker Cost." *Contra Costa Times,* March 14, 1976.

"Pavilion Program Previews Tonight." *California Transcript,* March 17, 1976.

Elwood, Phillip. "Weekend of Opening Concerts: Concord's Sunny New Pavilion." *San Francisco Examiner,* March 19, 1976.

"Council to Eye Speakers." *Contra Costa Times,* March 21, 1976.

Kuehl, Brooks. "Pavilion Termed 'Great' by Mitch." *California Transcript,* April 15, 1976.

Hertelendy, Paul. "Oakland Symphony Opener." *Oakland Tribune,* April 19, 1976.

Desser, Lou. "AIA Jury Picks Best-Designed Buildings for 1976: 10 Southland Companies Capture Design Awards—Gruen, Gehry Win Highest Honors." *Los Angeles Times,* October 31, 1976.

Seidenbaum, Art. "Filling in the Centers." *Los Angeles Times,* November 5, 1976.

Dreyfuss, John. "Job Center Does Its Job . . . and Architecture Excels." *Los Angeles Times,* January 23, 1977.

"Plans Finished for Cabrillo Marine Museum." *Southland,* March 27, 1977.

Dreyfuss, John. "Pavilion: Crater with a Stage at Bottom." *Los Angeles Times,* May 15, 1977.

"Concord Pavilion Tops Nation in Architectural Design." *San Francisco Examiner Home,* May 22, 1977.

Hartman, Jeannette. "Design Stressed over Materials." *Santa Monica Evening Outlook,* June 8, 1977.

Martinez, Don. "Concord's Invaluable, Indebted Arena." *San Francisco Examiner,* July 21, 1977.

Shaffer, George. "Model Exhibited in Preview of Valley Cultural Center." *Los Angeles Times,* August 7, 1977.

Seidenbaum, Art. "Opening Our Eyes to Buildings." *Los Angeles Times,* December 28, 1977.

———. "Arts Park L.A. Up for Debate." *Los Angeles Times,* February 10, 1978.

Dreyfuss, John. "Gehry's Artful House Offends, Baffles, Angers His Neighbors." *Los Angeles Times,* July 23, 1978.

Holmes, Ann. "Disregarding the Rules." *Houston Chronicle,* August 20, 1978.

Thorne, Will. "House that Gehry Built Stirring up SM Controversy." *Santa Monica Evening Outlook,* August 22, 1978.

Koris, Sally. "Architect Gehry Does Own Thing." *Los Angeles Herald Examiner,* September 17, 1978.

Gindick, Tia. "The Power of Positive Organizing." *Los Angeles Times,* April 5, 1979.

Dreyfuss, John. "A New Museum for Children." *Los Angeles Times,* April 5, 1979.

Goldberger, Paul. "A House Slipcovered in Metal." *The New York Times,* May 17, 1979.

Smaus, Robert. "Will It Ever Be Finished?" *Los Angeles Times* May 20, 1979.

Snyder, Camilla. "A Museum for Kids to Romp Through." *Los Angeles Herald Examiner,* June 5, 1979.

Kaplan, Sam. "Los Angeles Children's Museum: It's Child's Play." *Los Angeles Times,* June 11, 1979.

Giovannini, Joseph. "Photography the Final Winner of the Architectural Competition." *Los Angeles Herald Examiner,* October 24, 1979.

Campbell, Don B. "Warehouse among Top 4 AIA Awards." *Los Angeles Times,* October 28, 1979.

Werne, Jo. "Architects Clash on 'Morality' of U.S. Designs." *Miami Herald,* October 28, 1979.

Dreyfuss, John. "Gehry: The Architect as Artist." *Los Angeles Times,* November 7, 1979.

Anguiano, Joe W. "Loyola Law School Plans Expansion." *Los Angeles Times,* December 16, 1979.

Hine, Thomas. "A Careless Design—Carefully Done." *Philadelphia Inquirer,* January 13, 1980.

Crane, Tricia. "At the Children's Museum Touches Join Looks." *Valley News,* January 19, 1980.

Dreyfuss, John. "Bunker Hill Project under Wraps." *Los Angeles Times,* March 16, 1980.

Doubillet, Susan. "Gehry Wraps Old Homes in New Ideas." *The Globe and Mail,* March 27, 1960.

Giovannini, Joseph. "Big New Proposal for Bunker Hill." *Los Angeles Herald Examiner,* April 16, 1980.

Conroy, Sarah Booth. "The Remodeled American Dream, East, West." *Washington Post,* May 25, 1980.

Merkel, Jayne. "Awards Reflect Trends and Issues." *Cincinnati Inquirer,* June 8, 1980.

Kramer, Hilton. "Art: Russian Avant-Garde in Los Angeles." *The New York Times,* July 7, 1980.

Cariaga, Daniel. " 'Phoenix' Helps Launch 59th Summer Season for the Bowl." *Los Angeles Times,* July 10, 1980.

Kramer, Hilton. "The Daring of the Russian Avant-Garde." *The New York Times,* July 13, 1980.

Wilson, William. "Isms, Schisms, and Russian Avant-Garde." *Los Angeles Times,* July 13, 1980.

Giovannini, Joseph. "The Last Draw on Bunker Hill." *Los Angeles Herald Examiner,* July 16, 1980.

von Eckardt, Wolf. "The Good, the Bad and the Tricky." *Los Angeles Times,* July 18, 1980.

McClure, Clara. "Little Ones Stand Tall at the Children's Museum." *Weekend Outlook,* July 19, 1980.

Kramer, Hilton. "The Mystical Basis of the Russian Avant-Garde." *The New York Times,* July 20, 1980.

Merkel, Jayne. "It's Just a Colonial Turned Outside-In." *Cincinnati Inquirer,* August 3, 1980.

Giovannini, Joseph. "In Venice, an Idea House That's Not for the Timid." *Los Angeles Herald Examiner,* August 6, 1980.

———. "The Architect-Owner-Contractor Axis." *Los Angeles Herald Examiner,* August 13, 1980.

———. "Biennale Lays Bare Threat of Classical Revivalism." *Los Angeles Herald Examiner.* August 20, 1980.

Green, Roger. "Arts Laying Claim to Lafayette Square." *The Times-Picayune,* September 6, 1980.

Archer, B. J. "First Architecture Biennale in Venice." *International Herald Tribune,* October 4–5, 1980.

Moosbrugger, Ed. "Santa Monica Place to Open Thursday." *Santa Monica Evening Outlook,* October 15, 1980.

Bazyk, DeDe. "Frank Gehry." *Soho Weekly News,* October 15, 1980.

Giovannini, Joseph. "Shopping Center Well Place-ed in Santa Monica." *Los Angeles Herald Examiner,* October 20, 1980.

Fanucchi, Kenneth. "Mall's Pros, Cons Remain." *Los Angeles Times,* October 26, 1980.

Baird, Barbara. "Santa Monica Has a Place for Seaside Shopping." *Los Angeles Times,* October 26, 1980.

Childress, Deirdre. "Clutter Is Creative at Kids Museum." *Los Angeles Times,* October 28, 1980.

"Accolades Presented by AIA Chapter." *Los Angeles Times,* November 2, 1980.

Dreyfuss, John. "L.A. Will Get Two Modern Art Museums." *Los Angeles Times,* December 5, 1980.

Giovannini, Joseph. "Mural, Mural on the Wall." *Los Angeles Herald Examiner,* December 29, 1980.

Dreyfuss, John. "A Place in the Sun for Southland Shoppers." *Los Angeles Times,* January 8, 1981.

Mills, Kay. "Prefab Aesthetics." *Los Angeles Times,* January 18, 1981.

"SAG Acts to Set Up Merger Committee." *Los Angeles Herald Examiner,* February 2, 1981.

Giovannini, Joseph. "Flawed Remarriage of Art and Architecture." *Los Angeles Herald Examiner,* February 9, 1981.

Lehman, Jane. "Midtown Housing Complex Planned." *Atlanta Journal,* February 11, 1981.

"How Art and Architecture Look at the 80s." *The New York Times,* March 6, 1981.

"SM's Gehry to Design Big Atlanta Project." *Santa Monica Evening Outlook,* March 10, 1981.

Sorkin, Michael. "The Odd Couples." *Village Voice,* March 18, 1981.

Goldberger, Paul. "Where Are the Form Givers?" *The New York Times,* March 22, 1981.

"Southland Architect Plans Atlanta Project." *Los Angeles Times,* March 22, 1981.

Dreyfuss, John. "Doorways to L.A.'s Unique Environment." *Los Angeles Times,* March 26, 1981.

Giovannini, Joseph. "Architecture Enters the Age of Personality." *Los Angeles Herald Examiner,* April 20, 1981.

Goldberger, Paul. "Houses of Strength and Serenity by Arata Isosaki." *The New York Times,* April 30, 1981.

Giovannini, Joseph. "Art that Sells as Real Estate." *Los Angeles Herald Examiner,* May 4, 1981.

Dreyfuss, John. "Diversified Design, Talk Mark Parley." *Los Angeles Times,* June 7, 1981.

"Furniture by Architects." *The Christian Science Monitor,* June 12, 1981.

Giovannini, Joseph. "The Architecture of Light: Building Modern Mysteries." *Los Angeles Herald Examiner,* June 22, 1981.

Knight, Christopher. "Art Exhibit Recaptures the 60's." *Los Angeles Herald Examiner,* July 22, 1981.

Rauen, Chris. "SM Place Tops Projections." *Santa Monica Evening Outlook,* August 3, 1981.

Giovannini, Joseph. "Loyola Received Both Sides of the Architectural Case." *Los Angeles Herald Examiner,* August 24, 1981.

"Reality and Fantasy." *Los Angeles Herald Examiner,* October 1981.

Gallagher, Mike. "Architects, Students to Tackle Mall Study." *Kalamazoo Gazette,* October 12, 1981.

———. "Architects, Students Study Mall." *Kalamazoo Gazette,* October 15, 1981.

———. "Architects Meet Winds Down Here." *Kalamazoo Gazette,* October 17, 1981.

Giovannini, Joseph. "The AIA Awards' Blueprint for Design." *Los Angeles Herald Examiner,* October 19, 1981.

"Ten Projects Receive Design Awards." *Los Angeles Times,* October 25, 1981.

Giovannini, Joseph. "AIA Meetings Breaks with Convention." *Los Angeles Herald Examiner,* October 26, 1981.

Dreyfuss, John. "Lay Speakers High Point of AIA Session." *Los Angeles Times,* November 1, 1981.

"Moderator Puts Panelists to 'Meet the Press' Test." *CM Daily Pacific Builder,* November 9, 1981.

Goldberger, Paul. "Architects If Left Alone Begin to Probe Their Souls." *The New York Times,* December 10, 1981.

"Area Projects Capture Eight Coastal Awards." *Los Angeles Times,* December 13, 1981.

Dreyfuss, John. "New Museum Creates Sea Space Ashore." *Los Angeles Times,* December 25, 1981.

Knight, Christopher. "Can Architects and Artists Work Together?" *Los Angeles Herald Examiner,* March 8, 1982.

Freedman, Adele. "Fish and Flying Cubes Lead Gehry's Assault." *The Globe and Mail,* March 18, 1982.

Seeley, Rick. (Column.) *Santa Monica Evening Outlook,* April 1982.

Slesin, Suzanne. "The Studio House: New Trend-Setter from California." *The New York Times,* April 8, 1982.

Dreyfuss, John. "A Turning Point in Architecture." *Los Angeles Times,* May 21, 1982.

"Cardboard Makes Sturdy Furniture." *New Nation,* June 15, 1982.

Robertson, Rosanne. "Frank Gehry: Samll Buildings Getting Better and Better." *Sydney (*Australia*) Morning Herald,* June 23, 1982.

Slesin, Suzanne. "Cardboard Furniture Reborn." *The New York Times,* July 22, 1982.

Kay, Jane Holtz. "Frivolity in Design." *The Christian Science Monitor,* July 23, 1982.

Dreyfuss, John. "Exposition Park's Elements Linked." *Los Angeles Times,* August 27, 1982.

Campbell, Robert. "Architecture." *Boston Globe,* September 12, 1982.

"Evening at the ICA." *The Patriot Ledger,* September 14, 1982.

"Best Iconoclastic Building." *L.A. Weekly,* September 17–24, 1982.

"Public Gets First Look at Civic Center Design." *Beverly Hills Post,* September 30, 1982.

Dreyfuss, John. "Beverly Hills Civic Center a Challenge." *Los Angeles Times,* October 1, 1982.

"Beverly Hills to Remodel Its Image?" *Los Angeles Herald Examiner,* October 4, 1982.

Campbell, Robert. "Frank Gehry's Pop Perspective." *Boston Globe,* October 5, 1982.

Finley, Elizabeth Navas. "What We've Done to Furniture." *San Francisco Chronicle,* October 6, 1982.

Barrett, Judith. "Gehry's Cardboard: Bargain Elegance." *Boston Globe,* October 8, 1982.

Dreyfuss, John. "An Architect with the Soul of an Artist." *Los Angeles Times,* December 17, 1982.

"Beverly Hills Panel Chooses Design for a Civic Center to Fit City's Image." *The New York Times,* January 18, 1983.

Morgenstern, Joe. "Obsession of an Architect with Fish on a Grand Scale." *Los Angeles Herald Examiner.* March 4, 1983.

Giovannini, Joseph. "Architectural Imitation: Is It Plagiarism?" *The New York Times,* March 17, 1983.

Coombs, Robert. "Post Modernism Has Arrived. Collage, the Chicquest Technique in Architecture Comes to California." *Los Angeles Herald Examiner.* March 30, 1983.

"Temporary Museum May Stay Around." *Los Angeles Herald Examiner,* April 14, 1983.

"Gehry Unveils Plans for Temporary MoCA." *Los Angeles Herald Examiner,* April 14, 1983.

Degener, Patricia. "Daybreak Is Near for the Temporary Contemporary." *St. Louis Post-Dispatch,* May 1, 1983.

Slesin, Suzanne. "Technology and Tradition Mark Chicago Show." *The New York Times,* June 16, 1983.

Dreyfuss, John. "Design for the Hollywood Library Makes a Dull Read." *Los Angeles Times,* June 27, 1983.

Giovannini, Joseph. "Ten Architects' Bold Imaginings." *The New York Times,* July 14, 1983.

Dreyfuss, John. "Throwing Stones at L.A.'s Monotonous Glass Boxes." *Los Angeles Times,* July 24, 1983.

Robertson, Allen. "Bells Are Ringing." *Village Voice,* August 9, 1983.

Drohojowska, Hunter. "MoCA & Available Light." *L.A. Weekly,* September 23, 1983.

Swed, Mark. "Critics Choice: Available Light." *L.A. Reader,* September 23, 1983.

Bromberg, Craig. "Abstracting Time Space With Childs." *Los Angeles Times,* September 25, 1983.

Isenberg, Barbara. "A Museum at Home Away from Home." *Los Angeles Times,* September 25, 1983.

Sterrity, David. "Lucinda Childs Choreography Offers Elegance, Precision." *The Christian Science Monitor,* September 26, 1983.

Knight, Christopher. "MoCA Sheds Light on Its Future." *Los Angeles Herald Examiner,* September 29, 1983.

"Most Creative Law Building." *L.A. Weekly,* September 30, 1983.

Perlmutter, Donna. "MoCA Debut Fails to Live Up to Its Billing." *Los Angeles Herald Examiner,* October 1, 1983.

Bernheimer, Martin. "Post-Modern Dance Ritual Offers Little Heat and Less Light." *Los Angeles Times,* October 1, 1983.

Wilson, William. "Lucinda Childs & Company Portend the Tack MoCA's Art Will Take." *Los Angeles Times,* October 1, 1983.

Drohojowska, Hunter. "Available Light." *Los Angeles Herald Examiner,* October 6, 1983.

Giovannini, Joseph. "Designs for Today's Kitchens: A Place to Work and Live." *The New York Times,* October 6, 1983.

Borger, Irene. "Performance Piece for a New Museum." *The Wall Street Journal,* October 14, 1983.

Stark, Sherie. "Illusions of Space in Small Places." *L.A. News West,* October 21, 1983.

Kisselgoff, Anna. "Dance in Brooklyn, Premiere of Available Light." *The New York Times,* October 29, 1983.

Kaplan, Sam Hall. "Dworsky Firm Big Winner in L.A./A.I.A. Awards." *Los Angeles Times,* October 30, 1983.

______. "Bay Area Design Community Has a Ball." *Los Angeles Times,* November 2, 1983.

Goldberger, Paul. "Some Modern Follies to Amuse and Entertain." *Los Angeles Times,* November 3, 1983.

Stuart, Judith. "Childs in N.Y. Dance Premiere." *The Phoenix,* November 3, 1983.

Kisselgoff, Anna. "There's More Than One Way of Viewing Dance." *The New York Times,* November 6, 1983.

Knight, Christopher. "This Sculpture Turns Art History on Its Head." *Los Angeles Herald Examiner,* November 6, 1983.

Wilson, William. "Germans Explore Man, Machine, Mankind." *Los Angeles Times,* November 6, 1983.

Drohojowska, Hunter. "Birth of the MoCA." *Los Angeles Herald Examiner,* November 13, 1983.

Wilson, William. "Post Modern: Is It Part of the Future?" *Los Angeles Times,* November 13, 1983.

Jowitt, Deborah. "Minimal with Knobs On." *Village Voice,* November 15, 1983.

Wilson, William. "Temporary Contemporary: Its Time Is Now." *Los Angeles Times,* November 20, 1983.

Pally, Marcia. "Rite of Way." *New York Native,* November 21, 1983.

Russell, John. "Art: Coast Gets Home for Works since 1945." *The New York Times,* November 21, 1983.

Giovannini, Joseph. "A New Museum Has an Instant Impact." *The New York Times,* November 27, 1983.

"Dictara Aqui Conferencia." *La Estrella de Panama,* December 19, 1983.

"Dictara Conferencia F. Gehry." *"Ya" Tienes la Verdad,* December 19, 1983.

Clurman, Irene. "City Spirit Offers Aesthetic Explosion." *Rocky Mountain News,* December 23, 1983.

Kisselgoff, Anna. "New Works, New Dancers Come to the Fore." *The New York Times,* December 25, 1983.

"Expositor Norteamericano." *La Estrella de Panama,* December 27, 1983.

Kaplan, Sam Hall. "Skyline in '84: Up, Up and Diverse." *Los Angeles Times,* January 1, 1984.

Venant, Elizabeth. "Czar of the Arts." *Los Angeles Times,* January 15, 1984.

Morgenstern, Joe. "Tempo Contempo Is Art sans Hype." *Los Angeles Herald Examiner,* February 20, 1984.

"Gehry Nominated for Challenging Tradition." *Westside Life,* February 23–29, 1984.

"Gehry Rejoices over Masterpieces for MoCA." *Westside Life,* March 15–March 21, 1984.

Kampler, Roger. "Frank Gehry: Understanding the Urban Campus." *The Loyola Reporter,* March 1984.

Feeney, Susan. "Music on the Mississippi." *The Times-Picayune,* March 18, 1984.

"Loyola Uses Manville Asbestos in New Construction." *The Loyola Reporter,* March 29, 1984.

"Festival—An Olympic Celebration of the Arts." *Los Angeles Times,* April 15, 1984.

Miclean, David J. "Substance at Last." *The Loyola Reporter,* April 30, 1984.

"Do Tell: PDQ at PDC." *Los Angeles Herald Examiner,* May 1984.

Goldberger, Paul. "Reality Squeezes out Fantasy in Louisiana Fair's Architecture." *The New York Times,* May 13, 1984.

Gagnard, Frank. "Even Empty, the Amphitheater's a Winner at the Fair." *The Times-Picayune,* May 20, 1984.

"It's not Business as Usual at the L.A. Museum." *Los Angeles Times,* May 25, 1984.

Dreyfuss, John. "Olympian Interest Around the Coliseum." *Los Angeles Times,* May 31, 1984.

Slesin, Suzanne, "Accessories by Architects." *The New York Times,* May 31, 1984.

"Prelude to the Olympics." *Los Angeles Times,* June 1–August 12, 1984.

"L.A. Arts Leaders Take Their Pick from Festival." *Los Angeles Times,* June 9, 1984.

"Frank Gehry..." *Westside Life,* June 21–27, 1984.

"Click... Architects Unite" *Los Angeles Herald Examiner,* July 5, 1984.

Temko, Allan. "L.A. Museum Shows How." *San Francisco Chronicle,* July 7, 1984.

Kaplan, Sam Hall. "Aerospace Museum Is Geared for Maiden Flight." *Los Angeles Times,* July 20, 1984.

Whiteson, Leon. "Frank Gehry's Buildings Invent Their Own Order." *Los Angeles Herald Examiner,* July 29, 1984.

"Max Palevsky...." *Westside Life,* August 2–8, 1984.

Giovannini, Joseph. "The Look of Urban Confetti." *The New York Times,* August 10, 1984.

"David Hertz...." *Westside Life,* August 16–22, 1984.

Whiteson, Leon. "An Architect Captures L.A. Tensions in Solid Form." *Los Angeles Herald Examiner,* August 26, 1984.

"Best New Building." *L.A. Weekly,* September 28–October 4, 1984.

Kaplan, Sam Hall. "Museum Design Wins." *Los Angeles Times,* October 21, 1984.

Green, Roger. "Fair Missed Potential for Design." *The Times-Picayune/The States-Item,* November 10, 1984.

Slesin, Suzanne. "Lamp Shapes: A Pisces Effect." *The New York Times,* November 22, 1984.

Gildea, Michael. "Frank Gehry's Post-Kelbo's Transgressions." *L.A. Reader,* November 30, 1984.

Russell, John. "Lamps by Frank Gehry." *The New York Times.* November 30, 1984.

Video and Film

Frank Gehry: Counter Statements (audio tape interview). Pigeon Audio Visual. Distributed by World Microfilms Publications (London): 1981.

Blackwood, Michael. *Beyond Utopia: Changing Attitudes in American Architecture* (film). Michael Blackwood Productions, Inc. (New York): 1983.

Periodicals

"Japanese Garden Shared with Public." *Architecture West,* September 1964.

"Where Architects Hang Their Hats." *Architecture West,* August 1965.

"Exhibition Installation by Gehry and Walsh, Architects." *Arts and Architecture,* July 1966.

"The Architect's Own Office: Show Place and Work Space." *Progressive Architecture,* September 1966.

"The Merriweather Post Pavilion of Music." *The Architectural Forum,* November 1967.

"Architect—The Award Winning Scene: Merriweather Post Pavilion, Columbia." *Maryland Living/The New American Magazine,* November 12, 1967.

"South Coast Plaza, Joseph Magnin Store Features Thin Coat Plaster by Varner." *California Plasterer,* May 1968.

Olyshant, Kenward S. "Unique Acoustical Control by Bixby Green." *California Drywall Industry,* July 1968.

Hallstead, William F. "Music Comes to the Woodlands." *Maryland Magazine,* Autumn 1968.

"Conversation with Inbrani." *Dance,* September 1968.

"The Quiet Townhouse: This Project Goes All the Way with Noise." *House and Home,* December 1968.

"Lustra Crystal and Tempered Starlux in Novel West Coast Store." *Creative Ideas in Glass,* Spring 1969.

"Commercial Interiors: A New Dimension to the Shopping Syndrome Makes Going to the Store a Pleasure in Itself." *Designers West,* May 1969.

"Interview with Frank Gehry." *Designers West,* May 1969.

Risser, Arthur C. AIA. "Alfresco Spectaculars." *AIA Journal,* August 1969.

Southern California Institute of Architects. "Award Winners Named." *Bulletin,* November/December 1969.

Terbel, Melinda. "Bengston and Westerman." *Arts,* December 1969/January 1970.

"Southern California AIA Triennial Program Cites 12 Buildings." *Architecture West,* December 1969.

"Jim Rouse's Satellite City." *Look,* February 10, 1970.

Gebhard, David. "L.A.—The Stuccoed Box." *Art in America,* May/June 1970.

"U.S.A.: Une salle de concert en carton." *Techniques et Architecture,* September 1970.

"Twelve-Year-Olds Build a City." *Smithsonian,* May 1971.

"Children Plan Future Cities." *My Weekly Reader,* November 15, 1971.

"Joseph Magnin, San Jose: Dynamic Store, Dynamic Design." *Stores,* December 1971.

"New Sounds for (Hollywood) Bowl." *Architectural Design,* February 1972.

"Cardboard Furniture." *Los Angeles,* April 1972.

"Innovations: Easy Edges Does It." *The Architectural Forum,* April 1972.

"A Wiggle's Worth." *Interiors,* April 1972.

Skura, Norma. "Paper Furniture for Penny Pinchers." *The New York Times Magazine,* April 9, 1972.

MacMasters, Dan. "Easy Edges: Why Didn't Somebody Think of This Before?" *Los Angeles Times Home Magazine,* April 30, 1972.

"Cardboard Comfort." *Parade,* April 30, 1972.

Chapman, Pat. "A Case for Paper Furniture is Revised." *Furniture Design and Manufacturing,* May 1972.

Lewin, Susan Grant. "Furniture Liberation. . . ." *House Beautiful,* May 1972.

Platt, Elise. "Laminated Fiberboard Liberates Furniture Design." *House and Home,* May 1972.

"Paper Currency." *Industrial Design,* May 1972.

"Practical Fantasy." *Interior Design,* May 1972.

"Budget Furniture for a Sheltered Patio." *Family Weekly,* May 21, 1972.

Curry, Susan McGuire. "New for You." *Family Circle,* June 1972.

"Bachelor of the Month." *Cosmopolitan,* June 1972.

"Bloomingdale's Goes Blond." *Interiors,* June 1972.

"Easy Edges Cardboard Furniture." *Playboy,* June 1972.

"Easy Edges: Completely New Furniture Concept." *The Dallas Marketplace,* June 1972.

"Living . . . New Pale Furniture." *Vogue,* June 1972.

"On and Off the Avenue . . . About the House." *The New Yorker,* June 16, 1972.

"Etcetera: Cardboard Cut-ups." *Progressive Architecture,* June 1972.

Brown, Helene. "Furniture You Have to Touch." *American Home,* July 1972.

"Easy Edges Cardboard Furniture." *Budget Decorating and Remodeling,* July 1972.

"Paper Chaise Lounge." *Esquire,* July 1972.

"Cardboard Furniture." *New York,* July 10, 1972.

"Cardboard Is for Jumping." *Life,* July 14, 1972.

Yeates, Terri. "A Paper Place: Desks." *Budget Decorating and Remodeling,* September 1972.

"Accessories to Make or Buy for Less than $50 . . . Study Corner Sophisticate." *Woman's Day,* August 1972.

"The Changing Shape of America: Interior Space Age." *Harper's Bazaar,* August 1972.

"New and Newsworthy." *1001 Decorating Ideas,* August 1972.

"Ready-to-go Zest: Cardboard Furniture." *House and Garden,* August 1972.

"Awards: Resources Council Honors the Designers and Manufacturers of 17 Furnishing Products." *Interiors,* November 1972.

"Apartment Ideas: One Room That Lives like Three." *Better Homes and Gardens Apartment Ideas,* Winter 1972–1973.

"Reflection of Views with Frank O. Gehry: Leading Architect Discusses Finishing's Role in Innovation." *Finishing Highlights,* December 1972.

"Look What They Are Doing with Cardboard." *Ideas for Better Living,* January 1973.

"Resources Council... The Award Winners." *Designers West,* January 1973.

"News of the Shopping Center Industry." *ICSC Newsletter,* April 1973.

Norris, Joanne. "Dining at the Hollywood Bowl." *Long Beach Independent Press-Telegram Sunday Magazine,* June 24, 1973.

"Exhibition: Musee des Arts Decoratifs, Pavillon de Marsan, Palais de Louvre." *Domus,* August 1973.

"Provisorischer Aukustischer Einbau in das Hollywood Bowl." *Baun + Wohnen,* October 1973.

"Roof and Seats Make Up Theater-in-the-Ground." *ENR,* October 18, 1973.

"New Ways to Sit." *San Diego Magazine,* December 1973.

"Ideas: Looking Back—and Ahead." *Finishing Highlights,* March/April 1974.

"The Rouse Cool Conception." *San Diego Magazine,* April 1974.

"Buildings for Recreation." *Architectural Record,* June 1974.

"Cochiti Lake Recreation Center." *Architectural Record,* June 1974.

McCoy, Esther. "Report from Malibu Hills." *Progressive Architecture,* July 1974.

"Concord Pavilion: Music in the Hills." *PG & E Progress,* July 1975.

"1975 Design Awards Program." *L.A. Architect,* July 1975.

MacMasters, Dan. "Q and A—Ron Davis: He Plays Tricks with Dimensions." *Los Angeles Times Home Magazine,* August 17, 1975.

Ryder, Sharon Lee. "Musical Acoustics—Some Sound Advice." *Progressive Architecture,* November, 1975.

Goldberger, Paul. "Studied Slapdash." *The New York Times Magazine,* January 18, 1976.

Ryder, Sharon Lee. "A Rousing Place." *Progressive Architecture,* February 1976.

Nairn, Janet. "Frank Gehry: The Search for a 'No Rules' Architecture." *Architectural Record,* June 1976.

"And Then There Were Twelve... The Los Angeles 12." *Architectural Record,* August 1976.

"Real Dream Houses." *Newsweek,* October 4, 1976.

"Concord Pavilion." *Baumeister,* November 1976.

"Stahl: Concord Pavilion, Kalifornien." *Baumeister,* April 1977.

"Davis Studio/Residence." *G.A. Houses,* no. 2, April 1977.

"Amphitheatre de plein air, Concord Californie, Etats-Unis." *Architecture Francaise,* April 1977.

Balzarini, Joan. "Music under the Stars." *California Life,* May 1977.

"Concord Pavilion." *AIA Journal,* May 1977.

"Trois Architectes francs tireurs." *Neuf,* July/August 1977.

"Southern California Chapter AIA—1977 Design Awards." *L.A. Architect,* July 1977.

"Jungian Institute, L.A., California." *Progressive Architecture,* August 1977.

"When Architects Pick America's Best Buildings." *U.S. News and World Report,* August 15, 1977.

"Toward a Paper World." *MODO,* November 1977.

Goldberger, Paul. "Corporate Architecture: A Study in Banality." *Saturday Review,* January 21, 1978.

"The Office of Frank O. Gehry and Associates." *L.A. Architect,* May 1978.

Stephens, Suzanne. "Where Categories Collide." *Progressive Architecture,* September 1978.

Ryder, Sharon Lee. "Legal Establishment." *Interiors,* October 1978.

Goldberger, Paul. "California Corrugated." *New York,* October 23, 1978.

Harris, Steven. "Frank Gehry at P.S. 1." *Skyline,* November 1978.

"Southern California Chapter AIA: 1978 Design Awards." *L.A. Architect,* November 1978.

Gehry, Frank O. "Suburban Changes: Architect's House in Santa Monica 1978." *International Architect,* volume 1, no. 2., 1979.

Hughes, Robert. "Doing Their Own Thing." *Time,* January 8, 1979.

Koris, Sally. "Renegade Frank Gehry Has Torn Up His House—and the Book of Architecture." *People,* March 5, 1979.

"Law Offices, Los Angeles." *The Architectural Review,* May 1979.

"Offices and Warehouse, near Baltimore, Maryland." *The Architectural Review,* May 1979.

"The Gehry House, Santa Monica, California, 1979." *Archetype,* Spring 1979.

Georgis, William E. "An Interview with Frank Gehry." *Archetype,* Summer 1979.

"Building of the Quarter." *Archetype,* Summer 1979.

Filler, Martin. "Perfectly Frank: Mid-Atlantic Toyota Distributors Warehouse and Offices." *Progressive Architecture,* July 1979.

Gunts, Edward. "Parts, Arts and Architecture." *The News American,* July 22, 1979.

"All'Interno Prospettive Exxentriche." *Domus,* August 1979.

Goldberger, Paul. "Architects Move into the Office." *The New York Times Magazine,* August 5, 1979.

Tigerman, Stanley. "Stanley Tigerman vs. Frank O. Gehry." *GA Houses,* No. 6, Fall 1979.

Gehry, Frank. "Gehry's Residence in Santa Monica." *GA Houses,* No. 6, 1979.

"Demenil Residence, New York." *GA Houses,* No. 6, Fall 1979.

"Gunther Residence, Encinal Bluffs, California." *GA Houses,* No. 6, Fall 1979.

"Spiller Residence, Los Angeles, California." *GA Houses,* No. 6, Fall 1979.

"Wagner Residence." *GA Houses,* No. 6, Fall 1979.

"Familian Residence." *GA Houses,* No. 6, Fall 1979.

"Doreen Nelson Kitchen." *GA Houses,* No. 6, Fall 1979.

"Frank O. Gehry & Associates." *GA Houses,* No. 6, Fall 1979.

"In Californian un Oggetto Architettonicao." *Domus,* October 1979.

"Addition to Architect's House, Los A. ɜeles, California, 1979." *Domus,* October 1979.

Troutman, Anne. "A Delicate Balance." *Residential Interiors,* November/December 1979.

Ryder, Sharon Lee. "Brutally Frank." *Residential Interiors,* November/December 1979.

"Awards Coverage for 1979 Southern California Chapter AIA." *L.A. Architect,* December 1979.

"The 27th Annual P/A Awards." *Progressive Architecture,* January 1980.

Larsen, S. C. "Imagine a Space, a Form, a World: The Paintings of Ron Davis." *Art News,* January 1980.

"Une Maison qui joue l'ouverture." *Maison Francaise,* March 1980.

Goldstein, Barbara. "Frank O. Gehry and Associates: Firm Profile." *Progressive Architecture,* March 1980.

———. "Spaces in Between." *Progressive Architecture,* March 1980.

———. "Cabrillo Marine Museum, Wilmington, California." *Progressive Architecture,* March 1980.

Murphy, Jim. "Art on Melrose." *Progressive Architecture,* March 1980.

Stephens, Suzanne. "Out of the Rage for Order." *Progressive Architecture,* March 1980.

Boissiére, Olivier. "Ten California Architects." *Domus,* March 1980.

Willard, Patricia. "Jazz Artists Agree on Outdoor Pavilion." *Federal Design Matters,* Spring 1980.

Filler, Martin. "Tradition Transformed Knockout Kitchen." *House and Garden,* April 1980.

Skorneck, A. Jeffrey. "Bunker Hill Development Competition." *L.A. Architect,* April 1980.

Pastier, John. "Of Art, Self-Revelation and Iconoclasm." *AIA Journal,* Mid-May 1980.

"Frank O. Gehry House, Santa Monica, California." *AIA Journal,* Mid-May 1980.

Berman, Clifford. "An Artist's Studio in the Malibu Hills Balances Aesthetics and Function, Home and Work." *Residential Interiors,* May/June 1980.

"Casa Gehry, Santa Monica, California." *Arquitectura,* May/June 1980.

Odoni, Giovanni. "Un Arredo in Prospettiva." *Casa Vogue,* May 1980.

Pastier, John. "The Art of Being Different." *Pacific Southwest Airways Magazine.* May 1980.

"Eccentric Space: Frank Gehry." *Art in America,* June 1980.

"Frank Gehry." *Architectural Review,* July 1980.

Ross, Michael Franklin. "Paper Architecture: Late Entries to the Chicago Tribune Tower Competition." *L.A. Architect,* July 1980.

"Architect's House, Santa Monica, California." *A + U,* July 1980.

"Chiudi (e apri) la casa (a Santa Monica)." *Archittetura,* July 1980.

"A New Wave in American Architecture: Frank O. Gehry." *Space Design,* July 1980.

Mendini, A. "Dear Frank Gehry." *Domus,* August 1980.

Stevens, Mark. "The Russian Visionaries." *Newsweek,* August 4, 1980.

Filler, Martin. "Breaking the Rules and Getting Away with It." *House and Garden,* September 1980.

McGuigan, Cathleen. "The Architect." *TWA Ambassador,* September 1980.

"Late Entry to the Chicago Tribune Tower Competition." *Artforum,* September 1980.

Jencks, Charles. "In the Presence of the Past." *Domus,* October 1980.

Goldstein, Barbara. "Constructivism in L.A." *Progressive Architecture,* October, 1980.

"The Extension That Encompassed the House." *House and Garden,* October 1980.

"Gehry Residence, Santa Monica." *GA Document: 1970–1980,* 1980 (special issue).

Street-Porter, Tim. "The Outside-In House." *Belle,* November/December 1980.

Celant, Germano. "Strada Novissima." *Artforum,* December 1980.

"Retail Complex Renews City Commerce." *Contract,* December 1980.

"25th Annual Design Awards, LA/AIA." *L.A. Architect,* December 1980.

Giovannini, Joseph. "New West Side Story." *Interiors,* December 1980.

Healy, Dan. "Cabrillo Museum—Avant Garde Design in San Pedro." *Random Lengths,* Christmas 1980.

"Biennale, 1980." *GA Document 2,* January 1981.

"Architect Frank Gehry Wins AIA Award for Hollywood Bowl Modifications." *Performing Arts,* January 1981.

"First International Exhibition of the Venice Biennale." *A + U,* February 1981.

"Collaboration: Artists and Architects." *Architectural Record,* February 1981.

Carlsen, Peter. "Designing the Post-Industrial World." *Art News,* February 1981.

Skorneck, Jeffrey, and Barbara Goldstein. "Three Urban Shopping Centers." *L.A. Architect,* February 1981.

Gilbar, Anne. "Architects Who Live by Their Designs." *Los Angeles,* February 1981.

Filler, Martin. "Architect Frank Gehry Makes His Own Rules." *House and Garden,* March/April 1981.

Baalman, Dirk. "Frank Gehry's House." *Architect* (The Hague), March 1981.

Stern, R., M. Sorkin, and S. Stephens. "Special Issue: American Architecture after Modernism." *A + U,* March 1981.

Goldberger, Paul. "A Meeting of Artistic Minds." *The New York Times Magazine,* March 1, 1981.

"Considine Company Plans Major Residential Complex in Midtown." *Atlanta Business Chronicle,* March 2, 1981.

Davis, Douglas. "Mixed Marriages of Art." *Newsweek,* March 16, 1981.

Filler, Martin, "Tradition Transformed." *House and Garden,* April 1981.

Schjeldahl, Peter. "The Eye of the Revolution." *Art in America,* April 1981.

"Frank O. Gehry: Santa Monica to Atlanta." *Architectural Record,* April 1981.

McMillan, Elizabeth, with Leslie Heumann. "New Venice." *Society of Architectural Historians California Chapter Newsletter,* April 1981.

"Eight Strong Projects Win Downtown Awards." *Downtown Idea Exchange,* April 15, 1981.

Filler, Martin, "Collaboration Artists and Architects." *Art in America,* May 1981.

"On Architecture in the Future: 2010 Visions." *AIA Journal,* Mid-May 1981.

Cohen, Jean-Louis. "Charles Eames, Frank O. Gehry—La Maison Manifeste." *Architecture Mouvement Continuite,* Juin/Septembre, 1981.

Molinari, Paulo. "Non succede mai per incidente." *Il Piccolo 28,* June 1981.

"Architectural League/Bridges Project." *Gran Bazaar,* June 1981.

"Tables by the Slice." *Architectural Record,* June 1981.

"Visual Excitement." *The Baltimore Sun Magazine,* June 21, 1981.

Wakefield, Ian. "Arthur Erickson vs. the 'All Stars,' the Battle of Bunker Hill." *Trace,* July–September 1981.

Goldstein, Barbara. "A Place in Santa Monica." *Progressive Architecture,* July 1981.

"James Rouse, Pioneer of the Suburban Shopping Center, Now Sets Sites on Saving Cities." *People,* July 6, 1981.

Breckenfeld, Gurney. "The Rouse Show Goes National." *Fortune,* July 27, 1981.

Bourdon, David. "Collaboration: Artists and Architects." *Vogue,* July 1981.

Pastier, John, et al. "A Grand Avenue." *A + U,* August 1981.

"He Digs Downtown." *Time,* August 24, 1981.

"Gehry Named Architect of the Year." *Arts and Architecture,* Fall 1981.

Scalvini, Maria Luisa. "The Play of Roles." *Domus 620,* September 1981.

Ross, Michael Franklin. "Urban Design Comes Indoors." *L.A. Architect,* September 1981.

"Siège Administratif de Toyota á Glen Burnie, U.S.A." *Techniques et Architecture,* September 1981.

Reed, Rochelle. "California by Design." *California Magazine,* October 1981.

Filler, Martin. "The Shopping Mall as a Work of Art... Landseer, Master of Marvelous Monstrosities." *House and Garden,* October 1981.

"Map Guide to Recent Architecture in L.A. 1971–1981." *L.A. Architect,* October 16, 1981.

Israel, Frank. "Frank O. Gehry's California Framework." *Gentlemen's Quarterly,* December 1981.

"An Azure Triumph: Frank O. Gehry's Santa Monica Place Sign." *Sites,* 1982.

"Photocopying a Melrose Avenue Building." *Sites,* 1982.

"Frank Gehry." *Architectural Design*, No. 1/2, 1982.

"Stage Set—High Art." *Architectural Design,* No. 3/4, 1982.

"Frank O. Gehry & Associates." *GA Document 5,* 1982.

"Loyola Law School Addition, Los Angeles, California, Design: 1980, Completion: 1982." *GA Document,* 1982.

"Spiller Residence, South Los Angeles, California." *GA Houses,* 1982.

"Indiana Project, Venice, California, 1981." *GA Houses,* 1982.

"New Waves in American Architecture." *GA Houses,* No. 11 (special issue), 1982.

"Santa Monica Place, Santa Monica, California, 1981." *GA Document,* 1982.

"Cabrillo Marine Museum, Wilmington, California, Design: 1976–78, Completion: 1980." *GA Document,* 1982.

"Architectural Stylebook." *Brutus 43,* 1982.

Rinaldi, R. "Inside and Out, Irrespectively." *Domus,* January 1982.

"Santa Monica Place." *A + U,* January 1982.

Mutlow, John. "Loyola Law School." *L.A. Architect,* January 1982.

Royall, John. "The Corporate Dilemma: To Move or Renovate?" *Designers West,* January 1982.

"Vertriebsburo in Glen Burnie." *Baumeister,* January 1982.

"Houses Now, Young, Human, Fun." *House and Garden,* February 1982.

Miller, Nory. "Agitprop's Legacy." *Progressive Architecture,* March 1982.

"Formes d'avant-garde." *Vogue* (Paris), April 1982.

Fillion, Odile. "Cabrillo Marine Museum." *Architecture Interieure Cree,* April/May 1982.

Street-Porter, Tim. "Architecture Outside the Rules." *Belle,* May-June, 1982.

Wiser, Ann. "A Vision Made Real, A Contemporary Look at the American Dream." *United—The Magazine of the Friendly Skies,* May 1982.

Morgenstern, Joseph. "The Gehry Style." *The New York Times Magazine,* May 16, 1982.

King, Carol Souker. "Getting Tough with Economics." *Designers West,* June 19, 1982.

"Mid-Atlantic Toyota Leads the Way." *Corporate Design,* July-August, 1982.

"Shopping Centers in America." *Japan Interior Design,* July 1982.

"New Beverly Hills Fire Station." *Beverly Hills Newsletter,* Summer, 1982.

Giovannini, Joseph. "A House Divided." *Metropolis,* September 1982.

Lowe, Frank. "Issues of Architecture." *Communique,* September 1982.

Scalvini, Maria Luisa. "The Gehry Intersection." *Domus 631,* September 1982.

"People Are Talking About...." *Vogue,* September 1982.

Filler, Martin. "Gehry's Urbanism." *Skyline,* October 1982.

"Gehry's Residence." *Bunte,* October 1982.

"The California Condition." *Architecture California,* November-December 1982.

"Beverly Hills California Civic Center." *Skyline,* November 1982.

"Gehry in the West." *Architectural Journal,* December 1982.

Baeza, Alberto Campo et al. "Three Articles on a Recent Exhibition in Madrid, Showing the Work of Five Architects and Five Sculptures." *Q,* December 1982.

Cook, Peter. "Frank Gehry—Los Angeles: Links in a Context of Fragmentation." *Architectural Journal,* December 22–29, 1982.

"Three Artists' Studios, Venice." *Architecture California,* January-February 1983.

"Fantasms and Fragments: Expressionist Architecture." *Art in America,* January 1983.

Allies, Bob. "Architectural Import: Report of an Exhibition at the ICA in Their Series of Exhibitions 'Art and Architecture.'" *Architects' Journal,* January 1983.

"Interview: Frank Gehry." *Transition Magazine,* February 1983.

Bush, Malvina E. "Frank Gehry: El Arquitecto Vanguardista Cuyos Edificos Provocan Controversias Feroces." *Hombre,* March 1983.

Pastier, John. "MoCA Builds." *Arts and Architecture,* Spring 1983.

McMillan, Elizabeth. "Five Basic Classifications of Building Production." *LA/CA Journal* 36, vol. 4, Spring 1983.

"P/A Third Annual International Furniture Competition." *Progressive Architecture,* May 1983.

"Beverly Hills Civic Center." *Architecture California,* May-June 1983.

"Spiller House." *Architectural Record Houses,* Mid-May 1983.

Shapiro, Lindsay Stamm. "A Minimalist Architecture of Allusion: Current Projects of Frank Gehry." *Architectural Record,* June 1983.

Flanagan, Barbara. "Gehry as Goth." *The Architectural Review,* June 1983.

Laine, Christian K. "Architecture and Praxis: A Self-Analysis." *New Art Examiner,* June 1983.

"The Gehry House." *Toshi-Jataku,* July 1983.

"New Products." *Architectural Record,* August 1983.

"AIA Winners." *Interiors,* August 1983.

"Spiller House." *Nikkei Architecture,* August 1983.

"Introducing Colorcore." *Progressive Architecture,* August 1983.

Moss, Howard. "The Cream That Rises to the Top." *Vanity Fair,* August 1983.

Villecco, Marguerite. "Housing Designed for Special Needs." *Architecture,* October 1983.

Laine, Barry. "Next Wave Brooklyn Academy of Music. *Dance,* October 1983.

Filler, Martin. "A New Material's Dazzling Debut." *House and Garden,* October 1983.

Morozzi, Christina. "L'Anima a colori." *Modo,* October 1983.

"Sweet Clarity." *Vanity Fair,* October 1983.

"You Light Up My Fish." *Vanity Fair,* October 1983.

Walsh, Michael. "Minimalists 3." *Time,* October 10, 1983.

Rich, Alan. "Modern Music on Parade." *Newsweek,* October 24, 1983.

"California Counterpoint." *Arts,* November 1983.

MacAdams, Lewis. "Arts and Intrigue." *California Magazine,* November 1983.

"Design Awards." *L.A. Architect,* November 1983.

Brown, Patricia Leigh. "The No-Consensus Census." *Metropolis,* November 1983.

Apple, Jackie. "Focusing on Responsibility." *Artweek,* November 12, 1983.

Tobia, Tobi. "Fixed Ideas." *New York,* November 14, 1983.

Stevens, Mark. "Los Angeles's Place in the Sun." *Newsweek,* November 21, 1983.

Aloff, Mindy. "Dance." *The Nation,* November 25, 1983.

Sontag, Susan. "For Available Light: A Brief Lexicon." *Art in America,* December 1983.

"What is the Meaning of Architectural Style." *Orange County Architect,* vol. 4, issue 3, 1984.

"The Temporary Contemporary." *Architecture and Design Support Group Calendar,* 1983–84.

Spapira, Nathan H. "Los Angeles: Between two Olympics." *Abitare,* Winter 1984.

"The Big Splash." *Spectator,* Winter 1984.

Kuspit, Donald. "Follies." *Artforum,* January 1984.

McEvilley, Thomas. "Freeing Dance from the Web." *Artforum,* January 1984.

"Available Light." *Images and Issues,* January/February 1984.

Jencks, Charles. "L.A. Style/L.A. School." *AA Files,* January 1984.

Meyer, Jan. "Follies." *Arts Magazine,* January 1984.

Filler, Martin. "Shack of the New." *House and Garden,* February 1984.

Gilbar, Gary. "The Temporary Contemporary." *L.A. Architect,* March 1984.

Plagens, Peter. "Exemplary Contemporary." *Art in America,* March 1984.

Viladas, Pilar. "The Undecorated Shed." *Progressive Architecture,* March 1984.

"Revitalized Riverfront Is Legacy of New Orleans Fair." *Architectural Record,* March 1984.

"The Loyola Campus as Seen by Students Day and Night." *Loyola Lawyer,* Spring 1984.

"Low Tech." *Casa Brutus,* Spring 1984.

Chase, John. "Follie—The Line Between Folly and Foolishness IS Thin." *L.A. Architect,* April 1984.

Stephens, Suzanne. "The Fountainhead Syndrome." *Vanity Fair,* April 1984.

"Casa Role." *Metropolis,* April 1984.

Goldberger, Paul. "Genius or Eccentric?" *The New York Times Magazine,* April 15, 1984.

"Oldenburg e Gehry lavorano insieme." *Domus,* May 1984.

"Atlante comparato dell'archittura contemporanea." *Modo,* May 1984.

Paulis, Margherita Rossi. "Frank Gehry: Una Citta in Casa." *Casa Vogue,* June 1984.

"California Culture." *Arts and Architecture,* Summer 1984.

"Norton Residence, Venice, California 1982–84." *GA Houses,* July 1984.

Strathaus, Ulrike Jehle-Schulte. "Frank Gehry." *Werk, Bauen + Wohnen,* July/August 1984.

Welish, Marjorie. "Where Art Comes First." *House and Garden,* August 1984.

"Museum in Lagerha." *Baumeister,* August 1984.

Slavin, Maeve. "Out on the Table." *Interiors,* August, 1983.

van Bruggen, Coosje. "Waiting for Dr. Coltello." *Artforum,* September 1984.

"Monument Oder Schuppen." *Deutsche Bauzeitung,* September.

"Errors of Judgement." *Designers' Journal,* November 1984.

Woodbridge, Sally. "Architecture in Eden." *Architecture California,* November/December 1984.

Rico, Diana. "Frank O. Gehry." *City Magazine International,* no. 5, November 1984.

Goulet, Patrice. "Projets et Realisations." *L'Architecture d'Aujourd'hui,* December 1984.

Filler, Martin. "Tipping the Scales." *House and Garden,* December 1984.

Tabor, Paul. "Chain Link for Art's Sake." *World Fence News,* December 1984.

Warga, Wayne. "L.A.'s New Place to Fly." *Westways,* December 1984.

Tighe, Mary Ann. "The Collectors." *Vogue,* December, 1984.

Gandee, Charles. "The Right Stuff." *Architectural Record,* January 1985.

"Research Facility." *Progressive Architecture,* January 1985.

"Frank O. Gehry." *Space Design,* January 1985.

Viladas, Pilar. "Form Follows Ferment." *Progressive Architecture,* February 1985.

Photo Credits

Morley Baer
P. 84: 2,4,6

Henry Bowles, Jr.
P. 144: 3

Frank Gehry
P. 91: 3; p. 103: 4; p. 130: 1

Jim Gibbs
P. 152: 1

Larry Harris
P. 267: 3,4,6

Tim Hursley
P. 244: 1,2,3,4,5,6,7

Rudolph Janu
P. 264: 2

T. Kitajima
P. 60: 1,4,5,6; p. 62: 1; p. 76: 5; p. 92: 1,2,4; p. 94: 4; p. 134: 1; p. 138: 2,3; p. 142: 10; p. 144: 2

Richard N. Levine
P. 56: 9

Charles Lowrey
P. 248: 1

Norman McGrath
P. 78: 3; p. 82: 1,2,3,4,5,6

Ralph Morse
P. 68: 1

Michael Moran
P. 202: 3,5,6,7; p. 222: 2,3; p. 224: 3; p. 228: 1,2,3; p. 246: 1,2,3,4; p. 254: 6,7,8,9,10; p. 260: 2,3; p. 262: 3,4,5,6; p. 268: 2,3,4; p. 278: 6,7,8,9; p. 282: 1,2,3,4; p. 286: 2,3

Grant Mudford
P. 272: 3

Jayme Odgers
P. 70: 3,4; p. 72: 2,3,5

Douglas M. Parker
P. 254: 3

Kimberly Parsons
P. 238: 7,8,9

Tim Street-Porter
P. 104: 2,3; p. 106: 3; p. 114: 7; p. 142: 3,4,7; p. 156: 5; p. 158: 1,2,4,6; p. 170: 3; p. 174: 2,3,4,6; p. 210: 1,2; p. 214: 2,3

Marvin Rand
P. 18: 1,2; p. 22: 1,2,3,4; p. 26: 1; p. 30: 1,2,3; p. 36: 1,2,3,4,5,6,7,8; p. 40: 1; p. 42: 1,2,3,4,5; p. 48: 1,2,3,4; p. 52: 6,7; p. 54: 1,2; p. 56: 2,3

Otto Rothschild
P. 52: 2,3; p. 58: 5

Mark Schwartz
P. 118: 1,2; p. 126: 1,3; p. 148: 1,2,3; p. 184: 2,5; p. 198: 3,4; p. 212: 2

Gordon Summers
P. 21: 5; p. 46: 1,4; p. 50: 5; p. 52: 5; p. 56: 2,3; p. 66; p. 70: 1; p. 74: 3; p. 76: 2; p. 80: 1,2,3,4,5,6; p. 154: 1,2,3,4,5; p. 184: 1,7

Steve Tomko
P. 158: 11; p. 162: 1,2,3,4; p. 164: 2; p. 194: 1,3,4,8; p. 196: 3,4,5; p. 202: 1; p. 204: 2,3,4,5; p. 208: 3; p. 220: 4; p. 232: 4; p. 236: 3,4,5

Clay Tudor
P. 130: 3; p. 146: 2,3,4; p. 140: 3,6,7,8

George de Vincent
P. 34: 4

Tom Vinetz
P. 202: 2,4; p. 218: 1,2,3,4; p. 238: 4,5,6; p. 242: 1,2,3,4; p. 250: 3,4,5,6; p. 270: 2,3; p. 272: 2

Gregory Walsh
P. 90: 1,2; p. 92: 3; p. 114: 2,3; p. 116: 7; p. 174: 3,6

Peter Wexler
P. 54: 2